Dream Symbols of the Individuation Process

A list of Jung's works appears at the back of the volume.

Dream Symbols of the Individuation Process

Notes of C. G. Jung's Seminars
on Wolfgang Pauli's Dreams

C. G. JUNG

EDITED BY SUZANNE GIESER

PHILEMON SERIES

Published with the support of the Philemon Foundation
This book is part of the Philemon Series of the Philemon Foundation

Princeton University Press
Princeton and Oxford

Requests for permission to reproduce material from this work
should be sent to permissions@press.princeton.edu

Published by Princeton University Press
41 William Street, Princeton, New Jersey 08540
6 Oxford Street, Woodstock, Oxfordshire OX20 1TR

press.princeton.edu

Any unattributed illustrations and diagrams in this book are
reproduced by permission of either the Jung estate or the
Philemon Foundation.

The photographs in this book were taken in 1936 at the Bailey
Island seminars. The photographer's identity is unknown.

ISBN 978-0-691-18361-9
ISBN (e-book) 978-0-691-19194-2
Library of Congress Control Number: 2019948525

British Library Cataloging-in-Publication Data is available

Editorial: Fred Appel, Thalia Leaf, and Jenny Tan
Production Editorial: Karen Carter
Text Design: Pamela Schnitter
Jacket Design: Kathleen Lynch/Black Kat Design
Production: Merli Guerra
Publicity: Tayler Lord and Kathryn Stevens
Copyeditor: Kathleen Kageff

Jacket Credit: "Nuclear Space," 1946 (oil on canvas), Moholy-Nagy,
Laszlo (1895–1946) / Private Collection / Bridgeman Images.
© 2018 Estate of László Moholy-Nagy / Artists Rights Society
(ARS), New York

This book has been composed in Sabon LT Std

Printed on acid-free paper. ∞

Printed in the United States of America

10 9 8 7 6 5 4 3 2 1

Contents

Acknowledgments

The Philemon Foundation thanks former president Judith Harris for making this project possible and for her continued support; Fred Appel, Karen Carter, and Thalia Leaf at Princeton University Press for their editorial work and stewardship of the project; Stratos Malamatinas for providing a draft transcription of the seminars; Craig Stephenson for meticulous work checking and completing the transcription; Virginia Ling for the indexing; and Christopher Rodrigues for proofing.

This editorial work started ten years ago, in 2008, when I visited Toronto and the Second Philemon Seminar in Jung History held by the Philemon Foundation, to give a lecture on the relationship between the Swedish psychotherapist Poul Bjerre and C. G. Jung. This was my first meeting with the Philemon scholars and resulted in the proposal that I take on the editorial work of Jung's lecture series "Dream Symbols of the Individuation Process."

It has been a thrilling and stimulating journey to complete this work, and I would not have been able to do it without the help of many contributing partners. First and foremost I want to thank Judith Harris for her support of this project and general editor Professor Sonu Shamdasani for invaluable help and support. I also want to thank the community of heirs of C. G. Jung and the Foundation of the Works of C. G. Jung, especially Dr. Thomas Fischer, for helping me to access relevant material in the Jung archive at the Swiss Federal Institute for Technology (ETH) in Zurich.

The help of Professor Karl von Meyenn, physicist, science historian, and editor of the Pauli correspondence, has been pivotal to me since I first became aware of the dialogue between Pauli and C. G. Jung in 1986. He has also been a great help during the editorial process of these seminars, especially by providing a full list of Pauli's dream material.

My special thanks to Christopher Beach at the Main Jung Centre, who showed me around at Bailey Island to see the lecture hall at Bailey Island and the ancestral home of Kristine Mann, and also Mann's impressive house on the bank overlooking the ocean where Mann, Harding, and Bertine had their analytical practices. He also showed me the photo album and the short silent movie made at the occasion of the seminars.

A special thanks also to Jungian psychoanalyst, past president of the Kristine Mann Library, and faculty member of the C. G. Jung Institute of New York, Dr. Maurice Krasnow, who was of great help in identifying some of those who attended the seminars and also handed me relevant written testimonials from some of the participants.

The following persons and institutions also helped me with my research:

The Archive for Research in Archetypal Symbolism (ARAS) for providing information about the original illustrations used by Jung at the Bailey Island seminars, and the Kristine Mann Library for providing a copy of the photo album of the venue. I also want to mention Richard Brown of Bellarmine University in Louisville, Kentucky, and Aksel Haaning from Roskilde University for contributing valuable information.

Dream Symbols of the Individuation Process

Introduction

Suzanne Gieser

In 1936 and 1937, Jung delivered consecutive seminars in Bailey Island, Maine (see figure 1), and in New York City. The seminars ran for a total of eleven days, six days on Bailey Island and five days in New York. Jung's lecture series was titled "Dream Symbols of the Individuation Process." The dreams presented were those of physicist and Nobel Prize laureate Wolfgang Pauli (1900–1958). Jung went into far greater detail concerning the personal aspects of Pauli's dreams than anywhere else in his published work.

Central to these seminars was showing how the mandala as an expression of the archetype of wholeness spontaneously emerged in the psyche of a modern man, and how this imagery reflects the healing process. Jung defines archetypes as innate to man, having an invariable core of meaning that is "filled out" with experiential material conditioned by culture and environment. Therefore it was important to him to provide evidence for this hypothesis by holding up examples from different cultures and epochs, especially from the sphere of religious symbolism.

The themes that Jung chooses to pick up in these seminars are all related to his quest to develop and expound his theories of the psyche. In the lectures, Jung touches on a wide range of themes. He presents his theory of dreams; mental illness; the individuation process; regression; the principles of psychotherapeutic treatment; masculine psychology and the importance of the anima, shadow, and persona; psychological types; and psychic energy. He comments on the political currents of the time such as Nazism, communism, fascism, and mass psychology. He reflects on modern physics, causality, and the nature of reality. From the religious sphere, he chooses to illustrate his theories with examples from the Mithraic mysteries, Buddhism, Hinduism, Chinese philosophy, *The I Ching*, Kundalini Yoga, and ancient Egyptian concepts of body and soul. From the Christian heritage, he focuses primarily on Catholicism and the symbolism of the

Figure 1. Jung at the Bailey Island seminars.

Mass and the Trinity and also on the content of the newly discovered noncanonical gospels and Gnostic ideas. He also mentions the Dreamtime concept of Aboriginal Australians and their beliefs in healing objects, the Apollonian and Dionysian cults of ancient Greece, Nordic mythology, Pythagoras and Pythagoreanism, and the Khidr in the Koran. From the world of literature, he refers to Nietzsche's *Thus Spoke Zarathustra*, Goethe's *Faust*, and Meyrink's *The Golem*. He also discusses the Exercitia of Ignatius Loyola and the visions of Zosimos. The connections to Jung's further work on these topics is provided in the notes.

In summary, we see here many of the budding themes that germinated during the years 1937–57 in the ongoing development of Jung's psychology of religion. From his initial studies in mythology and religion from 1912 onward, in the early 1930s, Jung drew his comparison principally from Eastern esoteric practices, such as Kundalini Yoga and Daoism. After this, his focus shifted to the Western tradition, principally medieval alchemy and Christian symbolism. These themes were then deepened and further explored in the 1940s and 1950s.

What Is Unique about These Seminars?

Most of Jung's preserved texts and seminars in English have been either translated from German, or, when they were given in English, professionally transcribed and thereafter edited.[1] Moreover the translations of Jung's written works into English have gone through many revisions and "rewritings."[2] As a result, today's reader has been deprived of a valuable heritage, the fascinating evidence of the author's creative process.

These seminars comprise Jung's most extensive oral presentations in spoken English in front of an American audience. They were only very lightly edited, in order to, as stated in the introduction to the seminars by the Notes Committee, "keep the talks as nearly as possible as Dr. Jung delivered them." The Notes Committee consisted of three pioneering women doctors and Jungian analysts who lived in the United States: Kristine Mann, Eleanor Bertine, and Esther Harding. Here in this almost verbatim transcript is a chance to "listen in" to the way in which Jung spoke in English. Here also is textual evidence of Jung's intuitive, associative way of thinking, a style that would lead him to meander in many different directions, so much so that he was unable to keep to his original plan of covering the complete dream material—the eighty-one unconscious visions and dreams that he had selected to illustrate Pauli's individuation process—during his six days at Bailey Island. Of these eighty-one, he managed to cover only thirty-four. Just as important, here is a spontaneous survey of topics that were uppermost in Jung's mind during September 1936 and October 1937.

As the audience was composed of benevolent followers, Jung could allow himself to be informal. It was the explicit wish of the organizers that the seminars should be "as strictly private and informal as the [preceding]

---

[1] C. G. Jung (1959). *The Collected Works of C. G. Jung* (hereafter CW), vol. 9, part 1 (hereafter 9/I), *The Archetypes and the Collective Unconscious* (New York: Pantheon), 4.

[2] S. Shamdasani (2004), *Jung and the Making of Modern: The Dream of a Science* (Cambridge: Cambridge University Press), 22.

Harvard event had been prestigious and formal."[3] No newsmen were allowed. The lectures contain spur-of-the-moment responses to questions from the audience. They were given in front of a limited audience of especially invited people, usually Jung's followers, analysts, students, and analysands.[4] The seminars were turned into simple transcripts from shorthand notes made by a few selected seminar members, then copied, bound, and distributed before Jung had the chance to comment, change, or edit them.[5] Jung actually wrote to ask for a copy of the Bailey Island notes to review and edit in connection with a request from the publishing house Harcourt Brace and Company to publish the seminars. Jung requested that a note should be added to the introduction of the seminars that read: "Dr. Jung has consented to let these notes be distributed to those present at the talks without his final suggestions or corrections. Any errors or shortcomings that have occurred are the responsibility of the Notes Committee."[6]

The second part of the seminars, those held in New York in 1937, were originally not planned for, so that, in a sense, the seminars given at Bailey Island were at the time considered "completed." But even as Jung sent his request for a copy to review, there were budding plans for another trip to America for the autumn of 1937.[7] These plans may have played a role in holding back the publication of the Bailey Island seminars. In the end, these publication plans were never realized, but then, considering how much Jung disclosed in the seminars about Wolfgang Pauli's personality and family, what would have remained in a publishable version of the seminars?

---

[3] Claire Dewsnap (1975), "Seminars on an Island," in *Memories and Perspectives Marking the Centennial of C. G. Jung's Birth*, ed. Judy Rosenberg (New York: Analytical Psychology Club of New York), 20–23.

[4] One could raise the question if the patients of these early Jungian practitioners were primarily privileged members of the WASP establishment. We have no substantiated information on this. We certainly know some of this social background, but we don't have the overall picture. There has been little research on the patients of the early US Jungian analysts. There is little biographical work on any of them, let alone on their clientele. There are indications that there were a significant number of people in artistic and creative fields—prominently, figures such as Jackson Pollock and Martha Graham. From that it is legitimate to guess that the backgrounds were quite mixed. See Jay Sherry (2011), "Faint Voices from Greenwich Village: Jung's Impact on the First American Avant-Garde," *Journal of Analytical Psychology* 56 (5): 692–707; Beth Darlington (2015), "Kristine Mann: Jung's 'Miss X' and a Pioneer in Psychoanalysis," *Journal of Archetype and Culture* 92:371–99.

[5] H. Bancroft (1983), "Bailey Island: The Contribution of a Place to Analytical Psychology, *Spring: An Annual of Archetypal Psychology and Jungian Thought*, 191–97.

[6] Kristine Mann–Jung Correspondence, Jung to Mann, January 9, 1937, C. G. Jung Papers Collection, ETH-Bibliothek, ETH Zurich University Archives, henceforth abbreviated JA.

[7] Kristine Mann–Jung Correspondence, Jung to Mann, January 9, 1937, JA.

Instead, the seminars were (as was the case with many other seminar notes transcribed from Jung's lectures and speeches) printed and circulated privately to a restricted list of subscribers. For many years they were kept in Jungian libraries, accessible only to readers on approval, for instance, if the reader had completed a certain number of hours of Jungian analysis.[8]

The Circumstances Surrounding the Seminars at Bailey Island

In 1935 Jung celebrated his sixtieth birthday and was appointed titular professor of psychology at the ETH, the Swiss Federal Institute for Technology in Zurich. Two years before, in 1933, he had started to give lectures at the ETH that were open to the public, lectures that became so popular that it was difficult to find a seat.[9] In August 1935 Jung decided to give a lecture at the Eranos conference on a selection of Wolfgang Pauli's dreams, called "Dream Symbols of the Individuation Process," without disclosing the identity of the dreamer.[10] The lecture on Pauli's dreams was held less than a year after Pauli had ended analytical contact with Jung in October 1934.[11]

This was Jung's third lecture at the Eranos conferences, a yearly event held in Ascona, Switzerland, on the shores of Lago Maggiore. The Eranos meetings were initiated by Mrs. Olga Fröbe-Kapteyn, a Dutch woman with a strong interest in Jung's psychology, symbolism, art, and religion, especially the encounter between Eastern and Western religions and philosophies.[12]

---

[8] Foreword by William McGuire to C. G. Jung (1984), *Dream Analysis: Notes of the Seminar Given in 1928–1930* (London: Routledge and Kegan Paul), vii.

[9] Jung, C. G. (2019). History of Modern Psychology: Lectures Delivered at ETH Zurich, vol. 1, 1933–1934, ed. and trans. Ernst Falzeder (Princeton, NJ: Princeton University Press / Philemon Series).

[10] C. G. Jung (1936), "Traumsymbole des Individuationsprozesses," *Eranos Yearbook 1935* (Zurich).

[11] Pauli to Jung, October 26, 1934, in C. A. Meier, ed. (2001), *Atom and Archetype: The Pauli/Jung Letters 1932–1958* (Princeton, NJ: Princeton University Press), 7. Henceforth abbreviated as *PJL*. The original letters are in JA. Both the German and the English editions contain several errors. A correct version will be published in a supplementary volume to the Pauli letter collection, *Scientific Correspondence with Bohr, Einstein, Heisenberg*, Springer-Verlag, henceforth abbreviated PLC.

[12] Olga Fröbe-Kapteyn (1881–1962) had Dutch parents but grew up in the UK. Her father, Albert Kapteyn, decided to buy the Villa Gabriella on Lake Maggiore in Ascona that she inherited upon his death in 1927. There she founded the annual Eranos Conferences.

In August 1935, Jung had already received an invitation to Harvard University to participate in the tercentenary celebrations that were scheduled to take place from September 16 to 18, 1936, at the occasion. He was also to receive the honorary degree of doctor of science.[13] Once the news about his coming to the United States was released, he was swamped with requests for different kinds of engagements, social as well as professional. Kristine Mann, Eleanor Bertine, and Esther Harding invited him to come and give lectures to their circle. Apparently Jung gave them a choice of topics for the subject of the seminars, and they chose "the individuation process traced through a series of dreams or fantasies."[14]

During the early months of 1936 they made plans for Jung and Emma Jung's visit. They arrived on August 30 in New York. The Jungs had received many invitations and started their sojourn by spending the weekend at the home of Anglican bishop James De Wolf Perry, in Providence, Rhode Island.[15] (His son, John Weir Perry, was twenty-two at the time and

---

H. T. Hakl (2012), *Eranos: An Alternative Intellectual History of the Twentieth Century* (Montréal: McGill-Queen's University Press), 131.

[13] Henri F. Ellenberger (1970), *The Discovery of the Unconscious* (New York: Basic Books), 675. Apparently the tercentenary committee proposed to offer the honorary degree to Sigmund Freud but were advised by Erik Erikson (1902–94, psychoanalyst and developmental psychologist), who had moved to the United States, that Freud would not accept because of his advanced age and his illness (cancer), so instead of letting the remuneration pass to a rival department, the committee proposed to give it to Jung. P. Roazen (1986 [1976]), *Erik H. Erikson: The Power and the Limits of a Vision*, new ed. (New York: Free Press), 296. Henry A. Murray (1893–1988), director of the Harvard Psychological Clinic, claimed to be the initiator of Jung's honorary Harvard degree (see "Henry A. Murray" and "Harvard University" correspondences in the Jung letters at JA). Murray met Jung in 1925 and was deeply influenced by him. Murray is well known as the developer of personology, the integrated study of the individual from physiological, psychoanalytical, and social viewpoints and the primary developer of the Thematic Apperception Test (TAT). E. G. Boring and G. Lindzey eds. (1967). "Henry A. Murray" in A History of Psychology in Autobiography, vol. 5 (East Norwalk, CT: Appleton-Century-Crofts), 283–310. At Harvard, Jung delivered a lecture titled "Psychological Factors Determining Human Behavior." Cf. *CW* 8, 114–28.

[14] Eleanor Bertine–Jung Correspondence, Bertine to Jung, February 23, 1936, JA. Jung was paid $1,200 for the Bailey Island Seminar (approximately $30,000 in 2017) and $1,500 (approximately $26,000 in 2017) for the New York seminar. R. Brown (2011), "Carl Jung's Interpretation of Wolfgang Pauli's Dreams: The Bailey Island, Maine, and New York City Seminars of 1936 and 1937, *Dissertation Abstracts International* 71:6421.

[15] Sheets with information surrounding Jung's trip to Bailey Island with addresses, dates, where he stayed, and with whom, Jung Family Archive, Küsnacht (henceforth JFA). James De Wolf Perry (1871–1947) (1930), "Primate Perry, *Time* 15 (14): 28. Further names on the invitation list include Professor Raphael Demos (1892–1968), professor of natural religion, moral philosophy, and civil polity at Harvard University. (Roderick Firth, "Raphael Demos [1892–1968]," *Proceedings and Addresses of the American Philosophical Association* 44 [1970–71]: 208–9); Charles Durfee; Professor Wolfers; and Dr. Henry Murray.

later became a Jungian analyst and psychiatrist.)[16] During the Harvard celebration, the Jungs stayed with Stanley Cobb, professor of neurology.[17] After the tercentenary events, at which Franklin Delano Roosevelt was a featured speaker, Jung was interviewed and made statements about Roosevelt and world politics that he later may have regretted. He said: "Before I came here, I had the impression that one might get from Europe, that he was an opportunist, perhaps even an erratic mind. Now that I have seen him and heard him when he talked at Harvard, however, I am convinced that here is a strong man, a man who is really great." In the newspaper article, Jung was quoted as saying that he "paid his respects to dictators, explaining their rise as due to the effort of peoples to delegate to others the complicated task of managing their collective existence so that individuals might be free to engage [in] 'individuation.'"[18]

The seminars on Pauli's dreams were given at the small Library Hall at Bailey Island, off the coast of Maine, where Kristine Mann had her ancestral home. Her father, a Swedenborgian minister, had purchased a cottage on the island where Mann had spent her childhood summers, a location that was reminiscent of her mother's native Denmark. Beginning in 1926, during the summer months the three women had their analytical practices in Dr. Mann's house on the bank overlooking the ocean (otherwise, they had their practices in New York). The house, known locally as the "the Trident," had a posted sign at the doorbell advising, "Ring once for Dr. Mann; Ring twice for Dr. Bertine; Ring thrice for Dr. Harding."[19]

In January 1936 already more than a hundred people had applied to attend the seminars. Harding wrote to Jung that they would have to impose "drastic restrictions" to keep the number to what the Bailey Island Hall could handle.[20] There were also many requests for private sessions during his stay, and it seems that Jung at first declined but changed his mind, perhaps giving in to "clamorous" requests.[21] These sessions would have been given in the afternoons, while the seminars were held each morning for two hours. The lectures began with replies to written questions to the preceding lecture, if any had been handed in. The seminar event at Bailey Island was framed by festivities, all kinds of parties, where every-

---

[16] Daniel Benveniste (1999), "John Weir Perry 1914–1998," *Journal of Humanistic Psychology* 39 (2): 48–50.

[17] W. Kaufmann (1980), *Discovering the Mind*, vol. 3, *Freud versus Adler and Jung*. New York: McGraw-Hill.

[18] "Roosevelt 'Great' Is Jung's Analysis," *New York Times*, October 4, 1936, 4.

[19] Bancroft, 1983, 191–97.

[20] Esther Harding–Jung Correspondence, Harding to Jung, January 26, 1936, JA.

[21] Eleanor Bertine–Jung Correspondence, Bertine to Jung, February 23, 1936, JA.

body had the chance to contribute and to meet and talk with the Jungs.[22] A film called *The Mountain Chant* was shown to the participants of the seminar, made by Laura May Adams Armer. Mrs. Armer was almost certainly among the participants of the seminar. The film portrays the sacred Mountain Chant ceremony of the Navajo Indians.[23] There were also charades, dramatic sketches, singing, and folk dancing. Claire Dewsnap remembers participating in a charade representing the four psychological types, in which she took the part of intuition. Jung, who entered heartily into all these activities, guessed rightly and said, "That must be 'intuition' jumping up and down recklessly from the chair to the top of the piano." Those who got to be his partner in the folk dancing were especially elated. On the evening of the final seminar there was a snake dance.[24] The weather was rather cool, around seventeen degrees Celsius, with a light rain, and thick fog covered the island during the whole event; only at the very end, when they were leaving the island, a glorious sun appeared. Despite the fog, the Jungs seemed to have immensely enjoyed the Maine coast, exploring it by sailboat.[25]

Sadly, no list of participants has been found.[26] Of the hundred or so participants, only a few are identifiable. A great help in this regard has been the preserved photographs taken by Francis B. Bode at the occasion.[27]

---

[22] Bancroft, 1983, 195.

[23] There is a letter from Jung to Laura May Adams Armer, September 29, 1936, where he thanks her for letting the seminar group see the film. A copy of the letter is at the library of the Pacifica Graduate Institute. Mrs. Armer (1874–1963) was an American artist and writer who was known for her photographic work in the American West. She apparently was the first white woman to have a sand painting prepared in her honor and the first permitted to film the sacred Mountain Chant ceremony in 1928. She also wrote a book, *Waterless Mountain*, in 1931. She was also one of the editors of a volume on the Navajo "Beautyway" along with Leland Wyman and Maud Oakes. S. R. Ressler (2003), *Women Artists of the American West* (Jefferson, NC) McFarland; L. A. Armer and S. Armer (1931) *Waterless Mountain (London:* Longmans, Green); L. C. Wyman, B. Haile, M. Oakes, L. A. Armer, F. J. Newcomb, M. Singer, and W. Wilson (1957), *Beautyway: A Navaho Ceremonial* (New York: Published for Bollingen Foundation by Pantheon Books).

[24] Snake dance probably refers to a student celebratory parade. "Snake" refers to a line of students and "snake dance" is a traditional term. The University of Northern Iowa archives refer to snake dance as early as 1922. Dewsnap, 1975.

[25] Bancroft, 1983, 196; B. Hannah (1976), *Jung: His Life and Work; A Biographical Memoir* (New York: Putnam Adult), 237.

[26] In the Jung Family Archive there are a few sheets with information surrounding Jung's trip to Bailey Island. On this list are the names Dr. and Mrs. Stanley Cobb, Dr. Bertine and Dr. Mann, Dr. A. McIntyre Strong, Eugene H. Henley, PhD, Miss Lewisohn, Mrs. Crowley (handwritten), Dr. William J. Bell (in handwriting), Dr. E. A. Bennet, JFA.

[27] There are photos from the occasion that are not included in the album, for instance a photo of Jung, Harding, and Mann, reproduced in E. Harding (1957), "Conversations with Jung: 1922–1961," *Quadrant* 8:7–19.

There is also a short silent movie made by Dr. Eugene Henley capturing Jung and the participants gathering at Bailey Island Library Hall.[28] Henrietta Bancroft was one of four note takers; the others were Natalie Evans, Ruth Conrow, and Ruth Magoon.[29] Three of them took down Jung's words in shorthand during the first hour and transcribed the work in the afternoon. The fourth, who was a court stenographer, preferred to work alone and did the second hour of the lecture.[30] Afterward, all the notes were given to Sallie Pinckney, who edited and bound them and provided copies to the attendees of the seminar.

Jung in America and the Radicals around Beatrice Hinkle

One of the most influential persons present at the seminar was Dr. Beatrice Hinkle. She brought with her a large group of friends and colleagues. To understand Jung's relationship to America and Americans and the reception of Jung's ideas in America, it is crucially important to consider the role of Hinkle.

Recent research has made it clear that Jung's work was already known in its own right for several years before his trip to the 1909 Clark University conference with Freud and Ferenczi.[31] His experimental studies with the Word Association Test, conducted while working under the direction of Eugene Bleuler at the Burghölzli clinic, were recognized as pivotal contributions to psychiatry and were quickly translated into English by the Swiss-born psychiatrist Adolf Meyer (1866–1950) and the neurologist Frederick W. Peterson (1859–1938). The latter collaborated with Jung in 1906 and 1907, later sending his staff to do the same. Jung already knew English at the time, writing papers in English and treating American analysands. Later, he said that he gave seminars in English because the English and Americans were the first to recognize the value of his work.[32]

---

[28] Bancroft, 1983, 196.

[29] Henrietta Bancroft, teacher by profession, served the Analytical Psychology Club of New York in a variety of posts, including that of president. She was also the first secretary of the C. G. Jung Foundation of New York (Bancroft, 1983, 191).

[30] Bancroft, 1983, 196–97.

[31] C. G. Jung and R.F.C. Hull, trans. (2012), *Jung contra Freud: The 1912 New York Lectures on the Theory of Psychoanalysis* (Princeton, NJ: Princeton University Press).

[32] E. Taylor (1998), "Jung before Freud, Not Freud before Jung: The Reception Of Jung's Work in American Psychotherapeutic Circles between 1904 and 1909," *Journal of Analytical Psychology* 43 (1): 97–114. Peterson later sent A. A. Brill to study with Jung, after which Brill went in company with Ernest Jones to Vienna to study with Freud. Upon returning to the United States in 1908 Brill opened psychoanalytic practice and launched a project to translate Freud into English; W. McGuire (1995), "Firm Affinities: Jung's Relations with Britain and the United States," *Journal of Analytical Psychology* 40 (3): 301–26.

Both Meyer and Peterson had studied under August Forel (1848–1931), and Meyer was a classmate of Eugene Bleuler's. Meyer moved to the United States in 1891, where he was recruited by Stanley Hall (a psychologist and also president of Clark University) for Worcester State Hospital, and later he was invited by Peterson to serve as chief pathologist at the New York State Mental Hospitals. Influenced by Forel's revolutionary approach to psychiatric asylums, he engaged in transforming American hospitals, introducing a germinal form of what later became known as the psycho-bio-social approach to the treatment of mental illness. Peterson, later a professor at Cornell Medical School, had also studied the new dynamic psychology in Vienna and Zurich for a few years, and after working with Jung at the Burghölzli, he translated Jung's book on dementia praecox into English in 1909, the first book on psychoanalysis translated into English, before any book by Freud.[33] As a result, Jung, rather than Freud, was the main draw at the occasion of the twentieth anniversary of Clark University in 1909.[34] Through Meyer and Petersen came the Zurich connection to American medical psychology.

Cornell Medical School became a seedbed for the Jungian movement in the United States. In 1908 Beatrice M. Hinkle (1874–1953), by then a single mother of two children, joined the staff headed by Peterson's close associate Charles L. Dana (1852–1935), a leading neurologist who founded a psychotherapy clinic based on the latest techniques. A year later, Kristine Mann (1873–1945) came to study at Cornell, where she received her MD in 1913. Hinkle most likely attended the Clark University lectures in 1909. She was initially more taken with Freud; she traveled to Vienna to study psychoanalysis and underwent Freudian analysis that same year. In 1911 she accompanied Freud and Jung to the Psychoanalytic Congress in Weimar.[35] After returning she returned to the Cornell staff at the medical school and also opened a private analytical practice.

It is very likely that Hinkle attended Jung's lecture at the extension course in medicine at Fordham University in 1912, to which Jung was invited by Smith Ely Jelliffe (1866–1945).[36] Jelliffe was one of the founders of the *Psychoanalytic Review*, the first journal on psychoanalysis in the

[33] Taylor, 1998, 97–114.

[34] S. Shamdasani, "Introduction," in Jung and Hull (2012), xiii.

[35] J. Sherry (2011), 692–707; K. Wittenstein (1998), "The Feminist Uses of Psychoanalysis: Beatrice M. Hinkle and the Foreshadowing of Modern Feminism," *Journal of Women's History* 10 (2): 38.

[36] See also J. C. Burnham (1983), *Jelliffe: American Psychoanalyst and Physician* (Chicago: University of Chicago Press).

English language, in which Jung's Fordham lectures were published in the inaugural volume.[37] It was in this journal that Jung argued for the need of further developing psychoanalytic theory, referring to William James's pragmatic rule of scientific endeavor: that theories are instruments, not definitive answers to enigmas on which we can rest.[38] Jung thereby demarcated his freedom from the ideas of Freud.

Jung had left for New York in September 1912 just as the second part of *Transformation and Symbols of the Libido* had appeared in the *Jahrbuch für psychoanalytische und psychopathologische Forschungen*. Hinkle took it on herself to translate this work into English, in an edition printed in 1916 with the title *The Psychology of the Unconscious*. In 1913 Hinkle invited Jung to lecture at the Liberal Club. There is no record of Jung's March 27 talk, but the topic was dreams. There were also other reasons for Jung's visit to America in 1913: he went to analyze the heiress Edith Rockefeller, the daughter of the millionaire oil baron John D. Rockefeller. Jung had been introduced to him the year before by another of his analysands, Medill McCormick.

Hinkle was very active in a number of radical cultural organizations. She influenced the socialist magazine the *Masses*, the literary journal the *Seven Arts*, and the Provincetown Players, the first modern American theater company, to which playwright Eugene O'Neill belonged.[39] The Liberal Club had been started by the Episcopal minister Percy Stickney Grant in 1907, with the help of Charlotte Teller, a young Greenwich Villager. In 1912, Hinkle introduced Teller to Jung. Teller conducted a comprehensive interview with Jung that she published in the Sunday magazine section of the *New York Times* with the headline "America Facing Its Most Tragic Moment."[40] The Liberal Club discussed topics such as birth control, divorce, and the labor struggle. The club soon split into several factions, and a more radical subgroup functioned as an unofficial center for

---

[37] The second founder was William Alanson White (1870–1937), director of Saint Elizabeth's Hospital in Washington, the government mental institution. A. D. Mijolla (2005), *International Dictionary of Psychoanalysis = Dictionnaire international de la psychanalyse* (Detroit: Macmillan Reference USA). White was influenced by the Boston School of Abnormal Psychology or the Boston School of Psychotherapy, a dissociationist school inspired by the psychology of William James. E. Taylor (1996), *William James on Consciousness beyond the Margin* (Princeton, NJ: Princeton University Press), 75. Jung visited White in 1912 to study the dreams and visions of psychotic African American patients. W. McGuire, 1995, 301–26.

[38] Jung and Hull, 2012, 4 (CW 4, par. 86).

[39] Sherry, 2011.

[40] *New York Times*, September 28, 1912, 2.

creative young people in Greenwich Village. Hinkle introduced Jung to this circle, of which Kahlil Gibran, the Lebanese artist and poet, was a member. He did a pencil portrait of Jung.[41]

Jung also attended a dinner party hosted by members of another radical club, the Heterodoxy Club, America's first feminist group. Hinkle was a member, and a few members of the group were her analysands, including Margaret Doolittle Nordfeldt, the secretary-treasurer of the Provincetown Players, who was married to Bror Nordfeldt, a Swedish artist who painted the scenery for their theatrical productions. Margaret Doolittle Nordfeldt attended the Bailey Island seminar. Another attendee at the seminar from the Heterodoxy Club was Amy Springarn. She was married to Joel Springarn, cofounder of the publishing firm Harcourt Brace and Company, which published Jung's and Hinkle's books. Joel Springarn was well known for his effort to add a statement condemning racial discrimination to the platform of the Progressive Party. As well as for her radical affiliations, Hinkle may have been marginalized because of her eclectic approach to psychotherapy.[42]

Mann had been teaching English for four years at Vassar College in New York, where she developed lifelong friendships with three of her students, Cary Fink (later Baynes), Elizabeth Goodrich, and Eleanor Bertine. As mentioned above, she joined the Cornell Medical School in 1908, earning an MD in 1913. In 1917 she first encountered Jung's teachings in Hinkle's translation of "Transformations and Symbols of the Libido," and she became Hinkle's patient in 1919.[43] In 1920 Mann became director of the Health Center for Business and Industrial Women in New York. The same year she traveled with Hinkle and Bertine to England to attend Jung's lectures in Sennen Cove, Cornwall.

Mann studied with Jung during the 1920s and hosted a lecture by him in her New York apartment on Fifty-Ninth Street when he visited the United States in 1925.[44] She opened an analytical practice in New York

---

[41] Sherry, 2011.

[42] Sherry, 2011, 692–707.

[43] B. Darlington (2014), "Kristine Mann's Danish Inspiration: A Jungian Pioneer's Contribution to Jung's Collected Works, Volume 9/I, as 'Miss X,'" in *Copenhagen 2013: 100 Years On; Origins, Innovations and Controversies; Proceedings of the 19th Congress of the International Association for Analytical Psychology* (Einsiedeln: Daimon Verlag), 79.

[44] He gave a talk on racial psychology, the morphological changes of the skulls of immigrants to America, the lack of reverence for ancestors, and the single-mindedness of the Americans. Harding, 1957. See also P. Bishop (1994), "The Members of Jung's Seminar on Zarathustra," *Spring: A Journal of Archetype and Culture* 56:92–112. D. B. Lee (1983), "The C. G. Jung Foundation: The First Twenty-One Years," *Quadrant* 16:57–61.

and gathered people around her who laid the foundation for the Jungian community in New York. In 1928 she traveled to Zurich to begin an analysis with Jung that lasted until 1938, in which she produced paintings that Jung later published and commented on in several reworked editions, from the Eranos lecture 1933, "The Integration of the Personality" in 1939 to the volume *Gestaltungen des Unbewussten* (Formations of the unconscious) in 1950.[45]

Eleanor Bertine (1887–1968), born in Manhattan, graduated cum laude at Vassar College, where she encountered Kristine Mann as a teacher. She entered Cornell Medical School in 1909, graduating with honors and completing several internships in hospitals. In 1916 she practiced general medicine in New York City, and it was during these early days that she discovered Jung with Kristine Mann. At the end of World War I she accepted a position as head of the college division of lecturers, touring the country to introduce new approaches to mental hygiene.[46] She proved to be instrumental in dispersing Jung's ideas in America, when, for instance, she booked Beatrice Hinkle and Constance Long, the first British psychiatrist to follow Jung's methods, as speakers for the International Conference of Medical Women in 1919.[47] Long had studied with Jung at his Küsnacht home and also had arranged Jung's seminar in Cornwall on Arthur John Hubbard's *Authentic Dreams of Peter Blobbs and of Certain of His Relatives*.[48] In 1920 Bertine traveled to London with Mann to attend Jung's seminar and to begin analysis with Long. This encounter with Jung led Mann and Bertine to travel to Zurich from 1921 to 1922 to analyze and study with him there.

The Cornwall seminar was also attended by the English-born Mary Esther Harding (1888–1971). She graduated from the London School of Medicine for Women in 1914. During World War I, she conducted research on diphtheria, thereby contracting the disease, and for a period of time her life hung by a thread. After she recovered, she opened a private practice in London and rented a room to a consulting analyst, Mary Bell,

---

[45] Later included in Jung (1959), CW 9/I, pars. 525–626.

[46] E. Bertine (1967), *Jung's Contribution to Our Time: The Collected Papers of Eleanor Bertine* (New York: Published by G. P. Putnam's Sons for the C. G. Jung Foundation for Analytical Psychology).

[47] A. A. Paulsen (1963), "Origins of Analytical Psychology in the New York Area," *Contact with Jung: Essays on the Influence of His Work and Personality*, ed. M. Fordham (London: Tavistock), 185–90.

[48] P. Blobbs and A. J. Hubbard (1916), *Authentic Dreams of Peter Blobbs … and of Certain of His Relatives: Told by Himself with the Assistance of Mrs. Blobbs (by A. J. Hubbard, assisted by His Wife.)* (London: Longmans).

who introduced her to Long and to Jung.[49] She then also traveled to Zurich to study with Jung, and there she befriended Mann and Bertine. In 1923 she decided to move from England to join them in New York, where they all established their practices.[50] They became staunch allies of Jung and regularly traveled to Europe to attend his lectures and to continue analysis with him.

PICTORIAL DOCUMENTATION AT BAILEY ISLAND

A photo album (see figures 1–12) and a short silent movie document pictorially the events at Bailey Island. In one of the photos (figure 2), Jung, in a group of six, is speaking to two men on the left: these two men are identified as "Dr. Henley" and "Fowler." The second of the two men is probably, then, Harold Fowler McCormick Jr., the son of Edith Rockefeller McCormick. Both mother and son were in treatment with Jung, and Harold Fowler traveled with Jung in 1924 to meet a Hopi Indian called Mountain Lake.[51] A woman on the right (with her back to the camera) is identified as "M. McCormick," which means this could be one of Fowler's sisters.[52] The first of the two men is Dr. Eugene H. Henley (1884–1968), an American analytical psychologist and the first president of the Analytical Psychology Club of New York. His wife, Helen G. Henley, could be the woman facing M. McCormick. Both Eugene and Helen authored papers and reviews on analytical psychology.[53] The Analytical Psychology Club of New York had been inaugurated on April 17, 1936, a few months before the occasion of Jung's visit.[54]

One of Helen Henley's analysands, Mildred E. Harris, is visible in the short film footage of the Bailey Island seminars taken by Eugene Henley. Harris told the story that Jung briefly diagnosed her for her epilepsy ("Stick out your tongue") and predicted an unfavorable prognosis. Nevertheless she herself attributed her eventual recovery to years of analysis.

---

[49] Bishop, 1994, 92–112; Lee, 1983.

[50] Harding, 1957.

[51] McGuire, 1995, 301–26.

[52] Harold Fowler McCormick had two sisters, Muriel and Mathilde, so it could be either of the two. Photo album with photographs taken by Francis B. Bode, Kristine Mann Library at the C. G. Jung Center in New York. See also R. Chernow (1998), *Titan: The Life of John D. Rockefeller, Sr.*, 1st ed. (New York: Random House).

[53] Bishop, 1994, 92–112; Lee, 1983.

[54] W. McGuire (1983), "Jungian New York," *Quadrant* 16:39–44.

Figure 2. Participants at Bailey Island. Jung with, first on the left, Eugene Henley, and second on the left, Fowler McCormick; the woman on the right with her back turned is possibly either Murile or Mathilde McCormick.

Harris, a charter member of the Analytical Psychology Club of the C. G. Jung Foundation of New York, practiced physical therapy in which she combined Yoga, breathing techniques, and imagery work.[55]

In an essay written by Claire Dewsnap called "Seminars on an Island," she mentions Isabel Johnson and Eleanor Stone as attendees. They were among the first analysands of Harding (figures 7 and 8), Bertine (figure 8),

---

[55] Mildred Harris (1903–89) also taught training courses on relaxation and natural childbirth at Columbia University, and in 1988 she was a cofounder of the C. G. Jung Center for Studies in Analytical Psychology in Maine. See information on the homepage of the C. G. Jung Center for Studies in Analytical Psychology in Maine (www.mainejungcenter.org).

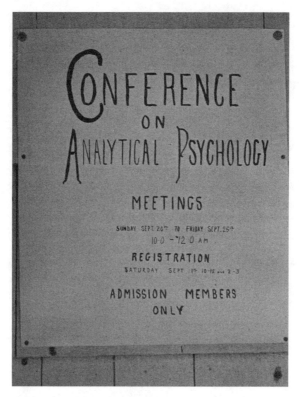

Figure 3. Poster for the Bailey Island seminars.

and Mann. Eleanor Stone was organizer of a Library Custodians Committee at the Analytical Club of New York.[56]

Still another participant was Harold Clarke Goddard (1878–1950), professor in the English Department of Swarthmore College, known for his work *The Meaning of Shakespeare*.[57] Another attendee, Alice Raphael, was a student of Jung's. Familiar with his writings since 1919, she traveled

[56] Dewsnap, 1975. Isabel Johnson provided living accommodations for attendees at Bailey Island at her place called the Willows, and later Eleanor Stone did the same at Summer Hill and at a place called the Robin Hood Inn, where also the reception for Jung was held in 1936. Among the first analysands of Mann, Bertine, and Hannah were Ruth Reeves, Anne Chapin, and Frances DeLeon, all of whom might also have attended the seminars. Bancroft, 1983, 192–96; Lee, 1983.

[57] A letter to Jung from the daughter Margaret Goddard dated March 15, 1951, confirms this (JA). See also H. C. Goddard (1960), *The Meaning of Shakespeare*, vols. 1 and 2 (Chicago: University of Chicago Press).

Figure 4. Participants at Bailey Island Hall.

Figure 5. Participants at Bailey Island Hall.

Figure 6. Participants at Bailey Island Hall.

Figure 7. Participants at Bailey Island Hall. The first woman on the left is possibly Esther Harding. The woman fifth on the left looking ahead is Eleanor Bertine.

Figure 8. Participants at Bailey Island. The first woman on the right is Rosamond Taylor. The first woman on the left is possibly Esther Harding.

to undergo analysis with him in 1927. In 1930, she translated the first part of Goethe's *Faust* into English, and in 1936 she worked on the second part. In her book *Goethe and the Philosophers' Stone*, she describes how, at the Bailey Island seminars, she spent one hour discussing with Jung the meaning of the second part of Goethe's *Faust*. She was convinced that the second part of *Faust* dealt with an alchemical problem.[58] Also

---

[58] Alice Raphael (later married with surname Eckstein, 1887–1975). Jung to Eckstein, March 28, 1936. Eckstein took a photo of Jung at Bailey Island. In a correspondence with her in 1955 Jung discussed the interpretation of the meaning of the murder of Philemon and Baucis in Goethe's *Faust* in relation to the figures of Philemon and Baucis in Ovid. She seems to have differed from Jung in her views of the importance of this relation. Jung scholars have shown that there are important relations between the figure of Philemon in Jung's *Red Book* and Philemon and Baucis in Goethe's *Faust*. The correspondence between Alice Raphael/Eckstein is preserved at Yale. S. Shamdasani (2007), "Who Is Jung's Philemon? An

Figure 9. Participants at Bailey Island. The first woman on the left is Margaret Doolittle Nordfeldt. The second woman on the left is Beatrice Hinkle.

accounted for in the photos are Rosamond Taylor (figure 8), Margaret Doolittle Nordfeldt and Beatrice Hinkle (figure 9), and Cary Jones (figure 10).

After the seminars Jung returned to New York. Here we know only a few details: He gave a lecture to "Dr. Strong's group" on September 30. He also offered analytical hours in the mornings of September 30 and October 1 and 2.[59] He rounded off his stay with a lecture titled "The Concept of the Collective Unconscious" at the Plaza Hotel in front of eight hundred people and with a dinner at the Analytical Club, of which Jung and his wife Emma were made honorary members.[60] Jung returned to Europe via London, where he gave the lecture a second time, at Saint Bartholemew's Hospital.[61]

Unpublished Letter to Alice Raphael," *Jung History* 2 (2): 5–7. See also A. Raphael (1965), *Goethe and the Philosophers' Stone: Symbolical Patterns in "The Parable" and the Second Part of "Faust"* (London: Routledge and Kegan Paul).

[59] Sheets with information surrounding Jung's trip to Bailey Island. A Mr. Bruher (?, handwritten) is noted on the sheet for Thursday October 1, JFA.

[60] McGuire, 1983.

[61] C. G. Jung (1959), "The Concept of the Collective Unconscious," lecture given at Saint Bartholemew's Hospital, *CW* 9/I, pars. 87–110. On the sheets in the Jung Family Archive the following addresses and names are noted for the stay in London: Hotel Albany House,

Figure 10. Jung with Cary Jones at Bailey Island.

The Dreamer and His Treatment

The subject of the seminars, the dreamer with whom Jung worked from October 1932 until, at least, the winter of 1942,[62] was Wolfgang Ernst Friedrich Pauli. Born in Vienna on April 24, 1900, Pauli was one of the many great scientists of the twentieth century involved in the discovery of quantum physics. He received his middle name from his godfather Ernst

Albany Street, Regent's Park, Dr. E. A. Bennet, Dr. H. G. Baynes, Dr. C. M. Barker (president of Psych[ology] Club), Dr. J. A. Hadfield, M.-J. Schmid c/o Mrs. J. Waldram.

[62] I.e., the four hundred dreams dreamt between February 3 and November 4, 1932. Pauli continued to send dreams to Jung until the very end of his life. S. Gieser (2005), *The Innermost Kernel: Depth Psychology and Quantum Physics; Wolfgang Pauli's Dialogue with C. G. Jung* (Berlin: Springer-Verlag).

Figure 11. Jung with a participant at Bailey Island.

Mach, the father of logical positivism, and was therefore in his own words "anti-metaphysically baptized."[63] Among his colleagues, he was known for his highly critical mind and sarcastic wit. At the age of twenty-one, as a student in Munich (where he befriended Werner Heisenberg), Pauli established himself with an article on the theory of relativity written at the request of his teacher Arnold Sommerfeld. This article earned the admiration of Einstein himself.[64]

Pauli met Niels Bohr for the first time on June 22, 1921, and was soon invited to Copenhagen. From 1922 to 1923 Pauli studied at the Institute

[63] Pauli to Jung, March 31, 1953, *PJL*.

[64] W. Pauli (1921), "Relativitätstheorie," in C. Enz and K. Meyenn, eds. (1988), *Wolfgang Pauli: Das Gewissen der Physik* (Braunschweig: Vieweg), 123–47. Albert Einstein (1922), "Besprechungen–Pauli, W. jun., Relativitätstheorie," *Die Naturwissenschaften* 10:184–85.

Figure 12. Jung at Bailey Island.

for Theoretical Physics in Copenhagen, an institute characterized by a fluidity of boundaries between the private and the professional, between work and leisure, science and philosophy. In 1924 Heisenberg also came to Copenhagen, and together Pauli and he formed the heart of the Copenhagen school of quantum physics. They remained in lifelong contact and in deep friendship with Bohr. In 1924 Pauli obtained a docentship in Hamburg, and in the same year he formulated the exclusion principle, for which he would be awarded the Nobel Prize in 1945.[65] In 1928 he was appointed professor of theoretical physics at ETH, the Federal Institute of Technology, in Zurich. During this period Pauli did a great deal of work on quantum field theory, of which he is one of the creators. He also

---

[65] He was first proposed for the Nobel Prize in 1933 by the Swedish physicist C. W. Oseen. Gieser, 2005.

took interest in beta decay, which led him in 1930 to surmise the existence of a new particle, the neutrino, a hypothesis that was verified by experiment in 1956. He was later to call this discovery "the foolish child of my crisis."[66]

In 1931 Pauli developed an acute depression, for which he sought the help of Jung in January 1932. In a late letter to Jung, Pauli recounts that his neurosis had already become quite apparent in 1926, while he was living in Hamburg. His exclusive preoccupation with science had suppressed all other human qualities and, in particular, harmed his emotional life. An expression of this imbalance was the vivid contrast between his daytime and nighttime personalities; it also manifested in his relationships with women. He developed a Dr. Jekyll and Mr. Hyde duality: on the one hand, he was the brilliant, famous "conscience of physics"; on the other, an alcoholic ruffian frequenting bars and getting into fights. He felt lonely and paranoid.[67] This condition worsened considerably in 1927 after his mother's death by a combination of pneumonia and poisoning.[68] He had had a positive relationship with her, but he felt hostile toward his father, who immediately remarried with a woman of Pauli's own age. He also allegedly despised his father for having converted to Catholicism, hiding his Jewish roots from his son (of which he became aware only at sixteen years of age).[69] In 1929 Pauli decided to leave the Catholic Church. In the seminars, Jung does not refer to this religious complexity in Pauli's background but states only that Pauli was Catholic.[70] In December 1929

---

[66] Pauli to Delbrück, October 6, 1958 (3075), W. Pauli, 2004, PLC IV/4, ii.

[67] Pauli to Jung, May 24, 1934 (30P), and October 23, 1956 (69P), "Statements by the Psyche," *PJL*; C. G. Jung (1935), "The Tavistock Lectures," in *CW* 18, par. 402.

[68] In some accounts it has been described as a suicide. See for instance A. I. Miller (2009), *Deciphering the Cosmic Number: The Strange Friendship of Wolfgang Pauli and Carl Jung* (New York: W. W. Norton).

[69] C. Enz (2002), *No Time to Be Brief: A Scientific Biography of Wolfgang Pauli* (Oxford: Oxford University Press), 5, 10. See also Pauli's letter to Jung, October 23, 1956; *PJL*.

[70] According to Karl von Meyenn, it was the physicist Markus Fierz who advised Jung not to include any information on Pauli's Jewish roots in order to preserve his anonymity (personal communication). Markus Fierz (1912–2006) became Pauli's assistant in 1936 and developed an intense exchange of ideas with Pauli on physics, the history of science, and analytical psychology from 1946. Markus Fierz's twin brother, Heinrich Karl Fierz, became a psychiatrist belonging to Jung's school of analytical psychology. Their mother, Linda Fierz-David, was a pupil of Jung's as well. Markus Fierz's father was Professor Hans Fierz, professor of chemistry at the ETH who helped Jung acquire his lectureship at the ETH (Enz, 2002, 313). The subject of his Jewish background seems to have been sensitive to Pauli. The first time he starts to discuss his Jewish roots is at the end of November 1950 in a letter to Aniela Jaffé. There he states that his solution to the problem of religious affiliation was to embrace Schopenhauer's position by lumping together the Old and New Testament and dis-

in Berlin, Pauli married the performer Luise Margarete Käthe Deppner. A couple of months later, she left him. She trained at the Max Reinhardt School for film and theater, the same Max Reinhardt who brought Pauli's sister Hertha to Berlin.[71] In November 1930, their separation was consummated. The loss of his mother, the failed marriage, and a professional standstill in the field of physics all contributed to Pauli's sense of personal crisis.

After having seen Jung for a twenty-minute interview, Pauli received instruction to drop by, concurrent with a lecture, at which time Jung slipped him a note, referring him to Erna Rosenbaum (1897–1957) for treatment. Pauli seems to have played down his condition in his first letter to Rosenbaum. Pauli's letter of introduction is worth quoting:

> I do not know who you are: old or young, physician or amateur psychoanalyst, completely unknown or very famous—or something in between these extremes. I only know that Mr. Jung quickly gave me your address after one of his lectures and mentioned that I should write to you, without an opportunity for me to ask him for details. The background is that I consulted Mr. Jung a week ago because of some neurotic symptoms which, among other things, have to do with the fact that it is easier for me to achieve success in academia than with women. Since for Mr. Jung the opposite is the case, he seemed the right person to ask for medical advice. My surprise was not little when Mr. Jung explained to me that this was not so, and it would be imperative for me to be in treatment with a woman. For I am very sensitive and easily distrustful vis-à-vis women, and thus I am somewhat doubtful about this. Anyway, I do not want to leave anything unattempted, and therefore I am now writing this letter to you. It would be very cordial of you to call me on the phone so we can make an appointment to meet.[72]

In February 1932, Pauli began analysis with Rosenbaum. He characterized her as "a young Austrian, pretty, fullish, always laughing."[73] Erna,

---

miss them both by labelling them "Jewish sabbatarian superstition." Pauli to Jaffé, November 2, 1950 (1172), PLC IV/I; Pauli to Jaffé, November 16, 1956 (2398), PLC IV/III.

[71] Enz, 2002, 209.

[72] Pauli to Rosenbaum, February 3, 1932, Enz, 2002, 240. A week before February 3 was January 27, and we know that Jung held a seminar on Christiana Morgan's visions that day, a series of seminars that Jung had been giving weekly since October 15, 1930. *Visions Seminars* 1 (1997), ed. Claire Douglas (Princeton, NJ: Princeton University Press).

[73] Pauli to Jung, October 2, 1935 (13P), Pauli to Jung, May 27, 1953 (62P), *PJL*; 121; Enz, 2002, 240.

or Nea as she was called, was of Jewish descent and had studied medicine in Munich and Berlin before she went to study with Jung. She first learned about analytical psychology in 1925 through Gustav Richard Heyer and his colleague Käthe Bügler; she studied with them from 1925 to 1928 in Munich and then from 1928 to 1930 with Toni Sussmann in Berlin.[74] She arrived in Zurich on October 1, 1931, and stayed for nine months to have a training analysis and to attend Jung's German and English seminars. That Jung described her as a beginner, largely unfamiliar with analytical psychology, seems strange.[75] She moved to England in 1933 to escape the Nazis. In a 1935 letter to Jung, she pleads that he should write a more personal letter of recommendation to the British Home Office so that she might be able to stay in England. The first letter he had written was apparently too impersonal to carry sufficient weight in support of her request to immigrate. She writes spiritedly: "Could you, after drinking a good drop of red wine, dictate another one?... My stay in England really depends on this letter."[76] She then salutes him from England by raising her glass of Chateauneuf du Pape to celebrate the tenth anniversary of getting to know his name. In January 1936 Jung composed a revised stronger letter of recommendation:

> I can warmly recommend Dr. Rosenbaum who is a pupil of mine. I have known her for ten years and can fully appreciate her human and professional qualities.... Her personality and her long experience in medical and social work make her not only an excellent doctor but also a very able psychotherapist. I should even say that there are few women doctors specializing in psychotherapy who

---

[74] Erna Rosenbaum–Jung Correspondence, Rosenbaum to C. G. Jung, December 31, 1935, JA. G. R. Heyer, a medical doctor working in Munich, started his career by treating somatic diseases with hypnosis. In the mid-1920s he trained with Jung together with his first wife, Lucie Heyer, who was a respiratory specialist. He opened a private practice and held study groups. He and his wife befriended Jung and are considered pioneers in psychosomatic bodywork. In 1937 Heyer joined the Nazi Party. Historians have a hard time figuring out where Heyer stood, as the sources give a very complex picture. Hakl, 2012. Toni Sussmann was a psychoanalyst trained by Jung. She moved from Germany to England in 1938 and died in 1967 in Brighton, England. She had a daughter called Vera Jensh.

[75] Jung, 1935, par. 402. Calling her a novice might refer to the fact that she had just started her own analysis, something that Jung states in the seminars. Doing one's own analysis with a trusted analyst was considered the most important way to learn about Jung's work C. G. Jung, 1984, vii.

[76] Erna Rosenbaum–Jung Correspondence, Rosenbaum to C. G. Jung, December 31, 1935, JA. Original in German, translated by the editor.

could show as much personal ability combined with a thorough medical training and a long practical experience.[77]

In London Rosenbaum married A. R. Redfern, one of the founders of the Society of Analytical Psychology in London (SAP).[78] On April 30, 1939, she asked Jung if she could consult with him for a couple of hours in July, to talk not about dreams but about her heavy heartache concerning the fate of the Jews. He responded that he would be on vacation in July but suggested that she should come to Ascona in August (to the Eranos meeting), where they might have some time to talk.[79]

DIAGNOSIS AND TREATMENT

When we look for a diagnosis of Pauli we encounter first the fuzzy term "neurotic symptoms," a term Pauli uses to describe his condition when presenting himself to Erna Rosenbaum.[80] In 1935 Jung described Pauli as one-sidedly intellectual with inner tensions that made him project his negative feelings onto other men whom he then perceived as enemies. This left him feeling isolated. To escape these feelings he drank and, once disinhibited, fell into quarreling and fighting.[81] In August 1934 Pauli described to his colleague Ralph Kronig that, as a result of a one-sided development of consciousness, he experienced a revolution from inside, from the unconscious, and so became acquainted with the "autonomous activity of the soul" and "its spontaneous growth products" that he designated "symbols."[82] To Rosenbaum he describes himself as suffering from recurring depressive states and a social phobia. He later also describes a wasp phobia that went back to his fourth year, as well as anxiety states caused by a great tension between opposites in his psyche.[83] To Jung, Pauli diagnoses

---

[77] C. G. Jung's letter of recommendation for Erna Rosenbaum to the Home Office, January 11, 1936. In the possession of the Foundation of the Works of C. G. Jung. I am immensely grateful to professor Richard Brown of Bellarmine University in Louisville, Kentucky, for sending me a photocopy of this document.

[78] See H. Westman (1958), "Erna Rosenbaum," *Journal of Analytical Psychology* 3:180.

[79] Erna Rosenbaum–Jung Correspondence, Rosenbaum to Jung April 30, 1939; Jung to Rosenbaum May 5, 1939, JA. It is worth noting that the Nazis had annexed Austria in March 1938 and Czechoslovakia in March 1939; a month later they were in Poland.

[80] Pauli to Rosenbaum, February 3, 1932. Correspondence Pauli–Erna Rosenbaum (JA).

[81] Jung, 1935, par. 402.

[82] Pauli to Kronig, August 3, 1934 (380), PLC II.

[83] See Pauli to von Franz, August 21, 1953 (1625), n. 5; W. Pauli (1999), PLC IV/II; Pauli to Jung, May 24, 1934 (30P), *PJL*.

himself by saying that behind the wasp "lurked the fear of a sort of ec-
static state in which the contents of the unconscious (autonomous part-
systems) might burst forth, contents which, because of their strangeness,
would not be capable of being assimilated by the conscious and might
thus have a shattering effect on it."[84] In the seminar, Jung concurs with
this diagnostic observation, saying that Pauli's condition could be compared to the kind of "complete disintegration" that can be seen in schizophrenia, a position Jung retains in his description of Pauli in *Psychology
and Alchemy*.[85]

The treatment for this serious condition was mostly left to Pauli himself, and Jung justifies this decision by describing him as a man with excellent scientific training and ability and a master mind with which he didn't
want to tamper. But he also rationalizes it because he wants to make "an
interesting experiment" to get pure archetypal material and to ensure
that Pauli's development proceeded without any personal influence from
Jung's part.[86] The task of the doctor was just "to observe the process."[87]
The greater part of the analytical work consisted in writing down and
reporting dreams, which were then passed on to Jung. Indeed, Jung makes
a point of mentioning that he did not meet Pauli at all during the first eight
months of his therapy. Thus 355 out of 410 dreams over a ten-month
period were reported dreamed without any contact with Jung.

As he explains in the seminars, Jung instructed Rosenbaum not to analyze Pauli's dreams, and when he himself took over the treatment he followed the same principle. He did not do any systematic dream analysis
with him. If Pauli posed a question, Jung would either reflect the question
back to him or he would share with him something from his own experience. But he also conveyed to Pauli to trust the helpful powers of the

---

[84] Pauli to Jung, April 28, 1934 (29P), *PJL*.

[85] Pauli to von Franz, August 16, 1953 (1624), plus appendix, August 21, 1953 (1625),
PLC IV/II. See also "Modern Examples of 'Background Physics,'" *PJL*, appendix 3.

[86] *CW* 12, par. 45; *CW* 18, par. 402. Pauli's second wife, Franca Bertram, whom Pauli
married after completing his analysis, considered this a frivolity on Jung's part. See C. Enz
(2000), "Wolfgang Pauli and Carl Gustav Jung," in *Wolfgang Pauli and Modern Physics*, ed.
ETH-Bibliothek (Zurich: ETH Zurich), 73.

[87] For a presentation of Jung's view on objectivity, and his epistemological standpoint on
"the reality of the psyche," see for instance Gieser, 2005, 111–25. Here it suffices to say that
Jung considered the psyche of man a piece of autonomous nature that can be studied on the
same terms as physical nature. The problem of the influence of the observer on the observed
is an integrated part of Jung's phenomenological standpoint and was crucial for Pauli later
embracing Jung's psychology as belonging to the new scientific paradigm alongside quantum physics.

unconscious. In the seminars, Jung says that the presence of the doctor functions in the process as "a sympathetic audience" and that it does not matter so much *what* the psychotherapist says, only that he say *something* to show that he is present with the patient and to react spontaneously to what he hears.[88] With regard to sanity, Jung says that the critical thing is to be able to explain yourself to your fellow beings, that is, he puts great weight on the human desire to communicate and to make oneself understood to one's fellows.

Pauli was able to see Rosenbaum in her practice at Hönggerstrasse 127 until the end of June 1932, when she left for Berlin. This means that they met for only five months. But even during this period she traveled, and Pauli tried to arrange to meet when they were both in Hamburg in April. They seem to have met several times a week. This is indicated in a note dated May 19, a Thursday. Pauli writes immediately after their session, to say that he is upset by a misunderstanding of the wording in a dream that he needs to correct straight away. The note ends with "See you on Saturday." In addition to their regular appointments Pauli sent her his dream material, which was so extensive that he felt he had to excuse himself.[89]

Although Pauli sometimes expressed satisfaction about the arrangement with Rosenbaum, as in March 1932 when he stated that things somehow functioned smoothly, his tone changed later.[90] During the summer of 1932 he writes her seven letters, describing his emotional difficulties (her replies have not been found). In July, after she left for Berlin, he fell into a deep depression. He mentions that this depression is different from the last one, which he had illustrated with a drawing of a crocodile. He goes on to say that his depressions often impinge on his capacity to work. This time around, he tries to handle his depression by stoically inviting it and keeping still. He thinks that the depression has a purpose: to force him not to run away. If he can manage to keep still, something will come of it. He explains that his ambition is to bring the wishes of the unconscious into harmony with those of his conscious life as a way to healing. But he misses his talks with Rosenbaum, and in two consecutive letters (in July) he asks for her phone number, for some sign of life from her. In a third

---

[88] It is worth noting that Jung does not mention transference or countertransference as important factors in these seminars. Jung's most worked through perspective on this issue was published in 1946 in the work *Psychology of the Transference* (CW 16) and is understood as best expressed by the ambiguous symbols in alchemy.

[89] Correspondence Pauli–Erna Rosenbaum (JA).

[90] Enz, 2002, 241. Also Correspondence Pauli–Erna Rosenbaum.

letter (also in July) he seems to have received a reply and feels happier. He informs her that he has thrown out his housekeeper, passed his driver license the same day, and is getting closer to his sister so that they soon will be on speaking terms again.[91]

Pauli's sister Hertha Ernestina Ashton-Pauli (her middle name was yet another homage to Ernst Mach) was six years younger, and they had a complicated relationship (see notes in the seminars). Pauli hardly ever mentioned his sister in his other correspondence, but in the letters to Erna Rosenbaum she is present. The only comment Pauli makes in the letters to Jung about his sister concerns the interpretation of dream number 16 on the ace of clubs and the number seven, when he doesn't fully agree with Jung's interpretation. Pauli associates the number seven to the birth of his sister in his seventh year and subsequently to the birth of the anima.[92] Although Pauli sends these associations to Jung in February 1936, Jung chooses not to include them in his presentation of the dream at the seminar. Jung may have decided against adding Pauli's corrections for reasons of confidentiality, but Jung actually did disclose a lot of information about Pauli's relation to his sister that is found nowhere else in presentations of Pauli's case. Jung uses the strong wording "infantile fixation" to describe it and states that Pauli fell in love with women who resembled his sister, that she had to give her blessing to the women he chose, and that he resented her for marrying. Pauli later developed a very affectionate relationship to his sister.[93]

Pauli's depression lingered on into August 1932 when he was in Engadin and later in Italy with a friend.[94] Even though he was physically active, swimming and rowing, outwardly looking healthy and suntanned, he felt depressed and afraid that he was becoming withdrawn and unsociable. He was getting increasingly impatient and sensed he was at a standstill in his personal development. After going to Venice he returned to Switzerland in September for a mathematics congress. In a letter he remarks that he is relieved to find that his sense of humor is not entirely

---

[91] Correspondence Pauli–Erna Rosenbaum.

[92] See Pauli to Jung, February 28, 1936 (16P) and June 16, 1936 (18P), *PJL*. The ace of clubs is a motif that reoccurred in Pauli's dreams. See Pauli to Jung, appendix to letter (1200), PLC IV/I.

[93] She was married for the first time in 1929 with a fellow actor named Carl Behr. The second time she married in the 1950s after moving to the United States, to another immigrant from Munich, Ernst Basch, who took the name E. B. Ashton. Enz, 2002, 17–18.

[94] The Engadin is situated in Switzerland south across the Maloja pass located in the Swiss Alps in the canton of Graubünden, a link to the Val Bregaglia and Chiavenna in Italy.

gone. He can still laugh at the world when he looks at the newspapers and reads about a new Prussian minister who is reported to be indignant about beauty queens in swimsuits receiving rewards. He asks Rosenbaum if she couldn't offer some psychological treatment "to the poor chap."[95]

His spirit is more upbeat when he writes to her from Venice, where he excuses himself for sending so many dreams (according to the complete dream records he recorded fifteen dreams between August 16 and 26).[96] He also wishes her well in the "2 ½ Reich," which is obviously a pun around the growing movement of National Socialists in 1932. In the last preserved letter from September, he sends her more dreams (seventeen according to the dream records) that he feels really point to a specific development. He is especially impressed by dream number 49, about a rotating star and pictures illustrating the four seasons.[97] It seems that Jung also found the dreams from this period important, since he chose five from these to be included in his presentation (nos. 46–50). (From the preceding period—July 18 to August 26, covering forty-six dreams—Jung chooses only two, nos. 44 and 45.) In his letter Pauli reports that his depression abated and changed into a kind of unrest that lasted for a couple of days before something came of it, about which he becomes conscious. These periods were accompanied by dreams of waiting or messages that things were still too premature.[98]

Rosenbaum returned to Zurich in September 1932, and there may have been a few sessions in October before they ended their contact and Jung took over.[99] It is therefore a bit surprising that, already in December 1932, shortly after taking over the treatment of Pauli, Jung planned to

---

[95] Correspondence Pauli–Erna Rosenbaum.

[96] The complete records are still unpublished, but the author has kindly received previews of the complete index from Karl von Meyenn. Henceforth abbreviated with CDM (complete dream material).

[97] C. G. Jung (1953), CW 12, nr. 49, par. 282; M 49 {0320}: fig. 39, "Rotating star figure with depiction of the seasons," dreamt on September 5, 1932. Jung has added a few sentences on the symbolism of the year and the seasons in the 1944 version. CW 12, par. 283. Apparently this dream made a deep impression on Pauli. Correspondence Pauli–Erna Rosenbaum, Pauli to Erna Rosenbaum, September 11, 1932.

[98] Correspondence Pauli–Erna Rosenbaum.

[99] Exactly when is not entirely certain. Jung says he didn't see Pauli for the first eight months of his treatment, i.e., February until September 1932. Jung also states that Pauli dreamt forty-five dreams while Jung was seeing him. If we compare this information with the complete list of dreams compiled by Karl von Meyenn, Jung would have started seeing Pauli again on October 10, 1932. See CDM. C. G. Jung (1953), "Psychology and Alchemy," CW 12, par. 45.

involve him in a joint international publication. The new journal, created by Jung, was to be called *Weltanschauung* and would offer "a synthesis of different disciplines."[100]

Pauli saw Jung continuously (although there is no available information about regularity and frequency) until October 1934. During the period of Pauli's treatment, January 1932 until October 1934, Jung was, among other things, busy giving a seminar in English on Christiana Morgan's visions at the Psychological Club in Zurich. It could be possible that it was in connection with one of these lectures, held on January 27, 1932, that Pauli received the note from Jung referring him to Erna Rosenbaum, as Pauli dates this event to one week before February 3.[101] It is also worth noting that, during his time in treatment, Pauli produced the first comprehensive overview of wave mechanics and also discovered that Schrödinger's wave mechanics were equivalent to Heisenberg's earlier quantum mechanics. This work is still today considered a great achievement in the history of physics, and it speaks to his mental functioning during this time.[102] Certainly, Jung was impressed by Pauli's way of working with his dreams, and he often used Pauli's dreams as key exemplars when presenting his theory of dreams.[103]

In April 1934 Pauli married Franca Bertram (1901–87) in London. They had met in 1933 at the home of a mutual friend, Adolf Guggenbühl, who was having a housewarming party. Franca originally came from Munich but had traveled widely.[104] At the end of October 1934 Pauli wrote

---

[100] In a letter to Jolande Jacobi, Jung writes about his plan to invite Hauer, Zimmer, and Pauli to collaborate with him on an international journal that he intended to create with the encouragement of the publisher Daniel Brody, who later published the Eranos volumes. Other names that were mentioned were Wolfgang Müller Kranefeldt, Erwin Rousselle, Leopold Ziegler, Hermann Keyserling, and Herman Broch. The project never came to fruition. Hakl, 2012, 85. There is nothing in the correspondence between Pauli and Jung that corroborates this project. The Weltanschauung project is discussed in the Jung–Jacobi correspondence (JA); some of these letters are reprinted in C. G. Jung (1973–76). *Letters. 1, 1906–50* and *Letters. 2, 1951–61*, ed. Gerhard Adler and Anièla Jaffé (Princeton, NJ: Princeton University Press, henceforth abbreviated Jung, *Letters*, vol. 1, and Jung, *Letters*, vol. 2) in particular letter dated December 23, 1932, where Pauli's promise to contribute is mentioned in connection with the project, and letter dated April 10, 1933, where the end of the plans is alluded to. Further exchange of thoughts about the project are in the Jung–Zimmer and Jung–Hauer correspondences.

[101] *Visions Seminars* 1, 1997.

[102] W. Pauli (1933), *Die allgemeinen Prinzipien der Wellenmechanik*. Handbuch der Physik, 2. Auflage, Band 24, 1. Teil, 83–272, Berlin.

[103] Personal communication from Karl von Meyenn, who has edited the complete dream material.

[104] Enz, 2002, 284–88.

to Jung that he wanted to discontinue his analysis. Pauli marrying Franca Bertram was seen as an important step in Pauli's recovery. Although Pauli stopped receiving regular analysis, he continued to send his dreams to Jung and to discuss his personal problems with him.

Pauli stayed in touch with Jung and his circle for the rest of his life, and in his later years he deepened his interest in depth psychology, dreams, the theory of archetypes, and other topics central to analytical psychology like myths and alchemy. But he specifically linked Jung's psychology to an understanding of the history and theory of science. He was particularly interested in new conceptions of the relationship between mind and matter and supported Jung in his formulation of an acausal and psychophysically neutral natural law expressed in the principle of synchronicity.[105]

Treasure Hunting for Alchemy

Readers of the seminars can bear witness to the editorial emergence of the texts that were eventually published in 1944 in the volume entitled *Psychology and Alchemy*. Apart from the introduction, this volume consists of two essays. The second text, "Religious Ideas in Alchemy," is a thoroughly reworked version of Jung's 1936 Eranos lecture, "The Idea of Redemption in Alchemy."[106] The first text, "Individual Dream Symbolism in Relation to Alchemy," is based on Pauli's dreams and was first presented as an Eranos lecture in August 1935. What is immediately noticeable is that the original title, "Dream Symbols of the Process of Individuation," makes no allusion to alchemy. Originally, then, Jung presented the Pauli material as an example of an emerging archetype of wholeness, the mandala.

When did the shift from the focus on mandala motifs as an expression of the individuation process to that of alchemical symbolism occur? It is worthwhile noting that Jung's alchemy copybooks attest to the fact that his detailed reading of alchemy starts in the autumn of 1935, later than is

---

[105] Gieser, 2005.

[106] According to Aniela Jaffé, this lecture was almost not given: Jung had already at the Eranos meeting in 1935 declared that he would not be able to attend in 1936 because he would be at Harvard. Aniela Jaffé claims that Fröbe-Kapteyn soon after visiting Jung in Küsnacht gave him an ultimatum: that if he would not come, it would be the end of Eranos altogether. Suddenly he then accepted. See A. Jaffé (1975), "C. G. Jung und die Eranostagungen," *Eranos Yearbook* 44:10; Hakl, 2012, 97.

usually assumed.[107] In most accounts, Jung's engagement with alchemy began in 1928 when he read *The Secret of the Golden Flower*, but his immersion in the subject started much later.[108] In the Bailey Island and New York seminars, Jung presents Pauli's dreams only in the context of mandala symbolism. Alchemy is mentioned, but not as the main reference for understanding the dreams. In the English edition of the Eranos lecture, translated in 1939 in a volume entitled *The Integration of the Personality*, Jung retains his original title with no reference to alchemy, and this despite the fact that in this edition he chooses to publish the text with an introduction that emphasizes the role of alchemical symbolism in the dreams of his patients. This also holds true for the first text of this 1939 volume, which is an expanded version of his first Eranos lecture called "A Study in the Process of Individuation" (1933), in which he presents the series of paintings made by Kristine Mann.[109] The additions made to this text especially focus on alchemical symbolism. Only one reference in the 1933 version can be linked to alchemy: the patient herself identified the serpent with Mercury and with Hermes the Psychopomp. In 1939 Jung added the following ideas from alchemy: the all-round being (*rotundum*); the stone that contains *pneuma* (spirit) that is identified with Mercury; the *ouroboros*, the tail-eating serpent; the sword that divides the egg; the *prima materia* as "lead"; the philosopher's stone represented as a living, winged hermaphroditic being; the four colors in alchemy; the peacock's tail; and the visions of Zosimos.[110]

In the English edition of *The Integration of the Personality*, Jung was keen to emphasize that his interest in alchemy was recent and that none of the patients mentioned were under his care once he had begun his study of alchemy (if this were so, his studies of alchemy would then have started after 1934). More important, he reports that the patients had no knowledge of the tradition.[111] However, Jung acknowledges that Mann's

---

[107] This point is also made by Thomas Fischer, who has assembled the background information on how and why Jung assembled his collection of rare books in the 1930s. T. Fischer (2011), "The Alchemical Rare Book Collection of C. G. Jung," *International Journal of Jungian Studies* 3 (2): 169.

[108] S. Shamdasani (2012), *C. G. Jung: A Biography in Books* (New York. W. W. Norton), 188.

[109] In German, "Zur Empirie des Individuationsprozesses"; in literal translation it means "On the empiricism of the individuation process."

[110] C. G. Jung (1939), *The Integration of the Personality* (London: Routledge and Kegan Paul), 41–51.

[111] Jung, 1939, 28.

father was a Swedenborgian, and Swedenborg associated his teachings with hermetic philosophy.[112] The introduction entitled "The Meaning of Individuation" was revised in 1939 as "Conscious, Unconscious, and Individuation," to be published later in the ninth volume of Jung's *Collected Works*, together with a still more expanded version of the interpretation of Kristine Mann's paintings published in 1950 (i.e., several years after *Psychology and Alchemy*). Although Jung claims that Mann's visionary dreams from 1928 first made manifest the parallels between the psychological process of individuation and alchemical symbolism, he chose not to include that material in *Psychology and Alchemy* (1944). He stressed this again on January 24, 1941, in a lecture on alchemy given at the ETH.[113] However, in 1950 Jung chose to publish his interpretation of Mann's paintings in *Gestaltungen des Unbewussten* (*Formations of the Unconscious*) together with texts concerning rebirth, poetry, and (coming full circle) mandala symbolism. From the start and consistently through different versions, he presented Pauli's dreams as an example of emerging mandala symbolism: in 1936, 1937, 1939, and in *Psychology and Alchemy* in 1944.

There are already references to alchemy in Jung's 1912 work *Transformations and Symbols of the Libido*, in which he refers to the imagery of cooking found in the visions of Zosimos.[114] Jung himself claimed to have discovered alchemy in 1914 through the works of Herbert Silberer. Jung mentioned Silberer as precursor in his Eranos lecture "Redemption Motifs in Alchemy" (1936). But in "The Meaning of Individuation" Jung qualifies this, saying Silberer's book did not convince him that alchemy was the missing link between the ideas of Gnosticism that he had studied for twenty-five years and the parallels he was tracking in the symbols of individuation.[115] According to Jung in his last (1959) entry in *The Red*

---

[112] Jung, 1939, 47.

[113] C. G Jung, E. Welsh, and B. Hannah (1990), *The Process of Individuation: Alchemy I: Notes on Lectures Given at the Eidgenössische Technische Hochschule, Zürich* (Largs, Scotland: Banton). These lectures were given from November 8, 1940, to July 11, 1941, and are published in two volumes, *Alchemy I* and *Alchemy II*. In a letter to H. G. Baynes he describes them as lectures "about the individuation process in the Middle Ages." Jung to H. G. Baynes, August 12, 1940, Jung, *Letters*, vol. 1, 286.

[114] Shamdasani, 2012, 167.

[115] Here he dates his acquaintance with Gnosticism to the year 1914, but we know that this is incorrect as has been shown by later research. See also B. Jeromson (2007), "The Sources of Systema Munditotius: Mandalas, Myths, and a Misinterpretation," *Jung History* 2 (2): 20–22.

Book, he renewed his acquaintance with alchemy in earnest in 1930, a decision so pivotal that he stopped the work on *The Red Book*, to which he had committed himself since 1913:

> I worked on this book for 16 years. My acquaintance with alchemy in 1930 took me away from it. The beginning of the end came in 1928, when Wilhelm sent me the text of the "Golden Flower," an alchemical treatise. There the contents of this book found their way into actuality and I could no longer continue working on it. To the superficial observer, it will appear like madness. It would also have developed into one, had I not been able to absorb the overpowering force of the original experiences. With the help of alchemy, I could finally arrange them into a whole.[116]

In 1928 the sinologist Richard Wilhelm sent Jung his translation of the Taoist treatise *The Secret of the Golden Flower*, asking him to write a commentary. Jung worked on the commentary during the winter of 1928–29, but only later did he realize that the text had anything to do with alchemy.[117] So what happened in 1930? In interviews for the preparation of *Memories, Dreams, Reflections*, Jung told Aniela Jaffé that the second part of *Artis Auriferae*, which contains the *Rosarium Philosophorum*, fell into his hands in 1930, and that he started to read it in 1931. He immediately recalled a dream from 1926 in which he "got caught in the seventeenth century." Jung also told how, while working on the commentary to *The Golden Flower*, he had asked an antiquarian bookseller in Munich to forward to him any European books on alchemy he happened across.[118] It was through this bookseller that he received his first alchemical collection, the *Artis Auriferae volumina duo* (printed in 1593), which included the *Rosarium Philosophorum* and the *Turba Philosophorum* (also called the *Codex Rhenoviensis* 172). The edition did not include the first part of the *Artis Auriferae*, because the sixteenth-century printer Conrad Waldkirch considered that the text profaned "the Christian mys-

---

[116] C. G. Jung and S. Shamdasani (2009), *The Red Book = Liber Novus*, 1st ed. (New York: W. W. Norton), 360. Hereafter referred to as *RB*.

[117] C. G. Jung (1938), foreword to the second German edition, "Commentary to 'The Secret of the Golden Flower," Jung (1967), CW 13, *Alchemical Studies*, 4.

[118] C. G. Jung and A. Jaffé (1993), *Memories, Dreams, Reflections* (London: Fontana), 204. Henceforth abbreviated *MDR*. See also *The Protocols of Aniela Jaffé's Interviews with Jung for Memories, Dreams, Reflections*. Library of Congress, Washington DC, and ETH Zurich Hs Hs1171:3, microfilm. Henceforth abbreviated *AJ Protocols*.

teries by applying them to alchemy," that is, by identifying Christ with the mystery of the philosopher's stone.[119]

Jung struggled with this material and finally decided to come to grips with it by creating a lexicon of cross-references, a project that he named "treasure hunting," initiated in the autumn of 1935 (after giving his lecture on Pauli's dreams).[120] This process can be rendered explicit by following the Vision seminars held during the period 1930–34. There, in February 1931, one finds the first reference to alchemy.[121] In November of the same year, Jung mentioned a lecture at the Psychological Club on alchemy by Dr. Thadeusz Reichstein. In his lecture, Reichstein concluded that the alchemical process must be seen as the process of individuation.[122] In December Jung brought to the seminar a little book on alchemy that Reichstein had given him, and he displayed and discussed a detail called "the Pandora woodcut" from the book.[123] He reproduced this woodcut in *Psychology and Alchemy*, identifying the figure as the female part of Spirit Mercurius.[124] References to alchemy increased steadily after that.

---

[119] A. Haaning (2014), "Jung's Quest for the Aurora Consurgens," *Journal of Analytical Psychology* 59 (1): 8–30. Cf. M. v. Franz and C. G. Jung, eds. (1966), *Aurora Consurgens: A Document Attributed to Thomas Aquinas on the Problem of Opposites in Alchemy; A Companion Work to C. G. Jung's "Mysterium Coniunctionis"* (New York: Bollingen Series), 6. Jung's alchemical rare books collection has been fully digitized and is accessible via e-rara.ch (http://www.e-rara.ch/cgj/nav/classification). See also Fischer, 2011, 169.

[120] Shamdasani, 2012, 172.

[121] *Visions Seminars* 1, 1997. In the Dream Analysis seminars that were held between 1928 and 1930, alchemy is mentioned in only three places, first in February 1929 in connection with the alchemical retort. *Dream Analysis I: Notes of the Seminar Given in 1928–1930 by C. G. Jung* (1984), ed. William McGuire (London: Routledge, Taylor and Francis Books), 108.

[122] Shamdasani, 2012, 69.

[123] Thadeusz Reichstein (1897–1996), a Swiss chemist born in Poland, became a professor at the ETH and would receive the Nobel Prize in Medicine and Physiology in 1950 for his work on hormones. He and his brother Ignaz Reichstein were both attending Jung's seminars and were members of the Psychological Club. *Visions Seminars*, 1, 1997, 436. See also C. G. Jung (1996), *The Psychology of Kundalini Yoga: Notes of the Seminar Given in 1932 by C. G. Jung*, ed. Sonu Shamdasani (Princeton, NJ: Princeton University Press); and C. G. Jung (2008), *Children's Dreams: Notes from the Seminar Given in 1936–1940*, ed. Lorenz Jung and Maria Meyer-Grass (Princeton, NJ: Princeton University Press), 382. Today there is a Museum of Pharmacology at the location of the former Institute of Pharmacology in Basel where Reichstein held his chair of pharmacology between 1938 and 1996, displaying among other things a life-size alchemical laboratory. The same house was frequented by Paracelsus and Erasmus.

[124] *CW* 12, 419 (fig. 231). This is an emblematic image or woodcut printed by Hieronymus Reusner, Basel, 1588 (1st ed. 1582). See the digitized "pandora woodcut" from Jung's copy of the Reusner edition under http://www.e-rara.ch/cgj/content/pageview/2032778. These

In the first published version of the Eranos lecture on Pauli's dreams, there are about twenty-five references to alchemy, most of them referring to the two treatises in *Artis Auriferae*.[125] But there are two more references to other alchemical works: to *Tractatus Aureus* attributed to Hermes Trismegistus and to *Mutus Liber*. These references, both placed in footnotes that were removed in the English edition (1939),[126] provide clues to Jung's ongoing discovery of alchemical texts. With regard to dream number 10 in the second series (the dream of the man with the pointed beard and the strange doll-woman), Jung recounts how he compared different editions of *Tractatus Aureus* to verify a saying by Hermes: "I, the lapis, beget the light, yet the darkness is of my nature."[127] After the Eranos lecture on Pauli's dreams in Ascona, on the occasion of his Tavistock lectures in London (held from September 30 to October 4, 1935), Jung visited the British Museum. In his second lecture at the Tavistock, he alludes to the fact that he went to the British museum to find references in medieval Latin manuscripts in order to understand the symbolic products of the unconscious and mentions discoveries that he is about to publish "in a little book."[128] He must surely be referring here to his plans to publish Pauli's dreams containing mandala symbolism. He also implies that the publication may outrage many of the English psychiatrists currently sitting before him. At the end of the fifth and last Tavistock lecture, Jung actually mentions Pauli's case (without disclosing his identity). This is the first time he refers to Pauli's case to an English-speaking audience,[129] but in this instance he refrains from connecting the case with the upcoming publication mentioned on the second day of the Tavistock lectures.

---

images were derived from what was probably the first German alchemical manuscript, *Das Buch der heiligen Dreifaltigkeit* (The book of the Holy Trinity), dated 1414 and 1419 at the Warburg Institute. Jung revised his comment on this image for the second 1952 edition of *Psychology and Alchemy*. The first edition of 1944 had "and when Ripley speaks of the tree of Christ, he is identifying the wondrous tree with the cross of Christ." In the 1952 edition the wording is changed to "and when Ripley speaks of the 'Crowned Maid' (*virgo redimita*) we at once recognize the anima mundi." I am indebted to Maury Krasnow for pointing out this revision. This is one of the few additions to the 1952 edition of *Psychology and Alchemy*, par. 499.

[125] The references are on pp. 26, 33, 35–38, 43, 49, 56–58, 62, 64, 68, 82, 88–89, 91, 93–94, 98, 100, 110, 114, and 118; Jung, 1936.

[126] Footnotes on pages 35, 68 and 114; Jung, 1936.

[127] Jung, 1936, 57. Jung used this saying and made an inscription of it (in Latin) in his bedrooms in his tower at Bollingen alongside a mural painting of Philemon. *RB*, 317.

[128] CW 18, par. 139. I am very indebted to Aksel Haaning for making me aware of this passage.

[129] CW 18, pars. 402–6.

Before going to London to lecture, Jung had written to Pauli on September 21, asking him for permission to include the dream material in a publication. Pauli answered the letter on October 2, explaining that the letter had to be forwarded from Zurich to Princeton. It is unlikely, then, that Jung received Pauli's letter of consent before he mentioned his case on October 4.[130]

According to Barbara Hannah, Jung also presented three lectures on alchemy at the Psychological Club in the late autumn of 1935, after returning from London.[131] He purchased a copy of *Mutus Liber* in December 1935.[132] All this leads to the conclusion that in October 1935 Jung was still writing and editing the text that was to be published in the Eranos yearbook under the title "Dream Symbols of the Process of Individuation," and that he had not yet discovered the information that he would place in the footnotes about his sources, when he gave the lecture in August.

Jung probably embarked on his "treasure hunting," that is, on his journey into the alchemical treatises and in his creation of a lexicon in the autumn of 1935, while in London, then upon returning to Zurich, and finally in Basel during the winter. In the first volume of his alchemical copybooks, there is a receipt from the university library in Basel dated October 26 for the loan of several alchemical books: among them, *Tractatus Aureus* and *Tabula Smaragdina*, both attributed to Hermes Trismegistus.[133] It is interesting to note that in the beginning of the same October (1935), Pauli sent Jung his own draft of a lexicon of parallels between the language of modern physics and the vocabulary of analytical psychology. Pauli sent this in a letter from the Institute for Advanced Study in Princeton, where he spent the winter term 1935–36 working with, among others, Einstein.[134]

Significantly, after having given his lecture on Pauli's dreams, the first product of Jung's treasure hunt was the Eranos lecture given in August 1936, titled "The Idea of Redemption in Alchemy." As noted earlier, this lecture almost didn't happen. Again, the probable scenario is that the published text of the lecture "The Idea of Redemption in Alchemy," printed in 1937, differed a great deal from the version presented to the audience

---

[130] Pauli to Jung, October 2, 1935; Meier, 2001. Unfortunately Jung's letter is not preserved.

[131] Hannah, 1976, 235.

[132] Fischer, 2011, 169.

[133] Shamdasani, 2012, 188.

[134] Pauli to Jung, October 2, 1935; Meier, 2001; Enz, 2002, 294.

in 1936, as Jung constantly reworked his lectures. In the published text, he made extensive use of *Aurora Consurgens* for the first time. In a footnote he acknowledges the contribution of his wife, Emma, who found a complete version of the text in Paris to replace the mutilated copy to which he had access. She was researching the Grail legend in Paris when she came across this volume in the Bibliothèque Nationale.[135] This reference to Emma disappeared from the later editions of this text, as did the reference to Marie-Louise von Franz, who helped him to read and transcribe *Aurora Consurgens*.[136]

Jung mentioned in the seminar that Pauli made his own drawings to his dreams, but he never showed or discussed these in detail, as he did the more elaborated paintings of Kristine Mann.[137] Today, two of Pauli's drawings have been published: one illustrates the dream "The House of Gathering" and the other, "The Vision of the World Clock."[138] The Eranos lecture on Pauli's dreams contains no illustrations, only a few geometrical figures. The seminar notes included diagrams and drawings: for instance, in the seminar Jung discusses the tail-eating or rotating snake in connec-

---

[135] Jung, 1936, 114; "Die Erlösungsvorstellungen in der Alchemie" (Redemption motifs in alchemy), Jung, 1936, 85, 86. I am very grateful to Aksel Haaning (2014) for mentioning this disappearance of the reference to Emma in his paper on Jung's quest for the *Aurora consurgens*. Still the question remains who took the decision to remove these references, Jung himself or the English translator, Stanley Dell? So the steps in Jung's search for the original handwritten manuscript could have been that he first received a copy of *Artis Auriferae volumina Duo* (1593) from his bookseller in Munich around 1930–31, missing the first part of the *Aurora*, then found a printed copy at the British Museum including the first part in the autumn of 1935, thus obtaining the wording of the first paragraph but with traces of revisions that prompted Jung to search further. The search was facilitated by searching for the manuscript by the incipit, which proved successful when Emma Jung was at the Bibliothèque Nationale, at the earliest during the winter of 1935. In his seminars on alchemy at the ETH 1940–41 Jung states that he himself found the manuscript in Paris. See Jung, Welsh, and Hannah, 1990, 109. See also v. Franz and Jung, 1966, 25–27.

[136] v. Franz is on the other hand thanked in the foreword to the volume of *Psychology and Alchemy*.

[137] Pauli started to illustrate his dreams in connection with his sixth dream {0006} of the veiled figure on the stairs. He also states that he made figurines in plasticine. All in all there are about 175 figures, some of them in color. The drawings were made without consideration for technique, but they became more and more stylized, as he started to use ruler and dividers. Information from Karl von Meyenn, the editor of the complete dream material of Wolfgang Pauli.

[138] For the drawings, see K. v. Meyenn (2011), "Dreams and Fantasies of a Quantum Physicist," *Mind and Matter* 9 (1): 9–35. It is interesting to compare Pauli's drawing of "The House of Gathering" with the alchemical illustration chosen (by Jolande Jacobi) to illustrate this dream, called "The Mountain of the Adepts," taken from Stephan *Michelspacher's Cabala* from 1654. Cf. CW 12, 195. In the complete dream recordings there are many more drawings by Pauli.

tion with several dreams. But in the 1944 edition of the text "Individual Dream Symbols in Relation to Alchemy" in *Psychology and Alchemy*, he doesn't illustrate the motif with images. Jung brought five images of mandalas to the Bailey Island seminars but, it seems, no illustrations to the New York seminars. Only one of the mandalas used in the Bailey seminars was included in *Psychology and Alchemy*, but not in the part dealing with Pauli's dreams; instead, it shows up in the third part of the book, dealing with the religious ideas in alchemy in the chapter on the lapis-Christ parallel.[139]

Olga Fröbe-Kapteyn provided Jung with the rich alchemical imagery used in his publications, and she was also pivotal in creating the forum of Eranos, where Jung first lectured on alchemy. She gathered six thousand illustrations over the years, at museums in Rome, Paris, London, and New York.[140] Her interest in symbolic images, which began long before she met Jung, was inspired by the poet and mystic Ludwig Derleth (1870–1948), who had been close to the circle of poets, aesthetes, and esotericists of Stefan George (1868–1933). Derleth first introduced Fröbe-Kapteyn to mythology and mystery teachings and encouraged her to study symbols and images. She was very much into exploring spiritual disciplines when, in 1930, she founded together with the theosophist Alice Bailey "a School of Spiritual Research" that was to be "free of dogma and sectarianism." They organized their first event in the summer of 1930: Bailey and Roberto Assagioli lectured.[141] That same year, she met Jung at Count Hermann Keyserling's School of Wisdom in Darmstadt.[142] (Jung also met the

---

[139] *CW* 12, 369, illustration no. 197. The text to the illustration says: "Christ in the midst of the four rivers of paradise, evangelists, Fathers of the Church, virtues, etc.—Peregrinus, 'Speculum virginum' (MS., 13th cent.)."

[140] *CW* 12, "Foreword to the Swiss Edition," x. Hans Bänziger (1955), "Das Eranos-Archiv," *Du. Schweizerische Monatsschrift* 4:8–10. Bänziger (1895–1956) was a noted psychiatrist from Zurich who had been Fröbe-Kapteyn's adviser for many years, especially concerning the Eranos Archives for the Research on Symbolism. See R. R. Bernardini, G. P. Quaglino, and A. A. Romano (2013), "Further Studies on Jung's Eranos Seminar on Opicinus de Canistris," *Journal of Analytical Psychology* 58 (2): 184–99.

[141] Roberto Assagioli (1888–1974) was a psychologist and founder of the Italian school of psychosynthesis. On this occasion he met Alice Bailey for the first time, which vastly influenced his system of psychotherapy, although he had already been in touch with theosophy as a child, through his mother. Before that he had studied and collaborated with Freud and Jung. Hakl, 2012, 29–30.

[142] Count Hermann Keyserling (1880–1946) was an important figure in intellectual Weimar Germany, married to a granddaughter of Bismarck. His book inspired by his travels around the world, *Travel Diaries of a Philosopher* (1919) became a best seller. With the patronage of Grand Duke Ernst Ludwig of Hesse he founded the School of Wisdom in Darmstadt, which lasted until the early 1930s.

sinologist Richard Wilhelm there.)[143] Others who participated and lectured at the school—Leo Baeck, Gerardus van der Leeuw, and Erwin
Rousselle—all later appeared at the Eranos meetings.[144] Fröbe-Kapteyn
invited Jung to lecture at her summer school in 1931, but he declined.
Hakl claims that Jung was displeased with her close connection to Alice
Bailey and Assagioli and that he pressured her to turn away from them.[145]
In 1932 the two women went separate ways, and Bailey left Ascona. At
the same time, Hermann Keyserling's School of Wisdom, which had been
offering events since 1920, formally stopped meeting.

It was in this context that Jung's first lecture at Eranos in 1933 took
place, in which he chose to present Kristine Mann's visions under the title
"A Study in the Process of Individuation." The conference was titled "Yoga
and Meditation in East and West." Approximately two hundred people
attended. Two years later, in 1935, Jung lectured on Pauli's dreams. It was
perhaps then that Jung encouraged Fröbe-Kapteyn to obtain photographs
of paintings and other works of art from diverse public libraries, at her
own expense.[146] Jung even gave her a letter of recommendation for this
research. As she lacked expertise in art history, she used an ancient divi-
natory method to compensate: she simply poked a long needle into the
card index of the archives and then demanded the book catalogued on the
card that the needle had indicated.[147] After her financial situation became
strained, in 1937 Paul and Mary Mellon agreed to pay for her expenses,
so that she could travel to Italy and Greece to collect pictures with arche-

---

[143] Richard Wilhelm (1873–1930) was a sinologist, theologian, and missionary, and translator of the *I Ching* and several other works from Chinese philosophy.

[144] The name Eranos was suggested by the scholar of religion Rudolf Otto, who coined
the term "the numinous." Hakl, 2012, 49.

[145] Fröbe-Kapteyn made a great effort to invite different famous people to her school for
the program in 1931, for instance Albert Einstein and the translator of the so-called *Tibetan
Book of the Dead*, W. Y. Evans-Wentz. Hakl, 2012, 30.

[146] Hakl, 2012, 30. In the book on the history of Bollingen, McGuire claims that Fröbe-
Kapteyn was inspired by the "the pictures from alchemical manuscripts that Jung had shown
during his lecture" in 1935. I doubt that any alchemical illustrations where shown at the
time. No alchemical pictures were included in the printing of this lecture, and the theme of
alchemy was very deemphasized. Also the fact that Jung showed no alchemical illustration
at the Bailey Island seminars in 1936, but chose illustration of mandalas, strengthens my
assumption. At the lecture in 1936 on the other hand, it is very probable that alchemical
illustrations where shown. The correction of these dates are relevant for tracing the exact
timing of Jung's researches into alchemy. W. McGuire (1989), *Bollingen: An Adventure in
Collecting the Past* (Princeton, NJ: Princeton University Press, 1989), 28.

[147] Hakl, 2012, 333.

typal motifs for the forthcoming conference "The Great Mother."[148] (A story recounts how, in 1941, Fröbe-Kapteyn fell under the scrutiny of the FBI on a return flight via Stuttgart for carrying "cryptic" pictures in her luggage.)[149] It is perhaps safe to assume, then, that the mandalas shown at the Bailey Island seminars were given to Jung by Fröbe-Kapteyn. Also the illustrations to the 1936 lecture "The Idea of Redemption in Alchemy" must have stemmed from her researches. All these and many more were then included in Jung's *Psychology and Alchemy*.[150] In the foreword to that volume, Jung thanks Olga Fröbe-Kapteyn for obtaining the photographic copies of alchemical pictures and Jolande Jacobi for choosing and arranging the illustrations for publication.[151]

Immediately after giving the Ascona lecture in August 1936 titled "The Idea of Redemption in Alchemy," Jung traveled to the United States to attend the Harvard University tercentenary celebrations, giving a lecture titled "Psychological Factors Determining Human Behavior," and to deliver his seminars at Bailey Island. There are traces in the seminars of new alchemical motifs employed as amplifications to Pauli's dreams that are not in the Eranos lecture from 1935. For instance, in the seminar Jung

---

[148] Hakl, 2012, 110. This material became the basis for Erich Neumann's book *The Great Mother*. McGuire, 1989, 29.

[149] Hakl, 2012, 131. Wolfgang Pauli was invited once by Fröbe-Kapteyn to lecture at Eranos in 1953. The topic was "Man and Earth." This was after Jung had stopped lecturing at Eranos. The last time Jung lectured there was 1951, on the topic of synchronicity, a theory that he developed jointly with Pauli. Pauli declined the invitation with the words: "I do not know anyone who is more unsuitable to participate in a conference on this subject than I," and "I don't see it as a general opposition against your conferences but as a certain opposition towards 'Mother Earth.'" He claimed to have no relation whatsoever with the theme "Man and Earth." His friends and colleagues the mathematician Hermann Weyl and the physicist Erwin Schrödinger lectured at Eranos: Schrödinger in 1946 on the topic "The Spirit of Science"; Weyl in 1948 on "Science as a Symbolic Construction of Man." In a still unpublished letter to C. A. Meier from February 25, 1942, Pauli writes about his "Eranos-complex," which suggests his ambivalent feelings about the event (the letter will be published in a forthcoming supplementary volume in the PLC series). Pauli to Olga Fröbe-Kapteyn, December 23, 1952, unpublished, Eranos archive. See also Pauli to Jaffé, November 28, 1950 (1172), PLC IV/I.

[150] The illustrations from the Eranos lecture are found as illustrations 4, 144, 147, 168, 169, 179, 224, 232, 234, 235, and 242 in *Psychology and Alchemy*, CW 12.

[151] Jolande Jacobi (1890–1973), born in Budapest, fled to Vienna in 1919 after the communist invasion. She met Jung when he lectured at the Austrian Kulturbund in 1927, where she was vice president. She moved to Zurich in October 1938 (after a quite dramatic escape) and trained to become an analyst, writer, and prime mover behind the C. G. Jung Institute. M. Anthony (1990), *Jung's Circle of Women: The Valkyries* (rev. ed.) (Berwick, ME: Nicolas-Hays).

expands on the *anima mundi* as a round, perfect globe and refers to the round substance of the alchemists, a motif that is present neither in the 1935 Eranos lecture nor in the English translation from 1939. In *Psychology and Alchemy* Jung developed this theme further with a reference to *Theatrum chemicum*.[152] In the same way, Jung's description of the croquet ball as a symbol of wholeness makes reference to Paracelsus.[153] In addition, the seminars refer to the circulatory work of alchemy (*opus circulatorum* or rotundum), that is, to distill the quintessence through a circular movement or circumrotation, and to the ouroboros as the basic mandala in alchemy, a detail he will expand on in *Psychology and Alchemy*.[154]

During the winter of 1936, Jung cancelled ordinary activities such as his ETH lectures and his English seminar and reduced his analytical hours to a minimum. According to Hannah, he did so in order to immerse himself in alchemical texts.[155]

THE NEW YORK SEMINARS

There were originally no plans for Jung to give a second lecture series on Pauli's dreams. He returned to America because of an invitation to lecture on psychology and religion at Yale (the Terry Lectures). The Jungs traveled on the *Hansa* of the Hamburg America line, most probably from the port of Hamburg around October 8.[156] They had just attended the ninth conference of the International General Medical Society for Psychotherapy, held between October 2 and 4 in Copenhagen, where they had stayed at the Hotel d'Angleterre.[157] It is probable that they went directly to Ham-

---

[152] CW 12, par. 116.

[153] CW 12, par. 150.

[154] CW 12, par. 165.

[155] Hannah, 1976, 238. Another reason for these cancellations could very well be the invitation to lecture at Yale. He must have needed some time to prepare the Terry Lectures to be delivered during the autumn of 1937. The length of the manuscript is approximately 115 print pages. The invitation to the Terry Lectures was a great honor, and there is a fair chance that Jung took a leave of absence from the ETH lectures in winter 1936–37 to properly prepare his upcoming lectures.

[156] Its route was Hamburg–Southampton–Cherbourg–New York, a trip that took about six to seven days.

[157] The conference was arranged by Poul Bjerre (1876–1964), a Swedish doctor and psychoanalyst who introduced psychoanalytic and psychodynamic ideas to Sweden, together with his Danish colleague Oluf Brüel. S. Gieser (2014), "From Copenhagen to the Consulting Room: Pauli and Jung in Copenhagen," *Journal of Analytical Psychology* 59:165–73; Jung to Poul Bjerre, August 26, 1937, Poul Bjerre collection at the Swedish Royal Library. Jung had

burg after their stay in Copenhagen. Their arrival in New York was noted in the newspapers.[158]

The seminars in New York were given before and after the event of the Terry Lectures. While at Yale, Jung was a guest fellow at Jonathan Edwards College. He dined in the hall, and the master of the college, Robert Dudley French, arranged that two or three undergraduates should lunch with him. Among others Jim Whitney and Robert Grinnell were chosen, and Grinnell remembers animated discussions and tea at the Elizabethan Club. Both young men would become involved with analytical psychology.[159]

Having the onrush of attendees to the Bailey Island seminars in fresh memory, Harding planned the New York event on a much larger scale from the beginning. She took it on herself to look for a suitable lecture hall and recommended to Jung the MacDowell Club at 166 East Seventy-Third Street in Manhattan, for its considerable capacity.[160] Of course, these New York seminars were much more formal; indeed, they were "as huge and formal as Bailey had been the opposite."[161] And again, Jung also planned to give private sessions.[162] The seminars were held from 8:00 p.m.

---

wanted Poul Bjerre to reserve three single rooms for him. As his friend and English colleague Dr. Helton Godwin Peter Baynes (1883–1943), translator of many of Jung's works, was presenting at the conference, maybe Jung reserved a room for him. The other room could have been for Emma Jung, who was traveling with him. Baynes was presenting on the topic "Psychological Demonstration of Drawings of a Schizophrenic Artist" on October 4. Program of the Ninth Congress in Medical Psychotherapy, Bjerre collection, Swedish Royal Library.

[158] "Dr Carl Jung Arrives," *New York Times*, October 16, 1937, 3; "'Voice' of Dreams Called Superior," *New York Times*, October 22, 1937, 21.

[159] Robert Grinnell was president of the Association for the Study of Analytical Psychology, and associate professor of philosophy at Stanford and of medieval studies at Berkeley; James Whitney, a medical doctor and Jungian analyst in San Francisco. R. Grinnell (1976), "Jung at Yale," *Spring: An Annual of Archetypal Psychology and Jungian Thought*, 155.

[160] It could hold up to 270 people. Esther Harding–Jung Correspondence, Harding to Jung, correspondence of July 4, 1937, JA. The MacDowell Club of New York City was established in 1905 and disbanded in 1942. It was among the biggest clubs by the same name around the country honoring the legacy of Edward MacDowell and supporting the MacDowell Colony, the artists' retreat in Peterborough, New Hampshire. The club funded and awarded a resident scholarship at the MacDowell Colony and made regular financial contributions. The club charter declared the main goals of the club as, among others, to discuss and demonstrate the principles of the arts of music, literature, drama, painting, sculpture, and architecture. Club membership included writers, musicians, performing and visual artists, theater and film actors, sculptors, and architects.

[161] Dewsnap, 1975. Dewsnap also recounts that she saw Mrs. Jung sitting in the rear of the hall, arms folded comfortably in front of her, head nodding, obviously sound asleep. She felt a deep affection for Emma Jung ever after.

[162] It is obvious from the correspondence that private sessions were planned. They were scheduled from 9 a.m. to 12 noon and from 3:00 p.m. to 5 p.m. each day except Sunday. Eleanor Bertine–Jung Correspondence, Bertine to Jung, September 8, 1937.

to 10:00 p.m. for five days, from Saturday October 16 to October 18 and then Monday October 25 and Tuesday October 26. The Yale lectures were held between October 20 and October 23, and it seems that Bertine drove the Jungs from New York to Yale and back in her car.[163] The announcement of the seminars indicated that only suitable applicants would be considered as participants, and that it was desirable that all attending should read the Bailey Island seminar notes beforehand. Harding expressed concern that people would attend who had not any "experience of the unconscious," or who were not sympathetic to Jung's work. She was afraid that such people could spoil the event for those who came to listen "with understanding ears."[164]

This time, the Analytical Psychology Club of New York was also arranging social events around Jung's visit. On October 17 a club tea was arranged between 4:00 and 6:00 p.m. at the Architectural League, 115 East Fortieth Street, for the members and their friends. Admission requests had to be communicated to Sallie M. Pinckney, the secretary-treasurer of the club. On the evening of Tuesday October 26, after the last seminar meeting, all members of the seminar were invited to a formal "Club supper" in honour of Dr. and Mrs. Jung at the Biltmore Hotel, Forty-Third Street and Madison Avenue.[165] It was at this dinner that Jung gave a most moving speech, and Barbara Hannah had the impression that "he knew he was speaking his last words to many of his audience," speaking as it were "directly from the unconscious." Indeed, this proved to be Jung's last visit to America, although no one thought this at the time. Jung spoke about living one's life as fully as possible and to "do just what Christ did. We must make our experiment. We must make mistakes. We must live out our own vision of life."[166]

One of the attendees at the seminar in New York was W. Stanley Dell, translator of Jung's work, and his wife. Also Paul and Mary Conover Mellon (1904–46) participated. On the last day Maud Oakes, a friend of Mary's from the Pacific Northwest who had studied art at Fontainebleau,

---

[163] Bertine–Jung Correspondence, Bertine to Jung, November 2, 1937, and November 11, 1937.

[164] Correspondence Esther Harding–Jung, Harding to Jung, July 4, 1937, JA.

[165] The cost of the supper was $2.50. Newsletter, summer 1937, document found in the basement of the Kristine Mann Library at the C. G. Jung Center in New York. I am indebted to professor Richard Brown of Bellarmine University in Louisville, Kentucky, for sending me a photocopy of this document.

[166] Hannah, 1976, 238–39. This speech is printed in W. McGuire, R.F.C. Hull, and C. G. Jung (1977), C. G. Jung Speaking: Interviews and Encounters (Princeton, NJ: Princeton University Press), 105, "Is Analytical Psychology a Religion?"

attended.[167] In 1934, Paul and Mary Mellon had read Jung's *Modern Man in Search of a Soul*,[168] and they started to consult with Ann Moyer, later Ann van Waveren, wife of Mr. Erlo van Waveren.[169] They first met Jung at the seminars in New York, and the next year they traveled to Switzerland to attend his Zarathustra seminar and to Ascona to meet Olga Fröbe-Kapteyn. They returned to Zurich the following year and started analysis with Jung and Toni Wolff.[170] Mary Mellon established the Bollingen Foundation in New York, dedicated to the dissemination of Jung's work.[171]

The author and screenwriter Philip Gordon Wylie (1902–71), one of the founding staff of the *New Yorker*, attended the seminars. He came with his analyst Dr. Archibald M. Strong and his wife.[172] Wylie had started analysis with Strong in 1936 because of a drinking problem.[173] The analysis continued for two years, two hours a day, six days a week, in the Harkness Pavilion at Columbia Presbyterian Hospital. During this period Wylie read analytical psychology. This new interest influenced his writings, and he used to boast that Jung had commented on his book *An Essay on Morals* (1947) and that he understood Jung's theories better than anyone else in America.[174] When Jung visited New York in 1937, he and Emma Jung stayed at Wylie's home at East River, Connecticut, for over two weeks, together with Dr. Strong and his wife, intensely discussing Jung's psychological concepts. In 1942, Wylie achieved prominence with a best seller, *Generation of Vipers*, a severe critique of American society

---

[167] McGuire, 1989, 18. The first Bollingen publication, in December 1943, was a book on a Navaho Indian ritual by Maud Oakes, *Where the Two Came to Their Father*, with a commentary on mythology by Joseph Campbell. McGuire, 1995, 301–26.

[168] This book is shown in the beginning of the film *The Petrified Forrest* (1936), featuring Humphrey Bogart.

[169] Erlo van Waveren, Dutch-born American analyst who trained with Jung in the early 1930s, brought there by his future wife Ann Moyer and was founder of the Ann and Erlo van Waveren Foundation. He had also been Alice Bailey's "business manager." Hakl, 2012, 109. See also Bishop, 1994, 92–112. The van Waverens were instrumental in spreading Jung's ideas to many future American Jungian analysts.

[170] McGuire, 1983.

[171] W. J. Schoenl (1998), *C. G. Jung: His Friendships with Mary Mellon and J. B. Priestley* (Wilmette, IL: Chiron).

[172] In the C. G. Jung letter collection edited by Gerhard Adler it is stated that Wylie met Jung already in 1936. Could he have attended the Bailey Island seminars? See Jung, *Letters*, vol. 2, xxxvii.

[173] Dr. Archibald McIntyre Strong (1881–?) was a psychiatrist and Jungian analyst in New York City. See Bishop, 1994, 92–112.

[174] Jung commented on the book with the words "I must say your book is difficult.... I couldn't imagine how you can hope to overcome the prejudice and shortsightedness of your public by a rather abstract demonstration of the moral issues of my ideas." See Jung, *Letters*, vol. 2, xxxix.

and especially of the American "Mom" that he equated with the "destroying mother."[175] In his introduction to the twentieth printing of *Generation of Vipers* (1954) Wylie declared that his gloomy "predictions" in the book tallied with reality because he used the logic of Freud's and Jung's psychodynamic laws as a basis for his "experiment." Using the language of reason and science he pleads that more people should pay attention to and understand science, so that disasters would be made foreseeable and avoided in the future.[176] In a letter, Jung commented on the book to Victor White: "Such a book would be impossible in Europe, because it kills itself.... I don't think Wylie's book defeats its own end in America. The general hide is enormously thick. W. is ethical, but he does not—not yet—understand religion."[177] Wylie also wrote a novel entitled *Night unto Night* (1944) that Warner Brothers made into a movie (starring Ronald Reagan and Swedish actress Viveca Lindfors). Later, in 1949, Wylie defended Jung in the newspapers against accusations of being a Nazi sympathizer. He stated that Jung had made it clear to him, while a guest in his house, that the Nazi leadership was all insane.[178]

JUNG AND ANTI-SEMITISM

We will now shortly speak to the issue of the allegations toward Jung that he was an anti-Semite and Nazi sympathizer. The subject is vast, and many scholarly works have analyzed the subject, and this contribution is in no way exhaustive.[179]

The accusations started in 1933 when Jung took over the presidency of the General Medical Society for Psychotherapy. The society was initiated in 1926 by German-speaking doctors who wanted to promote psy-

---

[175] P. Wylie (1955), *Generation of Vipers*, 20th ed. (London: Muller), 49, 204.

[176] Wylie, 1955.

[177] A. C. Lammers, A. Cunningham, and V. White, eds. (2007), *The Jung-White Letters* (London: Routledge), Jung to White, December 19, 1947, 102–4.

[178] R. H. Barshay (1979), *Philip Wylie: The Man and His Work* (Washington, DC: University Press of America). See also R. J. Plant (2012 [2010]), *Mom: The Transformation of Motherhood in Modern America* (Chicago: University of Chicago Press).

[179] See for instance G. Cocks (1985), *Psychotherapy in the Third Reich: The Göring Institute* (New York: Oxford University Press); S. Shamdasani (1998), *Cult Fictions: C. G. Jung and the Founding of Analytical Psychology* (London: Routledge, 1998); A. Maidenbaum and S. A. Martin (1991), *Lingering Shadows: Jungians, Freudians, and Anti-Semitism* (Boston: Shambhala); J. Sherry (2010), *Carl Gustav Jung: Avant-Garde Conservative* (Basingstoke: Palgrave Macmillan); C. G. Jung, E. Neumann, M. Liebscher, and H. McCartney (2015), *Analytical Psychology in Exile: The Correspondence of C. G. Jung and Erich Neumann* (Princeton, NJ: Princeton University Press).

chotherapy as a separate science and had the ambition to become an international association.[180] Jung had been a member of the society since 1928 and was elected vice president in 1930. The president at the time was Ernst Kretschmer.[181] The annual conference that was to be held in Vienna April 6–9 was cancelled, and Kretschmer resigned. The Nazi regime introduced legislation depriving civil servants considered enemies of the Reich, like communists and Jews, of their jobs and positions (Law for the Restoration of the Professional Civil Service). The regime proclaimed that all professional organizations had to be coordinated (*gleichgeschaltet*) and Jews excluded. Jung was urged to take over the presidency and finally did so with the understanding that he would only be the president of a reorganized international society composed of different national groups. He took office in June the same year and also became the editor of the journal belonging to the society, the *Zentralblatt für Psychotherapie*. Jung could, because he came from a neutral country, initiate a transformation of the society into an international society consisting of national groups that did not have to abide by German laws. Jung put a lot of effort into trying to limit the influence of the overpowering German group. He drafted bylaws that stated that no national group could control more than 40 percent of the votes, and that individuals not belonging to a national group could become members. This allowed the German Jewish members to stay in the organization as individual members. He solicited a Jewish lawyer, Wladimir Rosenbaum, member of the Psychology Club in Zurich, to help him formulate them "as little nazi-like as possible and in such a double meaning to make it possible to slip out of this whole Nazification." Rosenbaum also remembered Jung saying that the Nazis were all really crazy.[182]

This rearrangement was accepted by the board in October 1933. Also the journal was split into an international edition and a specific national supplement. It was planned that each national group would have their

---

[180] The founders were from Germany, the former Habsburg empire, Austria, and Switzerland. U. Zeller (2001), "Psychotherapie in der Weimarer Zeit—die Gründung der Allgemeinen Ärztlichen Gesellschaft für Psychotherapie (AÄGP)" Inaug. Diss. Medizinischen Fak. der Eberhard-Karls-Univ. Tübingen.

[181] Ernst Kretschmer (1888–1964) was a German psychiatrist who researched the human constitution and established a typology. The law in question dictated that non-Aryans and members of the Communist Party were not allowed to practice their profession and that they should be dismissed if they were teachers, professors, or judges, or had government positions. Shortly afterward, a similar law was passed concerning lawyers, doctors, tax consultants, musicians, and notaries. Although Kretschmer resigned at the time, months later (November 1933) he signed a public letter claiming allegiance to Hitler.

[182] Sherry, 2010, 129.

supplement sent out only to the members of that national group, while the international edition would go out to all members. Thereafter there started an intense period of recruiting new national groups that could work as a counterweight to the very large German group, headed by Hermann Göring's cousin Matthias Heinrich Göring. The new organization was finalized in 1934, with German, Dutch, Swiss, and Danish national groups; only later (in 1936) a Swedish group joined.[183]

The first issue of the journal after these events was published in December 1933, wherein Jung wrote an opening address as the new president expressing the importance of not confusing Jewish and Germanic psychology. In the German supplement M. H. Göring wrote an editorial proclaiming the allegiance of German psychotherapy to the ideology of National Socialism. This supplement was distributed along with the international edition to all members, without Jung being informed. In the next issue of the journal, published in 1934, Jung contributed with a piece with the title "The State of Psychotherapy Today." Here he chose to focus on criticizing Adler and Freud's theories as materialistic and soulless in a quite derogative way and again stressing the difference between Germanic and Jewish psychology, seeing what was happening in Germany as a rejuvenating process. He also made statements about Jews not having created a cultural form of their own, being dependent on a host culture.[184] These utterances from Jung started the suspicion of Jung being a Nazi and an anti-Semite. It generated a strong reaction among his Jewish followers and was also debated in the press. We can follow these discussions in the published correspondence among others between Jung, James Kirsch, Gerhard Adler, and Erich Neumann, all Jewish Jungians.[185] Here Jung mainly makes a difference between his race psychological ideas and anti-Semitism, fervently denying that he was an anti-Semite. His race psychology is based on his belief that the ethnic and cultural history of man is imprinted and a living fact of his unconscious psyche. Of course race psychological ideas were held by many scientists at the time, also by Jewish psychologists, as the discussion between Neumann and Jung shows.

---

[183] Cocks, 1985; letter from Walter Cimbal to Poul Bjerre (L 171), January 21, 1934, Poul Bjerre Archive, Royal Library of Stockholm; Gieser, 2014, 165–73.

[184] C. G. Jung (1934), "Zur gegenwärtigen Lage der Psychotherapie," *Zentralblatt für Psychotherapie* 7 (Leipzig): 1–16.

[185] Jung to Kirsch, May 26, 1934, in C. G. Jung, J. Kirsch, A. C. Lammers, and U. Egli (2016), *The Jung-Kirsch Letters: The Correspondence of C. G. Jung and James Kirsch*, rev. ed. (New York: Routledge/Taylor and Francis); Jung, Neumann, Liebscher, and McCartney, 2015.

It seems that Jung was genuinely surprised by the reactions, and it becomes obvious—but no less flattering—that his attacks on "the Jews" was rooted in his ambitions to establish a position for his own school of psychotherapy quite distinct from psychoanalysis. He took the opportunity to get back at Freud and the Freudians for accusing him of anti-Semitism for twenty years, just because he didn't accept the reductionist theory of sexuality. As he argues in a letter to Gerhard Adler, his main critique had to do with Freud denying his own roots by claiming that psychoanalytic theory was objective and valid for all humans, while Jung was convinced that every theory bears the mark of its author (personal equation). He claimed also to speak up for every Jew, yes every person of any ancestry, who wants to find their way back to their own nature.[186] That Jung used vocabulary borrowed from Nazi propaganda against "Jewish science" like "mechanization," "obscene," "undermining," "hostility to life," and "filth" is undeniable, but even psychoanalysts who where defending psychoanalysis slipped into using this kind of language.[187] According to James Kirsch, Jung at the time did not realize the danger of the Nazi movement and thought that it would be over in six months.[188] The same naïveté pertained to Wolfgang Pauli, who did not believe that the development in Germany would lead to war, until the very last minute, when he had to flee Switzerland in 1940.[189]

The further history of the General Medical Society for Psychotherapy shows how Jung continued to strive for a true internationalization of the society, diminishing the power of the German group. A conference was planned in Holland in 1936 but cancelled because of the political situation. At this time Jung wanted to hand in his resignation from the presidency but was urged by his Swedish colleague Poul Bjerre to stay and fight for the salvation of psychotherapy in Europe. Bjerre promised to do everything in his power to organize an international conference in Scandinavia and to recruit new national groups, and he succeeded together with his Danish colleague Olof Brüel in 1937, when a conference was held

---

[186] Jung to Gerhard Adler, June 9, 1934; Jung, 1973.

[187] "Psychoanalysis works to remodel incapable weaklings into people who can cope with life,... those enslaved by their instincts into their masters, loveless, selfish people into people capable of love and sacrifice ... and is able to give valuable service to the principles ... of a heroic, constructive conception of life, attuned to reality." S. Frosh (2003), "Psychoanalysis, Nazism and 'Jewish Science,'" *International Journal of Psychoanalysis* 5:1315.

[188] J. Kirsch (1986), "Reflections at Age Eighty-Four," in J. Marvin Spiegelman and Abraham Jacobson (1986), *A Modern Jew in Search of a Soul* (Phoenix: Falcon).

[189] Pauli to Charlotte Houtermans; M. Shifman (2017), *Standing Together in Troubled Times* (Singapore: World Scientific).

in Copenhagen. At this conference thirteen countries participated, and lectures were given in French, English, and German. An Austrian national group joined the federation, while French and Romanian groups were in formation.[190] With combined forces another conference was pulled off in Oxford in 1938, where an English group joined, with Strauss (who was Jewish) as president of the new group. Jung convinced Dr. Hugh Crichton-Miller to become vice president and thereby replace M. H. Göring. Jung was working to have an American group to join in. At this conference eighteen countries where represented, and it had three hundred participants.[191] In August 1939 a meeting of the delegates was held in Zurich, where Jung finally handed in his resignation. This was in connection with the application of three new national groups, an Italian, a Hungarian, and a Japanese group. As these three were all pro-German, Jung felt that he had failed to turn the society in a democratic direction, and his resignation was finalized in September 1940.[192] The same year Jung's books had also appeared on lists for banned books in Germany.[193]

Matthias Göring wrote to Poul Bjerre on November 12, 1940: "We should not forget that Jung has completely dropped Germany and that he in his latest book 'Psychology and Religion' severely attacks us. It is only thanks to the generosity of our propaganda ministry that this book is allowed to be sold in Germany."[194]

Oddly enough the rumors of Jung being a Nazi took time to reach his followers in the United States. In a letter from Beatrice Hinkle, probably sent to Jung's wife, Emma, she asks about the rumor, allegedly spread by Freud, that Jung had joined the Nazis and was spending time at Berchtesgaden as Hitler's chief adviser. Jung asked from whom she got this information and was informed that she heard it through a friend of Henry A. Murray, a Dr. Hadley Cantril, who worked at Princeton University.[195] Can-

---

[190] C. G. Jung (1938), "Presidential Address to the Ninth International Medical Congress for Psychotherapy, Copenhagen, 1937," *Zentralblatt für Psychotherapie* 10 (Leipzig): 139; 561.

[191] *Zentralblatt für Psychotherapie* 11, 1939, 1. Letter from Jung to Bjerre, December 19, 1938, Poul Bjerre Archive.

[192] Jung to Bjerre, July 12, 1940, Poul Bjerre Archive.

[193] Sherry, 2010.

[194] M. Göring to Bjerre, November 12, 1940, Poul Bjerre Archive. Translated by the author.

[195] Henry A. Murray (1893–1988) was an American psychologist at Harvard University. He was director of the Harvard Psychological Clinic in the School of Arts and Sciences after 1930. Murray developed a theory of personality called personology, based on "need" and "press." Murray was also a co-developer, with Christiana Morgan, of the Thematic Apperception Test (TAT). After falling in love with Christiana Morgan he became interested in

tril had met Freud, who had told him this.[196] She also added: "Nobody that knows you could possibly attach Nazism to you."[197] In December 1944 Eleanor Bertine wrote to Jung that she was interviewed by an agent of the FBI, in an effort to find out whether Jung was connected with the Nazis and whether he was anti-Semitic. She told him that she was fortunate to have several letters from Jung that cleared up the first point, and apparently the man took her word concerning the second point. She considered giving him the name of Eugene Harding as being able to give rather conclusive evidence on that point, but the reference was never followed up. She asked the agent what possible concern the FBI might have with the opinions of a Swiss citizen, but he said he was not allowed to tell her that they had received suspicious information including that Jung at the present time actually was in the United States.[198]

Others have documented the context of this rumor. It is possible that it originated from Jung's connections with conservative oppositional circles in Germany, and among other individuals the surgeon Ferdinand Sauerbruch (1875–1951), who was spending time at Berchtesgaden treating Hitler and his closest men, but who also became involved with Claus

---

Jung's psychology and went to meet him in Zurich in 1925. Christiana Morgan (1897–1967) was an artist, writer, and lay Jungian psychoanalyst that attended Jung's Vision seminars, 1930–34. Claire Douglas (1998), *Translate This Darkness: The Life of Christiana Morgan, the Veiled Woman in Jung's Circle* (Princeton, NJ: Princeton University Press).

[196] Hadley Cantril (1906–69) was an American public opinion analyst. He joined the Princeton Psychology Department in 1936, of which he later became chairman. In 1939, he established the Princeton Listening Centre to study Germany Radio Propaganda. During this time he also received a grant from the Rockefeller Foundation to establish an Office of Public Opinion Research. This brought him in contact with George Gallup and Archibald Crossley, two of the most groundbreaking public opinion pioneers of the period. During the Second World War, he worked as an adviser to FDR on public opinion toward involvement in the conflict unfolding in Europe. He also served as an agent for British Security Coordination during the war. In 1948 Dr. Cantril became a program director for UNESCO in Paris studying the role that international tensions play in causing wars. During the postwar years, he was a founding member of the Society for the Psychological Study of Social Issues and president of the Eastern Psychological Association and was awarded the American Association of Public Opinion Research Award for distinguished achievement. In 1955, Dr. Cantril left Princeton to found the Institute for International Social Research with his colleague Lloyd Free, where they studied transactional psychology. In 1965, Cantril published his most successful work, *The Patterns of Human Concerns*, which linked survey research data with findings in laboratory environments and is notable for creating Cantril's Ladder. By his death in 1969, Hadley Cantril had written over one hundred journal articles and eighteen books.

[197] Correspondence between Jung and Beatrice Hinkle, undated and from November 26, 1938, JA.

[198] Bertine to Jung, December 10, 1944, JA.

von Stauffenberg—whom he had treated after he had been injured in Africa in 1943—and his group of conspirators who later tried to assassinate Hitler on July 20, 1944. They were apparently allowed to use Sauerbruch's home for some of their secret meetings. Jung had probably known Sauerbruch since before World War I, since he had been a professor of surgery in Zurich at that time. They met several times during World War II in Zurich in connection with the Swiss Paracelsus society, to which they both belonged. Sauerbruch informed Jung about Hitler's deteriorating mental status. This information Jung then brought on to Allen Dulles, an American diplomat who set up the OSS intelligence operation in November 1942 in Bern. Jung assisted him with his analyses of German national psychology.[199]

In summary it can be said that Jung had racial ideas and prejudices about Jews, but that he was willing to discuss these conceptions with his Jewish disciples; and that during the period 1933–37 he seemed to have thought that something positive could come out of the Germanic and Nazi movements, in a sense of Germans "going back to their roots," to the fruitful soil of the collective unconscious. He also saw a chance for lobbying for his own brand of psychotherapy now that "Jewish" psychoanalysis was under attack. His criticism of psychoanalysis stemmed of course from long before the 1930s and had overlapping arguments with the racist critique coming from the Nazi ideology, that is, that psychoanalysis was materialistic, mechanistic, "degenerate," and soulless. Jung seemed to have definitively changed his mind about Germany around 1937, and became increasingly concerned about its development. He also engaged more in doing his part to assist the allies and to move the General Medical Society for Psychotherapy in a "Western" and democratic direction.

It should also be noted that Pauli had regular sessions with Jung during the period from November 1932 until October 26, 1934, when Pauli decided to stop seeing Jung. It was precisely during this time that Jung was heavily accused of being an anti-Semite. There is no mention of this in Pauli's letters. We know that Pauli was engaged in helping his fellow scientists that were affected by the anti-Semitic laws and who needed to flee from Germany.[200]

---

[199] Allen Welsh Dulles (1893–1969) was as an American diplomat and lawyer who became the first civilian and third director of Central Intelligence Agency and was its longest-serving director to date.

[200] Shifman, 2017; W. Pauli (1985), *Wissenschaftlicher Briefwechsel mit Bohr, Einstein, Heisenberg u.a. Bd 2, 1930–1939* (New York: Springer-Verlag).

INDIVIDUAL DREAM SYMBOLS IN RELATION TO ALCHEMY

In the Terry Lectures, 1937, Jung addressed an academic audience for the first time about the importance of alchemical philosophy. Here Jung chose to discuss Pauli's dream of the reconstruction of the gibbon (no. 16) and the church dream (no. 17), which he had started to discuss at Bailey Island and picked up again for the beginning of the New York seminars. He also discussed the dream of "The House of Gathering" (no. 54) and "The Vision of the World Clock" (no. 59), which were not covered in the seminars. These were two dreams that occurred after Jung had taken over Pauli's treatment from Erna Rosenbaum, and both were illustrated with pencil drawings by Pauli.

In the Yale lectures, Jung highlights the contrast between the principles of the Dionysian and Christian cults, as he does in the seminars. He discussed the lack of the Dionysian element and ecstasy in connection with Pauli's dream of the Catholic Church, a dream that Jung had started to discuss at Bailey Island. The topic, which recurs in Jung's work from his early reading of Nietzsche, pervades these seminars.[201] In *Psychology and Alchemy*, the interpretation of Pauli's church dream is amplified with this theme of emotions and affect that find no suitable religious outlet in a Christianity that is too Apollonian.[202]

In the 1937 seminars in New York, Jung employs twice as many references to alchemy as in the earlier seminars on Bailey Island. He illuminates motifs such as the philosophical tree and the *soror mystica*, which are not to be found in the essay "Individual Dream Symbolism in Relation to Alchemy," in *Psychology and Alchemy* (even if they are concretely present in the illustrations). In 1937, Jung was also absorbed in the visions of Zosimos. He had just recently lectured at Eranos on the topic,

---

[201] This is a topic that had interested Jung since his reading of Nietzsche in his youth. The topic is present everywhere in Jung's work and is also referred to in the 1935 lecture on Pauli's dreams. He also gave his seminars on Nietzsche during this period of 1934–39. *CW* 12, par. 118; Paul Bishop (1995), *The Dionysian Self: C. G. Jung's Reception of Friedrich Nietzsche* (Berlin: Walter de Gruyter); C. G. Jung (1988), *Nietzsche's Zarathustra: Notes of the Seminar Given in 1934–1939* (Princeton, NJ: Princeton University Press).

[202] *CW* 12, par. 182; *CW* 11, par. 43. For further explanation on Jung's views on the Apollonian and Dionysian cults, a view strongly influenced by the philosopher Friedrich Nietzsche, read seminar text below.

Figure 13. "The House of Gathering" was dreamt on October 16, 1932, Meyenn, 2011, 9–35.

which shows influences in the New York seminars.[203] References to Zosimos also find their way into the text of *Psychology and Alchemy*: the interpretation of vision number 6 of the veiled female figure on a staircase, and again the motif of the ladders in dream number 12.[204] In the New York seminars, Jung expanded on the alchemical idea of *massa confuse*, and this was added to the texts in *Psychology and Alchemy*.[205]

In the published version of Pauli's dreams in *Psychology and Alchemy* from 1944, launched with the title "Individual Dream Symbols in Relation to Alchemy," are several new references that reflect Jung's continued immersion in alchemical texts after 1937. In 1952, Jung republished the book with a few minor changes, including passages derived from his trip

---

[203] C. G. Jung (1938), "Einige Bemerkungen zu den Visionen des Zosimos" (Some remarks on the visions of Zosimos), *Eranos Yearbook* 1937 (Zurich), considerably expanded in "Die Visionen des Zosimos" (The visions of Zosimos), in *Von den Wurzeln des Bewusstseins: Studien über den Archetypus (Psychologische Abhandlungen)*, vol. 9 (Zurich, 1954); cf. CW 13, pars. 85–144.

[204] CW 12, par. 66; par. 80.

[205] CW 12, par. 244.

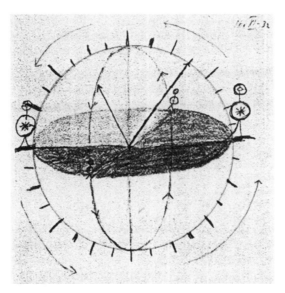

Figure 14. The vision of the World Clock from November 4, 1932, Meyenn, 2011, 9–35.

to India in December 1937, during which time he was introduced to Lamaic mandalas.[206]

Jung recounts that he was deeply occupied with *Psychology and Alchemy* in the summer of 1939 when he was giving his seminars at the Eidgenössische Technische Hochschule (ETH) on the spiritual exercises of Ignatius of Loyola.[207] At this time he beheld a fascinating but upsetting vision of a life-size Christ figure with a body of greenish gold on the Cross. This introduced to him an analogy of Christ with the *viriditas* (greening) of the alchemists, the life spirit or anima mundi that animates the whole cosmos, that pours itself into everything, infusing even inorganic matter such as metal and stone.[208] After his seminars on Loyola he gave a lecture series on alchemy at the ETH starting November 8, 1940, and ending July 11, 1941.[209] These were the last lectures that Jung gave at the ETH, the culmination and finale of the ETH lectures series that he started in 1933.[210]

---

[206] CW 12, par. 123.

[207] Martin Liebscher is editing a book on this topic for the Philemon Series, Princeton University Press, in preparation.

[208] Jung and Jaffé, 1993, 237.

[209] Ed. Martin Liebscher.

[210] In 1933 Jung received a *venia legendi* (right to lecture) at the ETH, the professorial title (*Titularprofessor*) being bestowed on him two years later in 1935.

In these lectures on alchemy, Jung starts with Pseudo-Demokritos, moves on to Zosimos, then addresses the *Tabula Smaragdina*, the *Rosarium Philosophorum*, and the axiom of Mary of Egypt. He revisits the Kristine Mann case material that led him to alchemy, discusses the *Turba Philosophorum*, and the influence of alchemy on authors like Goethe and Meyrinck. He covers several themes from alchemy such as the mountain, the treasure, the *arcanum*, the *mysterium*, and the secret language. By the summer term of 1941 he discusses the concept of *anthropos*, the links to Eastern alchemy, the attitude of the alchemist, meditation, the concepts of *scientia*, *sapientia*, and the prima materia. Jung also linked alchemy explicitly to the process of individuation.[211] But Pauli's dreams are not mentioned at all in these lectures.

Another important step toward publishing *Psychology and Alchemy* was, in 1941, the celebration of the five hundredth anniversary of the death of Paracelsus, on which occasion Jung was invited to give the keynote address in October at the Schweizerische Paracelsus Gesellschaft in Einsiedeln. This prompted Jung to immerse himself in the teachings of the medieval doctor, and he discovered the extent to which Paracelsus was influenced by alchemy. Jung states that it was through Paracelsus that he was finally "led to discuss the nature of alchemy in relation to religion and psychology or, to put it another way, of alchemy as a form of religious philosophy." The results of this exploration inform *Psychology and Alchemy*.[212]

In the summer of 1942, Jung made studies of the spirit Mercurius that were published in the *Eranos Yearbook* and then revised during the period 1943–48.[213] During this time, Jung must have been working on *Psychology and Alchemy* in order to have it ready for printing during the autumn and winter of 1942.[214] Additions to the text "Individual Dream Symbols in Relation to Alchemy" reflect this.[215] The lengthy passage on the gibbon and the association of the dog-headed baboon to the Egyptian Thoth-

---

[211] Jung, Welsh, and Hannah, 1990. The ETH lectures will be published in eight volumes by the Philemon Foundation.

[212] Jung and Jaffé, 1993, 256. All the references to Paracelsus in *Psychology and Alchemy* are added after 1935–36. Paracelsus is not mentioned at all as an influence on Jung's interest in alchemy in the ETH seminars on alchemy from 1940 to 1941; CW 12, par. 165. Jung, "Paracelsus as a Spiritual Phenomenon" in CW 13.

[213] CW 12, par. 172–73, "Der Geist Mercurius," *Eranos Yearbook* 1942, expanded published in CW 13.

[214] The foreword to *Psychology and Alchemy* is dated January 1943.

[215] CW 12, pars. 84–85; par. 150; par. 210; par. 244.

Hermes is surely a fruit of these studies.[216] Jung added a passage concerning the evasive nature of Mercurius as *cervus fugitivus* (the fugitive stag) and the concentration required in alchemical work. Connecting possibly to the case of Pauli, Jung linked this motif to the moral obligation to stop running away from and to face up to the questions of life.[217] He also introduced long passages on the transition from three to four and to the axiom of Maria Prophetissa, and on the idea of the anthropos as a representation of human wholeness.[218]

Jung added references to the sixteenth-century German Christian mystic and theologian Jakob Böhme. Jung read Böhme in his student days, and perhaps he rediscovered him during his "treasure hunt."[219] He did not discuss Böhme in the 1936 and 1937 seminars, but now he included an illustration of a mandala taken from Böhme's opus. For some reason Jung chooses not to include this illustration in *Psychology and Alchemy*. In an added passage in "Individual Dream Symbols in Relation to Alchemy" Jung compares the wheel as a recurring symbol for the circulating process in alchemy to the mystical role of the wheel in the opus of Böhme. Jung emphasizes how much Böhme was influenced by the ideas of alchemy. The idea of an impregnated jelly-like life mass, associated with glue or gum in alchemy, is also added.[220] Lions and wild animals indicating latent affects come as an addition.[221] There is a passage on the Fire Mountain and the seven stars that are more associated with Gnostic ideas added to the interpretation of the dream of "The Solemn House."[222] The motif of the children's play in alchemy as a symbol for cooperating with infantile forces has been added.[223] The phoenix or eagle emerging from the egg as a symbol for the liberated soul is new in "Individual Dream Symbols in Relation to Alchemy."[224] To illuminate "The Vision of the World Clock" Jung adds a passage on the idea of the three *regimina* and the creation of quintessence, and the alchemical hermaphrodite is drawn on.[225] One paragraph is added in the 1952 edition in which Jung compares the thirty-two

---

[216] *CW* 12, par. 175.
[217] *CW* 12, par. 187.
[218] *CW* 12, pars. 209–10.
[219] Jeromson, 2007.
[220] *CW* 12, par. 244.
[221] *CW* 12, par. 277.
[222] *CW* 12, par. 298.
[223] *CW* 12, par. 302.
[224] *CW* 12, par. 306.
[225] *CW* 12, pars. 310–11; par. 313.

pulses of Pauli's World Clock with number mysticism in the Kabbalah.[226] This is the last addition to a text that started out as a lecture on the emergence of *one* symbolic product in the individuation process, the mandala, and transformed over the years into the text "Individual Dream Symbols in Relation to Alchemy."

This process of transformation is even more apparent in the third part of *Psychology and Alchemy*, in the revision of the text "The Idea of Redemption in Alchemy" into "Religious Ideas in Alchemy." Here the additions are so comprehensive as to render the original text unrecognizable.[227] For example, on the subject of *Aurora Consurgens* there is an approximately fifteen-page addition.[228] Jung had apparently already in 1942 planned for the publication of the full text of *Aurora Consurgens* translated by Marie-Louise von Franz, as he states in a footnote to the first edition of *Psychology and Alchemy*.[229] But when von Franz asked Jung to contribute a preface, he became so fascinated with the material that he asked whether she would mind if he wrote a whole book on it. His preface swelled into an eight-hundred-page book, *Mysterium Coniunctionis*, to which *Aurora Consurgens* became a supplementary volume more than ten years later.[230] This work started before he suffered his myocardial attack in February 1944, and he is reported to have told von Franz that his illness, near-death experience, and visions had been necessary for him to fully "know" the reality of the *mysterium coniunctionis*.[231]

Jung obviously decided to include Pauli's dreams in *Psychology and Alchemy*, although in the beginning they were presented as an example of emerging mandala symbolism. Nothing in the Pauli correspondence indicates that Pauli found it in any way strange to publish his dream material in the context of alchemy. The first time Pauli mentions alchemy in his correspondence is on May 24, 1937, after Jung sends him his Eranos essay "Redemption Motifs in Alchemy." Pauli states that the essay is of great

---

[226] CW 12, par. 313. Jung had some strong visions with Kabbalistic contents in connection with his heart attack in 1944. See Jung and Jaffé, 1993, 354.

[227] Just to mention the largest changes: pars. 361–80, pages 285–87, pars. 420–21, pars. 426–32, pars. 456–61, pars. 464–78, pars. 497–500, pars. 502–8, pars. 510–12, pars. 515–55, par. 565 are added in *Psychology and Alchemy*. The English version from 1939 published in *The Integration of the Personality* is only slightly revised from the Eranos version. There are some footnotes that are removed and a few passages that have been moved to the beginning of the text.

[228] CW 12, pars. 464–79.

[229] Haaning, 2014, 510.

[230] Shamdasani, 2012, 196.

[231] Hannah, 1976, 279. Jung's near death experience is described in Jung and Jaffé, 1993.

interest to him both as a scientist and in the light of his own personal dream experiences. He also confirms the relevance of the link between concepts describing physical processes and psychological processes, saying that "even the most modern physics also lends itself to the symbolic representation of psychic processes, even down to the last detail," and after 1935 he refers to the role played by the "the radioactive nucleus" in his dreams after 1935 as a parallel to the philosopher's stone.[232]

Jung gradually amplified Pauli's dreams more and more in the light of alchemy. Jung's thorough reading of Paracelsus and his discovery (or rediscovery) of Paracelsus's concept of the *lumen naturae*—the light of nature, the divine spark buried in the darkness of matter, in the innate intelligence in animals and plants, and also in man—contributed to the decision to include the physicist's dreams in *Psychology and Alchemy*.[233] Perhaps Jung considered it symbolically appropriate to include the dreams of Pauli as quantum physicist and modern alchemist, a man combining a deep knowledge of the mysteries of matter with a devout observation of his unconscious psyche. Pauli embraced a similar idea in his historical work *The Influence of Archetypal Ideas on the Scientific Theories of Kepler*. Starting in 1946 after a compelling dream, Pauli studied the debate between the astronomer Johannes Kepler and the alchemist Robert Fludd, focusing on that point in history when the shift occurred from the older hermeneutic worldview to an emerging newer one characterized by a strict demarcation between subject and object, between soul and matter. The older hermeneutic view included a feminine element in the form of the anima mundi (world soul) who stands in direct relation to the human soul, macrocosm to microcosm, connected. What intrigued Pauli was not only quantum physics' renewed interest in the problem of the demarcation between subject and object, but also his own differentiated identification with both parties in the historical debate: "I myself am not only Kepler but also Fludd."[234]

---

[232] Pauli to Jung. May 24, 1937 (22P), *PJL*. See also Pauli to Kronig (807), March 10, 1946, where he (for the first time?) to a physics colleague mentions Jung's interest in alchemy and the link between alchemy, his dreams, and the experience of psychological transformation, with the comment, "There are obviously very deep connections between Mind (Seele) and Matter and thus also must be between the physics and psychology of the future," PLC III.

[233] C. G. Jung (1942), "Paracelsus as a Spiritual Phenomenon," in *CW* 13.

[234] Gieser, 2005; R. Westman (1984), "Nature, Art, and Psyche: Jung, Pauli and the Kepler Fludd Polemic," in *Occult and Scientific Mentalities in the Renaissance*, ed. Brian Vickers (Cambridge: Cambridge University Press), 177–229. Pauli to Fierz, January 19, 1953 (1507), PLC IV/II.

Bailey Island Seminar, 1936

Lectures 1–6

PREFATORY NOTE TO THE MIMEOGRAPHED NOTES OF THE BAILEY ISLAND SEMINAR

THESE NOTES are for the use of the members of the Bailey Island Seminar with the understanding that no part of them is to be copied, loaned, or quoted for publication without Dr. Jung's written permission.

The difficult task of taking down these talks in shorthand, as nearly verbatim as possible, and transcribing them, was done by four members of the group: Natalie Evans, Chairman, Henrietta Bancroft, Ruth Conrow, and Ruth Magoon. The Committee desires to express to them its appreciation for their part in making this valuable material available to all present; also to Sallie Pinckney for her help in the editing for final publication.

The aim of the Committee, in response to the request of many members of the Seminar, has been to keep the talks as nearly as possible as Dr. Jung delivered them, thereby conserving the informality of the spoken lectures.

Dr. Jung has consented to let these notes be distributed to those present at the talks without his final suggestions or corrections. Any errors or shortcomings that have occurred are the responsibility of the Notes Committee.

KRISTINE MANN, CHAIRMAN
M. ESTHER HARDING
ELEANOR BERTINE[1]
Notes Committee

---

[1] For information about the women mentioned here, see introduction.

Lecture 1

Ladies and gentlemen, I must tell you first that I am really very grateful to you and to the committee for giving me this opportunity to say a few things about my special interests.[1] Though I am a practical man and have done much work with patients, I am also interested in scientific pursuits, and, as you know, I have been chiefly concerned with the peculiar processes of our unconscious mind. I consider the unconscious mind of man as something very important. Many people even in our day are convinced that there is no such thing as the unconscious mind. They think that the human mind, the human psyche, is just the conscious and its contents, and that beyond that there is nothing but physiology, namely, peculiar processes in the brain cells. But our experience with insane and neurotic patients, with dreams, and with the documents of history has shown very clearly that beyond the conscious there is a sphere of the mind that is not the object or content of the conscious; something which is invisible, unknown, yet most influential with respect to our conscious processes.

Our conscious processes, as a matter of fact, depend usually upon the functioning of the unconscious—so much so that if the unconscious should prefer not to function on a certain day we should be absolutely unable to say a word because it would not come into our mind. When I talk to you I depend entirely upon the functioning of my unconscious, which may give or withhold the word. If the unconscious should prefer not to give the word then I could not think of the word; it simply would not enter my mind, and I would be cast ashore and wrecked. I could not even say, "Good morning," because I could not remember the words *good morning*; the unconscious could withhold them. As you know, that happens every day. So, when you seek a name and want to introduce somebody, often the unconscious isn't on the spot, and you don't find the name, though it is perfectly well known. Of course, there are certain reasons why

---

[1] This lecture was held on September 20, 1936.

the unconscious at times refuses to work. In pathological cases it may refuse to function in a wide area of the mind.

Now you see this unconscious mind is not complete darkness, an indefinite field of things we do not know. We can make out something about it in an indirect way, namely, by means of those materials of our consciousness which clearly derive from somewhere else than from this visible world of experience. And by that I mean chiefly from dreams, just to mention one source. Of course, there are many other manifestations of the unconscious, but dreams are those products that are closest to our immediate awareness.

When I want to say something about the unconscious I am always in a certain difficulty; there are so many things one can say about it. It has so many aspects that it is often quite difficult to find a single topic of which one could treat in a short series of lectures. It is particularly difficult to find something complete and standing by itself, because in the unconscious everything merges with everything else, and under certain conditions anything may become anything else. One calls this peculiar condition the contamination of one content of the collective unconscious by others. The contents are likely to be contaminated, though they are not always so; but we must assume that in a condition of complete unawareness, of complete unconsciousness, all contents of the unconscious are merged, practically, into one indistinguishable complete unit which, because it cannot be differentiated, cannot be conscious.

You also see that when things are dimly conscious they still carry the characteristics of contamination; but the more they become conscious the more they are distinguishable. As a matter of fact, to call contents "distinguishable" means "capable of being conscious"—they are synonymous terms. In spite of the fact that the contents are merged we can distinguish certain strata of the unconscious, certain contents, as for instance, those of the personal unconscious and those of the collective unconscious.[2]

By the personal unconscious I understand contents which were once part of our conscious life, things that have been forgotten, things that are repressed, overlooked. I would also include subliminal contents which are not now conscious and have never been conscious, but have been acquired

---

[2] C. G. Jung developed the notion of the "collective unconscious," though the concept was of a later date, in his work *Wandlungen und Symbole der Libido: Beiträge zur Entwicklungsgeschichte des Denkens* (1912), translated into English in 1916 under the title *Psychology of the Unconscious*; see also CW 5, preface to the 2nd and 4th editions. He first used the term "collective psyche/unconscious" in *The Structure of the Unconscious* (1916); see CW 7, pars. 437–507.

during our personal life. These subliminal contents play sometimes quite a role; they enter our unconscious mind, this personal subconscious, through the sense organs, our hearing, our seeing; but they are of such small intensity that they do not become conscious. Psychic processes must have a certain intensity in order to reach consciousness. If they do not reach that intensity, they do not become conscious, but still they enter the subconscious mind. We can hear something but may not know that we have heard it. Yet it is in us as if we had heard it and really works in us as if we had heard it.

Beyond this we have the collective unconscious, which is of entirely different quality and structure, something we have never acquired; it is born with us, came into the world with us, born within the brain structure; something which is identical with the structure of the instincts. It has the form of an instinct, the image in which an instinct functions; and we call these "images" archetypes. This term is of very ancient origin. You will find it in the writings of Pythagoras. It was frequently used in the centuries immediately before Christ, and immediately after. Later Saint Augustine took it up again, and there I got it.[3]

Now these archetypes are, as I say, a form of instinct. If you observe the instinctive functioning, for example, of an insect, you will see that this instinct has a certain definite form. For instance, a certain insect performs a certain act on a plant, doing it always in the same way, not being taught. Born with that instinct, it will invariably carry out an instinctive action the moment it comes into contact with that plant. We must ask ourselves: How does this insect know that this is the plant upon which such and

---

[3] Cf. Jung, "Aion," CW 9/II, pars. 74–91. In his earliest texts Jung refers to Saint Augustine as a source of the archetype concept. In 1954 he reports as his sources the Greek theologian Saint Irenaeus, whose *Adversus haereses* presents the ideas of the Gnostics. He also refers to *Corpus Hermeticum* and to Dionysius the Areopagite's *De divinis nominibus*. Cf. Dionysius the Areopagite (1897), *Works, the Divine Names*, section 5 (1–127). Jung already refers to Gnostic systems in his doctoral thesis from 1902, "On the Psychology and Pathology of So-Called Occult Phenomena," CW 1, par. 149. In 1948 Jung confessed that the term does not come from Saint Augustine. Jung to White, September 24, 1948, in *Jung, Letters*, vol. 1, 507: "S. Augustinus does not use 'archetypus' as I once erroneously surmised, only the idea, but it occurs in Dionysius Areopagita." Although delivered initially in 1934 as an Eranos lecture, Jung revised the paper twenty years later. Jacobi notes that Jung "was drawn to the term above all by Saint Augustine's definition of the *ideae principales*, the Latin equivalent of the Greek ἀρχέτυπον. J. Jacobi (1968 [1943]), *The Psychology of C. G. Jung* (New Haven, CT: Yale University Press), pp. 39–40. Cf. C. G. Jung (1928), "Instinct and the Unconscious" (1919) in *Contributions to Analytical Psychology* (London: Routledge and K. Paul), 279 (cf. CW 8, par. 275), and "The Archetypes and the Collective Unconscious," CW 9/I, par. 5.

such a thing should be done for the propagation of the species? There must be an archetypal image in the insect which begins to function when the stimulating form appears in the outer world—the sort of reflex image in the animal that is identified directly with the flower in real existence. So when the insect finds the flower, this instinct instantaneously begins to work, and the insect must often perform a very complicated action which is usually for the propagation of the species.[4] The same process is found throughout all living nature; and so also man has similar instincts of specific forms, which are congenital and inherited, never acquired. How they originally came into existence at all is a matter for speculation. I know nothing about that. I only know that as far back as we have any records of man's mental activities we see that these archetypes have always been in existence. They are really identical with the "eternal ideas" of Plato.[5] They are the archetypal or image world, by means of which we are able to grasp the world at all so that we are not absolute strangers here. We are already acquainted with this world when we come into it; there is from the beginning a peculiar identity between the inner and the outer.

These archetypes are, despite their contamination, quite recognizable, and they were recognized long before I came upon them. We find them in comparative mythology as the so-called mythological motifs, and we also find them in the psychology of the primitives.[6] Contemporary research has established their presence there. (Cf. Lévy-Brühl, *Représentations Collectives*.)[7]

Now as a possible subject for our seminar I have chosen such an archetype, and I shall try to show you in the actual material produced by a dreamer the peculiar life such an archetype lives in the unconscious. It is like a living organism, and it develops, differentiates itself, and has something like a life of its own. Now this is, of course, a pretty new idea, and I shall try to be simple and clear about it. The particular archetype I have chosen is an image that often occurs in dreams and that plays a very great and important role. I will explain to you later what it is all about.

---

[4] Jung, 1928. See *CW* 8, par. 268.

[5] See Plato, author, and B. Jowett, trans. (2000 [1894]), *The Republic* (Mineola, NY: Dover), 149.

[6] Jung's usage of expressions such as "Negro(es)" or "primitive(s)" was consistent with the customary vocabulary of his time and has been kept in the translation.

[7] This reference is in the original manuscript of the lectures. L. Lévy-Bruhl (1910), *Les fonctions mentales dans les sociétés inférieures*; in English, L. Lévy-Bruhl (1985), *How Natives Think* (Princeton, NJ: Princeton University Press). Jung read his work while preparing his book *Transformation and Symbols of the Libido* around 1910. Shamdasani, 2012, 53.

First I must say a few words about the case from which I got the series of dreams in which the archetype is contained. It is that of a young man. He was about thirty-two years old when he came to me.[8] He is a highly educated person with an extraordinary development of the intellect, which was, of course, the origin of his trouble; he was just too one-sidedly intellectual and scientific. He has a most remarkable mind and is famous for it. He is no ordinary person. The reason why he consulted me was that he had completely disintegrated on account of this very one-sidedness. It unfortunately happens that such intellectual people pay no attention to their feeling life, and so they lose contact with a world that feels and live in a world that thinks: in a world of thoughts merely. So in all his relations to others and to himself he had lost himself entirely. Finally he took to drink and such nonsense so that he grew afraid of himself, could not understand how it had happened, lost his adaptation, and was always getting into trouble. This is the reason he made up his mind to consult me.

I saw him at first for only twenty minutes. I instantly perceived that he was in a way a master mind, and I decided not to touch his intellect. I therefore proposed to him to go to my then most recent pupil, a woman doctor who knew very little about my work.[9] She was right in the beginning of her own analysis; but she had a good instinctive mind. She was not a fool, had a good deal of common sense, and was, of course, highly surprised when I told her that I was going to send such a fellow to her. Naturally I had to do some explaining. I told her why I was doing it and also suggested to her how to deal with him. I told her I had instructed him to present his dreams to her; that he must write them out very carefully, and that she should listen to them and nod her head and, in case she was astonished or puzzled, should say so. She should not, however, try to understand or analyze these dreams. I said, "You won't understand them at all, so you had better not touch them." Now she was, of course, quite glad that she had to play a more or less passive role, and astonishingly enough that man incidentally saw the point too. He understood what I

---

[8] Wolfgang Pauli (1900–1958) first saw Jung at the end of January 1932. According to the findings of Karl von Meyenn in the CDM Pauli was inspired to go to Jung through a dream he had in January 1932 (dream {0256}) where his friend the mathematician Erich Hecke (1887–1947) tries to persuade Pauli to go and see Jung. Pauli was thirty-one years old at the time. See *PJL*.

[9] Erna Rosenbaum (1897–1957) was an Austrian analyst who studied in Berlin before coming to Jung in Zurich, then moved to England in 1933; she married A. R. Redfern and was one of the founders of the Society of Analytical Psychology in London (SAP). See Westman, 1958, 180.

told him. I said, "I don't want to influence your own mind, which is valuable. You can do the whole thing by yourself, and then you will be convinced. If I should do it for you, you would never be convinced, therefore I shall not even try. You go to this woman doctor and she will listen to your dreams." She did. There were certain dreams in which she noticed nothing and others in which she noticed queer material. Other dreams were not clear, but she felt that there must be something back of them, and then she asked a question. Or she felt about certain points that they were not well worked out, and she told him. That was enough. He went home and continued dreaming, and the next time he brought new material with him. And so before he came back into my hands we had a series of over four hundred dreams and visual impressions. He had the gift of visualizing things, and so he had spontaneous fantasies. I count them as dreams—they are just as good as dreams. You can have your dreams in the daytime.

That material was collected in eight months. He spent five months with the woman doctor and then three months all alone.[10] By the time he came to me he was quite certain of the functioning of his unconscious; he knew that he could trust that functioning, and he knew exactly when something had been told him from outside and when it came out of himself spontaneously. There was absolutely no chance of putting anything into him unless he could agree with it, unless he had felt the same thing. When he was in my immediate care I really had to say very little. Occasionally he said, "Now could you explain this and this" or "I do not understand this peculiar thing." Then I merely told him from my experience and knowledge what I knew about it, and he went away and dreamed again. I never did anything like systematic dream analysis with him. He could do it all by himself in his own peculiar way.

Now as to the contents of his dreams. I must say that his dreams were consistent from the beginning. My pupil, of course, brought them to me, so I could follow up the whole development; and it looked exactly as if at the moment of our first consultation something had been touched upon— something had been started in him—which expressed itself in a peculiar symbol, and that is the symbol of which we are going to speak. But before we come to that I should like to say a few words about dreams.

---

[10] Pauli's first contact with Rosenbaum was in the form of a letter dated February 3, 1932. They had regular sessions (at Hönggerstrasse 127) until the end of June, when Rosenbaum moved to Berlin. She returned in September 1932. They end their contact in October 1932. See Correspondence Pauli–Erna Rosenbaum, JA. Also Gieser, 2005.

Dreams are particularly apt material because we do not interfere with them. We *cannot* interfere with dreams. We can't say we will dream about such and such a thing or have any particular dream. The dream is a natural product like an apple on a tree, like an animal, made by nature, not by man. We could say therefore just as well that dreams are not made by man. They are not made at all. They grow. They come up naturally like a spring. A dream is a series of representations, of images, starting from an underlying unconscious process. Since a dream is a series of images, I assume that these images are caused by an invisible process of an unknown nature, and that is what we call the unconscious. The dream itself in its composition is not unconscious, otherwise you would not know of it. You know of the dream itself, and you conclude as to the underlying processes. These processes are unconscious, that is, not capable of becoming conscious. So whenever you deal with a dream you deal with something that begins and ends in the unconscious and is carried by that unconscious mind, which we shall never know. We only know images of that process; the cause of that process is not known. We have, of course, many speculations about it, but only speculations.

It is often questionable whether this unconscious process has any cause at all. We can ask whether dreams have a cause. That is a fair question, but it is very insufficiently understood as yet. However, we have evidence that makes it highly probable that the unconscious is a continuous process without beginning or end. In other words, we can't apply categories like beginning, end, causality to it. We can imagine it to be a sort of stream that is always flowing past like the series of events in the physical world. It is a continuous stream that begins nowhere and ends nowhere; in other words, our mind has no means of determining a beginning or end.[11] We can speculate about it but have no means of proving anything about it. This formulation probably fits the nature of the unconscious very much

---

[11] This notion was most probably influenced by William James's (1842–1910) concept of "stream of consciousness." James describes consciousness as continuous. Not even sudden events are entirely divorced from what was before and what comes afterward. Although consciousness is seen as continuous, this "stream of consciousness" does not flow uniformly, but with a particular rhythm that alternates between rest ("substantive parts") and motion ("transitive parts"). The purpose of these transitive parts of consciousness is to lead us from one substantive conclusion, where thought can find a contemplative state of rest, to the next. The actual transitions from motion to rest form an indivisible whole and cannot be subjected to detailed analysis. At the very instant we try to stop and contemplate the transitive part, it ceases to be in motion. If we wait until we have reached a "resting point," the motion has passed. See W. James (1981 [1890]), *The Principles of Psychology* (Cambridge, MA: Harvard University Press), 236.

better than if we assume that a dream has a cause and an ending. The dream itself has a beginning and an end, but that is not the same as the process underlying it. The dream is a series of representations that more or less incidentally become conscious.

We must assume that the dream process, that process that causes a dream to be, that carries a dream, takes place continuously as a stream of psychical life that happens in us or which we contact. Only occasionally, however, under certain circumstances, do we become aware of it. That occurrence which is represented in a dream is just one event in the stream of psychic events that goes on all the time. So you can catch a dream even in the daytime, when you are conscious. For instance, when you suffer an *abaissement du niveau mental,*[12] or when you are tired, right in the midst of your conscious thoughts certain phenomena begin to appear, which, if they become more intense, can develop into hallucinations. The same thing happens with people who are intoxicated; certain automatic phenomena begin to appear. Visions or whole passages of dream contents may arise as soon as they are a bit tired or drunk. In other words, when the conscious loses its intensity, then the unconscious can appear. Then it is just as if there were an opening somewhere in your consciousness—a hole through which you become aware of the presence of an entirely different functioning of the human mind. You see that particularly in cases of schizophrenia and certain forms of insanity—the voice changes, the expression changes, the thought contents change completely. It is just as if something quite strange had suddenly appeared and then as suddenly vanished. That is a hole, a split, in our consciousness through which we can become more aware of the peculiar contents of the unconscious.

We could therefore represent a dream in the following way.

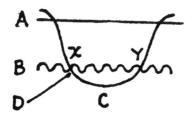

---

[12] "Lowering of the mental level" is a term coined by Pierre Janet (1859–1947), designating a psychic state caused by strong affects, fatigue, intoxication, or pathological brain processes. It results in a narrowing of consciousness and a lowering of the levels of attention and orientation. In this (mostly temporary) disintegrated state, unconscious contents break into consciousness, so that consciousness cannot control these unconscious "ideas." Energy

Suppose this line A represents the level of consciousness. Now here in the unconscious B you have a process. When the level of consciousness sinks—that is, when you lose your intensity of consciousness—then you have this curve, C, and at this point, D, the unconscious becomes visible. Now this is the normal way it happens in dreams during sleep. In sleep you have a gradual descent of the intensity of consciousness until you become aware of the unconscious processes. When you wake up, the intensity of consciousness is increased, and this intensification of consciousness wrecks the world of the unconscious, so that it is just as if your unconscious had disappeared again. But the dream is visible only in this part (x to y).

The function of dreams or the function of the underlying unconscious processes can be determined by the quality of the conscious contents of a dream. Ask yourselves, "Why do I dream like that? Why do I think in such and such a way in the dream?" Then you will discover a peculiar relationship between the dream contents and your conscious, namely, a relationship of a complementary or compensatory character.[13] For a simple example: suppose you are not aware of the existence of a conflict in your conscious mind. If in your conscious mind you are more or less at peace, then you are likely to dream of conflict. That means that the opposing forces in the conscious or the unconscious compensates the tranquility of your conscious mind by representing a storm or a fight or a fire, or any other emotion. So it happens that in a time when you are happy during the day, you may have more or less disagreeable dreams containing conflict.

Or, suppose you are conscious of a conflict; you are conscious that your mind is not at peace; you are a bit restless or nervous; or you even suffer intensely from a conflict in consciousness. Then the dream may show

---

is withdrawn from certain conscious contents so that they are blacked out or become unconscious. See P. Janet (1903), *Les obsessions et la psychasthénie I* (Paris: Alcan), xviii.

[13] In his Eranos lecture held in 1935 (henceforth EYB 1935) concerning Pauli's dreams Jung comments that he abstains from going into an analysis of the different connotations of the concepts of complementarity and compensation. See Jung, 1936, and also *CW* 12, par. 48. This comment was probably motivated by Pauli introducing the concept of complementarity from physics to Jung, and suggesting that it might be better to perceive the relationship between the conscious and the unconscious as a complementary one, i.e., that they stand in a mutually excluding relationship to each other instead of seeing the one as a part of the other. See Pauli to Jung, October 26, 1934 (7P), *PJL*. Compensation has more to do with the notion that the unconscious balances the one-sidedness of the conscious attitude. This footnote is not included in "Dream Symbols of the Process of Individuation" in C. G. Jung (1939), *The Integration of the Personality* (London: Routledge and Kegan Paul), 96–204 (henceforth "Dream Symbols"). See also *CW* 12, par. 48.

tranquility, may make use of symbols that represent a union of opposites. Then your unconscious is obviously trying to produce peace. That is what I mean by compensation. Usually, or at least very often, people cherish the idea that they are living at peace with God and man and that there is no trouble whatever, until they are disturbed by something—an uncomfortable symptom—and then they believe, of course, that it has to do with the body and with food. They develop a sort of phobia, become food fiends, eating only certain things. They believe the body is what they eat and try to eliminate the disturbance by changing the food. Now of course such a thing does not help. It may help some people for a while, as anything you believe in can help for a while.

When, however, you are not cured, you go to the doctor and tell him about the symptoms, and he will inform you that this is a psychogenic disturbance; that there is something on your mind that worries you. But quite likely you don't want to know about it because it is against your philosophy; things ought to be normal at all times, and here is something that disturbs you, and this should not be, according to your idea. There is a conflict because your philosophy is not at one with nature. And then the doctor plays that awful trick upon you, by telling you these symptoms have appeared because you are not at peace with yourself. When at last you become conscious that you are a battlefield of opposing forces you are likely to conclude that you are the only one human being in existence that is entirely wrong, because you realize that this is a conflict while everybody else seems to consider that everything is quite all right. The bad people are never living on the same street with you nor in the same house, and only bad people have conflicts. Also nobody will help you very much because the whole world tries to believe that the human being has no conflicts and that to have them is all wrong. So the more impressed you are with the fact that now you have a conflict, the more you feel yourself to be a bad person. You are thoroughly worried, and that is the conflict in consciousness.

Then, if you observe, you will discover that the unconscious produces peculiar dreams that try to overcome that conflict; the unconscious is attempting to create a new personality that is capable of dealing with opposites. First you are a mere ego that prefers to imagine there is no such thing as conflict; then you fall into the conflict between yourself and the strange fellow that is also in yourself, a sort of shadow of your ego-personality, indubitably you yourself, but painted quite black and producing things for which you would not stand; things impossible and immoral; things that depress you and that you fight against. Then the unconscious is trying to produce a personality that can cope with man as he really is rather than as he is supposed to be, capable of coping with the real man, namely, the man that consists of light and darkness.

Now in such a state the unconscious will produce a certain symbol which we designate as a *mandala*, a Sanskrit word meaning "circle," "magic circle."[14] We owe this term to Eastern philosophy, wherein the Tantric and Lamaistic texts elaborate descriptions of it occur. It exists not only in the East but is also to be met within the West. It is very old, existing from the earliest beginnings, one of the few great symbols that can be found in all times where we have evidence of the existence of mankind. The oldest mandala symbol I have come across belongs to the Paleolithic age. We find it in the Paleolithic drawings of Rhodesia where it has color and form and is about like this:

It is a circle containing a star-like figure that always forms a cross. It has a fourfold division. Now ethnologists often call this the sun wheel, but I must draw attention to the fact that this sun wheel was made when no wheels had been invented. The wheel is a late invention of man, dating from the Neolithic age. Hundreds of thousands of years elapsed between the making of this symbol and the actual making of a wheel. One therefore should not use the term *wheel*, but *mandala*. It usually appears in the form of a circle or a globe, also in the form of the cross, fourfold or eightfold, or in the form of the square, usually divided by four or eight. It often contains four colors representing four different qualities, which may perhaps be symbolized as four peculiar beings standing in the four corners of the symbol, demons, or I don't know what. Then the element of rotation is very often given at the same time in the symbol, that is, the whole thing is represented as revolving. Almost always the center is of greatest importance, though in individual cases it is not filled in by significant symbols. But this latter would be, of course, a particular case which is not

[14] Cf. EYB 1935, p. 14; CW 12, par. 45.

normal. We use these facts for diagnosis with reference to the stage of development of the individual.

The meaning of the symbol is a crossing. When two things cross they form a center; they come together, a symbol of the union of opposites. We have that symbol in Christianity, Christ being the unifying or reconciling symbol on the Cross between the two thieves, the one who is going with Christ to heaven and the other one who is going with Christ to hell; for as you know, after His death Christ went to hell. The one thief is meant for hell and the other thief for heaven. We find this same symbolism, only differently expressed, in the Mithraic cult.[15] There in the center instead of the Christus, instead of the crucified victim, is the god sacrificing the bull and the bull is himself. On either side is the torchbearer (*dadophoros*), who is a youth usually standing in a peculiar position, with one leg crossed over the other. One dadophor holds the torch pointing down, the other up-down, and up. Above the whole scene there are often the signs of the zodiac and the sun or a day rising on one side and the night going down on the other side of the picture, a sort of rotation.

The circle means completion, roundness, also union of opposites, making a whole. So the circle also means wholeness, therefore the complete or perfect thing has always been understood to be round. Plato says that the primordial man who was the complete man, the perfect man, was an all-round being, who had four arms and four legs and being hermaphrodite, when cut apart, made man and woman.[16] The older philosophers, as for example, Empedocles, held that the most perfect being would be the so-called *sphairos*, or globular being.[17] This being is one who does not exist in the beginning, but rather in the end of the world, namely, when things attain to the perfect condition. He called that being divine, a god, *theos eudaimone statos*, "the most blissful God," because all the different elements of nature and of the world are united in him by love, by friendship, by *philia*. They are brought together in a perfect form. Now this is also such a psychological symbol.

Since that complete or perfect being cannot be brought about without a process of union of opposites, this symbol of the mandala also has the

---

[15] Mithra or Mithras refers to a sun god worshipped since ca. 1000 BC in Iran. His cult "Mithraism" was spread in the first century AD by Roman soldiers and was based on the opposition between good and evil and was serious competition for early Christianity. Jung read *A Mithraic Liturgy* by Albrecht Dieterich in 1910. Shamdasani, 2012, 51.

[16] Described in Plato's *Symposion*. Plato (1978 [1951]), *The Symposium*, rpt. ed. (Harmondsworth: Penguin), par. 190b.

[17] Empedocles (ca. 490–430 BC), Empedokles, and W. E. Leonard, trans. (1973), *The Fragments of Empedocles*, new ed. (LaSalle, IL: Open Court), 29, fragment 27.

meaning of transformation, or rebirth; and it is always understood that the center, which is emphasized in this most archaic form, is the place of transformation or of rebirth. It is the place where the secret transformation is brought about. In the Chinese Yoga they call it the germinal vesicle, the bladder in which the transformation takes place.[18] In Western philosophy it is the so-called vas Hermeticus, which is an alchemical vessel in which transformation or transubstantiation occurs. It is the equivalent of the Christian chalice in which transubstantiation in the communion takes place. Those are the historical interpretations of the symbol. Psychologically it would mean then that it is the transformation, the unification, the reconciliation of the opposites in man. This is what we call in psychology the individuation process, namely, when we become what we are, when we bring together everything we possess, and particularly all the complexities and contradictions of which we necessarily consist. Then we are what we are, and that is individuation. You see these conflicts are given by nature. They are a collision of instincts. If that were not so, if we had no conflict, then we would have no energy. Energy is only to be found where there is opposition. This is an absolutely necessary source of any energy. There is no energy in nature if there is not an opposition of above and below, hot and cold, and so on.

Before I begin with the actual dreams I should say a few words about the material we are dealing with. I have extracted from the dreams and visions fifty-nine that contain this particular symbol, and I will show them in their natural sequence so that you can see how this symbol behaves, how it develops. Of these more than four hundred dreams, only forty-five were dreamed while I was seeing the patient.[19] As I saw the patient at the beginning for only twenty minutes, and nothing was said about these symbols, it is certain that I have not suggested the whole thing to him, but that the production of the symbols is really absolutely spontaneous; no invention, no cheating about it. I'm sorry I have to insist on such things. People always think I invent them. It is merely their fathomless ignorance

---

[18] Cf. R. Wilhelm and C. G. Jung (1962 [1931]), "Origin and Contents of the T'ai I Chin Hua Tsung Chih," in *The Secret of the Golden Flower: A Chinese Book of Life* (1962 [1931]) (London: Routledge and Kegan Paul), 70. There it is stated: "The germinal vesicle is an invisible cavern which has neither form nor image. When the vital breath stirs, the seed of this vesicle comes into being; when it ceases it disappears again. It is the place that harbors truth, the altar upon which consciousness and life are made. It is called the dragon castle at the bottom of the sea, the boundary region of the snow mountains, the primordial pass, the kingdom of greatest joy, the boundless country. All these different names mean this germinal vesicle."

[19] Jung took over from Erna Rosenbaum from early October 1932, in connection with dream {0355} October 4 (not published). See CDM.

that makes them talk like that. If they had a little knowledge of the history of the human mind they would be aware that I am talking about things very well known in certain quarters. Only they have never come across them. That is their funeral.

It would not be quite a fair presentation if I should give you merely the selected dreams, therefore I would like to give you first a series of twenty-two dreams, very short ones. I have cut out all the material which is of no importance and which is merely personal, as I am also not allowed to bring this in because I must be very discreet about the case. These are the first twenty-two dreams he had. Among these are to be found those dreams which contain the mandala so that you can see how it appears in a perfectly natural sequence of unconscious productions that have not been disturbed in the least.

Immediately after the first interview with the woman doctor, the patient dreamed the first dream of the series: He was in a social gathering at which there were many indistinct people. He had rather a vague feeling of people around him who were more or less familiar to him. As he was about to leave the party, he picked up his own hat, as he supposed. But when he put it on, he discovered that it was not his, but one strange to him. That is the whole dream.[20]

Now, of course, if a patient should tell me such a dream, I would feel rather hesitant about interpreting it because it was just a little fragment; and one has to be careful not to say too much about such a dream because one may go entirely wrong. In the light of subsequent events, one feels a bit safer. But if the patient should have insisted that I give him my thoughts about it, then I would say, "Of course, I don't know what that dream means in your personal psychology at this moment." For one must make that differentiation between an individual or personal meaning and a general meaning. Those symbols which are of an archetypal nature have a general meaning that can be established apart from a personal psychology. For example, in this dream, the symbol of the hat would suggest that part of a man's attire which covers his head. The head is the seat of consciousness, of the conscious mind, and anything that comes from the conscious mind is a general idea. In the German language we use the metaphor *verschiedene Sachen unter einen Hut zu bringen* in order to express the idea of a complete subsumption, which means that when we have any conceptions or notions from which we create a general idea, we say "we

---

[20] Cf. "Dream Symbols," nr. 1, p. 102, and CW 12, nr. 1, par. 52. I 01 {0001}: "Dream of the strange hat," dreamt on February 5, 1932, CDM.

gather many notions under one hat." Also the hat may designate the general idea we have about the function of a man. For instance, if he is a very prominent individual, then he is "crowned." He has a peculiar kind of hat, the sun hat, the crown of a king; and the crown of a king is the sun's halo with the rays. The king is that human individual who is transformed into the sun. As the sun is in the heaven, so is the king upon earth. As the sun is radiant, so the king is radiant. As the sun is ruler of the universe, so the king or emperor wears the mantle covered with stars, just as the universe wears the celestial mantle. So the Roman emperors, and also the old Babylonian kings, wore mantles bedecked with stars like the medals or orders of today. This is the last remnant of the idea that an individual can be made into a cosmic being—into a sun. Also a doctor's cap or hat is used to designate that particular individual as a scholar.

So you see when the dreamer gets a strange hat it means he is not under his own ideas. A strange idea has caught hold of him. His unconscious has given him a new idea under which he is now. This has been made use of by a writer, Meyrink, of whom you may have heard. He wrote a book, Golem, in which he describes the case of a man who by mistake picked up the wrong hat.[21] On examining it he found in it the name "Athanasius," which means "the immortal one." This would mean that he has put on the hat of an immortal one; he is under the idea of an immortal one. Then Meyrink goes on to describe what happens to the man who put on the strange hat, the hat of the immortal one. He is involved in a series of extraordinary events of a mystical nature. He is invaded by the collective unconscious.

In our case we can assume that by putting on the hat the dreamer will pass under a peculiar influence, presumably the influence of the unconscious, and will enter a new world of experience, namely, the experience of the collective unconscious. That is, he will be surrounded, invaded, influenced by ideas or events that come up from lower levels, up from the basic structure of the mind. Now we shall see if this hypothesis holds water or not.

In the next dream, the second, he was in a train, standing at the window, looking out at the passing scene. He obstructed the window completely

---

[21] Gustav Meyrink (1868–1932), pseudonym of Gustav Meyer, Austrian author. See G. Meyrink and E. F. Bleiler, trans. (1986; 1976), The Golem (New York: Dover), 10. Two copies of this book are in Jung's private library: a 1915 edition (dedication to C. G. Jung by "Carl Picht") and a 1917 edition (dedication: "zum Geburtstag 1922, Dein Sohn"; translation: Happy Birthday 1922, your son); as well as four other additional titles by Meyrink in the Jung library.

and realized that other people were there who wanted to get the view too. He felt that he should give way to them; so he withdrew from the window.[22]

That is the main part of the dream. In this dream we become acquainted with the fact that he is surrounded by other beings—as was the case in the former dream. Again he doesn't know who is there. In the first dream the people seemed vaguely familiar; in the second, they were all strangers.[23] Literally, this means there are other contents in his sphere represented by the other people in the car. They want to get at the view, which means to become aware, to become conscious. To look out means to become conscious of something. So you can see he is in his head—he is, as it were, looking through the window of his head, through the eyes of his consciousness. He should give way to those behind him, whom he does not see, as that sphere behind is the unconscious space. Therefore the Greeks call those that are following us, the invisible ones whose presence we dimly divine, the *synopadoi*, which means "those who are following us from behind," the name for the demons who always accompany man.[24] This idea is merely a consciousness of the fact that when I think I am alone I become aware of an unconscious, invisible presence. This is an experience which is not common to the white man of today, therefore it seemed to William James so extraordinary that one should have such a feeling that he mentioned it at length in his book *Varieties of Religious Experience*, where he describes his own case.[25] He would not have had this feeling of strangeness if he hadn't lived always with people. We live so much in large crowds; but if we live alone, away from man and man's accumulations called cities, then such a thing quite regularly happens—that we feel invisible presences.

I have had this experience in the Alps, and in the bush in Africa. In primitive nature, there is nothing human, and you become aware of the

---

[22] Cf. "Dream Symbols," nr. 2, p. 103, and CW 12, nr. 2, par. 54. I 02 {0002}: "Dream of the blocked railway window," February 5, 1932, CDM.

[23] The stranger, or the strangers, was to become a central motif in Pauli's dreams recurring until the end of his life, and he always interpreted it as contents of the unconscious still not assimilated to consciousness. See for instance Pauli to Fierz, March, 21 1957 (2588), PLC IV, part IV: A.

[24] Editor's note: *Synopados* (συνοπαδὸς) means the follower and companion but doesn't refer specifically to demons. See Plato's Phaedrus 248c where the soul is described as *synopados* of the God. Plato, author, and B. Jowett, trans. (1931), *The Dialogues of Plato*, 3rd ed. (London: H. Milford/Oxford University Press).

[25] William James (1842–1910): "It is if there were in the human consciousness a *sense of reality, a feeling of objective presence, a perception* of what we may call 'something there,'" in "The Reality of the Unseen," in W. James (1960), *The Varieties of Religious Experience* (1901–2) (London: Collins), 73.

presence of the collective unconscious. It is not a nice feeling exactly; you feel observed, you feel observed from behind. I remember experiencing this once when I was in the jungle in Africa. I had gone there with a friend, but he had left with two native guides to find an animal he had wounded and wanted to get. I preferred to remain in a lovely spot near a brook where there was a huge tree from which extended enormous roots. The place impressed me. I thought I would like to stay in such a nice place smoking a pipe instead of creeping with the others through the dirt and ferns. I had my heavy rifle; I felt safe; no reason why I should be afraid. I lit my pipe and was sitting on one of the huge roots thinking the world was perfectly all right. My conscious felt free from conflict, my mind at peace, and then the unconscious began to work instinctively and to brew trouble. I felt somebody was looking at me from behind. I said to myself, "This is foolish." I looked behind; I thought it better to turn round and watch behind. But when I looked behind I saw nothing, so I turned round again, but it was still behind. I thought I would go around the tree and sit by another root with my back against the tree. So I did. Then the effect was of somebody looking down from above. It must be a monkey. Then I thought I had better watch; it might be a leopard, since they often sit on the upper branches waiting to drop down on their prey. That is why the Negroes carry their spears upright—then the leopard jumps onto the spear.[26] The leopard knows that, so he does not jump. Then I felt watched from below. I felt no peace anywhere. I began to walk around the tree. Since my friend did not come back for a whole hour, I walked around the tree for a whole hour. My mind was not at peace at all.[27] That is likely to happen; one feels observed in the unconscious presence. At night many people become suspicious of invisible presences; they hear a little noise somewhere. That is an old instinct. It is due to the working of the archetypes in the unconscious, which come to life when there is silence.

In this second dream the dreamer is in a car which is in movement, that is, he is on the move; things are going to happen. He is going to experience something new. Those behind him want to come up into consciousness, to have a look out, and he feels he ought to give way to them, out of

---

[26] Jung's usage of expressions such as "Negro(es)" or "primitive(s)" was consistent with the customary vocabulary of his time and has been kept.

[27] Jung went to Africa with his friends Dr. Helton Godwin (Peter) Baynes (1883–1943) and George Beckwith in the autumn of 1925 and returned to Zurich on March 14, 1926. There is a chapter about his experience in Africa in *MDR*, but this particular episode is not included. Burleson relates many more passages where Jung experienced "presence" when he was in Africa, which caused him to lose his cold reason, sometimes causing panic attacks. B. W. Burleson (2005), *Jung in Africa* (New York: Continuum), 154–56, 197; *MDR*, 254.

politeness. He should be polite. That is a very nice way in which the unconscious puts it; it is always compensatory to the conscious. Had he known the meaning of the dream, he would have said it was all rot and nonsense. Or he would have been afraid. People are afraid when they feel observed. He is afraid of the idea of going crazy; there are apparitions of things that do not exist. But the unconscious puts it nicely: for the sake of politeness you should give room to those behind you. There is nothing to be afraid of, but please be polite to the invisible presences. It is that politeness which has great importance for primitive peoples. When the Romans came to a new place they put a little stone there, an altar, to the unknown genius or god of this place.[28] They did not know who the presence was in that place but felt they had better do something about it and be polite and greet it. So they dedicated a stone or altar to the invisible genius of that place. That is the primitive politeness to the existence of the invisible unconscious.

The third unconscious product was a vision: he saw the shore of the sea. As a matter of fact, he was standing on the shore, when suddenly a huge wave washed up to the place where he was. He was on a sort of little mound or hill, and it seemed that the sea covered all the land so that he found himself on an island where he sat alone.[29]

This shows now very clearly what is happening. The sea is eternally the place of origin of all living beings; it is the mother of life, and it is a very apt symbol to express the unconscious. It is just as if we were in a boat, or swimming on the surface of the sea, that is, we are on a sort of impenetrable shining surface. At certain places we can look into the depths, but we can never penetrate the deeper levels of great darkness. Many forms are hidden in the sea and can come up suddenly. So, often unconscious contents suddenly appearing on the surface, that is, entering our consciousness, are symbolized as fishes.[30] They come up suddenly from the depths, appearing in our field of vision. Also like the sea, the unconscious has a certain rhythm which has much to do with the phases of the moon so that those people who are inundated by the unconscious are called lunatics. When something drops down into the water, it is removed from sight. You can't see it any more as it is covered by the sea, by the sheet of water. That experience is also expressed by this symbol.

---

[28] In classical Roman religion a genius loci was the protective spirit of a place. Genius (Latin: "begetter") loci (Latin: "place").

[29] Cf. "Dream Symbols," nr. 3, p. 103, and CW 12, nr. 3, par. 56. I 03 {0003}: "Vision: coast with sea irrupting," February 6, 1932, CDM.

[30] Jung had a special interest in the fish as a symbol of unconscious content. See *Aion*, CW 9/II, pars. 127–49.

Then you realize that you are really like a man alone on a small island; you are isolated in your conscious, surrounded by the great sea of the unconscious. This is an important realization for a scientific man like my patient. We usually assume that there is a sort of continuity of consciousness; that we are always in this reasonable and nice world and that nothing separates us from our neighbor. We do not realize at all that we are in reality surrounded by an abyss of unconsciousness or that we are out on the sea like a ship, that our consciousness is really only just a speck of light, or little area lit up by the projection of our psychical intensity. And this spot is surrounded by an intensity of darkness of which we are not aware because we do not see it. But it does exist, it functions as such, and that is the important realization that the dreamer has to make at this moment. Also we learn from that vision that the unconscious is thoroughly stirred and that a huge movement is going to take place. It is as though a big wave was about to break on the shore of his consciousness.

The next unconscious product, the fourth, is a dream which now takes on a more specific form: He finds himself surrounded by a great number of indefinite female figures and suddenly he hears a voice say, "I have to leave the father first." That is the whole thing.[31]

The surrounding sea is now personified by female figures. Personification is often found in poetry, in which a river, a tree, the mountains are represented by nymphs or fairies. He realizes nothing of the significance of these figures. He just perceives indefinite female forms. That they are feminine must be explained by the fact that he is a man and his object is always a woman; and to a woman, of course, it is the other way round. A woman's object is a man, or men. These figures have different characters according to the quality of consciousness. You know in mythology, there are multitudes of such figures: the white virgins, the Valkyrie, fairies, and numbers of others. Fairies can be very dangerous, as the lamiae of antiquity.[32] The vampires of the Middle Ages called succubae were women who slept with men and drew their blood.[33] There are also in literature

---

[31] Cf. "Dream Symbols," nr. 4, p. 104, and CW 12, nr. 4, par. 58. I 04 {0004}: "Shadow-like female figures," "I have to get away from the father," February 8, 1932, CDM.

[32] In Norse mythology, the Valkyries, servants of Odin, escorted the brave who were slain in battle to Valhalla and took care of them. Lamia is a child-eating monster or witch; in folklore a corpse that rises at night to drink the blood of the living. In Greek mythology Lamia was the daughter of Belos and Libye. When Zeus fell in love with her, she was driven into a rage by Hera, in which she first devoured her own children, then all the children she could get hold of. In historical times Greek mothers used to threaten their children with her story.

[33] Latin *succuba*, harlot, from Latin *succubāre*, to lie beneath. Female demon fabled to have sexual intercourse with sleeping men, especially appearing in their dreams. Compare *incubus*, who is a male counterpart.

little creatures which hardly have a name. To give an example: There is a famous book, very little known in these days, but well known for two centuries. It was written in the fifteenth century by an Italian monk, Francesco Colonna, and has a funny title which I won't try to explain. It is called *Poliphilo* and means "lover of Polia," who is one of the virgins at the court of the queen, Venus.[34] The whole book is a dream of the monk who wrote it. It was later on taken as a highly mystical book, and I think it really is one. You see its theme was repeated rather often: that of a man coming into a peculiar place on an adventure, a quest, a spiritual venture, where he is met by a multitude of virgins and maidens. Just so, Poliphilo enters the lost city in the midst of the big forest and meets with these women. Some have positive and some negative qualities which are simply personifications of his surroundings, dead objects filled with the life of the adventurer, the hero. So Poliphilo projects the life of his unconscious or finds it personified in his surroundings.

This is like an insane person who hears voices out of the walls or houses or trees, and so on, merely a vivification or animation of his surroundings by projections of the unconscious. The unconscious behaves as if it were not in you; it constellates your reaction as if it were outside of you. So you never suspect its presence; you assume it is somewhere else. Even if you know it is psychological, it actually appears as if it never happens in you, but always outside of you. It happens in your friends, it happens anywhere else but never in yourself. You are always convinced it is somewhere else; it is in this or that object. Everybody has a so-called black beast, the bête noire, the animal. Your best enemy is always in someone else, naturally. You find, for instance, your own blackness always somewhere else. It is the same politically; it is so between nations. The foreigner is a bad fellow, you know, and if he is killed it is good to kill foreigners, because they are bad. That is the primitive point of view. During the war, you could see this kind of projection strikingly exemplified in the newspaper, because we are all convinced that the foreigner is a devil. We have our weapons only for self-defense against all the devils in the world around us. And finally nations fight each other out of mere self-defense.

---

[34] Cf. Poliphilo is also discussed in "Dream Symbols," 202n4, and *CW 12*, par. 61. Francesco Colonna, *Hypnerotomachia Poliphili, ubi humana omnia non nisi somnium esse ostendit, atque obiter plurima scitu sane quam digna commemorat* (Venice, 1499). Bib. Class. Ravenna (Inc. 652). F. Béroalde de Verville, *Le Tableau des Riches Inventions ... qui sont Représentées dans le Songe de Poliphile* (Paris, 1600). See also L. Fierz-David (1950), *The Dream of Poliphilo* (New York: Pantheon).

In this case we are considering, the animation of the surroundings begins out of nothing; a multitude of female figures appears, denoting that now his unconscious begins to operate, to function; and it is just as though it were coming from without. Again the unconscious is very careful not to arouse suspicion. These indefinite female figures are not offensive but are very pleasant. A man thinks he can cope with such a proposition, though there are some men who are not so certain.

And now he hears a voice. This is again a symptom of the animation of his surroundings. That voice is not his; it is strange to him; and yet it is a voice of great authority. Whenever this appeared in subsequent dreams he felt overcome, completely convinced. He knew that what it said was right; it always hit the nail on the head, and whenever it spoke there was no contradiction; there was nothing to say against it. Therefore the voice usually appeared at the end of the dream; it was as if it said, "This is so." Even if it went against the grain of his conscious convictions, he gave way at once. It was the voice of authority. In later dreams it was sometimes the voice of a general, a captain of a ship, or an old wise man. Then under my treatment, it was my voice, apparently, but always it carried absolute authority. Now you see that if that voice had taken place in reality as a hallucination, the man would be definitely insane, or he would have a tremendous mystical experience, and then it would seem as if God had spoken. But it is important to mark this phenomenon of the voice because it is the experience in a very simple form of something you know in an entirely different way. It is that voice heard by the prophets, which, like the word of God, is a definite psychological phenomenon. There are not a few cases in which it is heard in dreams, and it always tells something which is valid and cannot be contradicted.[35]

That voice, completely strange to him, says he has to leave the father first. Yet it is as if he had said this to himself. For the voice told him the very word that should be heard at this moment, namely, that he isn't up to dealing with the animated surroundings, that is, the collective unconscious, until he has left the father. He himself does not understand what that means. He did not know that he was clinging to the father, who had died long ago.[36] He thought himself a perfectly independent man. While this idea was strange to him, it is really very clear. He was clinging to a father,

---

[35] Jung does not emphasize the meaning of the voice in "Dream Symbols," or CW 12 in connection with this dream.

[36] This is not accurate. Pauli's father was alive, and he died in 1955. It is unclear why Jung makes this statement. It could maybe be to preserve Pauli's anonymity, or he might be unaware of Pauli's relationship with his father.

and the father was his scientific point of view. That was his father. If you said anything was scientific, that settled the whole question; for he believed that the ultimate truth is necessarily scientific. He was absolutely convinced that this world can be explained in a rational way, and eventually become quite reasonable, thus settling the whole problem. Also that you can tell people the way to act and that they will do what is obviously right to you. You just tell them, and it is all right—as if anyone were inclined to listen and carry it out. In reality few people ever do. You cannot tell people. You can tell them to give you a piece of bread or mail a letter for you. But you cannot tell them the Truth. That is out of the question. That you can is an old-fashioned idea. Fewer and fewer people believe you when you tell them something. As long as you cherish such rational ideas you cannot cope with the collective unconscious.

It is a terribly irrational thing for a perfectly balanced individual to be afraid of an invisible presence, as in my jungle experience. I have seen many a patient who says, "You see, Doctor, I am convinced this idea is perfect nonsense. I know it is nonsense, but it is there." People of reason and intelligence can have such ideas, and they simply can't cope with them unless they have given up a certain traditional attitude of mind. The father is a symbol of the traditional mind, a traditional way of dealing with the living experience. So you see a father can be philosophical teaching or religion, which tells you things are so and so—particularly that kind of teaching which deals with ultimate philosophical truth. For instance, the father could say: This world is reasonable and can be explained on a reasonable and rational basis, or this is the best world possible or the worst world possible, and you have to behave in such and such a way to be up to it. So the dreamer has to leave the father, that scientific mind. He has the rational, scientific attitude which he must leave to be able to cope with absolute facts.[37]

The next unconscious product, the fifth, was a visual impression. He suddenly saw himself standing upright and rooted in the ground like a tree and with an instinctive feeling of being unable to move away. Now the question is: Why should he be rooted like that? He would be rooted like that if he was in the presence of something very disagreeable and uncomfortable from which he tries to move away but can't. He is spellbound,

---

[37] This corresponds to Jung's own crises as he describes it in the *Liber Novus* or *The Red Book*. "The spirit of the depths has subjugated all pride and arrogance to the power of judgment. He took away my belief in science, he robbed me of the joy of explaining and ordering things, and he let devotion to the ideals of this time die out in me. He forced me down to the last and simplest things." *RB*, 229.

rooted to the spot. Suddenly a huge snake appeared moving around him in a circle.[38]

This symbol is highly mythological. A circle made around one is always a matter of magic, and he is again as if on an island surrounded by animated consciousness. Things happen as if objects were threatening him by their independence and their behavior which he might not be able to explain. It is not scientific at all that one should hear a voice. He has an instinctive fear of anything so irrational. Man always has been and still is afraid of untoward events that threaten to disrupt the order of things. He is afraid of an ultimate chaos that might be impending and at the same time is tremendously fascinated and struck by a panic which roots him to the spot, so that he is exposed to these powers. These powers can now come up. The unconscious like the sea comes up, and he is rooted to the spot. He might drown; he thinks of the assault of enemies, of wild animals, and can't get away. He is in an utterly exposed situation. He has to realize he can't move away, he can't escape the onslaught of unconsciousness, and he needs protection badly. This protection is given by the snake that describes the circle. This brings up a symbol motif. It is that of the snake that swallows its tail, the tail eater. You find this symbol all over the world—ouroboros—you find this as late as the seventeenth to nineteenth centuries in the Sanskrit writings as symbolizing the continuous revolution of natural processes.[39]

---

[38] Cf. "Dream Symbols," nr. 5, p. 106, and CW 12, nr. 5, par. 62. I 05/M 01 {0005}: "Vision of a snake orbiting the dreamer," February 15, 1932, CDM.

[39] The tail-eating serpent, ouroboros or uroboros, is not mentioned in "Dream Symbols," nor in CW 12 in connection with this dream but is represented with several illustrations in CW 12, i.e., illustration no. 7 p. 46, illustration nos. 46 and 47, p. 103; and it is discussed in passages that where added for the 1944 edition of *Psychology and Alchemy* (*PsA*), as in par. 165. Jung explored the ouroboros in the Eranos lecture of 1936, "Die Erlösungsvorstellungen in der Alchemie" (Redemption motifs in alchemy), EYB 1936, 43, which later, very much revised and extended, became the third part of CW 12, *Religious Ideas in Alchemy*.

In this dream the snake describes a magic circle around him in order to protect him against the ghosts that are animated in the atmosphere. He doesn't know about these things at all; he just gets certain impressions. He has no idea of the things I am telling you. The magic circle has an apotropaic effect, meaning "a way to ward off," or "hold off." It is a sort of gesture that conquers magic influence, the dangerous figures that threaten with their presence. The magic circle is used by the magician who tries to call up hidden devils or ghosts. To protect himself he makes a magic circle. When the Romans founded a new city, they made this so-called circle, a furrow, the *sulcus primogenitus*,[40] which they drew with the plow. Perhaps you read in the newspapers that when Mussolini founded a new town in the palatinate swamps he made the circle with a motor plow, in modern fashion.[41] He drew a furrow around the area in which he was to build the settlement. Usually in the middle of the circle they made a hole in the earth, a so-called *fundus*,[42] into which they put a sacrifice to propitiate the ghosts of the earth. The circle was intended to ward off the evil which might come by making a sort of specially sterilized area protected against spiritual enemies around it and, by thus propitiating the gods of the soil and earth so that whatever was built there was safe, protected by the propitiated gods.

This snake making the circle then is a very common symbol; it occurs in the East as a mandala symbol, and in the West it is the magic circle. This snake encircles the dreamer's totality. He is the island in his own sea. The snake is the personification of the unconscious, of the sea. That snake is also a serpent that can devour the world. It is like a big leviathan, which fills one-third of the ocean, the world-devouring dragon. It is the serpent

---

[40] Latin: original furrow.

[41] Benito Mussolini (1883–1945), *Il Duce* (The Leader), was an Italian politician, journalist, and the founder of Italian fascism. As leader of the National Fascist Party he ruled Italy as prime minister from 1922 to 1943. In 1925 he set up a legal dictatorship. In 1938 Jung described Mussolini in an interview with H. R. Knickerbocker, where he compared Hitler, Stalin, and Mussolini. Here he compared these contemporary leaders with leading men in indigenous societies, identifying different types of men of strength. Hitler was defined by Jung as a "medicine man," a kind of inspired seer, fashioning his regime by powerful archetypal symbols, such as the wind metaphors (Sturm) and the swastika moving to the left, in a sinister direction. This kind of leader receives his power from what people project into him. Mussolini, on the other hand, was described as a "classical chief," a man of physical strength. Jung describes Mussolini as a likable leader with human traits, although a bit childish. Hitler on the other hand, is described as a scaffolding of wood covered with cloth, an automaton with a mask, a robot that makes you scared. C. G. Jung, W. McGuire, and R. Hull (1978), *C. G. Jung Speaking: Interviews and Encounters* (London: Thames and Hudson).

[42] Latin: bottom.

Figure 15. Thirteenth Century Christian Mandala. In the center God with Christ on His lap. Demons watching the Gates. Twelve rivers. This description does not correspond to the description of this mandala in the Archive for Research in Archetypal Symbolism (ARAS) library in New York. Here the mandala is dated eleventh to twelfth century (ARAS record 5Dk.311), with the Virgin Mary and the Christ Child at the center holding an open book on which is written *Si quis sitit, veniet et bibat* (if any man thirst let him come to me and drink; John 7:37); four rivers of paradise forming a cross of four quarters terminating in four horned, fork-bearded river gods personifying the Tigris, Geon, Euphrates, and Pison. Four Latin Fathers of the Church in medallions are positioned at the right of the gods, symbols of the four Evangelists in medallions at the left of the gods. Four trees supporting medallions with feminine personifications of the four cardinal virtues and flanking each of four tree trunks, two virgins personifying the Beatitudes. A mandala similar to this one, is reproduced in *CW* 12 as illustration no. 197, p. 369, in the chapter on the lapis-Christ parallel. The one published in CW12 is a thirteenth-century mandala with Christ in the center (ARAS record 5Ek.001).

of time which devours everything. Everything disappears in its belly, and since time is a revolution, the years are all revolution; months are revolution; for everything returns in great periods. So time is a dragon that chases its own tail. The zodiac is represented as a great serpent carrying zodiacal signs upon his back. Even Christ, who symbolizes the year of the church, is the serpent carrying twelve constellations upon his back, understood to be the twelve disciples, according to old church symbolism.

The patient is now rooted to the spot surrounded by the serpent; he is protected and exposed at the same time. He is the symbol itself; he is the symbol himself. He is the victim of his own symbolism. He is under the symbolism as he is under the hat. The hat already was that circular symbol, and we shall see in a later dream that the hat was really the first form of the mandala.

Lecture 2

DR. JUNG: Ladies and gentlemen: Here are quite a number of questions, and I am afraid that if I answer all of them fully our time will be completely exhausted.[1] Nevertheless I will try to say a few words about each. The first is very simple.

QUESTION: What is it in the unconscious which makes it attempt to reconcile conflicts?

DR. JUNG: This question is related to the fact that life is something which moves, and anything that moves needs energy. There is no energy, no potential, without pairs of opposites. If there is no conflict, there is no movement, no energy. Conflict is necessary.

QUESTION: Does complete individuation do away with conflicts?

DR. JUNG: That would mean you would come to a complete standstill. Individuation, on the contrary, means intense consciousness of conflict.[2] You never will be saved from conflict as long as you live, otherwise you would be dead before you die. Conflict cannot be removed. If it seems to be removed, that is imaginary. Conflict must be, if one lives at all. It is absolutely indispensable. But the way you deal with it, that is the question—whether you are overcome by the conflict, whether you get drowned in it, whether you get identified with one or other side of the conflict. Individuation simply means you find your place amidst the turmoil; you keep yourself in the midst of the conflict; you are in the conflict yet above it.

QUESTION: How may one cultivate deeper awareness of the unconscious?

DR. JUNG: Don't cultivate it. The unconscious comes to you. If you are not aware of the unconscious, consider the case as particularly favorable. It is not a particular joy to be aware of the unconscious, because it is a deep sea, you know, and if you are in a safe boat that keeps steady

---

[1]This lecture was held on September 21, 1936.

[2]Jung elaborates on these ideas in his work "On the Energetics of the Soul," CW 8, originally written in 1928.

even in a huge swell, then be thankful. One never should seek it. It is much better to let it come to you and then see what you are going to do about it.

Now here is somebody who is quite curious [*reading question*]:

QUESTION: If you found yourself again in the jungle, would you experience the same fears as you did the first time?

DR JUNG: Sure I would. Just give me the necessary time, you know. You see if a magician should transport me from this place right into the jungle, I should think it a huge joke and would not take the jungle for real. I should be curious and interested and would say, "Hello, how did I ever arrive here?" and, "This is obviously a stage performance," or something like that, and it would take me quite a while to become aware that I was in the jungle; but when I did realize it, then my consciousness would be profoundly altered. I would then be in an entirely different position, and after a short while my old animal instincts would come up and identify with the surroundings, and then more and more I become the primitive man, losing consciousness of myself as a civilized being, until my whole personality is fundamentally changed. That tendency is so strong that people living in such places find it necessary to maintain their customary standards in a most unusual way. They are frightfully conventional and all that, in order to maintain the dignity of the white man. Otherwise one "goes black"—that is the technical term people use in Africa—which means that one is tempted, or even forced, to adopt primitive ways in adapting to jungle life.[3] Even if I understand something of psychology, or even if I am a civilized man, it is quite certain that after a while I am in it; I have a different kind of attitude, a different outlook, for conditions are absolutely different.

QUESTION: Would you please say something about the part played by the woman doctor in the production of the dreams you are discussing? If the man had merely been keeping a record of his own dreams, do you think the same development would have come about? Or do you think the presence of an interested observer made a difference, even though she did not and could not interpret his dreams?

DR. JUNG: Of course it is quite certain that the presence of that doctor was important and the same development would probably not have taken place if the dreamer had not felt the presence of a sympathetic au-

---

[3] Jung writes about "going black" in "The Complications of American Psychology," in *CW* 10, par. 962.

dience. Most of the therapeutic effect in the analytical performance depends, you know, upon invisible things. I often say to my patients, "It does not matter *what* I say; it is important that I say *something*, that I am there, that I am on the spot with you. That is the thing that really counts." I often do not know what I am going to say, but what I say helps. I simply react, and if I am doing that, that is real therapeutic art. If I should map out some plan as to how to cure the patient, that would be a big mistake because it would be arbitrary and calculated, something which has nothing to do with reality. When two people carry on an analysis together, they follow a plan which is preexistent in the unconscious and works by thoughts which have been thought out before, but in the unconscious. We have to follow the lead of the unconscious and not the lead of the conscious process. Usually when there is a conscious purpose we are defeated because that has nothing to do with the unconscious. We are really up against something which is not identical with our conscious.

So the role of that doctor was in a way very important, as was the fact that she was a woman. She produced that substance or that secret which is characteristic of women, namely, a productive force, a pregnancy force. That is a very peculiar thing which cannot be defined intellectually because you can't see it, you can't touch it, you don't know what it is. It is a fact, nevertheless, that a woman can precipitate a man's thought. The man has the creative secret in his head, and, as a French writer once said, the woman has "le formidable secret dans ses hanches."[4] This has to do with the sympathetic nervous system, therefore the word *sympathy*. The woman doctor could sympathize with that man, which gave body to his suspended thoughts. He had thoughts, but they had no body. The woman can unconsciously give body to his thought so that it comes to earth, becomes visible. That is the extraordinary effect a woman can have on a man. It was the case here. His thoughts were suspended in the air, without tangible form, until through the sympathetic presence of that woman they became, as it were, real, and then they could develop. I am quite certain that his thoughts would not have been able to develop or gain definite form if it had not been for that sympathetic understanding. This is particularly important in the beginning when there are so many hostile forces in consciousness against the germ that begins to unfold in the unconscious. Nothing is better for carrying the germ of man's thoughts than a woman. She is made for that by nature.

---

[4] French: "the marvelous secret in her hips."

QUESTION: When in dreams the mandala rotates, or the sun wheel revolves, is the rotation or revolution clockwise or counterclockwise or sometimes one, then the other?

DR. JUNG: This is a point that plays a pretty considerable role in the dreams of our patient, but I can say only a few words about it. The moving mandala, the rotating mandala, always symbolizes a process that is actually going on. Now you know the clockwise movement is going with the sun, and going with the sun means remaining in the light. So when a thing moves clockwise it moves into or towards consciousness. When something comes up from the unconscious it moves into consciousness with the sun, clockwise. But if a movement, a development, goes down into the unconscious, it is anticlockwise, against the sun, and that means away from the daylight into the darkness. Therefore the Buddhists, particularly the Lamaistic Buddhists, when they circumambulate the shrine containing the relics of saints or of Buddha himself, always go round it clockwise, because they are seeking greater enlightenment, by gaining grace from the shrine, and bringing that grace up into consciousness. The goal after which they are striving is the perfect light, the perfect enlightenment, the abode of perfect truth. They attain it by a circumambulation towards the right, the side of consciousness.

If the movement is anticlockwise, it unwinds, it undoes the conscious purpose, and we are going away from the light into the darkness. The rotation to the left is always unfavorable and has much to do with magic. It is very interesting, for instance, that the German symbol of the swastika is turned anticlockwise. I was asked that question in Germany by the Nazis, and when I told them that this is an unfavorable sign, one man made a very apt remark, "When you are inside of the swastika then it turns clockwise."[5] And this is true. I said, "Yes, that is perfectly true, provided you are really inside." The trouble is that the whole thing is outside, and a big collective movement like that is likely to take its course into its own opposite. The danger in any big collective movement is that it too often goes back on its own principles. You see this in Russia where so-called communism which they were trying to establish has gone back to fascism. There is no tangible difference between them. Or look at Christianity. Christianity became in the course of a few centuries something quite different from what it had been at first. Any big movement that is against individuation is likely to falsify its own purpose, going back towards an

---

[5] Concerning Jung's relationship to German psychotherapy during the Nazi era, see Cocks, 1985.

unconscious condition. For, you see, when you become like everybody and identify with everybody, then you lose the consciousness of your self. You lose the conviction that you are the Lord's experiment on earth and that it is your own responsibility what you do with your life. You leave all this to sacred institutions and allow their prescriptions to fit you into a frame. All that has no merit whatever. Moreover when you heap up people of high qualities, moral or intellectual, you do not heap up their value. One hundred intellectual men together make only one hydrocephalus.[6] You can see that in committees, university committees, and such things. For virtues are qualities that never heap up; only bad things heap up.

The next question is very difficult and I am afraid that I cannot enter upon a satisfactory discussion of it.

QUESTION: Would Dr. Jung develop further the relationship between the statement that causality cannot be ascribed to the unconscious, and the statement that the unconscious—at least so far as it is revealed through dreams, and the like—is compensatory to the conscious? How far can purposiveness be attributed to the unconscious—as in a given dream sequence?

DR. JUNG: This is a question that must be answered by facts. If you simply look at the sequence of dreams or at a single dream, in a case where you are aware of the individual's general psychology, you can see that the unconscious behaves in a compensatory way. It always brings up that which is not seen or not considered enough in the conscious. How far that compensatory function is linked up with the problematical causality of the unconscious is a very difficult question. I would propose not to mix up the two questions, that is, the compensatory and causal aspects of the unconscious. You see this idea or hypothesis I allude to, of the causality of the unconscious, is most questionable. It is also based upon certain observations, but I am afraid it would lead too far into a philosophical discussion of the ultimate principles or laws of the unconscious. I am afraid I can't go into that; it would take too much time.

QUESTION: Would Dr. Jung care to discuss the relationship between the concept of the unconscious as an undiscriminated primordial totality within the individual and the philosophical concept of the undifferentiated continuum as the all-inclusive basic entity of experience?

DR. JUNG: That is a pretty tough proposition, but it isn't as bad as it sounds. The meaning of the question, as I understand it, is whether there

---

[6] Medical condition also known as "water in the brain," probably used as a metaphor for stupidity.

is a relationship between the collective unconscious and the continuum of events that underlies human experience. They are identical really; the collective unconscious *is* the continuum of experience. Of course, if you think that there is a reality designated by the Latin formula *esse in re*, a "being in the thing," an existence in the form of objective things, or if you assume that reality is *in intellectu solo*, "simply in the intellect," in either case you really can't answer the question; but if you assume that our world is our experience, which is the most evident thing man ever could say, then you argue that the reality of the world consists in our experience. For instance, take this glass. You could say this glass is real; but analyze it, and you come to the conclusion that it is merely the sum of the experiences through eyes, touch, et cetera, and all these are simply images in your psyche.

So our immediate awareness of a reality consists of images. We are living completely in a world of images, and we have the greatest trouble in saying anything valid about the objective reality of things. It boils down to a problem of physics. What is better? What is the real object? The physicists tell you something you don't even understand, so you can assume nobody understands what matter really is, but still objective existence is a thing in itself, quite apart from man's mind. I am tremendously impressed by the fact that whatever a physicist has to tell you about matter is expressed in psychological terms. Every word you say about matter is psychological, so the whole thing comes down finally to the fact that our world, in so far as we can experience it, is a psychical experience, an image, and as such, necessarily psychical.

Therefore I say the real answer to such a question is that the only form of experience we know is *esse in anima*, which means "being in the psyche."[7] Beyond that we have nothing to say. We can speculate, we can experiment, but we never shall get beyond the fact that whatever we can conceive of is an image, a psychical image. You are quite safe when you assume that you live in a world of psychic images and that that is your only reality. Any other realities are completely inaccessible. So we are quite safe in suggesting that the unconscious, being a continuity of images, is in itself the continuity of facts, of so-called external facts.

I am afraid this is a thoroughly Chinese piece of philosophy. It is the basis of Chinese thinking, and therefore to return to the earlier question, even our so-called causality is an image, and we have absolutely no means of establishing the existence of causality beyond our world of images.

---

[7] Jung discusses this distinction of *esse in intellectu, esse in re,* and *esse in anima* at length in his *Types*, CW 6, pars. 59–67.

Therefore I say the unconscious in its continuity does not necessarily follow the law of causality; there must be something else. If you study classical Chinese philosophy you will see that there are certain psychological facts which prove, or which make it at least most probable, that you can explain the world without the principle of causality.[8] For instance, according to this point of view causality would be magic, rather than what we like to term it, a scientific concept.

* * * * *

Yesterday I think we reached as far as the fifth dream, the circle described by the serpent, and I told you about the sulcus primogenitus[9] and the magic circle. You know when such an image as this—an encircling serpent with the conscious personality rooted in the center of the circle—is formed, it means that we have reached a very peculiar condition, namely, that the ego-consciousness at this point finds itself in the presence of a danger which makes it understandable why that serpent should make a magic circle. It is a situation of risks. It is the approach of the collective unconscious that makes one instantly assume the attitude of being under a magic spell. It might be, for instance, a sorcerer who keeps himself within the magic circle—a man who has called up the powers of the unconscious, demons, or something of the sort, and protects himself by that magic circle. So it is very probable that in the next dream or vision we shall find something that refers to the so-called constellated or activated unconscious.

The next unconscious product, the sixth, is a vision: he sees a veiled female figure on a staircase.[10] We have already encountered the *many* female

---

[8] This is obviously a reference to synchronicity. Jung's eyes were opened to Chinese thinking by Richard Wilhelm (1873–1930), with whom he published the book *The Secret of the Golden Flower: A Chinese Book of Life* (1962 [1931]) (London: Routledge and Kegan Paul). See also CW 13. For a documentary on Richard Wilhelm's life see, Bettina Wilhelm, dir. and writer, *Wisdom of Changes—Richard Wilhelm and the I Ching* (orig. *Wandlungen*) Cinema Documentary Feature, Triluna Film and Bettina Wilhelm Filmproduktion, 2011. Jung had at this time already formulated the concept of synchronicity; see W. McGuire, ed. (1984), *Dream Analysis: Notes of the Seminar Given in 1928–1930 by C. G. Jung* (London: Routledge and Kegan Paul), 44–45; but he had not yet published anything about it. Jung would later develop these ideas together with Wolfgang Pauli. See *Naturerklärung und Psyche* (Zurich: Rascher, 1952) and "Synchronicity: An Acausal Connecting Principle," CW 8. See also Gieser, 2005.

[9] Latin: original furrow.

[10] Cf. "Dream Symbols," nr. 6, p. 107, and CW 12, nr. 6, par. 64. I 06 {0006; fig. a, b} "Vision of a veiled figure on the stairs," February 15, 1932, CDM. Pauli made drawings of this figure.

figures, that multitude of magic or fairy-like beings. Now here we have the *one* veiled figure. The fact that that figure is veiled means secret, not understood; and a female figure—well, that would mean the personification of the object, namely, the psychic object, a strange psychic substance or experience coming up against the dreamer and taking the figure of the eternal object of man which is woman. And that object is not recognizable, therefore it is shown as veiled; and that figure now is on a staircase.

Here I must say something about the meaning of such a figure. As long as there is a multitude of these female figures we must assume that there is a multitude of objects, and that multitude reflects a peculiar condition of his own personality, namely, that his personality consists of a multitude of units appearing as personified in the mirror of the unconscious. It is as if he should look down into a well or into a lake, into quiet water, and see his own face transfigured and dissociated into many faces. That is the way in which the subconscious is personified. You can understand that the unconscious as a mirror reflects your unknown condition. Your unknown face is reflected in the unconscious. Or you can turn it round and say it is the unconscious that is in a condition of disintegration. There are many figures in the unconscious, which are not yet unified in consciousness and therefore that man's personality is a multitude of not yet unified units. It is really a question of two worlds, a world of the conscious and a world of the unconscious, and it is a matter of taste or preference or temperament whether you assume that this thing here, the conscious world, is the important and decisive factor, or whether the emphasis is on the unconscious factor.

If you go to India and study the mind of the Indian, you will see that it is based very much more on the reality of the unconscious than on the reality of the conscious. The Hindus would inform you that this world is the world of *maya*,[11] of illusion, and that this multitude of things is all illusion, for there is just the *one* Being, the one eternal consciousness, and our whole purpose is to remove ourselves as thoroughly and quickly as possible from the illusion of the multitude of things.[12] He will also live

---

[11] Sanskrit: from *mā*, "not," and *yā*, "this," the world of senses, the deity that manifests and governs the phenomenal universe and the impression that it is made up of a multitude of things.

[12] In 1937–38 Jung took the opportunity to make a three months' journey through India on occasion of the twenty-fifth anniversary celebrations at the University of Calcutta, to which he was invited by the British government. On his return he wrote his impressions in two articles: "The Dreamlike World of India" and "What India Can Teach Us" (see CW 12 and also *MDR*, 304–14). It is interesting to note that he already before his trip had formed

from that kind of conviction, from the unconscious intimation, that may take him out of his conscious existence at any time. This happened not long ago to a man, a statesman, a gifted person, with a very complete European education. When he was forty-five years old he was suddenly lifted out of this form of existence and went to live in the woods to become a yogi, something unheard of in our civilization. We would say such a man was quite unbalanced and would call for the alienist. Not so in India—there his actions would be considered the right thing. Of course, it has great merit, but everybody won't understand it. It is because Hindus base their lives upon the reality of the unconscious, and not upon the reality of the conscious world that makes their attitude toward it possible.

So when that figure of the unconscious, or the personification of the unconscious, appears as a multitude, then you can assume that the conscious is a multitude, or the unconscious is a multitude. The truth is probably that both are multitudes. On either side there is an incomplete condition, things are not unified, and therefore when the unconscious appears it must be a multitude. But if the germ of oneness, the essential thing, is touched upon, or impregnated, then the unconscious begins to reflect that unity which has lain inactive in the human personality; or you can say that the germ of consciousness that was latent has been touched upon and now causes a unification of consciousness. So we have the image of the man surrounded by a circle, and that means unity, completion. Instantly the unconscious is the same. But that image of unity, the magic circle, is not that man's invention, for it just came to him, it happened to him, the unconscious brought it to him as an object of vision. We can say just as well that the unconscious has done it, and the conscious has been the victim of it or is the object of that unconscious activity because it came to him as an objective vision; he did not seek it, or make it, or invent it; he doesn't even understand it; he doesn't know what is happening to him. We can even say that such an experience would rather prove that the unconscious is on top of the situation and has inundated the land. That man is "under the hat" of the unconscious rather than under the hat of his own invention. The unconscious is active and means more, is more influential, than the conscious.

If the unconscious appears personified as the one object, then it is very important to see what is happening to that figure or what that figure is doing. We call this figure of the veiled woman, this mysterious woman,

his view on Indian mentality. For a good introduction to Jung's relationship to India, see Jung, 1996, introduction.

anima, the Latin word for "soul."[13] That concept of the soul has nothing to do with the Christian concept of a metaphysical soul, which is rather a philosophical notion than anything else. This term *anima* is more a primitive notion, namely, it is *a* soul; it is not *the* soul, it is *a* soul; and I call it a primitive notion because primitives hold that you have more than one soul. You have several, up to six, or perhaps more, and at times a soul can leave you and wander away in the night and get lost, and in the morning you discover that you have lost a soul, not *the* soul, but *a* soul, a part of yourself, a part of your personality.

You see the anima is the female soul. This is not my invention. I gave it the name anima, but even that is not original, because these things were known long before my existence, known even to the medieval philosophers. I could quote you texts of the sixteenth century where a man says, speaking of that anima, "That is called Eve; man is Adam, and that is his Eve, whom he always carries with him inside, *in se circumfert*."[14] These people were quite aware of it. Or go back to India; there you will find any number of representations of the deity with the female consort either in a hole in the body of the god, or dwelling inside him. That refers directly to Adam, whose rib was made into a woman, because his female consort was thought to be living inside his body, a detachable female soul. God has simply pulled that thing out of him which was sticking in Adam like a rib, probably causing some trouble, as the female counterpart always does. Or you find the deity in an eternal embrace with his consort. It is the god and his Shakti.[15] Shakti is the one who *makes*; she is the maker of maya, and maya is building material. She gives body to possibilities. She is the maker of bodies. Maya is sometimes wrongly translated as illusion, for that illusion is very real, it is made of maya, of building material, made of earth or stone or wood. That is the material with which this goddess works.

Also this anima figure is active. She is representing something, and she appears on a staircase. Now that always suggests going up or going down. It means she is about to do something on these steps. She is perhaps going to go up or down. The staircase is a symbol which occurs in antique lit-

---

[13] For Jung's concept of the Anima and Animus, see CW 7, pars. 296–340, and CW 9 II, pars. 20–42.

[14] Latin: to carry or move around in himself.

[15] Sanskrit: from *shak*—"to be able," personification of divine feminine creative power. See also Jung's description of Shiva and Shakti, also as psychological principles such as "the contemplative consciousness" versus the "desiring consciousness" in Jung, 1996.

erature pretty often and played a considerable role, for instance, in the Mithraic[16] and many other mysteries. There often was in the temple a staircase consisting of seven planetary steps. This sort of astrological symbolism means that in the process of initiation you climb through the seven steps up to the seventh sphere, and ultimately you arrive at the sun which was supposed to be at the top, and the sun is the god. You find a very beautiful account of this in *The Golden Ass* of that old Roman poet Apuleius.[17] There he describes the initiation of the philosopher into the mysteries of Isis. And at the end you find the seven planetary steps to the *solificatio* or deification—the making into the Sun God. The initiant is crowned; there is a coronation ritual; and he is finally put upon a pedestal and worshipped by the assembled community as Helios, the Sun God.

So we can make the hypothesis that perhaps the stairs mean a possible going up to the seventh place, a transformation of the individual into a divine form. You know that is the purpose of the mysteries, to transform man, to give him rebirth into another form of existence which means that his ego-personality or his ego-consciousness is not sufficient to cope with existence, that he needs to have a different kind of personality; that his personality ought to change. Christian baptism contains the same idea, and there is any amount of other ethnological and historical material that substantiates this hypothesis. For instance, through baptism you are transformed from a mortal, merely human being, into the state of a child of God, and you partake in the wonder and immortal nature of the Deity and are granted the eternal vision of God. That is the belief in the Catholic Church, which says that when a child dies before baptism then the child is deprived of the vision of God. It is not exactly in hell; but it is deprived of the vision of God, which means it cannot partake of the perfection of the divine condition.

---

[16] See n. 15.

[17] Lucius Apuleius; ca. 125–ca. 180, Latin prose writer. In *The Golden Ass*, Lucius undergoes an initiation into the mysteries of Isis. He testifies: "I approached the very gates of death and set foot on Proserpine's threshold, yet was permitted to return, rapt through all the elements. At midnight I saw the sun shining as if it were noon; I entered the presence of the gods of the under-world and the gods of the upper-world, stood near and worshiped them." After this, he was presented on a pulpit in the temple in front of a crowd. He wore garments that included designs of serpents and winged lions, held a torch, and wore "a palm tree chaplet with its leaves sticking all out like rays of light." *The Golden Ass* (1984), trans. R. Graves (Harmondsworth: Penguin), 241. The significance of this account is that it is the only surviving description of such an initiation. Jung owned a copy of a German translation of this work, and it has a line in the margin by this passage. Cf. *RB*, 252n211.

Now we come to the seventh unconscious product, a dream which is now of the veiled woman.[18] He sees her as before, and now she unveils her face, and it is shining like the sun.

So you see our speculation as to the stairs comes off in a way, namely, this transformation or this performance of the anima means that she is transformed into the sun; she reveals herself as being of the sun, a deified, "solified" figure, anticipating what is going to happen to the ego-consciousness, namely, a transformation into a divine being. It is a transfiguration. Now this is the phenomenon. What does it mean psychologically? Psychologically it means an illumination, an enlightenment; the head transforms into the very source of light. A great light dawns upon her, meaning upon him, because she always mirrors his unconscious side. To his unconscious is happening the mystery of solification or illumination. A great light will come to him; he will see something; his consciousness will be enlarged beyond the human size to a divine consciousness, that means a nonhuman consciousness, something which reaches beyond the mere ego.

This statement of the dream is, of course, in most flagrant opposition or contrast to his conscious views. He is a scientific man, and he doesn't know about illuminations and such things. You know that is all terribly mystical stuff, and it is quite likely that it would get on his nerves, because a man like the dreamer can't swallow such things without a very irritated reaction.

To be sure, there are people who don't react like that, even scientific people. But it is an overpowering experience, when something happens to your unconscious side, to that which is behind you, and you see it portrayed in a vision before you. Your consciousness says that figure is all bunk, but it happens at the same time in you, and you get a warm glow so that you might be influenced; you might even lose your head, to a certain extent, and then the thing that happens to you is called inflation. Then your ego-consciousness getting that wonderful glow from behind swells up, and you feel grand, and you begin to consider yourself somebody.

We shall see what has happened to our dreamer, how he has taken this illumination. In the next, the eighth unconscious product, a dream, he sees a rainbow, and he knows that he ought to use this rainbow as a bridge.[19]

---

[18] In the Eranos text this is described as a visual impression, not a dream. Cf. "Dream Symbols," nr. 7, p. 108, and CW 12, nr. 7, par. 67. I 07 {0007}: "Vision of Woman unveiling her face," February 15, 1932, CDM.

[19] In the Eranos text this is also described as a visual impression, not a dream. Cf. "Dream Symbols," nr. 8, p. 108, and CW 12, nr. 8, par. 69. I 08 {0009}: "Landscape with rainbow bridge and falling people," February 15, 1932, CDM.

In other words, he ought to walk upon the rainbow; but instantly he is also aware that he should not walk upon it, that it would be frightfully dangerous, that those people who walk upon the rainbow bridge fall down and are killed; rather should he go below the bridge. That means he should pass under the bridge.

Now how does he happen to have this peculiar dream? The whole dream is an answer to an inflation. He got an inflation all right, and he instantly swelled up and became air-like. If you are air-like you can walk upon rainbows; then you are divine, because the rainbow bridge is the bridge of the gods. That means he has lost his body, has become entirely identified with the air-being, the anima. It is the feminine form of *animus*, which means "wind," "breath." The Greek *anemos* means "wind," "the breath of life," "the wind of life." He became identified with the wind. Wind, of course, can walk upon rainbow bridges. Therefore the first thought in the dream was "I can use this rainbow like a bridge to walk into the heavens and be like a god." Then instantly the reaction: "That would be terrible because I have a body and would fall down from that bridge and be smashed." Then he thinks better of it and says, "I ought to go below the rainbow bridge." Don't identify; don't get inflated; remember you are a mortal being; you have a body that is restricted in time and space. You are not air, but heavy matter, therefore walk humbly below the rainbow, as everybody should do.

Yet the rainbow is a bridge. Now what is below the bridge? Below the bridge is the water. There is the river, flowing below the bridge. That could be an allusion to the necessary course of human life, that it ought to be like a course of water, winding on the surface of the earth and finding its ultimate goal in the sea, passing under many rainbow bridges. This is for the time being a mere assumption, but it will be substantiated later on in other dreams where we shall encounter that magic water which means life and the course of life. The old Chinese philosophy of Laotze has used that simile.[20] It is certainly not this individual's own, but an old Chinese belief that the essential thing of life and existence is Tao, which is of the nature of water; it always seeks the deepest place, and that is how life moves. Water does not climb up; it flows down to its ultimate goal. That is very much in contradiction to attempts at spiritual flying, and identifications with spirit-like beings. It is a companion of the Chinese

---

[20] Philosopher of ancient China. According to Chinese traditions, Laotze (or Lao-tzu) lived in the sixth century BC, and he is best known as the author of the *Tao Te Ching*, founding text of Taoism.

belief in earth. We are made of earth, which is reality; we cannot jump out of our skins and become air-like beings as long as we are alive.

Now we shall see how the unconscious reacts to this new move. In the ninth unconscious product, a dream, he is in a green land, and there are many sheep pasturing. It is, as a matter of fact, the sheep land.[21] The feeling about this dream is a sort of Promised Land, a land of complete innocence, a pastoral land in every respect, and also there is a peculiar religious atmosphere about it. It is really the world of the sheep and of the shepherd. The dream is somewhat like a concretization of a verse from the psalms: "The Lord is my Shepherd," leading the sheep to the green pastures, and so on.

You see we could say instead of the identification with the spirit-like or wind-like being, it is the multiplicity or the multitude of animals. You know these sheep are a simile for a Christian community. For instance, if you have been in Ravenna you will have seen those beautiful mosaics where the early Christians are represented as sheep and the Good Shepherd is leading them to the water.[22] This dream looks like a regression into a sort of Christian mood, also rather like infantility, you know. It is a curious fact that Christian art in its beginnings had the peculiar infantile character. Even Christ is represented as a little lamb.[23] You find that again in the time of the Reformation, where people even adopted a quite infantile language, talking in diminutives and identifying with all sorts of little animals that creep about, even with maggots in wounds—just awful things. There is something of that in this dream. In one of the next dreams we shall find a confirmation of this peculiar atmosphere. Moreover, if such animals appear in dreams, they always allude to an unconscious instinctive form of existence because the animal is made of earth; it is nothing but nature; it is unconscious and fulfills the will of the creator in an absolutely perfect way. So one could say the animal is the most pious of all creatures because it fulfills the will of God. It has also a psychology of a kind which is not human. It is below the human, you would say, but inasmuch as it is below, it is also above the human. The animal represents the

---

[21] Cf. "Dream Symbols," nr. 9, p. 109, and CW 12, nr. 9, par. 71. I 09 {0010}: "Walk through the archway, view of many sheep," February 18, 1932, CDM.

[22] According to MDR and other sources, Jung visited Ravenna in 1914 (on a bicycle tour with his friend Hans Schmid-Guisan). A second visit took place in 1932 in the company of Toni Wolff. Jung writes about their experience in MDR. He was very impressed by the mosaics, which influenced his own paintings in the RB.

[23] In PsA Jung has added a footnote on the source of the Christian sheep symbolism. Cf. CW 12, par. 72.

will of the Deity. Therefore the animal is also the symbol of the Deity. The gods have always been represented in the form of animals everywhere, even in our times. The Holy Ghost is represented by the dove; the Evangelists, as you know, at least three of them, had animal symbols—the eagle, the ox, the lion, and the bird-man; Christ himself is the lamb. So whenever a deity was represented by an icon, by an image, it had animal attributes, even in Christianity, so much so that a Hindu who wrote a report about his visit to Europe, particularly to England, told his contemporaries that England had a sort of animal worship because he found any number of doves and pigeons and lambs and lions and eagles in their temples. You recognize them? Lions are at the base of columns. The dove is, of course, the symbol of the Holy Spirit. He thought that these objects were worshipped. As a matter of fact, you find them in the most prominent places, above altars, above the crucifix, in any number of pictures of the saints; they are all full of animal images. It is curious that in the New Testament animals are hardly mentioned, but happily enough, we have a most remarkable find in Egypt, fragments of a papyrus containing a collection of anecdotes of Christ and his disciples and associates. It is not a gospel but a collection of anecdotes. It was dug up in 1897 in lower Egypt, 150 kilometers above Cairo, in Oxyrhynchus, and there in that fragment we read of the importance of animals—a thing which is absolutely absent in the Gospels, as you know. It says that the animals are the ones that bring us, lead us, to the Kingdom. Christ himself says so to his disciples.[24]

When our dreamer is brought back to the green land, to the green meadow, where the sheep are grazing, we can say that this dream means: Now all that inflation stuff is nonsense. We bring you back to the sheep land, to the green meadows where you are like one of the sheep, like a child, or a little lamb. We bring you back to the state of innocence, of unconsciousness, where you will be law abiding, where you don't question,

---

[24] The Oxyrhynchus papyrus were three Greek papyrus fragments found in the Nile valley between 1897 and 1907, identified as sayings of Jesus. Only in 1945, in connection with the Nag Hammadi findings, it became clear that these sayings stem from the *Gospel of Thomas*, discovered there together with fifty-three other texts. One of those, *The Gospel of Truth* was purchased by the C. G. Jung Institute and presented to Jung in 1953 and named the Jung Codex in honour of Jung's interest in Gnosticism. See B. Walker (1989; 1983), *Gnosticism: Its History and Influence* (Wellingborough: Crucible), 27; and Shamdasani (2012), 122–23. (For the full story of the Jung Codex, see the article by James M. Robinson, "The Jung Codex: The Rise and Fall of a Monopoly," *Religious Studies Reviews 3* (January 1977): 17–30. See also Jung's address at the presentation of the Jung Codex, *CW* 18, par. 1826.

where you don't react with your consciousness because your consciousness will be absent; you will be like an animal so that you can learn to obey the Divine Will.

The next unconscious product, the tenth, is a visual impression.[25] He is in the sheep land once more, and there he sees the unknown woman who first appeared veiled and then with the face of the sun. Here she is again, and she points out the way he ought to go.

This visual impression shows that the dreamer has returned to the same place where he meets the anima figure. The green land, as you now know, is the land of innocence, of childhood, and of animal-like obedience, of utter docility, of which the sheep are characteristic. There he finds the anima figure. Now, you see, the anima is the personification of the unconscious which comes up against us, which is our object. Object comes from the Latin word *objicere*, meaning "to throw against." Something thrown up against me is an *objectum*. Now the anima personifies everything which is not given in consciousness, in other words, the whole of the unconscious, at least for a certain time. As long as the anima represents the whole of the unconscious, the anima figure is of the greatest importance. It is really important in a way that cannot be exaggerated. She stands for everything the unconscious could possibly mean. We find her here in a most important position, namely, pointing out the way, whatever that may mean. Probably it means the way into the future, the way into future development, and suggests further that she assumes the role of the *psychopompos*, meaning "soul-leader," which is really the attribute of Hermes, the messenger of the gods, who leads the soul into the land of the hereafter. In this case, she doesn't exactly lead him into the land of the hereafter, but to the next stage in the transformation of his personality, to a different situation, expressed in the form of a different country. A different country means a different kind of man, a different psyche, a different attitude.

This dream or vision helps us to understand why he had to return to the sheep land, or to the land of the children, the land of innocence and obedience. It was absolutely necessary for him to get away from his traditional ego-consciousness, from the traditional mind. You remember the voice said, "I must leave the father first," in order to come into the land of the sheep; which means to the land—to the condition—of innocence, of unconsciousness. He must return to a condition in which he cannot judge,

---

[25] Cf. "Dream Symbols," nr. 10, p. 109, and CW 12, nr. 10, par. 73. I 10 {0011}: "Strange woman in the 'land of sheep' = land of childhood," February 27, 1932, CDM.

in which he has to surrender to the instinctual basis of his personality, to the basic pattern that he is, and that is unknown to him. We all contain a pattern which neither we nor anyone else knows about. It is a basic pattern born with us, which only becomes known to us through what we do. Only in our deeds do we appear. We don't know who we are; we would never know who we were if we were brought up alone on top of Mount Everest. We need many deeds, many actions, many aspects of life to know how we react. We learn to our utter amazement who we are by the reactions we make to our surroundings. Nobody can tell beforehand who he is; only afterwards does he come to know who he is. And then he will have some indestructible memories of how he has reacted. He is that person who has lived such and such a life, and whether he meant to live it or did not mean to live it, whether he wanted to live that type of life or not, he is that person. Nobody could have told him, and he could not have imagined before that he would be such a person. This empirical personality is the pattern that is born with each one. It is the pattern of our fate no matter whether that fate is made by ourselves or has come to us. We cannot distinguish these two elements; things come to us because we are these things. Our fate comes to us because we are it, and the ultimate results of our lives will show quite clearly what we have always been, what we were when we were born.

Those among you who believe in astrology know that this is its basic idea, and those who do not believe in astrology would perhaps wonder at this miracle that one can make at least a chart of a human life at its nativity.[26] This is a problem which concerns the relativity of time. It is something which belongs to a chapter of which I shall not speak.

You see the situation in the vision where the anima points the way is exactly the situation referred to in the Oxyrhynchus papyrus. The anima personifies the leading element which also leads the sheep. She is the shepherdess. Of course, you could ask here why Christ, too, is the shepherd— why in that case it is a man. There is an explanation, but that would lead us too far afield. The situation described in the dream is, of course, a great difficulty to such an intellect as our dreamer possesses. We can imagine it would be pretty difficult for him to accept or assimilate such an idea, and as far as I am aware of what happened to him in the days when he had

---

[26] Jung started studying astrology in 1911, in the course of his study of mythology, and learned to cast horoscopes. Jung to Freud, May 8, 1911, S. Freud and C. G. Jung (1974), *The Freud-Jung Letters: The Correspondence between Sigmund Freud and C. G. Jung* (Princeton, NJ: Princeton University Press), 421.

these dreams, I must say he was utterly unconscious of their meaning, but there were symptoms which showed that he went through a pretty difficult time, because things came up to him which were entirely strange to his mind, as you can well imagine.

The next unconscious product, the eleventh, is a dream. The essential part of it is the voice which appears again and says, "You are still a child."[27]

That brings up a doubt in his mind: Why all this child stuff? I am not a child anymore; I do not want to hear all this nonsense. But the voice says, "You are still a child."[28] That is the voice of the superior insight—or whatever you like to call it—which simply makes this statement, and he has to give in; and he did. This means you are still in the land of the children, you belong to the flock; you are unconscious, and you ought to accept it. You can't jump away from the fact that you are still a child. Such a recognition is very important. If he refuses to accept it then he is obliged to identify with his intellect. He is a perfectly grown-up being, competent to deal with ordinary problems by means of his scientific intellect, but through his intellect he will never know of such things as these and would deny the reality of such a problem. Since he is still a child, the next dream will probably be concerned with the question as to what he can do about the fact that he is still a child and yet a grown-up man.

The twelfth unconscious product is a short, rambling dream of dangerous peregrinations with the father and mother up and down many ladders.[29]

Here is the up-and-down motive; climbing up and down means changing from one level to another, sometimes above, sometimes below. This, of course, signifies the turmoil going on inside him; sometimes he is up in the attic of his intellectual consciousness, and sometimes down below in the sheep land, the land of the instincts, below the diaphragm. Being a child he is always in the living presence of the father and mother, having, not a psychology of his own, but a projected psychology. The child is never its own; the child, to a great extent, is the father and mother. For many years he is a part of the parental atmosphere; he breathes the pa-

---

[27] Cf. "Dream Symbols," nr. 11, p. 110, and CW 12, nr. 11, par. 76. I 11 {0012}: "Everyone shouts: 'You are still a child,'" February 27, 1932, CDM.

[28] Here it should be noted that Pauli was known as the "infant prodigy" (*Wunderkind* in German = "wonder-child"). He later used to joke about it, saying: "Yes, the wonder passes, and the child stays." See Enz and Meyenn, 1988.

[29] Cf. "Dream Symbols," nr. 12, p. 110, and CW 12, nr. 12, par. 78. I 12 {0013, fig. 1}: "Dangerous wanderings with parents," February 28, 1932. Pauli made a drawing of this dream. CDM.

rental air, the parental psychological atmosphere. Before birth he was contained in the womb, a part of the mother's body, and for many years after birth the child is still a part of the psychology of the parents, which explains why children often react in a most upsetting way to the neuroses of their parents. When I have to deal with a child I always talk to the mother and make her more or less responsible, or I take both parents. A child cannot account for a neurosis; the child does not need the neurosis; it is the parents who need it.[30]

This climbing up and down ladders is also a kind of practice, or exercise, in moving the heavy body. You know that body played a very great role in Egypt. The Egyptians could not conceive of an entirely bodiless spirit, they assumed that the soul is partially body, and they named it Ka. The *ka* was a sort of semimaterial soul that dwelt in the tomb with the mummy. They put a little ladder or a simulacrum of a ladder in the tomb for the ka, which it could use to climb over the horizon into the heavens. Having a heavy body and not being able to fly, it had to have a ladder. In the Oxyrhynchus papyrus, already referred to, the disciples were worried about the problem of reaching heaven and questioned Christ: "Who then are they that draw us ... ?" Jesus saith, "The birds of the air, and the beasts, whatsoever is under the earth or upon the earth, and the fishes of the sea, these are they which draw you." Follow the lead of the innocent and pious animals, and they will lead you on the right way to heaven. He continues, therefore, "Learn to know yourselves first of all, since you are the city and the city is the Kingdom."[31]

The state of turmoil of the dreamer, in which he is climbing up and down, always seeking a place of rest and certainty, is due to the conflict between his grown-up consciousness and his dependence upon his parents, his infantility, his still existing childishness. However, it is not merely childishness, but also a necessity to go back to the place of his origin, because there he will find the formula that will enable him to unite the pairs of opposites, namely above and below, right and left. The problem is what to do with the heaviness of his material body, his bodily being, which cannot climb into the sphere of the breath-like spirit. Such a thing needs ladders. This belongs to the realm of the so-called personal subconscious, not the collective unconscious. We forget about our childhood; we

---

[30] On Jung's view of children's neurosis, see CW 17, i.e., introduction to Francis G. Wickes "Analyse der Kinderseele" and other works. His view that children's neuroses in actuality express the psychological problems of the parents makes him a forerunner of family therapy.

[31] See *Gospel of Thomas*, log. 80/22–26.

forget what we have been; we forget many things that are disagreeable; we repress them, and that forms the personal subconscious as I explained at the beginning. The subconscious is like a heavy stone around our necks; it does not allow us to identify with spirits and such light things.[32]

On the contrary, we have to go down into that period of our life when we experienced these things, which clearly show us that we are bodies, like the animals, not quite human yet. The unconscious is like an animal; and we have to carry with us this weight, the shadow that follows us. We do not have to climb with it to heaven. Man apparently has tried that for 1,936 years, and see where he has landed—nowhere in heaven. Sure not. If things were good for a time, man was always in between, halfway up and halfway down, but there were also particularly bad times when he was more than halfway down.

You see if he continues to climb up and down ladders he will mix up the above and the below, so that the pairs of opposites have a chance to come together. If they come together he will reach not perfection, but completion; he will become not a perfect, but a complete, being. He will possess everything that is his own; he will carry with him what is his. That is all we can do, and it is enough for any man to carry himself. He cannot carry more, only himself. It is heavy enough and difficult enough when he is able to make his personal subconscious his own, when he can say, "This is the fellow that has lived such and such a life, who has thought so and so, felt such and such things, has such and such surroundings, such and such thoughts, such and such troubles." After he knows all that and can say, "It is my own and I am responsible for this load put upon me by my parents, my grandparents, and the whole number of my ancestors," then he possesses everything he ought to be concerned with, and it is a burden heavy enough. But this means completion. If you realize what that means you will see something that is quite serious, whether you believe in Christianity or not.

But this is against our ideals. Our ideal is to identify with the spirit, to be nothing but good, to forget we have been bad, to forget all about it, to imagine we are perfect creatures. "Oh yes," we say, "that was a mistake; it should never have been—it never was." Everybody says you should not think back, you should remember it is unsound to do so, it is not right to dwell upon disagreeable memories. Everybody tries to persuade you to get

---

[32] Jung has added a passage on the ladder theme in the 1944 version, referring to the motif of transformation and Zosimos's ascent and descent of fifteen steps. Cf. CW 12, par. 80.

away from yourself, that it is morbid to think of yourself, as if man were always necessarily morbid inside. A funny kind of an idea, but an idea that is taught; we have all had an education along that line no matter how reasonable it may have been in other ways. The general atmosphere was such, and so you see this kind of realization goes quite against our grain. We hate to be reminded of the fact that we are still children or animals. We try to be decent and nice, ideal and spirit-like; we try to hide everything that could possibly remind us of our merely instinctual basis. It is against the traditional pattern.

So in the thirteenth unconscious product, a dream, he hears the voice of his father crying out anxiously, "That is the seventh."[33]

Now, which seventh? It must be an answer to something. We have encountered the seven steps before, the stairs.[34] It might refer to the stairs; then it would be the seventh step; and the seventh would be the one that leads him out of his human existence, his ego-consciousness, into the land of enlightenment. The traditional mind of his father would be quite clear about the situation. It would say, "For heaven's sake that is an 'illumination.' You have had an 'illumination.' That is terrible." That would mean that he had to recognize it as enlightenment. The seventh step becomes light like the sun, and that was the same thing he had had before which got on his nerves and he had tried to avoid. And here the mind recognizes he has reached the seventh level. That is the hypothesis. We shall see if it is true. It would mean that by a continuous up-and-down movement through the instinctual basis of man he had succeeded in completing himself, and that, by acknowledging what kind of man he had been, he had made a whole of himself.

This man had had some passages in his previous history that were a bit difficult to digest; he did not like to show certain chapters in his record; he would much prefer to say such things had never happened; but unfortunately they had actually occurred. So in his inventory of himself he had to mark them and declare himself as the fellow who had lived such and such things. To do that means completion. If you are completed in that

---

[33] Cf. "Dream Symbols," nr. 13, p. 112, and CW 12, nr. 13, par. 82. I 13 {0014}: "Father shouts: this is the seventh," February 28, 1932, CDM.

[34] See above. Jung makes the association of the stairs with the number seven, it is not in the dream material. Pauli remarked in a letter to Jung that he didn't agree with his interpretation of the meaning of the number seven here. For Pauli the number seven was associated with the birth of his sister Hertha (see below), which he described as "the birth of the anima," PJL.

way, if you have accepted your personal subconscious, with all the things you don't remember, or prefer not to remember, then you can say, "I am complete. I am not ideal at all, but I am at least complete." We now have the full inventory of that man's character, you see.[35] If he can acknowledge that his sun has a shadow, then he is in the position of the old alchemists who can make gold. They say you can make gold out of the sun and its shadow. See? And then the traditional mind says that would be the mystical thing; that would be the seventh step where man is transformed. As the anima has shown before, by anticipation, she becomes the sun. The intellect believes there is a god or believes, on the contrary, that there is no such thing as god—god is not. There are only the two things the intellect can make out: there is God, or there is not God. But in India, if you read the *Upanishads*, you will find that it is said there is being *and* non-being. It is a paradox.[36] That is what the traditional intellect cannot stand; it cannot stand a paradox. It must always be this truth *or* that truth. So you see when a man is in the Catholic Church he believes in God, while out of the church he is an atheist, that is, he denies God, but as fervently as he believed it before. So Bernard Shaw, being an Irishman, could make the joke about the man to whom something had happened which shattered his belief, and he says, "I have lost my atheism."[37] As a man says, "I have lost my belief in God."

---

[35] In the 1944 version Jung has expanded the section on "the seventh" with the pars. 84–85 in *CW* 12.

[36] *Upanishads*: *The Sacred Books of the East* (1975), vol. 15, trans. and ed. Friedrich Max Müller (Delhi: Motilal Banarsidass).

[37] George Bernard Shaw (1856–1950). In his play *Too True to Be Good: A Political Extravaganza*, written in 1931, Shaw describes modern man's lack of direction and indicates that he must reevaluate his aims and goals and discard worn out values that no longer describe either human nature or contemporary problems. In this play Shaw lets a sergeant discuss with an elderly man who has just lost his belief in the Newtonian universe, the stronghold of determinism. The elder says: "Determinism is gone, shattered, buried with a thousand dead religions, evaporated with the clouds of a million forgotten winters. The science I pinned my faith to is bankrupt: its tales were more foolish than all the miracles of the priests, its cruelties more horrible than all the atrocities of the Inquisition. Its spread of enlightenment has been a spread of cancer: its counsels that were to have established the millennium have led straight to European suicide. And I—I who believed in it as no religious fanatic has ever believed in his superstition! For its sake I helped to destroy the faith of millions of worshippers in the temples of a thousand creeds. And now look at me and behold the supreme tragedy of the atheist who has lost his faith—his faith in atheism, for which more martyrs have perished than for all the creeds put together." B. Shaw (1934), *Too True to Be Good, Village Wooing and On the Rocks: Three Plays* (London: Constable), 89. Jung also refers to this passage in his seminars on Nietzsche's Zarathustra, given on June 20, 1934 (Jung, 1988, 122). It should also be noted that Pauli loved to read and cite George Bernard Shaw. In his surviving private library, preserved in "La Salle Pauli" in the European Organi-

But the intellect cannot stand a paradox, so you see the dreamer's mind is revolting against this peculiar mixture of good and evil, of yea and nay, of right and left, or above and below.[38] To him that is impure logic; it is against the laws of thinking; it is not clear at all. It is just chaos, and man always tries to get out of chaos and to create order. To do so is a perfectly decent enterprise. He cannot throw intellect overboard; he must do something about it. Let us see what happens.

In the next unconscious production, the fourteenth, he dreams he is in America and there he seeks an employee with a pointed beard. He must have a pointed beard, and they say, "All people in America always have such an employee."[39] Now who is the man with the pointed beard?

ANSWER: The devil.

DR. JUNG: Yes, you are right. The man speaks German, he knows German. Faust has his Mephisto, that is, the man with the pointed beard. Now his dream shows him what to do with his intellect. Intellect should be an employee; it should not be the father, the authoritative principle which rules the psyche; rather it should be the employee, a servant, a very useful and dangerous servant, as Mephisto was.[40] Now, why in America? What do you think? Mind you that man was European; if he was an American he would not dream like this.

ANSWER: New country. Land of promise.

---

zation for Nuclear Research (CERN), there are ten books by Shaw, most of them with marginal notes. Some of these books presumably stem from the library of his mother, who was a socialist and had an extensive interest in philosophy and literature. See Gieser, 2005, 28; Pauli to von Franz, February 1955 (no. 2019), PLC IV/3; Pauli to Heisenberg, December 21, 1957 (2811), PLC IV/4 I.

[38] It should be noted that Pauli was quite familiar with thinking in paradoxes owing to his years with Niels Bohr (from 1922), who taught him "that every true philosophy must actually start off with a paradox." Pauli to Jung, February 27, 1953 (58P), *PJL*, 94.

[39] Cf. "Dream Symbols," nr. 14, p. 112, and *CW* 12, nr. 14, par. 86. I 14 {0015}: "Employee with pointed beard is being sought," February 28, 1932, CDM.

[40] Pauli's colleagues George Gamov and Max Delbrück created a physicists' pastiche of Goethe's *Faust* to celebrate the tenth anniversary of Bohr's institute held during the physicists' conference of April 3–13, 1932. Pauli was cast in the role of Mephistopheles, "the spirit that denies," because he was known for his sharp, sarcastic, and critical intellect. Pauli did not attend the celebration, so his colleague Léon Rosenfeld played his part. Pauli was working on his handbook article on wave mechanics at the time, which had to be finished during the spring of 1932. G. Segrè (2007), *Faust in Copenhagen: A Struggle for the Soul of Physics* (London: Jonathan Cape); "Die Faustparodie," *Niels-Bohr 1885–1962: Der Kopenhagener Geist in der Physik* (1985), ed. K. v. Meyenn, R. U. Sexl, and K. Stolzenburg (Wiesbaden: Springer). It is unclear if Jung knew how familiar Pauli was with the figure of Mephisto. In the 1944 version Jung has added several paragraphs on Mephisto and also makes connections between him and the alchemical figure of Mercurius. See *CW* 12, pars. 88–90.

DR. JUNG: It is the land of the west, the new country, the new continent, a peculiar country for a European. Why peculiar? Well, I was once driving with an American in Europe, in particular in Switzerland, which is an old country, and he cursed the roads because they were all crooked, winding trails, and he said, "In America the roads are much straighter. Why haven't you got straight roads?" That is what impresses an American in Europe, that the roads are so winding. You will find it in all countries that are old. The radius of the curve is sometimes ten yards, or a hundred yards. In primitive countries like Africa the radius is only three, four, or five yards. This means a snake-like movement. If you have a perfectly flat plain and follow a native trail, you will walk in serpentine curves, without any reason. To understand, you must watch the primitives, how they walk. In Africa we crossed a plain, and we walked more than six kilometers, which is four and a half miles, an hour, in a tropical sun. When you walk as fast as that you go more easily if you swing to right and to left. That means you walk more quickly along the serpentine way than in a straight line. Moreover, it is a most natural movement, the way of the snake; that is how the primitive walks, and therefore all primitive roads are like that, meandering like the course of water, like the movement of the snake, like the movement of nature.

In thought, movement is straight as an arrow flies. When you *think* a road, you make it straight, when you *live* a road, walk a road, it is never straight. It is as a snake goes, as a river goes. This is a rule of nature. America to us is a land of straight roads, where things are thought out. You think "This is good," and you apply it. In Europe we think it is good, of course, but we don't necessarily do it. Because we consider, "Well, anything good always has a long shadow, and there is just as much on the other side." We do not even believe that the good will win out. But, in this country plenty of people believe in the good, and that you can tell about it. You can say, "You see the truth is so and so," and you really expect people will accept it and behave accordingly. I think we have never had this belief in Europe. We are terribly skeptical about it. You see we are too much impressed with history, and history contains an awful record of mankind. Anyone who studies history carefully can tell what man really is, and then he doesn't believe that he can be told. If he could learn merely from being told, the world would have been in paradise in the old times, back in the seventeenth century BC, but it never has been. Mankind has been told the best things, things that would lead straight to paradise, but no paradise came into existence, and I doubt whether it ever will.

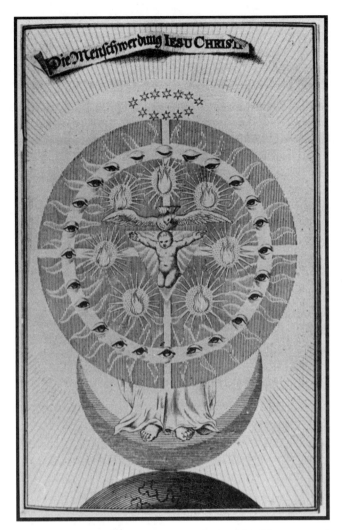

Figure 16. Jacob Böhme, *De Incarnation Verbi* (1620). "Representation of the
incarnation of Christ. Standing on a crescent is a figure with only the feet and the
lower portion of the robe visible, the rest hidden behind or represented in form
of a large light sphere surrounding a circle having thirty-two rays springing from
thirty-two eyes in next circle; from the other side of eyes emerge another thirty-
two flames into the inner circle, also containing eight large flames within circles.
The whole is crossed, at the center is an inverted triangle containing a kneeling
Christ with arms outstretched in the posture of the crucifixion; above the head
of the child, a dove with outstretched wings; at the head of the cross within the
outer circle of light, a crown of twelve stars, seven above, five below, titled 'Die
Menschwerdung Iesu Christi.'" (ARAS Record 5Gs.754). This mandala is not
reproduced in *Psychology and Alchemy*.

So when the dreamer is in America, he is in a land of straight roads, where one believes in common sense, in rational devices.[41] One believes in directness, and one thinks one can tell it to the people and they will listen. Moreover where public opinions and convictions are strong, they are generally shared by all. In the dream the dreamer hears that somebody says so; that people say everyone has such an employee. Now that is not exactly what one would say in America; one would not say that everyone has a Mephisto, or that it is necessary to have a Mephisto, as a secretary or an assistant. But if you think straight, if you believe in your conclusions and if you also allow your unconscious to tell you something, you will hear this good advice. Have your intellect, but as a servant; yet he is a dangerous one with a pointed beard, a devil. Faust would have been taken in by the devil in the end, but while he lived, he needed him.

Now the next unconscious product, the fifteenth, a dream, denotes an important change.[42] He sees his mother, and she is pouring water from one basin into another. It is a solemn ceremony of great importance to himself, as well as to his surroundings, even to the contemporary world. And while he is tremendously impressed by that ceremony, he suddenly becomes aware of the fact that his father has disinherited him, not only disinherited him, but exiled or excommunicated him. We will talk of that tomorrow.

---

[41] This long exposition on America cannot be found in the Eranos lecture nor in *PsA*.

[42] Cf. "Dream Symbols," nr. 15, p. 113, and *CW* 12, nr. 15, par. 91. I 15 {0016}: "The mother pours water into a basin," February 28, 1932, CDM.

Lecture 3

DR. JUNG: Ladies and gentlemen: here are several questions.[1]

QUESTION: Will Dr. Jung tell us whether, in collective material, symbols like the staircase can be thought of as having a fixed meaning, or whether they must be always interpreted in the light of personal associations?

DR. JUNG: It is an important question. As a rule, I consider the representations in dreams, the so-called symbols, as individual creations, and I would not attach any fixed meaning to such images. There are, however, certain exceptions. For instance, if you give me a dream of an unknown person and in the dream is the representation of a staircase, I should feel quite hesitant as to its meaning. I should need more material, at least a series of from ten to twenty dreams, in order to establish a more or less sufficient interpretation. If a patient is not going through the kind of process which I am describing here, then naturally I should try to establish the context first; I should inquire in what connections this staircase appears, for it might have an entirely different meaning. You should never rely upon a fixed meaning; such a thing practically does not exist. You know these dream ideas have many aspects, and it depends entirely on the context how you ultimately interpret them.

QUESTION: How can the dreams of the patient be considered as an unfoldment of his personality if he remains unconscious of their significance?

DR. JUNG: You must not be impatient. This patient produced a series of almost fifteen hundred dreams, and the first part of his development took eight months.[2] We are analyzing the twenty-two initial dreams where he could not possibly be conscious of what the dreams meant; but, you know, he is a very intelligent man, and after a certain while we surely can expect that he will begin to smell a rat and become more and more con-

---

[1] This lecture was held on September 22, 1936.

[2] As far as we know, Pauli recorded approximately one thousand dreams, with 410 of these during treatment with Jung and Rosenbaum. See CDM; also Meyenn, 2011, 9–35.

scious. There are quite a number of people among you to whom I need to tell only the text of the dreams when they begin to sit up and say, "Aha, that probably means so and so; it is going to such and such a goal." And that is what he did. After a while he became aware that these things really meant something, and he got a sort of notion. It would not be necessary to say much in such a case; it would be quite sufficient to give a man a single tip, and he would understand the whole thing.

QUESTION: Will you please explain what you meant by saying that Christ went to both heaven and hell when he died.

DR. JUNG: I mean nothing by that. I have not invented that story. Christ certainly went up to heaven, as you can read in the Bible, and he also went to hell, of which the Catholic Church made a very great story. He spent three days in hell, which was most significant.[3] He went there to complete the perfect integrating process of redemption. Hell is the shadow of heaven, the other side, the opposite world, the negative world. One has to put these two things together in order to make a complete mandala. That is why he went to hell. That is why you go to hell to a certain extent when you go through analysis, in order to put the two ends together. In medieval philosophy the conjunction of the opposites produces the precious substance which is able to reconcile that which is irreconcilable.

QUESTION: Was the parental image dominant during the Victorian era, and if so, is that why its voice speaks with such authority in dreams today?

DR. JUNG: That is a slight mistake. The parental image has a different meaning. If one speaks of the Victorian age, there were fathers that had beards and mothers that wore crinolines. They, of course, caused a very peculiar kind of parental image. You said, "Sir," to your father, and the parents were somewhere off in the clouds, sort of demigods. This caused a peculiar revolt in the next generations against fathers and mothers of such an authoritative character. But a parental image does not produce any authority in the unconscious; on the contrary, it only produces rebellion. When a voice of authority appears in dreams, it is by no means the voice of such a father or such a mother; it is something quite different. The real authority, the parent with that voice, of which I told you, is Yahweh and not at all the human father; it is the voice of the unconscious itself, which has an authority higher than anything we know of, absolutely compelling. When you get it from the unconscious there is no contradiction possible even. You are just compelled to do something.

---

[3] Jung writes about this already in *The Red Book*, "No one knows what happened during the three days Christ was in Hell. I have experienced it." *RB*, 243.

So you see you can't compare this authoritative voice with the voice of the parental image in the strict sense of the word. You can say it is the voice of the father perhaps, but the father is there the symbol, the image, of that authority which is innate in the unconscious. It is the personification of the power and influence of the unconscious, and the more you do *not* see that power, the greater is its authority, because the thing that grips you without your awareness, that grips you unconsciously, is the thing that you follow most blindly, and therefore obey completely, like an animal, without questioning. For instance, you never ask yourself, why did I do this or that, if you are moved to do something unconsciously. It is just as if your judgment were completely blind and silent; you can't even use your mind, you just react. Unless other people ask you, "Why do you do such things?" you do not realize that what you have said or done was rather peculiar. For if there is nobody to tell you, you are not aware of it. That is how the unconscious works, and therefore it works with the greatest authority.

QUESTION: When you define individuation as the understanding and acceptance of a preexistent and unalterable pattern imposed on the individual by his inheritance and culture, how do you relate it to social or racial evolution? Is evolution, in this context, an illusion, and racial experience merely cyclical?

DR. JUNG: I am afraid this is again a pretty complicated question, inasmuch as the question of an individual pattern is only very loosely connected with the idea of evolution. The individual pattern is the result of a coming together of very many elements or inherited units, or genes, as one says in biology. For instance, you have the genes of the father's tribe and of the mother's tribe. You are, strictly, not even born of your mother, that is, you don't repeat your mother; you are not made by your mother, but by the tribe of the mother, and by the tribe of the father. So children are really children of tribes and not children of individuals. Children may be very different from their parents, exceedingly different, and very often you don't really know where certain qualities come from. Often children don't even look like the parents. Then the individual pattern is also influenced by partly known, partly unknown considerations. For instance, children are very much influenced by the place in which they are born, and by the climate, perhaps. Many things, unknown influences, contribute to the fashioning of a definite pattern.

This idea does not, however, exclude evolution at all. For instance, it has nothing to do with the idea of the general evolution of the species, but surely it has much to do with the evolution of an individual. We gain through this idea a sort of new formula for the evolution of an individual, namely, a gradual filling in of a pattern, which is exactly what we are doing when we have a growing consciousness of our individuality as I describe it.

When you study children you find in the child a definite individuality; but when you meet the same person again in later years you find peculiar differences between the adult and the child whom you had known. Certain important strains have perhaps been excluded, others overdeveloped, and there may be a peculiar one-sidedness. One whole side of that child may have disappeared, in which case there may arise a neurotic condition which, if analyzed, discloses all those qualities that the child once exhibited, but which have disappeared in later years. For instance, very often those women who, when they were thirteen or fourteen years old, were quite boyish, climbed trees, and wanted to be boys in later life become hysterical and exaggeratedly feminine in character. The boyish side seems to have disappeared so that they have apparently become completely feminine. But if you analyze them you will find a powerful animus, a masculine figure, which has been split off. The cure of such a case consists in the bringing together of these two separated sides, of adding a great amount of masculinity to their exaggerated and neurotic femininity. The total then allows one to see in them the original pattern again.

* * * * *

I told you yesterday that dream (the fifteenth) of the mother who pours water from one basin into another. The dreamer sees his mother pouring water from one basin into another. It is performed with solemnity—important both to himself and to his surroundings, even to the contemporary world—and he is much impressed by this peculiar ceremony. Then, he suddenly becomes aware of the fact that his father has disinherited or exiled him or has excommunicated him. The dreamer used the German word that means all of that. Really what he means is a sort of excommunication.

In the preceding dreams, apparently his problem was to get away from the father. The voice told him, "You must get away from the father." The father represents the traditional mind. It is expressed in Latin by animus. Animus means wind. The father is often characterized by the wind, while the mother is characterized by the water, by the water of life, also by the vessel symbol, for obvious reasons. The child is contained in the mother, in the water, in the amniotic fluid, in the basin, in the magic vessel of creation. The mother really stands for that vessel. So we find here the mother pouring water from one basin into another which means from one woman into another woman.

Later on, in the twenty-eighth dream of the subsequent series, he suddenly remembered that he had had this dream and that in it he really had been aware of the fact that the other basin was that of his sister, which he had completely forgotten when he pulled out this earlier dream. So we can take it from subsequent remembrance that the second basin is that of his sister. This means that the mother pours the living water, the creative fluid, from her form into the form of the sister. In other words, the source of life-giving water, whatever that is, is no more in the mother basin but in the sister basin. The source of secret life does not well up any more in the mother, whatever she means, but now in the sister.

This refers to an important change in the anima image of the man. A man has his anima projection in the mother first. The mother represents the female object to him. If he gets stuck in that image, then his whole feeling life, his Eros, his relatedness, his emotional experiences, his ideals along that line, are completely identified with the mother.[4] Such a man will be enthusiastic over babies and have very nice feeling; he will be a "good" boy, not at all naughty. On the other side, he may be quite a man, but when it comes to the feeling life, he is just mother's good boy and quite ideal in that respect. For women he is not particularly ideal, unless they are mothers "born" or are identified with their mothers. Then they will be very enthusiastic over such a nice boy. The disagreeable thing is that the mother then has all the real feeling of the boy, his heterosexual feeling, and what is left is only an inferior feeling for women. To him,

---

[4] Jung uses the word *Eros* with different meanings. Here it is defined as the principle of feminine relatedness, which is usually put into contrast to the masculine principle of *Logos*, defined as "objective interest" ("Women in Europe," from 1927, in *CW* 10, par. 255) or "discrimination of opposites" ("Psychological Aspects of the Mother Archetype," from 1954, in *CW* 9/I, par. 178). But Eros is also put into opposition to the will to power ("The Problem of the Attitude-Type," from 1917, *CW* 7, par. 78). Although Jung experienced these two principles in his visions in 1913, recorded in *The Red Book* as the figures of Elijah (forethinking) and Salome (pleasure), he seems to have waited to define these and present them in his written work until much later. See "The Personification of the Opposites," from 1955, *CW* 14, pars. 224–25. He presents his thoughts on Eros and Logos to a wider audience in his 1925 seminar. See C. G. Jung (author), W. McGuire (ed.), S. Shamdasani (ed. and introduction) (2011), *Introduction to Jungian Psychology: Notes of the Seminar on Analytical Psychology Given in 1925*, Bollingen Series (Princeton, NJ: Princeton University Press), 98. His other definition of Eros stems from his need to differentiate his views from those of Freud's, where he widens Freud's sexual definition of Eros to bring it closer to the classical Greek definition that we find in Plato's *Symposium*, i.e., one that includes the spiritual aspects of Eros. Still another definition of Eros is to be found in *MDR*, where he describes it as "a *kosmogonos*, a creator and father-mother of all consciousness" (387).

women are either mothers or prostitutes, but not real women. Or even this adaptation to the woman may be too difficult, and then there is nothing left for him but to become a homosexual.[5] For a woman to marry a man of that type is no joke. He has wonderful feeling for men in general, especially for younger men; but they are really his mother's fantasy feelings. It occasionally happens that the mother develops certain fantasies in which she finds other men quite nice; but, if she is not aware of these fantasies in her unconscious, and, if the boy is closely identified with her, he will have no sexual feeling for the woman but will develop homosexual feelings for such nice young men. That is how such things go.

As long as this young man of the dreams has his life-giving water (whatever that means, we must talk of it), the source of his life in his mother, he is likely to repeat the mother's psychology and to behave more or less like a woman. This was the case with him. On the one side he was boyish and infantile, and the good boy in a way; and then on the other side he had no relation except to mothers or to prostitutes. The two things, of course, did not fit together. He had quite a number of so-called love affairs which were not matters of love at all, just foolishness, all to his own detriment. When the mother pours the water into the basin of the sister, then he is no more contained in the mother; he is contained in the sister. Now the sister is more or less of his own age, and that is better. One can never be as dependent upon the sister as upon the mother, because she has not given one life and existence. She is more parallel. The fact that one can never be contained as much in the sister as in the mother means a certain amount of liberation. The sister then becomes the second object for the projection of the anima. Thus we see bachelors living with their sisters, repeating father and mother together in platonic form, and they make a life of it.

The dreamer never got along very well with his sister.[6] Moreover she made the mistake of marrying, so she could not carry the anima image any

---

[5] For Jung's view on homosexuality, see for instance Robert H. Hopcke (1988), "Jung and Homosexuality: A Clearer Vision," *Journal of Analytical Psychology* 33 (1): 65–80.

[6] Pauli's sister Hertha Ernestina (reference to the philosopher and Wolfgang Pauli's godfather, Ernst Mach) Pauli was born in 1906. She became an actress and later an author. She was called to the famous German Theatre in Berlin by the famous actor/director Max Reinhardt (1873–1943). She collaborated on film and radio projects. On the rise of the Nazis she first returned to Vienna, where she wrote several books, before fleeing to Paris, where she was involved in the resistance. Finally she ended up in America, where she founded a theater school in Hollywood. She married and acquired the surname Ashton and became a US citizen in 1952. In her semidocumentary short story *Break of Time* she describes the persecution of political activists in Vienna and her flight to America after the German Anschluß.

longer. The pouring of water into the basin of the sister is entirely symbolical. The symbol refers not really to sister, but woman. Whenever he fell in love, it was either with a woman who had a certain resemblance to his sister, or with friends of his sister. The sister had to give her blessing, otherwise the woman wasn't good. But when she was blessed by a certain similarity or by being a friend of the sister, then there was the possibility for his feeling to creep from one object to another.

A man's anima is a peculiarly sluggish thing, like a woman's mind. (Excuse me!) It always needs a bridge. The object must be of a certain color if he is to touch it. In other words, a man whose feeling and relatedness are extremely influenced by the mother must at least see a maternal quality in the woman, otherwise he can't creep across from the mother to the other woman. It is as if the object had to be painted in a certain color or given a certain smell if he is to accept it. There must be the medium of the bridge of similarity, otherwise he does not get his feeling across the chasm to the object—the gap is too wide. As is the case with the feeling of the man, so with the thinking of the woman. In educating the mind of a woman, one must always first familiarize the mental image with her previous thinking, otherwise the thought can't creep across. So masculine feeling must also have a bridge; for, like feminine thinking, it cannot leap. Feeling for him is not a differentiated function, and only differentiated functions can leap. Inferior functions can't jump; they creep like snails.

The dreamer characterizes this exchange of basins as a most solemn ceremony, as a most important performance. Curiously enough it is important, not only for him personally, but also for his surroundings and even for the contemporary world, just as if this magic performance meant a tremendous change, that would influence also the world.

Now it is very difficult to see why this performance should have such an aspect. That comes from the fact that the sister is entirely symbolical. The sister in this case means the anima, the image of the female. As long as he has his feeling or his function of relatedness, his emotion, in the mother, he has it in the unconscious, because the mother symbolizes the unconscious, the source and origin of life, which is the unconscious. Consciousness wells up from the unconscious, rises like an island from the sea, from the darkness, and the mother is the darkness, the original unconsciousness. Out of the mother came individual consciousness. As long as

---

She died in 1973. Like her brother Wolfgang, she had no children. H. Pauli (1970), *Der Riß der Zeit geht durch mein Herz Ein Erlebnisbuch* (Wien); English title *Break of Time*. Enz, 2002, 17–19.

the water of life, the essence of existence, is in the mother, the man is in a more or less unconscious condition; he doesn't know he is related to the world. He finds himself contained in the world passively; he is as if suspended in the mother's womb, contained in the water, the amniotic fluid. Obviously he can't defend himself because everything is in the unconscious.

So the dreamer repeatedly found himself in the most amazing situations. For instance, once he found himself in the midst of a great row in a restaurant, and a man threatened to throw him out of the window on the first floor. Then he grew afraid of himself.[7] He did not understand how he got into such a situation. Anyone outside could see very clearly how he stumbled into it. But to himself, he was a victim of circumstances; he had no control over his outer conditions because he was still an embryo suspended in the amniotic fluid where things simply happen. He was a victim of circumstances in this way because he was not related. This is what happens to such a nice boy quite continuously. He has one affair after another, and is always a victim. He says, "What could I do?" like that, like a so-called innocent girl, "What could I do, he held my both hands and kissed me."

Now you see as long as he was in such a condition, having nothing but a traditional mind, he was dependent upon the parental image. With the traditional mind you can only think along the well-trodden roads of tradition, and you have no thought beyond. But he has given up that paternal inheritance, as you have seen in these dreams; and that is apparent in his unconscious before he is aware of it. A liberation is being prepared in the unconscious, namely, the liberation of his feeling from the mother, and its transference into the form of the anima. This means that he now becomes conscious of the unconscious—of the fact of the unconscious—which is a very important thing; so important is it that it even has significance for the contemporary world, for he is going to undertake a step which has not been undertaken before.

I must explain this further: the symbolism is very simple, and whoever understands it knows the whole story, but it is difficult to explain. The relationship to the maternal unconscious has always been taken care of by certain philosophies or religions. For instance, that symbolic mother that

---

[7] Pauli describes this in a letter to Jung (May 24, 1934, 30P): "The specific threat of my life has been the fact that in the second half of life I swing from one extreme to the other (enantiodromia). In the first half of my life I was a cold and cynical devil to other people and a fanatical atheist and intellectual 'enlightener.' The opposites to that was, on the one hand, a tendency toward being criminal, a thug (which could have degenerated into me becoming a murderer)." *PJL*.

contains our unconscious life has been, say, a church, or a certain creed. It has always been outside of ourselves—it is the world, or it is Mother Nature, in which we are contained—but we never thought of it as a psychological phenomenon within ourselves, because we did not think the church could be a symbol, for it was reality. The relationship to Mother Mary in the Catholic Church is this kind of relationship to a metaphysical object, and before that it was the relation to the Mother.

In all more or less civilized tribes and peoples there are initiations, secret ceremonies, that carry people over from the state of unconsciousness in their parents, to another state of unconsciousness, namely, the relation to the tribe, the identification with the tribe or with certain institutions, for instance, the church. Our initiations are baptism, confirmation, and all that, and then we become children or members of a Christian community, members of a church, children of God, and, if we are Catholics, our mother is Mary and the church, and the church is also characterized as *Mater Ecclesia*. Beyond that one has not developed. The general conception of our time is a mere negation. We say, "Oh well, those were historical ideas, superstitions perhaps," and we have chucked the whole thing; we don't bother about it anymore. But then we are bothered by the absence of such ideas, and the unconscious begins to grow. That is why we began to talk of the unconscious at all. Before that no one ever mentioned the existence of the unconscious, because it did not exist. It was all in such institutions, in such life forms.

The Catholic Church is a way of living the unconscious, and the dogmas of the Catholic Church contain all the history of the unconscious objectified. Whatever they represent as happening is what happens in the unconscious. There we have the Divine Mother, the Divine Father, the birth of the hero, the great dragon; we have everything we possibly could think of, all the essentials of the unconscious process established, as metaphysical realities. We have simply forgotten the meaning of these things, and we reject them as meaningless and valueless, because our unconscious has withdrawn from these expressions and has established itself as a psychological fact, and this gravely disturbs everybody because we have no expression for it. The source of our life has been poured into another basin.

The mother is the absolute object in which we are contained unconsciously like the embryo in the mother's womb. So a true Catholic is contained in his church in a most unconscious way. He is simply the object of the church; the church is the subject. Or, in primitive tribes, the tribe is the subject and the members are the objects. The tribe members individually are practically nonexistent. In a natural state such tribes are ruled by the unconscious completely, and the real ruler of such a tribe is the medicine man who has vision, who has heard the voice of the unconscious. The members of the tribe are exchangeable units with practically no individual existence. This is a very curious fact. But you can still find these facts in the Catholic mind of very highly educated people. I remember a medical professor at a European university. He knew I was a psychologist; he had heard of my books but, of course, could not understand them, for he had an entirely different mental makeup. He said to me, "Why do you worry about psychology? What is it after all? We don't worry about such things." I said, "How do you do it—surely certain problems arise?" He said, "No, there are none. If anything questionable arises I simply ask my father confessor, and he tells me. If he doesn't know he asks the bishop; and if he doesn't know, he writes to the College of Cardinals at Rome, where the records go back for two thousand years. These questions have all been perfectly answered long ago." This man is not concerned at all; he leaves all his questions to that body of truth represented by the church. All his philosophical life is entirely in the church, not in him.[8]

There was another case: I once had an interesting experience with some highly intelligent Frenchmen in Paris, men from the academy. They asked me about the collective unconscious. One man said it was entirely mystical. I said, "I don't see any mysticism in the collective unconscious. It is only another formula for the fact that we have collective instincts. Instincts that are not new. Sex and hunger are the same everywhere. You can prove it; indeed, it has been proved long ago; and we have the same motives in mythology and religion all over the earth. I really wonder why you say 'mystical.'" The Frenchman said, "What you have to say has nothing to do with psychology. For instance, you treat the symbolism of the golden flower or speak of the symbolism of the hero or the whale-dragon myth." I said, "Naturally." He said, "C'est la réligion." For men who happen to be in the church, these things don't exist as scientific problems. The whale-dragon myth, for example, is a mere dim anticipation of the dogmatic idea of the devil, who is the whale-dragon that eats the hero. And this idea—that the hero is devoured by the dragon—is only an anticipation of the later revealed divine truth that Christ has gone down to

---

[8] This long passage on the Catholic church is not included in the Eranos version or *PsA*. Jung states in an interview with Aniela Jaffé, April 30, 1958, that he had been writing on the Catholic mass during the summer of 1936. He gave a lecture on it at the Psychological Club in 1941. The text was published in 1942. See *AJ Protocols*, 361, and also "Transformation Symbolism in the Mass" (1942) in *CW* 11.

hell to redeem even the dead. Or take the Virgin Birth. There were plenty of virgins and virgin births in the time before Christ. They are all thought to be nothing but anticipation of the truth that Mary as a virgin was to bear the Redeemer. When I say to a Catholic that that dogma is symbolic and simply reveals a psychological truth, he cannot follow. To him it is there, embodied in real events that have actually taken place and which have nothing to do with psychology. So when I speak of symbols Catholics say, "la réligion." That is being in the mother. They are still in the mother. They believe they are concerned with those things as little as the embryo believes that he is concerned when his mother gets shaken or falls downstairs. *He* has nothing to do with it, even if he dies. That happens in the surrounding world; it is not he that has fallen down the stairs. That is how these people behave. I even have to say, "My dear man, this thing concerns you—you are in it." He does not know it. Many people don't know where they are living; they are not aware. I say, "You are in mortal danger." They don't realize it. They happily doze on for twelve years in a dream that other people are responsible or that father will pay for it, or something like that.

So when that source of life is changed into another form, into the sister, then something very important has happened, namely, that whole projection is withdrawn, and he becomes aware of the fact that he himself is the maker of dogmas. "*I* have made Christ, *I* have made Mary, they came out of *my* psychological suffering." And then he can't say any more, "C'est la réligion." He must say: "I am responsible for that myth; I am the source of it, because in my anima, my unconscious, is really the source of all these things." These myths, for example, that Christ really has existed, are not necessarily even historical; they came from man's unconscious. Now if I am aware of the fact that *I* am really the source of all that, then I gain new importance. Man gains new importance; for he then realizes himself as the source of psychological existence, and that is the most important step in the evolution of mankind; it means an enormous extension of consciousness. Of course, looked at from the standpoint of any church, it is a terrific heresy, almost blasphemous. It lends a value to human existence that has only been accredited to the gods. You can accredit a god with the faculty of creating myth, but man has always been the victim of it. That man should now be the subject, the origin of all these things is too much; our contemporary mind cannot grasp it yet.

But the dreamer's mind, unconsciously at least, got hold of it. The moment he gives up the traditional mind, he is able to realize that he is unrelated. The traditional mind tells him this is the normal condition in which one lives, but when he gives up this attitude he becomes aware that he lives really in a very funny way and is conscious that he produces many effects which he formerly attributed to circumstances.

Like the well-known phenomenon one experiences with patients. They tell you that all people are very bad and that they are the most innocent victims of these bad people. They never realize that wherever they go they carry their specific devil who always creates a situation for them. They think the pope, perhaps, has foreseen bad circumstances for them. The idea never enters their heads that in every situation they are themselves and if there is a devil in that situation, they have brought it in. Thus people live perhaps ten to twenty dramatic episodes, and each takes the same course, but to them every case is new and most astonishing. A man marries five different women, all behave quite badly, in different ways; but *he* is perfectly innocent. He never thinks that he has brought an element into the relationship which has caused the situation. Such a mind is absolutely caught in the unconscious in an embryonic way. The moment one gives up that way of thinking one becomes aware that things are not as they should be.

So it dawned upon this man that when he gets into rows like the one I have just spoken of in which he is injured, he is irritating to other people, he is offensive; he is the real cause of his misfortune. And now he asks, "Who in me arouses all that mischief?" He knows his mind; he knows himself, that he went to that restaurant in a perfectly peaceful mood in order to have a good meal and a bottle of wine and to meet certain nice friends. Then suddenly a row, and all around *him*. How did it happen? He never bothered to ask, even, until it became too thick, and then his mind told him and helped him. But he could not think like that until he had given up his traditional way of thinking which says: "Whatever happened to you, poor child, is not your responsibility; that happens to you and injures you because there are very bad people. You don't exist as a responsible factor."

Now when he is able to come to the realization that he is the cause of all the mischief around himself, then the question arises in him, "Who then? If I don't do it with my conscious intention, who is then the author of all the evil?" And then he becomes suspicious, but still he doesn't see that anything came from his hands. He turns round to see whether somebody is behind him who has thrown that object. He says, "What is the matter? Here is something that causes trouble." And then he discovers the unconscious as a real fact. That is the anima. The anima is the personification of the unconscious.

So when the mother pours the living water from her basin into the basin of the sister, it means he becomes aware of the existence of his anima. Now as to the water. The water of life is a very old and widespread idea; for instance, the essential idea of mother in the old hymns of the church, is called *pege*, meaning "the source," "the stream"; and in the litany it is often called *fons signatus*, meaning the "sealed well." You know that water plays a very great role in Christian symbolism, for example in the teaching about Christ, where he is called the Water of Life. Water is also the transforming fluid of baptism, which represents the fact, the biological fact, that we are made in the amniotic fluid. So, when we are immersed in the water which has the power of regeneration through the blessing of God bestowed upon it, we are made over and given rebirth. In the Catholic Church, on the night of the *sabbatum sanctum*,[9] the night between Easter Saturday and Sunday, there takes place the special ceremony, called the *benedictus fontis*,[10] which bestows the power of regeneration on the water. In that ceremony the priest performs the sacred union between the masculine element, the light, and the feminine element, the water, by immersing a burning candle three times into the basin. After the light is extinguished by the water, he divides the water into four parts (this belongs to mandala symbolism) and evokes the Holy Spirit to descend into the water and give to it the quality, or faculty, of regenerating power, so that people immersed therein may be reborn into a new childhood and that a new offspring may be born to the church of God. This water is always used in churches, as you know, for baptism; it has apotropaic[11] power, a magic power of cleansing; it is sprinkled on coffins, on altars, and on the community also, to disinfect them and whatever they are concerned with, from the admixture of evil spirits. It is magic water. Magic water played a great role in antiquity. In the circle of hermetic philosophers it was called the *hydrathuon*, the divine water; in Latin, *aqua permanens*, the everlasting water, and also *aqua nostra*, our water. This magic water was applied to the impure metals or impure chemical substance, in order to transform them into silver or gold, or to transform dead matter into living matter. These are just a few examples of the peculiar nature of this water.

Now psychologically, if water is stagnant, it is usually a symbol for the unconscious. But if it is flowing, it means the river of life, the meandering

---

[9] Latin: Holy Saturday.

[10] Latin: blessed fountain.

[11] To ward off evil: from Greek *apotropaios*, from *apotrepein*, to ward off: *apo-*, *apo-* + *trepein*, to turn; see *trep-* in Indo-European roots.

snake, the serpent—the Tao in China. You know all these metaphors. It is the fertilizing agent that makes plants grow and gives life to man; it quenches their thirst and produces their food. Primitive man always lived near rivers, which were his life; they gave him food and drink. The coast was always inhabited because the sea contained food and was life-giving. So you see water, psychologically, must symbolize something which is tremendously important for man. It means life to man. What is this thing that means life to our psyche? What is the real life giver? What do you think? Just give it. Risk it.

ANSWER: The living spirit.

DR. JUNG: No, that is much too thin; that is wind.

ANSWER: The unconscious gives it.

DR. JUNG: No, that is the mother, the seed. But the flowing water, the water of a well, instinctive forces, what do we call it psychologically?

ANSWER: Libido.

DR. JUNG: Libido is the term—desire—that is what makes us live. If you have no desire, you do not live; you are stagnant; you become unconscious. It is desire that makes you move. If you have a new desire, a new hope, a new outlook, you move. It is energy.

FROM THE AUDIENCE: Enthusiasm.

DR. JUNG: Yes, that is one form, a peculiar outburst of life-giving force. So you see our energy, our psychological energy, is expressed by that water. Or you can say, by that eternal symbol of water, man is given a new symbolical interpretation of our so-called scientific concept of energy. The course of the water is the union of opposites, therefore it is life giving. You are forced to stand still at attention because of the mere existence of pairs of opposites. Then when something happens between the opposites, that is energy; it is the flow of life; it is movement; it is the process of all things, inasmuch as things live and move. Really the flowing water symbolizes released, psychical energy.[12]

When the water flows from the mother, however, the source of life is unconscious. We do not know where it comes from; we do not know the source. If it comes from the anima, we know that the flow, the well of our life, comes from the unconscious, and that it does not come from altar, church, or creed. It comes from nothing outside, but from what we call the unconscious, namely, from an unknown place with which we are eternally in contact. Mind you, we do not know what the unconscious is,

---

[12] Jung uses the analogy of water in his essay on psychic energy, originally published in 1928 as "On the Energetics of the Soul," Cf. CW 8, pars. 1–130.

therefore, we call it unconscious. It is the utterly unknown. But we have a definite feeling that we are connected with it quite intimately, and that the source is somewhere inside ourselves and wells up from there somehow, because we feel the source of energy must be within us. Not up here [*indicating the head*], but we find that it comes from down below, from the lower regions of the body, usually from the center, below the diaphragm, the solar plexus. The term *plexus solaris*, meaning the "center of the sun," has been given to the accumulation of sympathetic nerves in the abdomen because it is the equivalent of the sun in heaven, according to an old idea, the sun being the origin of life. It is not the bright light of the sun above, but the dark light below.

We know that for our dreamer, the source of life, the source of energy, has been transferred from the mother to the sister, which means from one unconscious condition to another, but now to one that is psychological, while the former was merely unconscious. In other words, in the former condition one does not know and does not bother where life is coming from, while in the latter one knows that life is really coming from the unconscious, and one now even has an idea of the nature of that unconscious. One knows it approaches us in the form of the female figure, in the form of the anima. When that is the case all former beliefs change their faces; the origin of our life is no more in a dogma, which is really outside ourselves, but in us, in our unconscious, whatever that is. We now cease to appeal any longer to anything outside of ourselves; we appeal to something which touches us in ourselves, and the ultimate authority is no more in the saying of a father, or the fathers, or of a church or a dogma, but is a voice within ourselves. It is as if that voice came out of our own depths. This is an exceedingly heretical thought, a thought not allowed to exist in the precincts of the church. Whoever cherishes such a thought is excommunicated from the church, the ecclesia. The church means the community, so the dreamer finds himself excluded from the community, because the community is always under one idea, under one authority. If everyone had his ultimate authority in himself there could be no such community. The father lets him know that he is exiled, excommunicated. He is no more in the church, no more in the community of men, but is outside of the community or of communal belief and creed.

A man in such a condition is isolated and will naturally ask himself, "But what is authority? What is father? Or mother?" As long as he is in the church, he knows quite well what father is. For instance, the pope is Papa, his father confessor is his father; Mater Ecclesia is Mother Church. But now what should be his authority? Very often people get into a panic at this point. "For heaven's sake," they say, "we are all alone, and there is nothing left but this ego-consciousness, and that should be authority. That should be God." This attitude would amount to a sort of neurotic individualism. There are many people who think like that, but they don't feel too good about it. But if one has an objective mind and can weigh things, then one comes to the conclusion that even if one is quite alone, one is never quite alone because there is something in the invisible space behind consciousness. You receive all the time from that source; there is not one thought in your head which has not been received. You do not make thoughts; they come to you. If the unconscious chooses to interfere with things, it can do anything it likes to do. It can make you forget things, or put things in your mind you don't want there, disagreeable things. It fills you with emotions you haven't made, and things happen to you which you have not chosen. Every night you have dreams you have not created. You are all the time surrounded by peculiar psychological conditions over which you have no control. You find yourself in the midst of conflicts you hate to have, and hate to admit that you have, while thoughts you don't want keep pressing in upon you. Who is the maker of your thoughts? Who is the feeler of your feelings? Obviously, there is something behind your consciousness that produces all these phenomena, for you and against you. What is it? That is the question.

The next unconscious product, the sixteenth, is a dream, a very short one: On a table is a card, a playing card, the ace of clubs, and beside that the dreamer sees a number seven.[13]

The ace of clubs is very baffling, I admit, but the seven we have already heard of. Seven is the highest number, the highest stair of the staircase. It would be the sun step, the step of completion. So we can assume this seven means completion. He arrives at the topmost place beyond which there is nothing because he arrives at the sun, and we can't imagine anything beyond the sun. What about this ace of clubs? When such a symbol occurs in a dream, very often the dreamer has no associations with it whatever.[14] It is too strange. Then the analyst must step in and ask about it. Has it form? Has it shape? What would you say about the shape?

---

[13] Cf. "Dream Symbols," nr. 16, p. 116, and CW 12, nr. 16, par. 97. I 16 {0017, fig. 2}: "Ace of clubs and the seven," February 28, 1932, CDM.

[14] In this case we actually know that Pauli had associations to the ace of clubs and the number seven, and he didn't fully agree with Jung's interpretation. Pauli associates the number seven to the birth of his sister in his seventh year and subsequently to the birth of the anima, and the ace of clubs to "the cause of the birth of the anima," a conscious archetype of power, a wish for power and the dark side of Christianity. See Pauli to Jung, February 28,

ANSWER: It is threefold.

DR. JUNG: That is obvious, and what more?

ANSWER: It is like a clover leaf.

DR. JUNG: Yes, quite, it really is like a clover leaf.

FROM THE AUDIENCE: The cross.

DR. JUNG: Yes, now, what about the cross?

ANSWER: Sacrifice, the opposites.

DR. JUNG: Naturally the cross reminds you of the central symbol of the Christian religion. It might have to do with the Christian religion.

FROM THE AUDIENCE: What about the three, the Trinity?

DR. JUNG: That also plays an important role in the Christian dogma. This is a Christian cross, and perhaps it refers to the Trinity. That is the main thing we can make out. Has there been any question of Christianity just now? Well, to explain the dream before, we have had to talk a lot about it. We just said that the old, the most important idea, of Christianity, the ecclesia, the community, has been overcome in a way. The water has been poured into a new basin. In the next part of the dream the seven tells us the dreamer has probably reached the top, for the number seven is completion.

Now the ace of clubs not only has a shape but also has a meaning, you know; it is an ace. What about the ace?

ANSWER: The highest card.

DR. JUNG: Yes, the highest card. You know its value is number one. Numbers one, two, three, four, five up to ten are the number cards, the lower cards, and the ace by all accounts should be the lowest card, but it is the highest. The lowest is highest, the highest is lowest.

FROM THE AUDIENCE: The beginning of a new scale.

DR. JUNG: We must consider that afterwards. We have that card which is the lowest and the highest. There are even certain games where the ace is lowest, where it is one; but usually it is the highest and strongest. If it is the highest, below it come the king, the queen, and the knave, and then the number cards. Now who is on top of the great hierarchy of the world? God. God is above the king. You see the king is already the sun because he is crowned with the sun. He is made similar to the sun. Above the sun is only God, the Maker of kings, the King of Kings. So the ace is God, God according to the Christian interpretation, which is triune, a trinity. So this is the symbol of the Christian God, very obviously. And then follows the

---

1936 (16P), and June 16, 1936 (18P), *PJL*. The ace of clubs is a motif that reoccurred in Pauli's dreams. See Pauli to Jung, appendix to letter 1200, PLC IV/1.

seven, which is a sort of hieroglyphic. The conception of the Christian God, of the triune deity, comes first and afterwards the seven. The seven steps are stages of transformation after which you arrive at a new level. That is, the idea of the Christian deity, which is the essence of the Christian creed, will be followed by a new development, the seven steps, which invariably mean a transformation. We shall now see whether that fits with things that follow afterwards.

But I want to say here that the thought of the cross followed by the process of transformation is an idea that had already occurred in the Middle Ages. There was a secret movement which held that the cross is not the definite goal but that there is something beyond, expressed in the formula, *per crucem ad rosam*, which means, "through the cross to the rose." This is the mystic rose of the Middle Ages, which is the mandala. If we apply that symbolism here, it would indicate a process of development that will lead us through the cross to something like the sun, to the rose. The dreamer simply repeats what has happened long before in the Middle Ages, reproducing unconsciously that attempt of Western man to develop beyond the Christian symbolism and find a new level of consciousness, a new explanation of old truths.

There was another movement in the Middle Ages, which contained the same idea, only expressed in an entirely different form. The goal of any transformation is, of course, to produce a more precious substance, a better condition. For instance, the seven steps lead up to the sun. First you have in Saturn the lead, gray and heavy, a cheap metal, and gradually through transformation you work up to silver and then to gold, which is the sun. That idea has been expressed in philosophical alchemy. The alchemists even tried to copy the sun material, but mainly their attempt was philosophical. They tried to produce out of cheap and inconspicuous materials the beautiful and precious metal gold. They even say, "Our gold is not the common gold, *non aurum vulgi*, not the gold of the vulgar. Only ignorant people think we are seeking the metal, the material gold. What we are really seeking is our own gold, the most precious substance, the sun substance." It was an attempt on their part to go beyond Christianity, beyond the symbolism of the Christian Church. So they called the precious substance which they were seeking *aurum nostrum*. Also, they spoke of it as a golden flower, a beautiful flower of gold, exactly as the old Chinese designated it, their most precious substance, the golden flower. You know that from the book I published with Wilhelm, *The Golden Flower*. You remember there was no outward connection between our Western alchemy and the Eastern alchemy. That they produced exactly the same symbols, the same thoughts in the Far East as we did in the West, is just due to the fact of the collective unconscious.

It is quite natural that the dream which follows, the seventeenth unconscious product, begins again with the motive of a long peregrination, meaning the subsequent stages of transformation. In the end this dreamer is wandering on a long road beside which he finds a blue flower.[15]

It is most interesting that the last trace of the idea of the symbol of the *rosa mystica* is the blue flower. In the beginning of the nineteenth century, in the school of the Romantics in Germany, the last remnant of the old metaphysical philosophers were asking questions about that blue flower, which had very much the meaning of the wonderful thing they were seeking.[16]

The next dream, the eighteenth unconscious product, shows a man offering the dreamer gold coins upon his open palm, which he rejects violently, throwing them to the floor; then he immediately repents and is sorry he has not accepted them. The scene changes into a ritual within a delimited space, perhaps a square, or something like that.[17]

This is a peculiar parallel to a story by Meyrink, an Austrian writer. In that story there is an important scene, but it never becomes quite clear what it really means. Nevertheless, there is depicted a decisive moment when a phantom appears and offers the hero a handful of grain or seeds or something; the hero knows he ought to accept or reject them; he must make a decision; and his decision is to reject them. And that is the fatality of the story. Now here this man, not knowing of that story, has exactly the same symbol, namely, a man, an unconscious figure, brings up the treasure in the form of gold coins, and the dreamer follows his natural impulse to reject them, which is regressive.[18] He ought to accept these things. Then he immediately afterwards repents, he thinks better of it, and, of course, all that is needed is the dreamer's realization that he should have accepted the coins. The question of accepting them is really of minor importance; he must only change his attitude about it.

---

[15] Cf. "Dream Symbols," nr. 17, p. 118, and CW 12, nr. 17, par. 100. I 17/M 02 {0018}: "Long wanderings; finding of the blue flower," February 29, 1932, CDM.

[16] The last sentence on the symbolism of the flower Jung has added in *PsA* version CW 12, par. 101.

[17] Cf. "Dream Symbols," nr. 18, p. 119, and CW 12, nr. 18, par. 102. I 18/M 03 {0019}: "Knocked out golden coins; Vaudeville," February 29, 1932, CDM.

[18] Pauli had very probably read *The Golem* prior to meeting Jung. It is to be found in his library. "The 'Golem' by Meyrink has always greatly fascinated me." Pauli to Jaffé (1172), November 28, 1950, and n. 4, PLC IV/1, 201.

What is the meaning of these gold coins? Gold means precious substance, but its form is questionable. It appears in the form of separate elements, coins which have a banal aspect. It is money, something every man has and knows and sees everywhere. Moreover, in our days, it is very precious because it is not in evidence but is all hidden away in banks. Yet it is the basis of our currency; everybody talks of it; you read about it in every newspaper; but there is something hateful about it. That is accounted for by the fact that it is just money, a banal thing, which everybody wants and nobody has. So the dreamer rejects it. Then, obviously, he becomes suddenly aware of the fact that it is a symbol, that all that money means something. Now what does money mean?

ANSWER: Libido.

DR. JUNG: Again libido, coined energy, a form of energy. You see, you can buy an automobile; you can buy gasoline; and you have energy in the form of movement. Money is coined energy. As gold it means the highest value. It is only because it is in the questionable form of money that he rejects it.

This is exactly what the old alchemists say about the material out of which the precious substance is to be made. They called the gold, the lapis, the philosopher's stone, *substantia materia prima*,[19] the first material. "It is most inconspicuous, and you find it everywhere. Everybody handles it, and nobody knows what it is worth. You find it on mountains and in valleys; you find it thrown out into the street. Nobody knows what it is worth. If the merchant in the market knew what that thing is worth which they sell so cheaply, they wouldn't even sell it." They call this material *lapis excilis*,[20] the inconspicuous stone. In any kind of obvious material which you find everywhere there is something exceedingly banal. The alchemists had a nice hexameter verse about it, which translated means, "Here you find it, a cheap inconspicuous material, a stone, and concerning the price, very cheap. It is despised by all stupid people, but all the more appreciated by those who know."

The same idea, that the most precious material appears in a despicable or cheap form, is expressed in Spitteler's *Prometheus*. I have dealt with this in the fifth chapter of my *Types*.[21] There the jewel was ejected into the road,

---

[19] Lat.: *substantia materia prima*, the substance of the first matter.

[20] Lat.: *lapis excilis*, paltry stone.

[21] In his book *Psychological Types* (1921), Jung analyzed Carl Spitteler's (1845–1924) epic poem *Prometheus and Epimetheus* (1881). CW 6, par. 275. In Greek mythology Prometheus created mankind out of clay. His name means "forethought." C. Spitteler (1931), in J. F. Muirhead, ed. and trans., *Prometheus and Epimetheus* (London: Jarrolds).

stepped upon, and thrown into the fire. Nobody saw the value of that jewel. If you go back to the Christian symbols regarding Christ, it is said in the prophecy of Isaiah that he has no beauty and is of an ugly appearance. The Servant of God is inconspicuous, and his value is not obvious, yet he contains the greatest value and is, indeed, the greatest of values.

The next unconscious product, the nineteenth, is a visual impression of a depressing nature. He sees a skull, and that skull is uncannily near him, as if it wanted to approach him. He tries to kick it away, but he doesn't succeed. As he kicks, the skull begins to glow with an inner light and is transformed into a red, glowing ball. The ball is transformed into the head of a woman, and suddenly the face of the woman begins to radiate like the sun.[22]

We have here the same vision as before, the head of the anima transformed into the sun. What has happened in this vision? You see he has reached the treasure, and this treasure was the secret of life; it is energy. If he rejects the energy of life, the living water, he would die—something would die in him. So death in the form of that skull is approaching him, a sort of spiritual death. He tries to get rid of it, but he can't. By a violent struggle with it he gets more and more energy into it so that it is transformed into a glowing sun. The sun, transformed through the anima, makes its appearance. That means he was able through that struggle to carry over the source of energy into the unconscious, and now he is able to accept it. This same situation occurred in *Hamlet* as well as in *Faust*.[23] In

---

[22] Cf. "Dream Symbols," nr. 19, p. 121, and CW 12, nr. 19, par. 107. I 19/M 04 {0020}: "The transformation of a skull; the red ball," February 29, 1932, CDM.

[23] W. Shakespeare (1969 [1623]), *Hamlet* (Menston: Scolar):

"To be, or not to be: that is the question:
Whether 'tis nobler in the mind to suffer
The slings and arrows of outrageous fortune,
Or to take arms against a sea of troubles,
And by opposing end them? To die: to sleep;
No more; and by a sleep to say we end
The heart-ache and the thousand natural shocks
That flesh is heir to, 'tis a consummation
Devoutly to be wish'd. To die, to sleep;
To sleep: perchance to dream: ay, there's the rub;
For in that sleep of death what dreams may come."

J. W. Goethe and G. Madison Priest, trans. (1952), *Faust: Parts One and Two* (Chicago: Alfred A. Knopf):

Here shall I find what is my need?
Shall I perchance in a thousand volumes read
That men have tortured themselves everywhere,

these plays both Hamlet and Faust talk to the skull; both talk about the meaning of life, which means nothing and therefore is worth nothing. It is transitory; it has no value. This is a sort of intellectual depression, intellect despairing about the ultimate meaning of life. Now through that struggle an *enantiodromia* takes place. That is perhaps a difficult word. It is a philosophical term from the sixth century before Christ, meaning "a transformation into the opposite," transformed from yea to nay, for example, the transformation of pleasure into pain or of pain into pleasure. You see through this most negative symbol a change takes place so that death becomes something positive, provided he can accept the fact that his unconscious is really the source of life.

Now the relationship between the anima and that ball is very curious. One would not assume that the anima would be a ball, but there is an antique idea that the anima, anima mundi, the soul of the world, is round, like a layer or stratum.[24] The ultimate stratum of the universe is fire, and around the fire is another stratum, and that is the anima; it is a perfect globe. The philosopher Empedocles so described the perfect man, whom he called the sphairos. The anima appears round, not on account of her own characteristics, but because she contains something that is round; and that is the mandala, the Self, which is round because it is complete. The circle, like the globe, is therefore the most perfect figure. All finished things, all perfect things symbolically are round. The old alchemist also assumed that that substance out of which you make the philosophical gold or the precious stone must be round. They said: "Take it from the round substance."

This idea of the globe comes up in the next unconscious product, the twentieth, a dream. There is a globe. Upon this globe stands the figure of a woman, an unknown woman, the anima, in adoration of the sun.[25]

Now this dream states that the anima is not round in herself, which explains exactly what we have said before, that the roundness comes from something else, namely, from two cosmic bodies. Obviously the globe upon which the anima stands must be the earth, as opposed to the sun. The anima

---

And that a happy man was here and there?—Why grinnest thou at me, thou
    hollow skull?
Save that thy brain, confused like mine, once sought bright day
And in the sombre twilight dull,
    With lust for truth, went wretchedly astray? (verse 50)

[24] The concept of anima mundi has been added in a footnote in *PsA*; it is not mentioned in the Eranos lecture.

[25] Cf. "Dream Symbols," nr. 20, p. 122, and *CW* 12, nr. 20, par. 110. I 20/M 05 {0021}: "Vision of a nude woman on a globe, worshipping the sun," February 29, 1932, CDM.

is in adoration of the sun, the other globe, the shining globe, the source of life. Consciousness makes a difference here. It is not that the anima is round or complete, but that completeness is in the earth and the sun, in those two things. Now we say in alchemistic language, the earth is prima materia or the material of which the sun is made, for the sun is the gold, the seventh step. The earth is dark and cold; that is the beginning; and the sun is the other opposite. In between is the anima, the bridge of life, the anima worshipping the sun.[26] Now this worshipping of the sun is an antique idea, which no longer exists in our day. We have no sun worshippers any more in our midst. It is in a way a regression to an antique belief. Such a regression always takes place before one comes to a decisive realization, before one understands a new formulation. It is what the French mean when they say, "*reculer pour mieux sauter,*" meaning, "one withdraws in order to take the leap."

---

[26] Jung has expanded on this topic in *PsA*, par. 116.

Lecture 4

DR. JUNG: Ladies and gentlemen: Here are some questions.[1]

QUESTION: Will you explain more fully the significance of the Rosicrucian position; of the step or stage beyond the cross to the rose?

DR. JUNG: That is a medieval development which is in a way an anticipation of what those dreams speak of. I hardly need to make any explanation; these dreams will show you what that step is. They simply repeat historical processes which I could describe in the terms of history. I could give you the necessary materials of an historical nature from the documents of that period, but it would lead much too far afield; it would need a special course of lectures. The Rosicrucian movement began within Protestantism and is a development from medieval alchemy.[2] Its point of view is really very modern; it contains the mandala symbolism. That is all I can say now.

QUESTION: Would you not say that animals were mentioned in the New Testament, as the lamb, sheep, swine, the dove, and fish?

---

[1] This lecture was held on September 23, 1936.

[2] Rosicrucianism is a philosophical, esoteric movement stemming from the seventeenth century, said to be founded by Christian Rosenkreuz in late medieval Germany. It includes aspects from hermetic philosophy, alchemy, and mysticism. Between 1607 and 1616 three anonymous manifestos were published that became fundamental sources to the movement: *Fama Fraternitatis* (The Fame of the Brotherhood), *Confessio Fraternitatis* (The Confession of the Brotherhood), and *Chymische Hochzeit* (*The Chymical Wedding of Christian Rosenkreutz*), claimed to be written by Johannes Valentin Andreae (1586–1654) (there is a copy of this volume in Jung's library). The ambition of the movement was to radically reform religion, science, and art. Their central symbol is the Rosy Cross, which symbolizes the union of love/eros with the suffering of the soul. Early seventeenth-century philosophers such as Michael Maier (1568–1622) and Robert Fludd (1574–1637) were interested in the Rosicrucian worldview (several volumes of M. Maier and Robert Fludd are in Jung's library). See Tobias Churton (2009), *The Invisible History of the Rosicrucians* (Rochester, VT: Inner Traditions). In *Psychological Types* (1921) Jung comments on Goethe's (1749–1832) poem "Geheimnisse": "Here the Rosicrucian solution is attempted: the union of Dionysus and Christ, rose and cross. The poem leaves one cold. One can not pour new wine into old bottles." CW 6, par. 314, n. 31.

DR. JUNG: I made an observation that animals play no role in the New Testament. Of course, there is plenty of animal symbolism, but that is not what I mean. Animals don't play a role in their own character as animals; they are merely used as symbols. For instance, the Galilean swine are mentioned, but just as suitable bodies for evil spirits. The animals play no role of their own because they do not appear in their own right. I quoted an example where the animals do appear in their own right, where they appear as functioning entities and not as mere symbols.

QUESTION: If the authoritative parent produces in the child a rebellion, which does not express itself in outer action because the child is too weak and the authority is too overpowering, but takes the form of inner seething and the denial of parental values, how would this affect the unconscious of the child?

DR. JUNG: I think we have spoken of that at length. The authority of the parents causes a certain rebellion in the child, then naturally the unconscious has a compensatory attitude. If the conscious of the child tries to be reasonable and tries to adapt to the authority of the parents, then the unconscious invents all sorts of compensations. For instance, the mother and father are then described in the unconscious of the child as being beasts, tyrants. All sorts of thoughts appear, ridiculous thoughts. That is the effect on the unconscious.

QUESTION: Is the blessing of the waters on Easter Eve an accepted Catholic ritual or is it only done in special places? Where can one find an account of it?

DR. JUNG: I am not sure that this ritual is carried out everywhere, but you find a detailed account in every *Missale Romanum*—Mass Book. There you will find the *benedictio fontis*[3] with every detail you desire.

* * * * *

You remember yesterday we had the visual impression, the twentieth unconscious product, of the unknown woman standing on the globe in adoration of the sun, and I told you that the globe means the earth and the sun, the source of life, both shown as differentiated from the anima. This is a process of differentiation taking place in the unconscious. The important point is that the anima is in adoration of the sun, which leads right back to sun worship. I have already mentioned this fact. Sun worship is a very special step in the evolution of the human mind. For instance, our living Pueblo Indians still have that direct sun worship which has otherwise died

---

[3] Blessing of the baptismal water.

out except with certain primitive tribes. But in no civilized community do we have real sun worship. Back of *real* sun worship lies the idea that the sun, as we see it, is the god. The Christian standpoint is a very markedly different one. Even if the sun is used as a symbol, it is no more itself, in its own right, but is used, exactly as the animals were, as a symbol.

In early Christianity you can still see the transition. Eusebius,[4] a famous historian of the early church, relates how the early Christians, chiefly in Asia Minor, used to prostrate themselves before the rising sun and direct their prayers to it, saying, "Oh, Lord, have pity upon us." He shows it as a sort of heretical mistake. Even Saint Augustine in one of his sermons has to say to his congregation, "Not this sun is the Lord, but the One who has made it."[5] These cases illustrate the transition from pure sun worship to the worship of a creative spirit who is the maker of the sun.

Here in our case we have a clear regression to antique sun worship where all the contents of the collective unconscious were still identified with the objects of nature: the sun, the moon, and so on. This state prevailed until the early Middle Ages, one would say, because we can't assume that such a state of mind disappeared right away. A very special educational development was required to detach the so-called spiritual contents of the collective unconscious from their visual objects, and this development took place in Scholasticism.[6] Scholasticism was a form of education which enabled thinkers to detach their spiritual ideas from objects. It was for this reason that they dealt with such grotesque or ridiculous problems, which we quote in order to ridicule the thinking of those days. For instance, one such problem was "How many angels can stand on the point of a needle?" A perfectly nonsensical question to us; but not so in those days, for they were determined to learn to think without objects. The moment the object was mentioned, it was no longer the object

---

[4] Eusebius of Alexandria, a person well known in the sixth and seventh centuries, was an ecclesiastical writer and author of a number of homilies (from *homilein*: to have communion or hold intercourse, "speak with," "sermon"). There has been much dispute regarding the details of his life and the age in which he lived. Jung refers to his work *Constantini Oratio ad Sanctorum Coelum*, in which he describes solar worship among the Christians. CW 12, par. 112, n. 39.

[5] "The Lord Christ is not the sun that was made, but He by whom the sun was made. For all things were made by Him, and without Him was nothing made." Augustinus, *Tractates (Lectures) on the Gospel of John*, tractate 34.

[6] Scholasticism: a method of critical thought that dominated teaching by the academics (scholastics, or schoolmen) of medieval universities in Europe from about 1100 to 1500. See also Jung's discussion on scholasticism in *Transformations and Symbols of the Libido* (1912), CW B, par. 30, and CW 6, pars. 56–67.

that was of importance, but the thought. And so they invented perfectly absurd problems which had no connection with reality, merely hypothetical questions which would exercise their thought, quite apart from any object. For instance, take this problem: "What would have happened if Christ had come to earth not in the form of a man but in the form of a green pea? Could he have done his work of redemption just as well?" You see it is quite apart from any object; it is not only absurd, but grotesquely abstract, and they had to deal with such things in order to release the mind from its attachment to objects.

In our modern science we have gone back again to objects, but it has taken us centuries to get back in the proper way, and this return has had a certain influence on our thought. We have again become rather concrete, so that we are often unable to think without objects, to think by ourselves, as it were; because when we touch upon the object we project our unconscious thought into it giving it a value it does not possess in itself. So the standpoint of science is quite valid as far as it goes; but it causes a certain attachment to the object which makes us peculiarly unfit to understand psychology. You see in psychology you have an invisible object, for thoughts themselves are the object of psychology, and when you deal with invisible things which you cannot touch, then you easily begin to imagine that you are dealing with mere inventions. So most people, even scientists, believe that psychology is a mere invention of certain thoughts invented for certain purposes; that you can really only observe those objects which are outside yourself—a very concrete experience. Therefore they say that science can exist only where you deal with a real object; and to them, thought is never a real object, but an invention. When they begin to observe the contents of their own minds they identify with them and assume that which they think is all their own invention.

This is the great difficulty still in our day. We are unable to see the mind objectively, to experience our own psychology. This comes chiefly from the fact that we have again turned our mind upon the object. If we go back to the Middle Ages, we see people particularly unable to maintain an abstract course of thinking. For instance, they had all the facts to enable them to make a steam engine, but they only played with the idea, that is, these thoughts played with them. They could not think with sufficient consistency to build a machine. They only made a sort of game of their ideas; they played with them, so that their mental activity never resulted in any serious mechanical invention.

Here in the case of the dreamer we have a peculiar regression to that state of mind where psychic contents became separated from the object

Figure 17. Harmonious Conception of the Light of Nature. From *Secret Symbols of the Rosicrucians*. The illustration comes from *Geheime Figuren der Rosenkreuzer, aus dem 16ten und 17ten Jahrhundert: Aus einem alten Mscpt. Zum erstenmal ans Licht gestellt: Drittes Heft* (1788 [1785]) (in English: *Secret Symbols of the Rosicrucians: The Teachings of the Rosicrucians of the 16th and 17th Centuries*) and has the text: "Harmonische Vorstellung aus dem Lichte der Natur. Daraus die Wiederherstellung und Neumachung aller Dinge *emblematice* abzunehmen ist" (In English: Harmonious Conception of the Light of Nature. From which you can deduce the restoration and renovation of all things emblematic). This mandala is not reproduced in *PsA*.

and led to a regression of the anima, for this is a phenomenon that generally takes place as soon as the intellect withdraws itself from the object. For instance, take Scholasticism as far as the Renaissance; in those centuries the mind went all by itself, quite apart from objects. So the object world was practically left to itself, and all the functions having to do with real objects became unconscious, that is, they came under the domination of the anima, and the anima made a regression into antiquity. While the mind was going forward with the development of Christian civilization, the anima went backward into late antiquity, and so there arose a tremendous split coincident with the Reformation and the Renaissance. Then suddenly a gulf became visible between one part of the mind and another part of the mind.

The classical book which contains the whole psychology of the Renaissance is *Poliphilo*, which I have already mentioned.[7] There in the form of a dream the monk-author describes the state of the unconscious in those days. His anima was Madame Polio, that is, she was the beloved of his heart, but he has separated from her and craves for a union with her, but he can't find her. Then he descends into the collective unconscious, where he finds the remnant of all past civilizations and symbols en masse. Finally, he discovers his dear Madame Polio at the court of Queen Venus. He goes through the labyrinths of bygone love affairs, through all their joys and woes, which he describes in the form of epitaphs on tombstones in the underworld, quite a touching part of the book. Finally, when he has recalled his anima, Madame Polio, he sails away with her in a beautiful vessel out of the west to the Islands of the Blest. The moment his golden ship touches the shore, he wakes up and hears the bells of the morn of the first of May, the month of Venus and of Mary. That is the situation of the Renaissance. This book unveils the whole psychology of that period.

Here in our dream series we have a different but parallel case. It is not a monk who has this dream, but an intellectual, a scientist who got away from his anima, and his dreams show him what his anima is doing while he is busy with modern science. His anima in a most absurd fashion is worshipping the sun. That has really to do with antiquity, as we shall learn.

In the next unconscious product, the twenty-first, a visual impression, he finds himself surrounded by nymphs, by antique demigoddesses, and

---

[7] See above.

the voice of one of the nymphs says, "We were always here with you; you have only not been aware of us."[8]

You see it is a case very much like the case of Francesco Colonna, the author of *Poliphilo*.[9] Instead of being a monk, the dreamer is a monk in his intellect, since he has replaced the church and the church belief; he has again been separated from the anima, and here he comes back to her. We have already had the gathering of virgins, of indefinite women, but they are more clearly defined as antique nymphs. This is certainly the situation of old Poliphilo when he enters the underworld. The first thing he meets is a gathering of naughty girls with flutes and guitars, and they represent temptation and vices and all sorts of funny things. But he always thinks of Madame Polio and is very sad and doesn't allow himself to fall into their trap. Later on, as a sort of reward, he meets the society of very wonderful girls who represent virtues, and they then bring him to the court of Venus. Even Olympus has become slightly more decent than in antiquity. Curiously enough you find in that book (the original is a priceless first edition of the fifteenth century, decorated with most precious woodcuts) one woodcut picturing him in an undignified role which shows that he is still an infant, exactly like our patient. He is represented there as a little boy who can't hold his water. It is like that famous fountain figure in Brussels.[10] He is represented as a little fellow held up between two of the virgins, with a Greek inscriptions *ogeloiastos*, meaning "the most ridiculous one." That occurs right at the beginning of his descent into Hades. Our patient is in the company of these nymphs on the way back to antiquity, and we do not know exactly how far back this regression will take him. If anyone should ask me: "What is your guess? Would you say he will go back still further or not?" I should feel some hesitation; I don't know what will happen next. Perhaps it is sufficient that he realizes that his Madame Polio, his anima, is among the nymphs; that would be pretty far

---

[8] Cf. "Dream Symbols," nr. 21, p. 124, and *CW* 12, nr. 21, par. 114. I 21 {0022}: "Vision of the unnoticed nymphs who where always there," February 29, 1932, CDM.

[9] Francesco Colonna (1433/34–1527), Italian Dominican priest and monk who is attributed to have written *Hypnerotomachia Poliphili*, published in 1499. Jung refers to a French edition called *Songe de Poliphile* (1600). (Jung had a copy of the 1600 edition in his library—acquired in 1924; also copies of the *Songe de Poliphile* of 1883, 2 vols.) *CW* 12, par. 61, n. 3.

[10] Manneken Pis (literally meaning Little Man Pee) is a famous small bronze fountain sculpture in Brussels (Belgium) depicting a naked little boy urinating into the fountain's basin designed by Jerome Duquesnoy and put in place in 1618 or 1619. (There was probably a similar figure perhaps as early as 1388.) Jung writes more about this motif in *PsA*, adding also an illustration. *CW* 12, par. 338.

back and might be sufficient as compensation for his advanced scientific standpoint in the conscious.

The next unconscious product, the twenty-second, is a visual impression. He finds himself in the jungle, in the primeval forest.[11] So you see he regresses still further, going right down into the primitive, close to animal psychology. In his fantasy is a huge elephant, which is apparently passive, but then becomes rather menacing. He is afraid of that elephant; then the elephant changes into one of the anthropoids, a big ape. The dreamer grows more afraid. Then the ape changes into something like a bear or a caveman with a huge club, and that fellow now shows a definite tendency to attack him, and he gets into a panic. But there is the man with a pointed beard, his Mephisto, who has magic power with which to fascinate the caveman, catching his eye and hypnotizing him so that he can no longer move. The dreamer is in a blue funk when the voice says, "Everything has to be ruled by the light."

This is the critical point. The regression leads right down into the primeval forest. He is like the animals, like the primordial man. Attacked by the caveman, he tries to catch hold of, to comprehend, that thing which comes up in him. This man knew how to handle a club but was otherwise in no way different from an animal. It is man's animal psychology which is threatening him, threatening to overcome him, which would, of course, mean complete disintegration of his modern and so-called rational consciousness. Practically it would mean schizophrenia.[12]

In those moments, and later on in similar moments, for these things repeated themselves several times—these advances and regressions—he was filled with a most uncomfortable apprehension that he might be crazy or could go crazy. This is the stuff that drives people crazy, because they can't catch themselves anymore; they can no longer control themselves when they have that animal psychology. It means they are driven by instinct. They see a thing and leap for it. That is the condition in schizophrenia, for all those things appear also in cases of insanity; they are dynamite that can easily explode in the human mind. Therefore it is important to know these things. If you know, and understand, you can integrate them into your modern consciousness, but if you are caught unawares by these contents then you can't explain yourself to people; and if you can't explain yourself any more to your fellow beings, you are in no way different from

---

[11] Cf. "Dream Symbols," nr. 22, p. 124, and CW 12, nr. 22, par. 117. I 22 {0025}: "Vision of threatening fightscene; the man with the pointed beard returns," February 29, 1932, CDM.

[12] Jung also makes this connection to schizophrenia in *PsA*, par. 116.

a crazy person. I tell my patients, "As long as you can explain yourself, at least to me, and I nod my head and show a sort of instinctive understanding, at least you are not crazy. But at the moment you cannot explain yourself anymore and run away in a panic of your own thoughts; then you are crazy, and no one can catch you back. You have left modern society. You could not, you did not want to explain yourself anymore, and that is the serious thing."

As long as man has the desire to explain himself, he is not crazy. Many people in such situations have a desperate desire to explain themselves. If those people to whom they speak are incapable of understanding, then the second step is that they begin to feel, "Now we are just over the border." Then comes the panic, and that is the fatal thing; then they explode. If they find a trace of understanding, if it is only an instinctive thing, if it is only the willingness of the partner to accept that there might be something back of it, then that is enough. Repeatedly such patients have told me things I simply could not swallow, my mind refused to accept these things; I felt that aversion one feels towards the morbid; but something in me had an instinctive feeling: "There is something back of that talk, no matter how absurd it seems to be; something is back of it, something I can't grasp." That was sufficient. They saw that flash in my eye, and that was enough for them. If one tries very hard one can understand something that is back of their peculiar experience. These people experience very queer things that are by no means nonsense, only they don't have the understanding or language which would enable them to explain themselves. Usually we are dealing with people who are miles away from that primitive standpoint which one needs in order to endure such primitive onslaughts. We should understand the primitive very thoroughly in order to understand the so-called psychotic experience, because it is an experience of primeval man, of the caveman. The mental structure of our mind is always threatened by the chaos of primitive nature and its terrors.

You see our man here is going through such an experience. If he tells you that it is a primeval force, one should not take it lightly. It is a real experience of the terrors of the jungle. When we talk here of the fears of the jungle it is only a figure of speech—poetic—but if you have experienced the jungle, being lost in the primeval forest, for example, you know what I am talking about. If a white man gets lost in the bush, the next day he tears all his clothes from his body, and if people come after him he runs away like a wild animal. He simply goes back to his former condition, to the man of ten thousand years ago. He doesn't know civilization; he doesn't know the white man. He cuts off with one cut his whole civilized world. In a milder way you find it also in the phenomenon of "going black." When you live under these conditions for a while, you see how all the other stages where you harbored civilized ideals are gradually depleted. You think your drawing room of civilized thoughts [are] still there. You go into that room and find it singularly empty because everything has gone down into a lower stratum. You are up against wild conditions, chaotic conditions; you don't need there any complicated or sophisticated things, so that room where you store all the things you need in civilized life becomes obsolete, becomes dusty, evaporates, when the primitive man lives. So white men living under such circumstances become black under the skin. The very first thing that goes back into the primitive is the anima. The anima instantly "goes black" in order to be adapted. We could not adapt if we had not that faculty of regression, that very important faculty. It is often the body or the mind, for that is identified with the body, that reacts first to such primitive surroundings.

The conclusion that is drawn from this regression comes from the voice that says, "Everything must be ruled by light." By light is meant the day or sunlight, the light of consciousness. Ruled by light means everything ought to be seen, everything ought to be understood; then a man can be safe against these primitive onslaughts. The onslaughts of primitive powers are very important in primitive psychology or in early civilized psychology. Primitives have special rites to identify them again with the primordial man so that they shall not lose connection with that original state. Semibarbaric tribes have a certain time in the year when they identify themselves with their ancestors—it may be as much as ten thousand years ago. Such rites do exist, for instance, among the central Australian natives, who, when they want to carry out a certain ritual, can't simply carry it out by making a decision. They can't make a decision. They first have to organize a certain psychological regression and identify themselves with their ancestors of the so-called Alcherringa time.[13] That is the time of the Homeric heroes. Just as the noble families of Athens or Greece in general boasted of having ancestors in the Homeric time, so these natives had their ancestors in an old heroic time. When they carry out their ceremonies they must first identify with the heroes of that time. These heroes are supposed to be directly the sons of the great serpent, who is the creator of all things.

---

[13] The Alcherringa or Dreamtime of Aboriginal Australians is a specific notion of time, where past, present, and future merge in a subtle, diffuse, and ambiguous way in a "forever" that surrounds the "now" like permeable membranes.

In Greece they had pretty much the same thing. Every one identified himself every year to half-animal man-satyrs, he-goat men. They performed dances and mysteries in which these he-goats played a decisive role. This ritual belonged to the cult of Dionysus; it is their reidentification to half-animal psychology. They had terrible orgies; women behaved like wolves and tore animals, and even human beings, to pieces. There is, for example, the myth of Pentheus, who was torn to shreds by his own mother and her Maenads, the raging ones.[14] It was a sort of ecstasy or frenzy, in which these women went through the ritual behaving like wild animals. This myth was reenacted at a certain time of the year, in the spring. These games developed into what was later called *tragos*, the he-goat, the tragedy.[15] The original theater is a representation in a delimited space performed by half-animal men, which means that they represented the events, the psychological events, of a time far back, thereby increasing their own strength. In this way they touched upon the collective unconscious again, and it was very important that they should do so in order not to get lost in the abstraction of civilization. As civilized beings they turned further and further away from nature and became incapable of dealing with natural facts.

In any civilization the danger is that man may lose contact with nature and get into perfectly impossible conditions. If we are caught in such a situation, we should seek reidentification with nature. Therefore all former civilizations, knowing this danger, had rituals which reidentified them with the original man, so that they never lost sight of him, or of his needs and purposes. So the Dionysian mysteries had this purpose of reidentifying man, reestablishing his contact with nature. This is the origin of our theater. Not all the people took part in the ceremonies; certain people were in charge of performing this reidentification, but the majority of the people sat in the theater watching the performance. This rite was also the origin of the carnival. In the carnival we take on other forms, wear animal masks, perhaps, or perform animal dances. It is a sort of orgy in which

---

[14] In *The Bacchantes* by Euripides (ca. 480–406 BC) it is described how the young king of Thebe, Pentheus, rejects Dionysus's divinity and tries to arrest him. In the end Dionysus drives Pentheus insane and leads him to the mountains, where his own mother, Agave, and the women of Thebes tear him to pieces in a Bacchic frenzy. Euripides (1995–2004), *Selected Fragmentary Plays* (Warminster: Aris and Phillips).

[15] Tragodia: "a dramatic poem or play in formal language and having an unhappy resolution," https://www.etymonline.com/word/tragedy#etymonline_v_16855, apparently literally "goat song," from *tragos* "goat" + *oide* "song." The connection may be via satyric drama, from which tragedy later developed, in which actors or singers were dressed in goatskins to represent satyrs.

people reidentify with a being of a lower mind and of lower morals, and by that they touch nature again. In Europe all sorts of things happen during the carnival; it is a pretty wild time.

In the early medieval church they respected the carnivals and celebrated them even in the monasteries; brothers became abbots and celebrated Mass, and instead of singing sacred hymns, they sang all sorts of *chansons de la rue*,[16] very obscene ones. Instead of the ritual of participating in the blood of the Lord, they drank themselves full of sweet wine and rolled out into the streets. This aroused so much scandal that finally the pope, in the early thirteenth century, issued an encyclical against keeping carnival in the church. Since then this kind of ritual has become obsolete. But it gave them strength. Their touch with Mother Earth, with the primitive man within them, gave them contact again with the live wire of their instincts. These celebrations were based on the eternal laws of nature, therefore the participants were again brought in touch with the natural functioning of their unconscious and therefore got a peculiar strength which benefited everything they did.

For instance, in Athens even until late times, the ladies who participated in the Eleusinian mysteries celebrated the same ritual in a very funny form. On a certain day a great dinner was given by the noble ladies of Athens, and the priestess of Demeter had the chair, and one of the ladies was the president. They had rich food and wine, and after dinner the ritual began. It had a special Greek name, and it consisted in their telling obscene stories and jokes of a most shocking kind. They supposed that this was good for the fertility of the earth in the coming season; the earth was supposed to be quite pleased by the telling of these obscene stories. It was simply a reidentification with the primitive layer of civilization which gave a peculiar strength to these women through its fun and indecency so that they then worked much better in the fields. This is why field cults are usually of a very obscene nature. The fields are more fertile, yield better results, because by such a ritual the people could pull themselves together to work in them with the energy of instinct. If you tell somebody, "It is your duty," he will go to work in a most hesitant way, for he hates to perform duties all the time. But if he is convinced there is some fun about it, then he works willingly. I am sorry man is like that; I have not invented man. There is no use in not seeing facts; if we do not see them, we get simply stupid and cannot explain any more why man is as he is. All that ought

---

[16] French: songs of the street.

to be understood; all that ought to be recognized; and that is the light referred to in this fantasy.

This dream about the ape-man is the twenty-second fragment or dream.
I have given you thus far a survey of the twenty-two unconscious products
which we observed. This last one shows you clearly what the task is that
lies before this man, namely, to understand everything that went before,
the secrets of the primitive man.

We now come to the second chapter of our patient's development,
namely, to the fifty-nine[17] dreams out of four hundred, which contain the
special kind of symbol that I am going to discuss, the mandala. We have
encountered this before in several dreams and fantasies cited: first in the
hat in the first dream, then in the encircling serpent, then in the delimited
space where a certain ritual takes place, already anticipating the Dionysian mystery play in which is represented the reidentification of modern
consciousness with primitive man.

The first unconscious product in this second series is a dream in which
he sees a woman, the unknown woman again, the anima, pursuing him.[18]
He is very much afraid of her, and she forces him to run in a circle. He
can't run away; he must run in a circle as if he were a horse.

This dream repeats the motive of the encircling serpent, where he
formed the center and the serpent encircled him. Now he is forced to circumambulate. This is a special rite which expresses concentration upon
the center of worship. When you walk around the center of worship, you
concentrate upon it; you act like the earth with reference to the sun, the
life-giving center. So circumambulation is used by the Mahayana Buddhists where part of the worship is the circumambulation of the shrine.
There is also a very famous shrine in Java, a huge temple, built in the form

---

[17] Unfortunately Dr. Jung had time to take up only the first twelve in the second series.
(This note is from the original seminar notes.)

[18] Cf. "Dream Symbols," nr. 6, p. 130, and CW 12, nr. 6, par. 129. M 06 {0027}: "At a
ball, running in a circle pursued by a strange woman," March 4, 1932, CDM. In the same
night Pauli dreams a dream where he plays with two girls from Mali, the mother appears,
and water is distributed in a basin {0028}. In connection to this dream there is a note from
Jung remarking that after this dream a long discussion with Pauli was undertaken about his
relationship to his mother. It is unclear if this discussion took place at the time of the dream,
in which case it stands in contrast to the claim that Jung didn't see Pauli during his treatment with Erna Rosenbaum. It could also be that Jung discussed the dream with Pauli when
seeing him in November 1932 after taking over from Rosenbaum. Personal information
from Karl von Meyenn, based on forthcoming publication of complete dream material. In
PsA Jung has added a section on his meeting with the Lamaic rimpoche Lingdam Gomchen
in 1938, who instructed him about the Tibetan mandala. Cf. CW 12, par. 123.

of a square spiral, and you have to walk up that spiral. It is like the Mexican pyramids. You walk up in a square spiral approaching the center, circumambulating the central shrine on top where no human thing is visible. That is the center of the mandala.

I think this is the place where I should tell you a little more about the mandala. The typical form of the mandala in history, as well as in dreams and visions, is just a circle. This circle is usually divided by four. The four points of the horizon, or the four gates, if the boundary is thought of as being a wall.

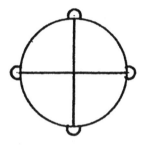

For instance, in the Mountain Chant of the Navajos, the performers of the ritual go to the east, west, north and south, throwing corn or scattering flour or water to the four quarters.[19] In the middle of the mandala would be the medicine lodge; there is the center with the four gates leading

---

[19] Navajo, also spelled Navaho, second most populous of all North American Indian peoples in the United States, with some three hundred thousand individuals in the early twenty-first century, most of them living in New Mexico, Arizona, and Utah. Jung does not mention the Navajos in the Eranos lecture or in *PsA*, but in the latter a Navajo mandala is reproduced in illustration 110 (*CW* 12, par. 327). Jung uses a variant of this mandala in his essay "Concerning Mandala Symbolism" from 1950, where he thanks Margaret Schevill for the pictures. See *CW* 9/I, par. 701, n. 33. It seems that she sent them to him in early 1934 (or maybe late 1933). In a letter from January 10, 1934, Jung thanks Schevill for sending him beautiful and interesting pictures and wants to know if she has some more information about "what the Indians think about their mandalas." She also sent him the book of the Night Chant by Dr. Matthews in the spring of 1935, together with another book on Navaho myth (Schevill to Jung, November 26, 1936, JA). Margaret Schevill Link (1887–1962), American ethnologist of Arizona who studied the Navaho nation, was Jung's patient in the 1920s and belonged to a group around the attorney Chauncey Goodrich and his wife, Henrietta, who analyzed with Jung in 1923. She worked with Jung during spring 1926, spring and autumn 1928, winter and spring semesters 1929, and autumn semester 1935 (Jung to Schevill, December 12, 1935, JA). See also Jung to Margaret Erwin Schevill, September 1, 1942; July 25, 1946. Jung, *Letters*, vol. 1, 57. See also C. S. Goodrich Jr. (1983), "Transatlantic Dispatches from and about Zurich," in *Spring: An Annual of Archetypal Psychology and Jungian Thought*, 183–90.

to the points of the horizon. Usually that division is given in the form of a cross, and the center is always emphasized. Now that partition can also be made in another way, by a division into eight, and then the four points are connected and the square is formed. That is the old problem of medieval speculation, namely, the square made out of a circle or the circle made out of a square. The center is often represented as a precious stone or a place where things are created, a golden vessel or a star, the sun, or an egg; and the outer circle is thought of either as just static or sometimes as rotating or circumambulating.

Sometimes a snake is shown revolving around that center, or the whole figure may be revolving. It then takes on this character of the swastika, as, for instance, such a form where the rotating movement is indicated by feet. That is the classical form. Only you can hardly say feet; it is more like legs. Sometimes, as a matter of fact, it is really legs, but that usually occurs in the *triskeles*, a Greek form meaning "three-legged." It is found chiefly on Greek coins and buildings, or on medieval arms.

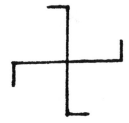

This mandala, for instance, would revolve clockwise, but there are also mandalas that go anticlockwise. Both are found; the one has positive, the other negative meaning. The clockwise one moves toward the right, the conscious side; and the anticlockwise one moves to the left, to the unconscious side.

There are also mandalas in which the circle is not visible; the figure then is simply a form of star with eight rays.

Or the mandala may be a square containing a circle subdivided into four parts with a cross.

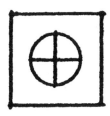

Or it can be a cross of equal branches having the circle at the intersection.

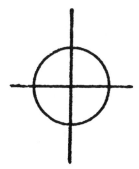

A pretty frequent symbol is the Christian cross with the elongated lower branch and the serpent crucified on it. It is Christ in the form of his own shadow, namely, the serpent crucified on the cross. This is the symbol of the *nous* which leads into Gnosticism.[20] Another form of mandala is the egg, or it can be a round body encircled by the serpent which is the

---

[20] *Nous* is Greek. There is no exact equivalent to the Greek concept of nous in English. It is translated as "mind," "spirit," the divine intellectual principle expressed in the world of ideas, the image of the One, the light by which the One sees itself. Plotinus (ca. AD 204/ 5–70), fourth and fifth Ennead. Plotinus (1952), in S. Mackenna, B. S. Page, eds. and trans., *The Six Enneads* (Chicago: Encyclopaedia Britannica).

Hindu representation of the god Shiva,[21] in his latent but creative condition, encoiled by Shakti, his female counterpart.

The center can also be a square, often understood to be a stone, encircled by a serpent.

The serpent generally means rotation, movement. If there is no movement in the mandala then it represents a static condition.

Now in this dream he is forced to make circumambulations. Nothing is said of the center, and the unconscious itself, personified in the form of the woman, is forcing him to make that circumambulatory movement. In medieval philosophy it is called the *opus circulatorium*. The term *opus* was used in the early Christian Church, in the order of the Benedictines, to designate the *officio divinum*, the divine service. The Mass, the prayers, the singing, the fasting, and other rules are part of the opus. Today in the Benedictine writings and ritual they still use the word *opus*. This opus played a great part in medieval philosophy. The opus circulatorium, the circulating opus, the rotating opus, means "manifold repetition," a circum-

---

[21] Shiva (Sanskrit: "auspicious one") refers to a major Hindu deity, the Destroyer or Transformer among the Trimurti, the Hindu Trinity of the primary aspects of the divine.

ambulation by which the gold that was sought for was to be produced. It was like a shrine in which a precious substance ought to be created or in which (and that is now in the Christian formula) is contained the relic, or witness, of the Lord Himself. In this case the circumambulating is done in order to partake of some of the grace stored in the sacred relic. Very primitive means are applied in the Catholic Church to obtain that grace, which they conceive to be a semisubstantial thing. They circumambulate the tomb of Christ, and then they go up to it and stand quite close to it while they rub it, and then rub their hands over their own bodies.

They do exactly as the central Australians do with their *churinga*. The churinga is a flat stone or slab of wood which is supposed to be charged with health power, health electricity.[22] When a man feels rotten, when a part of his soul has gone away in the night, then he goes out to the hidden place, the hollow tree, or cleft in the rocks, where he has hidden his individual churinga, which was given to him at his initiation. He takes it out and puts it on his knees and rubs it. And by that rubbing, which is a circumambulation done with the hands, he gets the health power out of the churinga; it goes into his body, and at the same time his rotten health goes into the churinga. Then when all the rotten health has gone into it, he puts it back into Nature, into the hollow tree or cleft of the rock, and leaves it there for several weeks, or months perhaps, until he feels rotten again. In the meantime Nature cures the ill health in the stone, and he can get good health out of it once more. That is psychotherapy among primitives.

With us psychotherapy still contains the same elements. For instance, you go and circumambulate your doctor, and you know many people have the fantasy of more than circumambulating him.[23] Then the doctor, by laying hands upon the sick man, treats him in the same way as the primitive does his churinga. That idea is still contained in our language. For instance, in German the word for treatment is *Behandlung*, which means "putting on hands." That is what the primitive medicine man does. He handles a patient like a churinga, and in rubbing him, a sort of magnetic process, he takes the rotten health out of his body and gives his good

---

[22] Churinga, also spelled tjurunga, is in Australian Aboriginal religion, a mythical being and a ritual object, usually made of wood or stone, that is a representation or manifestation of such a being. An Aranda word, tjurunga traditionally referred to sacred or secret, sacred things set apart, or taboo; for example, certain rites, stone, and wooden slab objects, bullroarers, ground paintings and earth mounds, ritual poles and emblems, headgear, and sacred songs. It was Jung's reading of Lucien Lévy-Bruhl that was the initial source of Jung's information concerning the *churinga*. Shamdasani, 2012, 53.

[23] Jung probably refers to the fantasy of having a sexual relationship with the doctor. Cf. "The Therapeutic Value of Abreaction" (1921), in CW 16, par. 276.

health-power to the patient and cures him by those means. The English word *treatment* comes from *tractum* (from the Latin word *trahere* meaning "to pull") meaning really to pull a man through, namely, through a hole, a hole in the wall, or between two trees, symbolizing the mother's womb. When a man is sick, the primitives make a hole in the wall near his head, and pull him out through the hole. After he is cured they give him a different name. There was such a clinic in Neolithic times. The Menhir Stone, Menantol, Cornwall, is a huge stone with a hole in it, just big enough for a man to squeeze through.[24] This was used as a clinic where a man was given health and rebirth, by the ancient rite of "pulling through." The word *treatment* goes right back to these ancient things.

So you see the circumambulation can mean: "I am getting power out of the center," or "I am giving power to the center." Now, of course, such old-fashioned things coming up in the mind of a modern scientist are terribly upsetting. As you can understand, this man became badly upset by such things. He felt that incomprehensible things were coming up against him, and he wanted to run away, to run away in reality by giving up that analytic business which he did not understand and did not want to understand and was, indeed, afraid of. But something held him back, and that was his anima holding his nose to the grindstone.

The next dream, the second of the second series, is again about the unknown woman, that anima figure.[25] She reproaches him that he does not care enough for her. Then he sees a watch that shows five minutes to ... ? he doesn't know what. Five minutes to what?

Now in this dream the anima obviously resents the fact that he is afraid, that he tries to run away, and doesn't want to run in a circle. She resents his conscious attitude of resistance and reproaches him for it. She behaves exactly like a jealous woman. She is jealous of the tendency of his conscious to run away from her, as if he belonged to her. That is the tendency of the anima to establish the connection between the conscious and the unconscious. Man is not allowed to run away from his unconscious and pays very dearly for that infidelity. Now he sees the watch which shows five minutes before ... ? Which conveys the idea that only a short lapse of

---

[24] The Mên-an-Tol is a small formation of standing stones near the Madron-Morvah road in Cornwall, United Kingdom. It is about three miles north west of Madron. It is also known locally as the "Crick Stone." The name Mên-an-Tol is Cornish language, literally meaning "the hole stone." J. Barnatt (1982), *Prehistoric Cornwall: The Ceremonial Monuments* (Wellingborough, England: Turnstone). Guided by his associate Helton Godwin Baynes, Jung visited and crawled through this stone in the summer of 1920 while in England to give a seminar at Sennen Cove. McGuire, 1995, 301–26.

[25] Cf. "Dream Symbols," nr. 7, p. 131, and CW 12, nr. 7, par. 130. M 07 {0040}: "Unsettling dream, clock shows 'five minutes to,' " March 13, 1932, CDM.

time separates him from a certain important moment. In our civilized life we live by the watch. The watch says, "It is now nine o'clock, and you have to do such and such a thing; now it is ten o'clock, and you must begin something else, and at four o'clock you are expected in such and such a place, and at five o'clock you must be back again." This is our daily life, so "five minutes to" means just a short space of time left. You might say: "I am glad I have five minutes, a short breathing space"; or, "It is already five minutes to; now, we have to hurry." You see it means a moment before something decisive is going to happen. It is urgent, so that it is as if the anima said: "Now look here: it is high time you did something; there is only a short time ahead of you."

This reference to time is taken up again in the next dream, the third: He is on a ship out on the sea, and he is occupied with making astronomical observations of his surroundings, in order to determine the position of the ship, the geographical place where the ship is.[26] He finds it a rather difficult task; sometimes his result is too far, sometimes too near. He knows the right place ought to be somewhere in the middle. Then he sees the map, and on the map is drawn a circle with a center.

This dream very clearly refers to the one before, the first in the second series, in which he is running in a circle without a center. He must find the center that was not shown in this previous dream. His anima is forcing him through a certain situation to determine the right place. That seems to be the important thing.

When he wrote that dream he suddenly remembered that on the same night he had another dream with a similar theme, namely, he was shooting at a target, sometimes shooting too high and sometimes too low. He ought to hit the center. This is the very same idea. The center which was formerly empty should be filled. For this reason he makes that circumambulation. He is going to create the center, find the center mark. The dream uses the symbol of astronomy, as practiced in navigation, that is, by the aid of the stars he can find that center. The center has to do with the stars and can only be found by their observation. Stars are far out in space; yet the center of the earth is found through its relation to the stars, the sun, and so forth.

This thought is taken up in the following dream, the fourth: He sees a clock with a pendulum.[27] The clock is running, but the weights that work

---

[26] Cf. "Dream Symbols," nr. 8, p. 131, and *CW* 12, nr. 8, par. 132. M 08 {0078}: "On a boat, occupied with new method of determining position," April 3, 1932, CDM.

[27] Cf. "Dream Symbols," nr. 9, p. 132, and *CW* 12, nr. 9, par. 134. M 09 {0089}: "Perpetually running pendulum clock," April 8, 1932, CDM.

the clock are not sinking down, yet the clock is continuously working. He is tremendously impressed.

Since he is a scientist, this naturally seems to him a miraculous thing. What kind of clock could that be? You know the name of that clock? *Perpetuum mobile*, a perpetual-motion clock. This idea is for metaphysical speculation, which concerned medieval philosophers, for such a clock has an incorruptible life; it has eternal life; it resembles the *elixir vitae*, the substance which creates eternal life, or sustains life perpetually.

So you see the patient is very much affected by those things which we have talked about previously. This dream has what I call metaphysical attributes or characteristics. By that word I do not mean anything mystical; I only mean that the attribute or quality of that which the man is seeking is stated in psychological terms. The unconscious says in so many words: "It is something you would designate as metaphysical," because perpetual motion is absolutely impossible. Any mechanical contrivance you can create must lose energy on account of friction, so that one cannot produce such a perpetual-motion machine. If such a thing should come into existence, it must be a superhuman or metaphysical invention. But the unconscious makes a statement about it which connects it with the mandala. The unconscious here represents the mandala as the clock where the hands go round as in a perpetual-motion machine, which is impossible, impossible, that is, for our minds, for we cannot grasp it. This is the first instance in the series of dreams where the mandala is represented as something we cannot understand. We obviously have to do with the fact that the mandala, being in the middle between the conscious and the unconscious, contains both.

This is a parallel to the concept of the Self. The conscious only covers a certain area; we are conscious only of a certain number of things. We experience a lot of things we don't know about, but which really do exist. They behave as if they were of psychological nature. The total of our human personality consists of things known and unknown, for it appears that some things are unconscious because they are unable to become conscious. So this area represented by the mandala is something we cannot grasp because it is greater than ourselves. Our consciousness is a small circle contained within the wider circle of our unconsciousness. The smaller cannot understand the greater, which corresponds with the saying of medieval philosophy: "The human soul is only contained in the body in its minority, its majority is outside the body, imaging the greater things which the body cannot comprehend."[28] That is the medieval statement

---

[28] This quote comes from the tract "De Sulphure" by Michael Sendivogius (or Michał Sędziwój (1556–1636), which is contained in his *Novum lumen chymicum* (A New Light

which coincides absolutely with the results of our psychological investigation, namely, that the unconscious mind covers an area of indefinite expanse while our conscious is very limited. In a given moment we can only hold a very few impressions in the conscious; all the rest is unconscious. We can turn the searchlight of the conscious projector from one field of experience to another, and so cover a very large area indeed. But though the consciousness of any individual can extend over a wide field, it cannot grasp the whole of human consciousness. We cannot reach with our human projector even the area which is covered by a public library, for there is no man on earth who could contain all the contents of a public library. You can only contain a very small amount, and even if you read and read and heap up knowledge, only a few things remain of all you have read; it has influenced you, but you could not for the world reproduce it, though you might get it back in a dream, or in the fantasy of a pathological condition. But to your consciousness it is extinct.

So you see our consciousness is always restricted, no matter how extended it is. You can by the artificial means of a public library extend your consciousness quite far, but even a library is limited. The British Museum library itself does not contain the whole world; it contains only man's thoughts about the world, not the world itself. So we do not know how far our unconscious reached. But the totality of our conscious and unconscious contains all; it is the thinker of our thoughts, the doer of our deeds, the feeler of our feelings. This is the philosophy of the *Upanishads*, the personal Atman versus the superpersonal Atman.[29]

From these ideas you can see how important it is to find this center, the Self, that compound of conscious and unconscious, which is the very central point which holds the whole thing together. In this dream we find a most peculiar symbol for that center, namely, a clock. This means that the center is something like a clock, that it is somehow identical with time, an

---

on Alchemy) from 1604. Z. Szydlo and R. Brzezinski (1997), "A New Light on Alchemy" (cover story), *History Today* 47 (1): 17. Jung uses this quote in his Eranos lecture of 1936, but here he calls the author "anonymous." He must later have found out the identity of the author of this tract. "Die Erlösungsvorstellungen in der Alchemie" (Redemption motifs in alchemy), EYB 1936, 35–36. Cf. *CW* 12, par. 396. In a translation the quote is rendered "but though the rational soul operates in the body, a more important part of its activity is exerted on things outside the body: it rules absolutely outside the body, and therein differs from the vital spirits of brute beasts." A. E. Waite (2007), *The Hermetic Museum: How That Greatest and Truest Medicine of the Philosopher's Stone May Be Found and Held* (London: Forgotten Books), 405.

[29] Atman: (Sanskrit: "self," "breath") one of the most basic concepts in Hinduism, the universal self, identical with the eternal core of the personality that after death either transmigrates to a new life or attains release (moksha) from the bonds of existence.

enigma of time. Time is created by our clocks which express a certain relationship of the earth to the stars, but we do not know whether time is
something real in itself. We have certain philosophical reasons why we are
in no position to answer that question. We cannot conceive of anything
that is not in time; we can talk about it, but we cannot understand it;
really we cannot think it.

So you see here is again a hint from the unconscious, that this thing we
call the Self, or the mandala, cannot be understood. It is beyond our
grasp, like the enigma of time: Is there anything like real time, or is time
created by a clock, in other words, by the human mind? Or is time, the
flow of events, perhaps the only reality? Or is the Self possibly a symbol of
man's relation to the universal stream of existence, much as the perpetual-
motion clock in the dream could be considered as a symbol for the movement of the earth through space? In this sense the conscious can call the
unconscious a clock. Well, this argument touches on another medieval
problem, namely, man's relation to the universe. The universe is the mac-
rocosmos; man is the microcosmos, not, of course, his body the flesh, but
his mind.

This theme is obviously very important, for the next dream, the fifth,
takes it up again in a peculiar form.[30] He finds himself in Zurich, in the
square place called the courtyard of Saint Peter. "Saint Peter's" refers to
the church which forms one side of the square. The tower of this church
carries a perfectly enormous clock. The dial is large enough to be seen
from distant parts of the town and from the lake and surrounding villages. Of course, it is a medieval church. There he finds himself in the
presence of an old acquaintance, namely, the man with the pointed beard,
who is otherwise unknown; and a physician also unknown, and an unknown woman who is called "the doll woman." You know the doll is the
object of the child. The woman doesn't talk and is not talked to, and he
does not know to whom she really belongs, whether she belongs to him,
to the man with the pointed beard, to the physician, or to someone else.
That he does not know worries him slightly; it seems uncanny.

As a matter of fact he really knows she belongs to him as his anima,
but he doesn't want to belong to her because she makes him run in circles, which he hates. The man with a pointed beard is Mephisto, his intellect; the physician is myself, perhaps. He was not under my treatment at

---

[30] Cf. "Dream Symbols," nr. 10, p. 132, and CW 12, nr. 10, par. 136. M 10 {0091}: "Together with doctor, man with pointed beard and the strange dollwoman at Peterhofstatt in
Zürich," April 10, 1932, CDM.

the time, but it is a slight allusion because it begins to dawn on him that analysis has played him a dreadful trick, and he knows analysis is the invention of that man Jung; it is he who has invented such things, getting people into trouble.

He used to feel you see, that psychology was an invention, not an experience. But already he is getting the idea that it might be an experience and senses how awful it would be if these things could be real. You cannot experience this if you believe it to be an invention; you must say that these things are, that there is an unconscious, there is an anima. But he realizes that that would be awful, for then the anima could really get at him, and that would be awkward. It is as if a certain woman could get at you. Then you would run away from the situation and escape. When you only see with the intellect you do not know how to live reality at all; you can only live as if you were in a picture. If things are real, however, and you experience that reality, then you are in it and something can happen to you. Now that was the thing he was most afraid of.

In the dream is that big dial, then the square, the delimited space. In antiquity that space was called *temenos*, designating the sacred precincts of the temple or the space in which a temple was erected, or a place delimited for certain purposes, a certain area tabooed for a certain purpose.[31] We can use this word *temenos* as a technical term to designate the motif of the delimited space, which often occurs in dreams. It can be a hall, a room, a certain place, a garden, a square in a town, a theater, or a circus. If the space delimited is emphasized at all, it most probably has the meaning of that place in which something is going to happen, the place where the pairs of opposites are being put together, which the philosophers of the Middle Ages called the *conjunctio*, in this case the place where the conscious and the unconscious are to be put together.

Now four people come together in this church square, and we must study these people. The dreamer is himself, his ego-consciousness, for that which I call myself, all that I know of myself, constitutes my ego. The man with the pointed beard is already well know to him; he is the clever fellow, you know, who thinks everything and disintegrates everything. He can think things away; he can even think reality away. As long as you can think things and can think them away, you can believe in everything. You can even think: "I did not do it," or, "Naturally, I did not do it." "I thought I had done it," you can say; and "I thought you wouldn't mind." Thus you

---

[31] *Temenos*: in Greek religion this is the name for the sacred precinct of temples and shrines.

excuse yourself by saying, "I thought." As if it matters what you think. But when people "think it" then something apparently happens to things which you know must exist or which do exist, as though the fellow with the wand, Mephisto, who gives apparent reality to nonreality, had changed them. We can say that the dreamer himself and the man with the pointed beard form consciousness. It is as if one said, "I know myself, of course; I know myself in a pretty good light." As a rule one has a pretty good idea of oneself, "but I have a sort of notion that this pretty good picture has some shadow, some dark aspects." We feel that for the sake of convenience we had better not mention the dark side, as it is disagreeable, yet we have a certain idea that somewhere hanging behind is a shadow. This man with the pointed beard is the dreamer's shadow; Mephisto who always accompanied Faust was very much his shadow. These two make the totality of consciousness, of his ego-consciousness, the known.

Then there is the unknown woman, who belongs to a different order of things representing the collective unconscious. And there is also a new figure, the physician, a person who possesses the secret knowledge by which healing is produced. He is obviously needed, and therefore he turns up. The dreamer ought to realize, you know, that he is now in a state of distress. There is not only the awful woman who chases him round in a circle, trying to get to him, for God knows what purpose, but also the physician who knows about curing him, who possesses, presumably, the means of curing this awkward situation. These four people form a square; they are the four points of a mandala. The situation is like this: Here is a square characterized as a sacred, or taboo, place because there is Saint Peter's Church, a Catholic church. This man is a Catholic. He is in the place bordering on the Catholic Church (Saint Peter's in Zurich is not a Catholic church, but the name Saint Peter's, of course, refers to the universal Catholic Church). And here are four people within the square.

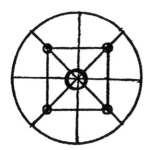

Two of these people belong to the conscious; they are above. And two belong to the lower sphere, the unconscious. These four figures in a way coincide with the four psychological functions of consciousness though, as a rule, only two are conscious.[32] For example, this man is a thinker, and besides, he is intuitive and has a very speculative mind. He uses two functions consciously, namely, thinking and intuition, but is not aware of the opposing functions, those that oppose thinking and intuition.[33] Feeling opposes the intellect, they never agree; otherwise they would become contaminated, impure; and sensation opposes intuition. Sensation is the concept of reality and intuition of possibilities. If you are intuitive, you do not perceive reality. Possibilities can never be perceived at the same time as reality. So to the intuitive, reality is the dead thing from which he escapes as soon as possible into a possibility, in order to get away from that odious reality; but sensation keeps him down to reality. Intuition makes us jump realities; sensation is afraid of possibilities, afraid that this reality might be something we would want to change.

So we can say, in this case, that the dreamer's shadow and his ego-consciousness would represent his intellect and his intuition. The woman and the physician together would represent feeling and sensation, the woman presumably the feeling because that is opposite to his main function, his intellect, and the physician, sensation, reality. Later I came to represent reality to him because I would say, "Now look here, you cannot jump over real facts as you do; you cannot think them away. Of course, that and this are possible, but never mind what is possible; create reality." For he considered that it was inevitable that an inveterate bachelor like himself should marry the woman who was looming on his horizon in a most menacing way. I had to call him back to reality.

So you see these four who make up the clock of the Self are qualities of the center. It is already what the old Greek philosopher Pythagoras called the *tetraktys*,[34] "the four at the basis of existing beings, especially living beings." I think it is particularly important in this case that the delimited

---

[32] Jung develops his ideas of the four functions in his *Psychological Types* (1921), CW 6.

[33] Jung here defines Pauli's typology as being an introvert thinking type with intuition as the auxiliary function, which puts feeling and sensation in the unconscious as "inferior functions"; much the same type as Jung himself (see Jung, McGuire, Shamdasani, 2011). Pauli gives another description of his typology in a letter to Anièla Jaffé, December 6, 1950 (1176), where he puts his scientific thinking in between sensation and thinking in opposition to his intuitive feeling. PLC IV/1.

[34] The Pythagoreans considered the number four to be holy; it is the most perfect number and the root of all things. It was associated with God and with the human soul. Tetractys was depicted like this and revealed the sum of the first four numbers: 1+2+3+4 = 10. In addition thirty-six was considered sacred because it forms the sum of the first four even and uneven numbers (1+3+5+7 = 16, 2+4+6+8 = 20).

space, the temenos, is bordering on the church, for it shows that the place is like a sacred precinct, or is an equivalent of the church. This gives the whole symbol a definitely religious character. We have historical parallels which show the ideas of the Self as anticipated, for instance, in the figure of Christ. You see he is the vine, and we are the grapes. He is the totality which carries the parts. Individual consciousness is only part of the great collective figure. That is very much the basic Christian idea, but it was never systematically expressed in Christianity to the same extent as in Gnostic texts. I should like to give you an inkling of the Gnostic teaching, as it resembles what we find in such dreams. There is a chapter in a Coptic treatise, of the *Codex Brucianus*, which was published a few years ago.[35] That text says, speaking of the so-called Monogenes, the Unigenitus, the Only Begotten, meaning the Self: "This same is he who dwelleth in the Monad, which is in the Setheus" (the Monad is the center of the mandala which is in the Unigenitus, which is in the Setheus—a name for the creative god) "and which came from the place of which none can say where it is. From him it is the Monad came, in the manner of a ship laden with all good things and in the manner of a field planted with every kind of tree, and in the manner of a city filled with all races of mankind.... This is the fashion of the Monad, all these things being in it. There are twelve Monads as a crown upon its head.... And to its veil which surroundeth it in the manner of a defense (fortification), there are twelve Gates.... This same is the Mother-City (metropolis) of the Only Begotten (Unigenitus)."

This allusion to the twelve Monads being the crown is literally represented in the classical mandala of Tibetan Buddhism, or Lamaism.

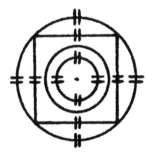

---

[35] C. Baynes and C. Schmidt (1933), *A Coptic Gnostic Treatise Contained in the Codex Brucianus*, Bruce ms. 96. Bod. lib. (Oxford: Oxford University Press). This book was published by Charlotte A. Baynes and Joan Corrie, two literary women from England. Joan Corrie was active in England as a pupil of Jung's. Baynes (apparently not related to the analyst H. G. Baynes) lectured at the Eranos conference of 1937. She was an anthropologist,

This is a city with four gates, not with twelve gates, but here in the center is the symbol of concentrated energy emanating in three times, or four times three, that means in twelve repetitions of this mandala. There is a circle like that in the illustration, and from that circle you have twelve emanations. That is the crown of the Only Begotten. The text says also that He is called the Dark Light, and also it is said of Him, "Thou art the House and the Dweller in the House." That means you are the house, the space you fill, and the contents of the space. Also the Monogenes stands upon a platform, supported by four pillars, referring to the four functions, the four qualities, just as Christ is represented in early ecclesiastical art, riding the four animals, the so-called *tetramorphos*, or standing upon four pillars meaning the four evangelists, the four Gospels.

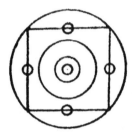

This text compares the Monogenes, the Only Begotten, to a city with four gates, and in each there is again a center. It is once more the Monad. As if in the gate of the city, there is again the city, again that Monad exactly as you find it in the Lamaistic mandala. The center is repeated four times in the gates, as the Gnostic text says. But Mahayana Buddhism only developed in that form after the third century, and the text, if not contemporary, was earlier than that, and mind you, written in Alexandria. My patient knew nothing of these things; he never came anywhere near to it. Moreover there are actually very few people in the world who have read this papyrus. So you see this symbol besides being very old is very original. Now this is the first dream in which the mandala symbol appears in an unmistakable form.

Soon after, he had this dream, the sixth in the second series: He was in an aeroplane with three unknown people, namely, the unknown physician, the unknown woman, and a pilot.[36] This time there was no Mephisto.

Oxonian scholar of Gnosticism, and OBE. She also worked on an archaeological dig in Jerusalem (see Jung, McGuire, Shamdasani, 2011).

[36] Cf. "Dream Symbols," nr. 11, p. 137, and *CW* 12, nr. 11, par. 147. M 11 {0098}: "In a crashed aeroplane with destroyed instrument of navigation," April 14, 1932, CDM. In *PsA*

Before we continue the dream, we want to establish the meaning thus far and what we can conclude from it. He is alone with three unknown individuals; the man with the pointed beard does not show up somehow. That means he has lost his shadow; the shadow has gone into the unconscious; in other words, the unconscious is now dominant. It is much stronger than he is, because it has even taken away his shadow. He is now a man without a shadow. Then, of course, his unconscious is frightfully strong, because it is three to one, as neither of the men is known to him. He is now threatened with invasion from the collective unconscious. He has lost his intellectual defense. What would happen now if the unconscious appeared as a bear or a caveman? With no shadow to protect him, no devil to protect him, the unconscious itself would be the devil.

Now see what happens. These three unknown individuals and he are flying high above the earth. The situation is slightly uncomfortable. Suddenly a projectile hits the navigating apparatus, which consist of a peculiar kind of mirror needed for directing the aeroplane. The projectile is a croquet ball; it flies into the mirror and destroys it, and the plane falls to the earth. The dreamer wakes up in the catastrophe.

Something very interesting has happened. His previous dreams had filled him with intuition; he began to sit up and say to himself: "Ah, that is most interesting, these four, that space, these people and then that doctor, that physician, most helpful." He knows all about it. He feels that he can trust that situation so he lets go of his inner self-control, his intellect, his understanding even, and trusts the unconscious implicitly. He has an inflation that takes him instantly up into the air. The aeroplane flies away with him, a dangerous situation. He lost the earth when he lost his shadow. Our shadow, our incompleteness, our somewhat negative qualities, you know, are very much of the earth. It is the remnant of the earth which makes the whole mixture a bit doubtful, somewhat dirty. When we have lost our shadow we are as white as snow, as light as feathers; then the Holy Spirit will enter, and up we go piloted by the unconscious. Very dangerous is the next moment; the clod of earth which has been lost flies into the aeroplane and destroys the navigation instrument so that the whole thing drops back to the earth. He has to go back to his earth again, since he is not an angel and not a pure spirit. It is a catastrophe.

Now, why a croquet ball? You remember the rainbow bridge over which the gods walked, but when mortals tried to walk over it they died? Men

---

Jung adds a paragraph on the anima representing the inferior function (feeling) opposed to the intellect. He also makes a reference to Paracelsus. *CW* 12, par. 150.

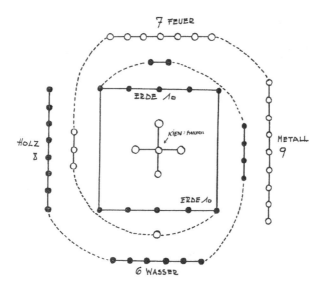

Figure 18. Diagram known as Ho T'su, the Yellow River Map, reproduced in the Richard Wilhelm edition of the *I Ching*, 309. R. Wilhelm (1977; 1967), *The I Ching; or, Book of Changes*, 3rd ed., Bollingen Series 19 (Princeton, NJ: Princeton University Press), rendered into English by Cary F. Baynes; foreword by C. G. Jung; preface to the 3rd ed. by Hellmut Wilhelm.

have to go below the rainbow bridge, and the croquet ball also goes below the wicket. It is a game which is played right on earth, no navigation in heaven. That ball is the thing that shoots him down. Once I had a very intuitive girl as a patient. She constantly had dreams of traveling in planes or balloons, and finally she had a dream where she was not even content to hang below the balloon; she was on top of it. But that was too much even for her, so she peeped down to earth and saw a tiny, tiny little man and that little man was myself, and he had a rifle which he aimed at the balloon. He shot it, and she came down with a thud. And she did in reality. It would go too far to tell you under what extraordinarily comical circumstances she came to earth; it was extremely funny.

Lecture 5

DR. JUNG: Ladies and gentlemen: We have some questions to answer.[1]

QUESTION: Would you please explain why the patient's shadow, Mephisto, carries the thinking function?

DR. JUNG: There seems to be some difficulty about the shadow and the functions. I admit this is a very complicated point. Of course, I cannot explain everything here, otherwise we shall never be able to continue our dreams. But I can see that this particular problem of the shadow and the functions might cause great misunderstanding. For instance, in our dreamer we have to deal with the fact that the ego-consciousness is accompanied by this Mephisto figure, which quite obviously represents the intellect, but we have also heard that the ego-consciousness is the intellect of this man. How does it happen that the shadow figure which one might expect to represent more or less the dark background, the unconscious, suddenly carries the intellect?

I think it will help you to understand the term "shadow" if you consider first its relation to the ego. Shadow implies that there is a source of light in front of your body which casts a shadow behind you. The source of light is consciousness. Consciousness like light casts a shadow. Always that function which is behind you or beside you, depending where the light is, is in the shadow.

Now this man is undergoing a peculiar change in his personality. He began with an entirely intellectual position, when the intellect and the consciousness were one. Thinking and consciousness were one. The shadow then fell upon the other functions, feeling and sensation, even intuition; all these were in the shadow. But when he began this process, this peculiar individuation process, then the position of the light changed. It passed over into intuition. If he is in his thinking, and thinking is identified with the conscious, then he is standing in the light; but if he steps into the shadow then he is in his intuition or any other function, depending, of

[1]This lecture was held on September 24, 1936.

course, upon circumstances, for whatever function his conscious is identified with is for the time being in the light.

You see thinking and intuition are closely connected in this man. Sometimes he is more intellectual, sometimes more intuitive. During the analytic process he became exceedingly intuitive, and the more intuitive he becomes the more light centers in intuition and the more the other functions are thrown in the shadow state of relative oblivion. If you are preoccupied with a particular situation which concerns you, everything else is in a state of oblivion, is in the shadow. The shadow, when personified, represents all those things which are in a state of oblivion. In our dreamer, the so-called auxiliary function, the intuition, was in the shadow; but when he moves into the intuitive process it is the intellect which is obscured. There are also feeling and sensation to be considered; but these two functions are split off because they are of an opposing, or contrasting, nature to the two conscious functions. They are thus in a place much more remote from him than thinking or intuition; they are contaminated by the collective unconscious, and are represented by the anima, because the collective unconscious is always represented by the anima in the case of men, by the animus in the case of women. These functions, as subconscious, are also in the shadow, and it depends upon the attitude of the conscious whether his unconscious appears under the aspect of Mephisto or under the aspect of the anima.

For instance, if the dreamer is conscious of the presence of his auxiliary function in the shadow, that means of his Mephisto, then he has practically no personal subconscious. He is aware of his shadow, of all his shadow qualities, of his inferior personality. When you are conscious that you are not an angel and that you really have some very dark sides to yourself, then you can assume that you have no repressions, that you yourself are human, the human animal, or the human beast. If you are conscious of that fact then you have no personal unconscious, and your unconscious will be represented by the anima. You will dream of the sun, inasmuch as you are aware of your shadow. If you are not aware of your shadow and think you are a Christ child or a little thing with golden wings, then naturally in that case your unconscious is represented by shadow; then you are up against a very bad world. The shadow is the unconscious cause of all your surroundings, and other people seem awfully bad. This problem will soon come to the foreground, for you will feel a tremendous need to improve the people in your surroundings. You will tell them all their faults. You are better in every case; you know where other people make their mistakes. You will run and tell them, because there is nothing in you left for possible correction. Those people who are always telling other people what they should do are unaware of their own shadow. They are like a man who leans over his garden wall and tells his neighbor all about *his* weeds, while his own garden is overgrown with weeds. A man who is aware of the weeds in his own garden will be confronted with the anima, or such a woman will be confronted with the animus, and will dream accordingly.

That answers practically two questions. Now here is another question.

QUESTION: Is the collective unconscious static, or are new forms of archetypes being constellated by continued race experience?

DR. JUNG: Well, you see the collective unconscious according to our knowledge and experience is a more or less static thing, but it is most probable that each period of time, each epoch, deposits a new stratum in the unconscious, so it is possible, even very probable, that the topmost layers of the collective unconscious in Europe are different from those in other countries.[2] There is something like racial or geographical differentiation in the unconscious. It is quite possible, for instance, that the Christian layer in the collective unconscious is a reality, that the Christian epoch has already left a certain deposit which is indestructible; something permanent remains. These things are all highly hypothetical. When I say anything about them I simply confess a certain opinion which I consider to be subjective.

QUESTION: Must there not be a fixed interpretation of dream material which has no possible source in actual personal experience, as, for instance, the eating of human flesh?

DR. JUNG: Well, it is true that when it is a matter of symbols which have no parallel in our actual life, the interpretation must be made more or less according to historical rules, that is, in such a case we have a more or less fixed interpretation because we have no other means. But if we take any particular instance of the appearance of a symbol such as, for example, the eating of human flesh, which, of course, is to us something that does not occur often, for it is not a conventional thing to do, it is yet subject to certain variations in interpretation.

It is always advisable to ask for associations; for much also depends on the context, the connection where the symbol appears, and so forth. Sometimes you have to present a certain thing in a certain light which is by no means conventional or fixed. Take anthropophagy, the eating of

---

[2]This geological model of the psyche is reproduced in Jung, McGuire, Shamdasani, 2011, 143.

human flesh. In one case it might have one nuance of meaning, in another it might be a bit different. For instance, one of the fixed interpretations could be the Christian symbol of the Communion, which is really anthropophagy of a very primitive nature, spiritualized under symbols.[3] But it can just as well mean integration of particles of the human psyche, such as certain inherited units or elements, which have not yet been assimilated by the individual.

There is in the Chinese *Book of Wisdom*, the *Yi King*, a special hexagram which contains this symbol; it is called "The Biting Through."[4] That is a hexagram which is especially applicable to cases where there are certain remnants or so-called inclusions, namely, traits or elements of ancestral character, which have not been assimilated in the individual, and where the task of analytical development is to integrate these elements. Such a thing might happen, for instance, if you had had an ancestor who was of a very particular, perhaps unique, character, having certain incompatible qualities. Then if you are the kind of person who is little inclined to accept or to integrate such an ancestral character, you will be born with a split personality. You may not feel it, but in the course of your life there will come to daylight the fact that there is in you a lump which simply refuses to be assimilated, to be made whole with yourself, and which will cause all sorts of disturbances. Then when you begin an analysis that thing will be constellated, and the *Yi King* will produce the hexagram of "The Biting Through." Then you have to digest that lump, and you will dream of eating human flesh.[5]

Of course, this is also a communion, because you eat the flesh in the Communion in order to integrate Christ into your system. You integrate the immortal, incorruptible flesh into yourself in order to transform yourself. One can say that this is an incompatible body, an uncomfortable lump, because man is mortal and an immortal substance does not agree with his system. So even that symbolism can be interpreted in different ways according to circumstances.

QUESTION: In the case, where a person is about to revert entirely to an instinctive level, to an animal state of unconscious, in which he does not

---

[3] Jung discusses this in his essay "Transformation Symbolism in the Mass" (1942), *CW* 11.

[4] *Yi King*, also spelled *I Ching*. Hexagram 21, Shih Ho: Biting Through. R. Wilhelm, 1977; 1967.

[5] Jung relates this kind of experience in his vision recorded in *The Red Book*, "The Sacrificial murder" which he introduces with the words "But this was the vision that I did not want to see"; *RB*, 290.

want to make another understand him, is the thing that holds him a bit of integrity that he has attained? Is the voice from behind projected to the doctor? Could this happen, that is, could he hold on, without the doctor actually being present?

DR. JUNG: In the analytic process the patient acquires a certain amount of integration. He integrates himself, he puts himself together—his conscious together with the unconscious. Inasmuch as he is able to do so he becomes more complete. But you see that has nothing to do with the voice at all. That integrity or integration is not the voice; that is his accomplishment; but the voice helps him. The voice is something that simply appears and is there whether he is integrated or not. The less he is integrated the more that voice could appear and make him integrated, and naturally inasmuch as the patient is rational and intellectual, he would assume that the voice is nothing but the ego, because he can't assume that there is something independent of himself within the sphere of his psyche. That is a thought very few people can realize. Therefore when such a reasonable voice appears, then only a lunatic can assume that this is the voice of the doctor. All rational people think, "This is just a part of my own psyche," and "That is myself; that is my consciousness." Our patient was accurate and scientific enough to see and feel instantly that this voice was not at all the doctor, not at all myself. He could not project that voice into his real analyst, who was a woman doctor, because she would not know about these things in the least. Moreover it was a male voice, therefore the dreams, when referring to that voice, called it the voice of the commander or general or captain or old wise man. Or it was an abstract voice that simply came out of empty space.

This is one of these phenomena that show you clearly that the collective unconscious is not oneself—it is collective. It is just as if I were in the presence of such a crowd as this. I think something, and suddenly a voice out of my audience makes a remark about it. In that case I should not think *I* have spoken or that I have projected it onto you. I should say, "Oh, what did you say?" I should instantly refer it to an objective event; I should not assume that you are a kind of hallucination. It is exactly the same with the collective unconscious. Our dreamer did not hesitate one moment; he saw and understood that the voice was an objective fact. He was a man with a great mind, so he observed accurately and instantly drew the conclusion, "That is a fact, that is not a projection, it is not an opinion, and moreover it does not belong exactly in my own psyche, despite the fact that it influences my psyche."

If, for example, I am talking to you when suddenly a voice shouts, "Fire," I should pay attention and not assume for one moment that *I* have meant fire. But when something comes from within that is what we usually do; we think, "I have done it." It is a foolish idea that we made the psyche, or that it is our own invention. This is the morbidity of our age; our consciousness has detached itself so much from its background that it assumes that whatever happens in us is made by our psyche, that we make it. Nobody questions; we cannot even imagine that we are capable of experiencing something that is psychical.

In this respect primitive man is in a much more favorable position than we are. He can experience something psychical. But if we are in a dilemma, or in doubt about something, then we say: "I must think it over." We handle it in our thoughts. We are doing the whole job. But the primitive man says, "I will talk it over with the spirits," and he goes into the woods; there he listens, and the trees begin to speak and to talk to him about it; they tell him what to do. If he is a medicine man he might say, "I must talk to my snake," meaning by that the anima, who is the wise snake. This means, "I must talk to the unconscious." The woods, of course, are always the unconscious, and the voice of the woods is exactly the voice in the dreamer's case.

With us, as you know, only lunatics hear voices, but if one is careful enough and observes critically, then one can make a distinction between the thoughts that are really our own and the thoughts that are intrusions. Certain thoughts occur within our reach; other thoughts are intrusions; we don't know exactly where they came from. They might come from the surroundings. That is quite possible because we are all living in the same psychical atmosphere, and then it is quite possible that certain thoughts in us or certain dreams come from the people with whom we happen to be living. Therefore in different surroundings, with different people, we get different dreams. Our dreams contain the problem of our surroundings, and we may dream the problems of others instead of our own.

There was a man once who wanted to be analyzed, but he had no dreams, and there were no problems in his conscious either. What can you do with such a fellow? I told that man, "Look here, you are aware of no conflict in your conscious, and you have no dreams, and you expect me to do something about it! Since you want to be analyzed and I know you are serious in your purpose, somebody in your surroundings has your dreams." And so it was. His seven-year-old son was having his dreams. The moment I said, "Somebody else has your dreams," he leaped up and said, "By Jove, that is my boy. Oh, he has the most extraordinary dreams. He keeps telling me his dreams, and I don't understand that stuff." The boy was always bringing him the message, and the fool of a father did not understand it. I said, "You put down all the dreams your boy has." Instantly the boy had a grand dream, and the father brought it to me. For two months we went on analyzing the boy's dreams as if they were the father's—and they were. The result was that, after seven or eight weeks, the father began to dream. The dreams then came to him. You see before that he simply would not accept them. He has such a thick skin; he was a terribly reasonable fellow, you know, and dreadfully dull. He simply exteriorized his dreams into his boy. Whenever I have such cases I say, "Someone in your surroundings has your dreams," and, believe me, it is true. For instance, when you are pathologically normal, then you can be sure someone has to carry your difficulties; you leave them to somebody else. People often say, "I have no problems; everything is perfectly OK." You see it written all over their faces that something is wrong. In that case somebody, the father or sister perhaps, is in the sauce.

QUESTION: If the patient had been a woman instead of a man, would the part the woman doctor played be the same, that is, would she also serve as a creative receptacle for a woman's thoughts?

DR. JUNG: Well, that is a technical question which goes pretty deep. It has to do with the peculiar effect a woman has on a man's suspended thoughts. She precipitates them; it is just as if she were lending body to a man's thoughts. In the reversed situation, there is also a peculiar effect. One could say a man makes a woman think. A woman usually begins to sit up when there is a man about, and men cause much thinking to women, so much so that I often have to send women patients away to a woman analyst because they get quite crazy; their animus gets stirred up in such a way, like a whirlwind, a frightful mess of thoughts. Then one sends them to a woman who weights the thoughts down, so that they become calm and the intoxication goes away.

Usually the analysis between man and man remains in a conscious and intellectual sphere, unless the unconscious is already in motion, when the analysis of the deeper layers can, of course, proceed. The same holds true when women consult an analyst of the same sex. If the unconscious is not already in motion then the analysis is likely to remain in the conscious sphere, concerning itself with personal relatedness, or Eros. But if the unconscious is already stirred, as is usually the case when the analysis is started, then it would not be different from a woman-to-man analysis.

If, however, I analyze a man and we have done what we could, and his anima has not become constellated at all, then his whole relatedness, his Eros, will remain completely unadapted. I can analyze a man as completely as possible and know all the time that he is like a little boy when it comes to a woman, and yet I can do nothing about it. If I send that man to a woman, he will be just like a little baby, and the woman doctor thinks, "Isn't it too funny for words; Dr. Jung has never seen it." Or a woman comes to me who has been analyzed by a woman, and, if her animus has not been constellated, she will show things to me that never came to light in her previous analysis.

So you see to a certain extent it is necessary that a woman should be analyzed by a man as well as a woman, in order to be complete. Usually in an analysis by one of the same sex, the day side, the adaptation side, the rational side becomes highly analyzed, but unless the unconscious has already been started, the dark side usually remains in the dark. If the analyst is changed to one of the opposite sex, however, you will get an entirely different picture, for then the dark side comes up. There are endless complications; for instance there are cases where you cannot start the unconscious because the conscious is not analyzed enough; and, as I have said, there are many where the unconscious has already been stirred by the conflict which has brought the patient to analysis; but these are technical problems. I could give you a whole book about these peculiar technical secrets, but I cannot go into all that.

* * * * *

We shall continue our dreams. We stopped yesterday with the dream of the aeroplane, the sixth in the second series. The patient was in the aeroplane with three other persons, the pilot, the physician, and the woman—all unknown to him—and I told you that in this situation the ego was alone against three in the unconscious; the game was one to three.

In such a case, of course, the unconscious prevails against the conscious, and so he is taken up into the air; he gets an inflation, and then he has to be shot down, and you know what rocket has done it. When he falls down to the earth, it is a coming back to hard realities, to the world as it is; for that is the earth, that is the place of battle and strife. Naturally when he is identified with the unconscious, he escapes the banality of life and the realization of facts, because in heaven you don't have to realize at all. Heaven is air anyway, and it doesn't matter what kind of air. That is why so many people like to fly off into space and converse with spirits instead of with human beings, because it isn't dangerous; it is only air. But the moment one comes down to earth, things become real, and then you get into hot water; there are consequences. In the realm of thought there are no consequences, unless you have a particular passion to make things real. Very few people have that; instead they use the mind as a safe refuge or as a safety valve. When they think a thing, they hope it doesn't come off.

When you come down to earth, and earth, reality, happens to belong to your inferior function, that is, if you are inferior in your adaptation to realities, then you are likely to fall into an infantile situation. The moment you touch upon your undeveloped side, your inferior function, you are in the realm of your inferior functioning, and that brings you back to the family. It is for this reason that so many people act as if they were still with the parents when they get into their inferior function. For instance, in business the boss is the father; and every woman is met as if she were the mother or the sister. And that is wrong. Now this man in coming down to earth has to take up his inferior function. As a matter of fact the croquet ball that shot him down is the globe, the earth, and he falls into his inferior function.

Therefore the next dream, the seventh, says he is with his father and mother and sister.[6] They are all clinging to the platform of a tramcar that is overcrowded and are in a very dangerous situation.

Now you see he is back in the family situation right away, because that is the only relatedness to life and to the world that his functions know of. Of course, with his mind he knows much better, but in actual fact he does not know any better. In reality he behaves as if all women were mothers and sisters, and all men fathers. For that reason he got into hot water and made one mistake after another. He trusted all women, and naturally women take advantage of such a situation; and he trusted men as if they were his father, and they also would take advantage of him or they would handle him as if they were really his father and he their naughty boy, and then they would beat him up.

So you see he falls instantly back into a sort of regression, into an infantile state, and gets into a very dangerous situation, hanging onto the platform of a tramcar. He is not even inside but outside. The tramcar is a very frequent dream symbol and always means the way in which most people move, for they move by streetcar, or by train. Anyone can be there, so it

---

[6] Cf. "Dream Symbols," nr. 12, p. 139, and CW 12, nr. 12, par. 151. M 12 {0112}: "With parents and sister Hertha in a dangerous situation at the platform of tramcar," April 22, 1932, CDM.

is an exceedingly collective way, the way most people go. Thus he falls into a collective situation; he is in the same boat with many other people, for most people like himself have an infantile adaptation.[7] This explains why everyone looks to see what other people are doing and expects them to do something; but they never realize that *they* themselves could do anything independently. Psychologically it is a complete circling; it is the psychology of the mob. For example, we have a perfectly infantile attitude to the state or government. We make the government father and mother. The state has an enormous udder, and everybody sucks, and nobody realizes that the state is a legend and does not really exist as a separate being; it is a mere abstraction. Governments do not exist; they are our own invention, and we think we have now invented a father or a mother to whom we can cling. This is the attitude of millions and millions of people. So when the dreamer falls down he simply falls to the ordinary level, but he ought to know better. He can't be a great mind on one side and a baby on the other.

Whenever such a man as this with a considerable mind or strong consciousness gets into such an infant situation, then a state of confusion or of disintegration is produced, because the family means the original state of our consciousness, and that is disintegration. When you think back you realize that consciousness begins with certain dispersed islands of memory which come up from the unconscious, from the darkness. You see a spot here and a spot there, and slowly they come together and form what you call the continuity of consciousness. If you go back into childhood you dissolve or disintegrate your consciousness in a similar way, and it becomes mere spots in the sea of the unconscious. At this point the condition becomes serious; it is a disintegration of consciousness; it could be a hysterical disintegration, or a schizophrenia. This man is always afraid of such a schizophrenic regression, because he is quite apt to make such regressions into early childhood, into the state where islands of consciousness begin to come together. And so when he came back to that place with the whole rush of a falling star, he might have fallen from the layer of childhood into the layer of nonintegration, and that would amount to a certain disintegration of consciousness, to schizophrenia, and he was afraid this might happen to him. There was some reason for his fear, because the greater the distance between the unconscious mind and the state of the undifferentiated functions, the greater is the tension and the greater the possibility of an explosion.

---

[7]This section on the tramcar is not in the Eranos lecture but is added in *PsA, CW* 12, par. 153.

In any case of schizophrenia you can observe a peculiar contrast between the two sides of the personality. On the one side, there is, perhaps, a normally developed mind, and on the other side, a childishness which simply cannot stand the reach of the mind. Then it is as if one side of the personality were too big for the other and the psyche is, as it were, exploded. Or the mind may be very narrow, and there may come a big vision, or a big dream which explodes the little brain box, and the whole thing is blasted to bits. Such difficulties often begin with an important and beautiful dream that would be a treat to a differentiated mind, but a narrow person simply goes to pieces over it, because he can't grasp it. If he could have grasped it nothing unfortunate would have happened; it would have been a gift of the gods. But it is a dangerous projectile that explodes the dream life of a childish person.

When consciousness moves down precipitately like that into the inferior function, into the danger of disintegration, it would amount to a fall into the sea, into the sea of the unconscious.

So the next dream, the eighth, contains the motive of the sea, that is, of complete unconsciousness.[8] He knows that there is a great treasure hidden at the bottom of the sea, and if any one were to try to get at that treasure, his task would be to dive through a very narrow opening. And he looked down into that opening. It was underwater, and he knew it was terribly dangerous to go down there. The danger seemed to be that one might get stuck in the opening because it was very narrow, and, in the dream, he is deliberating whether he should take the risk. He feels very much that he would like to go down there. Then he makes up his mind to leap. He leaps, and in the moment when he makes up his mind he knows that he will find a human companion down there, and that thought helps his decision. Then he takes the leap, and apparently nothing dangerous happens; he is suddenly at the bottom of the sea, and it is a beautiful garden of geometric form, and in the middle of it, in the center, is a beautiful fountain. Then he wakes up.

You see this dream is of the utmost importance, for it shows something exceedingly valuable, life saving even. He has been in a pretty critical situation before, for he fell down out of his illusions, his dreams, his hopes and expectations; he fell through the surface of the earth, that is, through consciousness, into childhood. He is now in a dangerous state of possible disintegration, and the question is, "But what can one do about it? How

---

[8] Cf. "Dream Symbols," nr. 13, p. 139, and CW 12, nr. 13, par. 154; M 13 {0126}: "Diving in the sea for a treasure; a garden with a fountain in the deep," April 29, 1932, CDM.

does one get out of such a situation?" This eighth dream says, "In this way, namely, that you understand the situation in a completely different way. You must learn that your childhood is built upon the basis of the collective unconscious, that beyond that dangerous condition which would be disintegration, the infantile disintegration of the mind, is an order, which is preestablished. Of course, the opening is very narrow; the door or path which leads to that place is narrow and very dangerous, beset by the danger of disintegration, or dismemberment. But if you are not afraid and make up your mind to dive instead of fall, or even if in the moment of falling you say: "This is diving; I *do* fall, but I *want* to fall; because I am diving, this whole thing is positive." But you must have courage. Then you are no more alone. That is the terrible fear when you begin to disintegrate; people begin to say things and to look at you. You are alone, you can't explain yourself anymore. In this dream his unconscious tells him, "You will find a companion."

No one can understand this dream unless he knows what it is to be confronted with such a problem. If you can put yourself into such a situation you will understand through sympathy. This man is in a conspicuous position in the world, and suddenly he has such thoughts. Let him tell his thoughts to his colleagues and see what happens. They will all say, "That man is stark mad." When I began to talk about such things, people looked at me as if I were crazy. I said, "In the end, we will see who is crazy." Many people haven't the knowledge, the power, the mental health to think such thoughts, to realize such things, therefore they have always been guarded as the treasure of mystery teachings which might not be betrayed. If anyone betrayed these mysteries he was killed, because it was considered exceedingly dangerous to know about such things at all. If we were in the year 1336 instead of 1936 I should be mighty careful to shut up about such things. Mind you there are plenty of things I shut up about today. That's no joke. We are not at the end of such days. People are still children. We can talk of these things pretty safely, though I would not risk saying many a thing I have said here in a scientific gathering; it would be pretty dangerous. I have risked my reputation more than once.

To this man the intimate knowledge of such realities came home more and more, and more and more made themselves felt. He feels, "If I don't go on with these things I am lost; I am stuck in the midst; I have lost the source of life. If I do go on with them I feel myself vibrating with them; I feel it makes sense." He realizes that he is in the current of life, but where does that thing lead to? His mind anxiously questions: "Where does this lead to; what will be the end of all this?" All the time he is confronted with the fear that this whole thing will end in insanity, in complete disintegration. He is not an alienist, so he doesn't know enough to answer this question; but even if he were an alienist or an analyst, it would help him very little, because no matter what one is, these things always appear in such a form that they arouse panic.

Now his dream tells him, "Forget about childishness. That is just a layer you will pierce; you will go deeper, and you will declare that falling is exactly what you want to do. You don't fall into the sea and get drowned; you are a diver." That is exactly the image I always use. I say, "You must not understand this whole thing as if you were a man drowning in the sea; it is diving. It is your own activity." It may be dangerous, but if you run away, you do not realize the nature of the danger, and that is much worse. If you do not allow yourself to experience it at all, you will resist it, telling yourself it should not be and thus protecting yourself in a reasonable way with your consciousness from any full recognition of your situation. Then you are dangerously in it because you do not want to be in it. When you are very much afraid of a thing then you can be sure it will happen. There is a secret fascination about things you are afraid of.

There is the case of a famous French officer, who was always a bit fearful as a boy. He was fascinated by history and particularly by terrible battles and such things. He was afraid of them, and so he became a soldier. Being an officer he once came to a Trappist monastery during maneuvers. He saw how the monks lived, how they dug their own graves, and sprinkled themselves with ashes, and how they did not talk. He grew afraid, thinking, "It is terrible to live like that." Immediately he entered the monastery. When he had lived that kind of life for several years some missionaries from Morocco came to the monastery and told hair-raising stories of their brethren who had been murdered by cannibals. Again he grew afraid and became a missionary to Morocco. There he was killed, murdered. What he feared became his task. He was a hero who admitted he was no hero. He was afraid, and fear fascinated him. And fear, the thing you are afraid of, often, you can say as a rule, comes to pass. This cannot be taken too literally, but sometimes things happen in just this way.

So you see in risking it, in making up his mind to take the risk of diving, the dreamer understands suddenly that the thing beneath does hold great danger, but in the loneliness of this problem he finds a companion. This again is a pretty famous motif. You know that people in loneliness and isolation often have the experience of meeting a companion. In recent days, for instance, it was Nietzsche who was confronted with an extraordinary problem, and it happened to him that he met a companion whom he called Zarathustra. We have a very precious confession of Nietzsche, in which he speaks of his time all alone on the mountains in utter desolation. For he had given up his professorship in Basel and had gone to live in the Engadine, six thousand feet up, in a place which was tremendously isolated, particularly in the fall and the beginning of winter. And there he felt that "one became two"; he became conscious of the presence of Zarathustra.[9] Zarathustra is an old teacher, really the teacher of personal religion, who lived about the ninth century BC.[10] Nietzsche realized that Zarathustra was the task, and so he wrote *Thus Spake Zarathustra*.[11] This task was a very mysterious one. Nietzsche understood that the peculiar split in Christian psychology, the split between good and evil, above and below, right and left, between God and Satan, between heaven and hell, was really due to the Persian influence in Judaism. Zarathustra first taught about the pairs of opposites, the day-and-night psychology, the eternal fight between the God of Light, Ormuz, and the God of Darkness, Ariman. Nietzsche's task was to reconcile these opposites and to undo the teaching of Zarathustra in a way. In the eternal return of things Zarathustra had come back to life to teach the opposite truth, namely, how man could be one and not two. First Zarathustra taught how man is two, and now he had come back to life in Nietzsche to teach man how he can be one, how he can become superman, man beyond good and evil.

The same phenomenon of aloneness is to be found in Goethe, who was a peculiarly lonely figure, despite his worldly life. His facial expression showed this. When Napoleon came to Weimar he saw Goethe at a social gathering in the palace of the grand duke. He did not know who he was

---

[9] In the poem "Sils Maria," Nietzsche writes:

"Here I sat, waiting—not for anything—
Beyond Good and Evil, fancying
Now light, now shadows, all a game,
All lake, all noon, all time without all aim.
Then suddenly, friend, one turned into two—And Zarathustra walked into my
    view."

F. Nietzsche and W. Kaufmann, ed. and trans. (1974), *The Gay Science: With a Prelude in Rhymes and an Appendix of Songs* (New York: Vintage), 371.

[10] Zoroastrianism, ancient pre-Islamic religion of Iran. Founded by the Iranian prophet and reformer Zoroaster in the sixth century BC, the religion contains both monotheistic and dualistic features. Zoroastrianism survives in isolated areas of Iran and in India, where the descendants of Zoroastrian Iranian (Persian) immigrants are known as Parsis, or Parsees. In India the religion is called Parsiism.

[11] Jung read Nietzsche's *Thus Spoke Zarathustra* in depth in early 1914, but he was acquainted with his works already in 1897. Shamdasani, 2012, 29. On Jung's reading of Nietzsche, see also Bishop, 1995.

but said to a bystander, "Voilà un homme qui a souffert beaucoup." There is a man who has suffered much. Goethe was an extraordinarily lonely man because he was a superior man, and to be superior is to be like a mountain that is higher than the surrounding mountains, that is, to be isolated. With him we see also the phenomenon of the companion, who in this case was Faust. Faust really accompanied him throughout his whole life from the first years of his manhood to his death—and even beyond death, because the second part of his famous tragedy, *Faust*, was a posthumous work. He worked on it continuously during his last days, and he always wrote in his diary, "Worked on the main work," *opus majus*, the greater work. At his death it was found that *Faust* was a more or less finished work.

The same thing is to be seen in other historical examples, for instance, when the two disciples went to Emmaus after Christ's death and were joined by the companion whom they did not recognize, but who was Christ. Then in the *Bhagavad Gita*, when the prince, Arjuna, goes to battle and is all alone with his thoughts, no one with him but his charioteer, it turns out that his charioteer is the god Krishna, who talks to him.[12] There is a particularly interesting report about the companion in the eighteenth Sura of the Koran. It is called the Kabal, which is the story of Moses, the prophet Moses mentioned in the Old Testament, and his servant Joshua. The story is that when Moses was eighty years old, he said to his servant Joshua: "Now let us travel. I want to seek the source of life." And so Joshua took a basket with provisions, bread and a fish, and they traveled together through the desert. And after a while old Moses felt tired, and they came to a spring, and he said, "Let us sit here and refresh ourselves." So they sat down for a short time and then continued their journey. Presently Moses said to his servant Joshua, "I feel hungry; let us eat." And Joshua gave him the basket; but when Moses looked into it he found that the fish was gone; and he asked, "Where is the fish?" And Joshua replied, "Well at that spring where we refreshed ourselves, a drop

---

[12] This must refer to the beginning of the *Bhagavad Gita* (chapter 1, verses 21–23) where Arjuna asks Krishna to draw his chariot between the two armies. Jung's reading that Arjuna is alone with his thoughts and then discovers that Krishna is his charioteer cannot be found in the original text. We know that Jung read the *Upanishads* in connection with the writing of the *Psychology of the Unconscious* in 1911–12. He owned Max Müller's fifty-volume series *The Sacred Books of the East*. See Shamdasani, 2012, 61. The charioteer/Krishna was an important dream image to Pauli, and he discusses this motif from a dream of October 6, 1949, with Jung (see Pauli to Jung, appendix to letter 1200, PLC IV/1) and also with Hans Bender (1907–91, professor of parapsychology at Freiburg) on April 30, 1957. See appendix to letter 2586, PLC IV/4 i.

of water fell upon the fish and instantly it came to life and jumped out of the basket into the brook and in a miraculous way took its course back into the sea." Then Moses said, "That was the spring of Eternal Life. Let us return to that place." So they went back, and the Koran says, "There they found one of our servants whom we have equipped with all our power and wisdom." And the commentaries say that this was Chidher, the Green One.[13] The early commentaries of the tenth century say that there Moses found a man sitting on the earth wrapped up in his burnous, and around him the floor of the desert was blossoming with spring flowers, because Chidher is the god of vegetation, the eternal renewer of life, the mystery god of the Sufis. This servant of God, the god of spring, was the companion; for when Moses saw him he said to him, "Let me follow you, and you shall teach me the wisdom of God, and I will always obey you and follow you in everything you do." And Chidher, or the angel, or whatever you call him, said, "You are not able to follow me." And Moses insisted, "I will follow you; you will find me always obedient and understanding." And Chidher said: "You are not able to follow me, but since you insist you can try." So Moses followed him, and many peculiar things happened. Perhaps I shall have an opportunity to tell you those adventures on another occasion. This story is particularly nice because it shows the finding of the companion at the well.

When the dreamer came down into this beautiful geometric garden, where was the companion, the one who had been promised? There was nothing there but the fountain, the spring. So we see that the spring and the companion are the same thing. The spring of life is personified as the companion. In the initiation of the Sufi cults even to this day, it is still taught that the companion is a returning, a self-renewing deity who appears in the form of a fountain, and the friend is revealed in the form of a garden.

When I was in Africa, I happened to have a Somali as head man who had had his initiation from a sheik who was a Sufi. This man, of course, assumed that I would know nothing of the Koran, that I was only a Christian heathen, and not a "Man of the Book." When I noticed what sort of countenance he had, I began to question him about the Koran, and then it turned out that he apparently knew nothing about it and was interested in my knowledge. So I asked him about the eighteenth Sura, the story of Chidher, and found to my surprise that he was well informed. He told me

---

[13] Also spelled Khidr. From the Koran eighteenth Sura. See also Jung, "Concerning Rebirth" (1939) where he goes deeper into this Sura. CW 9/I, pars. 240–58.

that his sheik had given him instructions about Chidher and had told him that he still appears to people in distress, but only to those who know about the book, the Koran. He described very dramatically how if a man unexpectedly comes to you when you are walking alone in the street or anywhere in the country and you know instinctively that this is Chidher, you should go up to him and take him by the hand and say, "Peace be with thee." He will then respond to you, and all your wishes will be granted. Only you must be conscious of your wishes at that moment. Or at night when you are asleep in your bed and you see a light, which has no smoke, which has no flame, which is a pure white light—that is Chidher. Then you must think of your wishes, and they will all be granted. And then he smiled and bent down to the ground and took a leaf of grass and said, "Also this can be Chidher." You see this means that God, this source of life, can take any form, and this is also true in psychology.

The garden which the dreamer discovers at the bottom of the sea is, of course, also the treasure which was the first motive in this dream, the treasure buried in the sea. This is also a well-known mythological motive. It is a jewel difficult to attain; often it is in the belly of the whale or dragon, or in the cavern where the dragon lives, or it is the treasure which the serpent guards; or it is defended by curses or by witchcraft. It appears in many different forms. Only the hero can recover that treasure, which usually means life energy, vital energy, or what is technically called psychic energy, libido. Its disappearance is the old, very primitive loss of a soul.[14] A soul has been lost or stolen, robbed, buried in the ground, or gone away, and one should recover it. When man has lost his soul, he does not live; he suffers from a condition of low tension and feels perhaps ill and that he ought to recover the lost part of himself, the lost soul, which is the treasure. This is a very general psychological condition; if he succeeds in recovering this lost treasure or soul, or lost fragment of his personality, then he is a totality, and the totality is the Self which consists of conscious and unconscious and is the great treasure, represented as the precious pearl, the diamond, the gold, the golden vessel, and so forth. The discovery of that lost treasure means the greatest discovery man can make, for in finding it he finds the totality of his life and existence. So the treasure when characterized by a symbol is spoken of as a city, a castle, a garden, sometimes as a beautiful garden, a marvelous, enchanted garden. It is a temenos, that sacred, delimited space in which the god dwells. Usu-

---

[14] For an overview of the ancient view that disease is caused by the loss of soul, see Henry F. Ellenberger (1970), *The Discovery of the Unconscious* (New York: Basic Books).

ally in the center of the temenos you find either the god, an icon of the god, or as in the Eastern mandalas, Shiva, the creative god, the god of life, the destroyer of life, with his Shakti, the one who builds maya, the illusion of the world. Also you find Buddha, Amitabha, or Avalokiteshvara in the center of the mandala, or one of the great Mahayana teachers, the venerable, miraculous, life-giving personalities of that particular religion.[15] And at that place where the spring comes up, the spring of life, Moses finds Chidher as I told you.

The idea of the temenos with the sacred and precious place in the center has been realized in many religious buildings. Examples are to be seen also in the Baptisterium, with the life-giving water in the center; in the *piscina*, also in the altar of a church which is usually at or near the center. One of the most striking examples is shown in the way in which the mosques are built. For instance, in the Achmed Ibn Tulûn in Cairo there is a wide courtyard, in the center of which is the life-giving spring. The fountain is right in the center, the place where the cleansing is done, the ritualistic washing, which means that man is made over, given rebirth into a sort of protected atmosphere, where he is contained in the water as the little fishes are. The early Christians carried rings with two fishes cut on the stone. They were called *pisticuli christianorum*, "little fishes of the Christians." Also the famous ring of the pope has the miraculous draught of fishes on it, meaning that he has spread his net like a fisherman and pulls in all the souls of the believers who like little fishes were contained in the sea of the unconscious, or worldliness and the flesh; he brings them like a sacrifice, to be integrated in man, in other words, to be eaten. You find the same symbolism in Christian buildings, where in the center of the cloister is the well. The same idea is to be found in the alchemical symbol, the so-called *rosarium*, the rose garden, in the center of which is always a spring.[16]

In that house, in that square building, somebody lives; the personification of the spring is the dweller in that house, and he is the house itself, the house and the dweller in the house, the friend of man, the Monogenes

---

[15] Amitabha (Sanskrit: Infinite Light) also called Amitayus ("Infinite Life"), a saviour figure predominantly in East Asia but also in Tibet and Nepal as one of the five "self-born" Buddhas (dhyani-buddhas) who have existed eternally. According to this concept, he manifested himself as the historical Buddha Gotama and as the bodhisattva "Buddha-to-be") Avalokiteshvara (Sanskrit: avalokita, "looking on"; ishivara, "lord") the bodhisattva ("Buddha-to-be") of infinite compassion and mercy, possibly the most popular of all Buddhist deities.

[16] Jung makes a detailed interpretation of the psychological meaning of the alchemical tract *Rosarium Philosophorum* (The rose garden of the philosophers) in his *Psychology of the Transference* (1946) in CW 16, pars. 402–539.

of the Gnostics, the Unigenitus in alchemy.[17] In alchemy the rose garden and the space delimited by a square is the *circulus quadratus*, the squared circle. It is also the wonderful stone, the precious stone, the stone more precious than any in the world, namely, the *lapis philosophorum*, which is at the same time a living being. It is not a dead stone; it is an animated being consisting of body, soul, and spirit. It is a superhuman being, really a superman, and is the friend or companion. There is a very ancient text, presumably of Greek origin but handed down through the Arabic translators, in which is contained an invocation or rather an exclamation of the stone, which speaks and says to man, "Protect me; I will protect thee. Give me my life, and I will help you." That shows very clearly the relationship of two friends where one can help the other. Now mind you, that is the so-called lapis philosophorum, the philosopher's stone. This quotation shows the protective value or meaning of the temenos or the mandala. It always protects against disintegration, and therefore our dreamer had this dream. His regression into childhood contains the danger of disintegration against which the unconscious gives the protecting symbol.

The dream expresses the idea of the mandala, rosarium, the rose garden, which is buried in the water; it advises him not to drown but to dive in order to attain the jewel which is difficult to attain, but when attained, will give him protection, hold him together, contain him as a mother does a child. The surrounding mother contains the child and holds the child together. That garden is like the mother; it is a piece of Mother Earth, a sacred mother that will contain him as the seed is contained in the flower. Anyone who is contained in that mandala is like a god, like a divine being living eternally in the mother, in the unconscious. Therefore the mandala contains the deity. It is part of the divine service, the Opus in the East, where the Yogin gradually enters the center of the mandala through the four gates, drawing himself together into the middle, until he is merged with the god. He contacts the god, is eaten by the god, or he eats the god and becomes indistinguishable from the deity. And as he comes out of that place again he is filled with the deity, with the source of life. He has rubbed his churinga; he has integrated within himself the health, the eternal and incorruptible life of the deity. So in the fourth and fifth dreams of

---

[17] The Greek work *Monogenes* in the New Testament is translated into "only begotten," as is Christ being the only begotten son of God. Jung refers especially to the idea of the Monogenes or Unigenitus in Gnosticism and its association with the Monad, the Mother-City, the temenos, etc. and links it to his concept of the Self (the eternal, indestructible center of the personality). In this context he often cites a book by C. A. Baynes (1933), *A Coptic Gnostic Treatise*, contained in the Codex Brucianus. See *CW* 12, par. 138.

the first series, we see the importance of the mandala. In the fourth he had to protect himself against a multitude of indefinite women, meaning *animae*, and in the fifth the serpent makes a circle around him to protect him, and he is rooted to the spot. We find analogous instances as I have already pointed out in that book, *Poliphilo*.

The fountain of life in the center of the mandala is ever flowing, a fountain of eternal life; it is the *aqua permanens*, the divine water, the everlasting water of the Greek and Latin alchemists. It is the *perpetuum mobile*, the clock with a pendulum which swings forever and whose weights never sink, or the fountain from which the life-giving water flows. Life is not always understood to be like water; sometimes it is understood to be fire. Heraclitus expressed that formula of the eternally living fire. Very often Christ is represented as the Deity in the center of the mandala. I have brought you some mandalas so that you may get an idea of these things (See figures 15–19)

We have a noncanonical saying of Jesus, "Whoever is near me is near to the fire, and whoever is far from me is far from the Kingdom."[18] This is, of course, a formulation which has much to do with Neoplatonic or Neopythagorean teaching. The life-giving warmth of the fire, the source of life, or the life-giving water are terms used in the philosophy of the Stoics.[19] They convey the idea of the primordial warmth which is the eternal living fire of Heraclitus, the source of life.[20] The medieval alchemists

---

[18] See *Gospel of Thomas*, log. 82/17–19.

[19] The stoics belonged to a school of thought "stoicism" that flourished in Greek and Roman antiquity. They put a high ideal on human conduct characterized by tranquillity of mind and certainty of moral worth. The stoics did hold that emotions like fear or passionate love either were, or arose from, false judgements. The later stoics of Roman imperial times, Seneca and Epictetus, emphasize the doctrines that the sage is utterly immune to misfortune and that virtue is sufficient for happiness. Dirk Baltzly (2000), "Stoicism," in *The Stanford Encyclopedia of Philosophy* (winter ed.), Edward N. Zalta, ed.

[20] Heraclitus, also spelled Heracleitus (ca. 540–480 BC) was a Greek philosopher born from Ephesus, Anatolia (now Selçuk, Turkey), conceived that the basic material principle of an orderly universe was fire. He is mostly remembered for his famous analogy of life to a river: "Upon those who step into the same rivers different and ever different waters flow down," illustrating the persistence of unity despite change. D. W. Graham (2011), "Heraclitus," in *The Stanford Encyclopedia of Philosophy* (summer ed.), E. N. Zalta, ed. Jung was especially attracted by the philosophy of Heraclitus and had a copy of Hermann Diels's *Fragments of the Presocratics*. In this he underlined the phrases in Heraclitus fragments 41, "wisdom resides in unity," and 45, "you will never find the boundaries of the soul, whether you travel every road, so deep is the ground." Shamdasani, 2012, 19. He also carved in a sentence by Heraclitus in his stone at Bollingen, a stone inspired by the *lapis*, the alchemist's stone: "Time is a child—playing like a child—playing a board game—the kingdom of the child." *MDR*, 254.

Figure 19. The editor could not identify this mandala.

also said that aqua nostra, our particular water, *aqua non vulgi*, the water not of the vulgar, was the everlasting water, the source of life, and was the same as the fire. So they say literally, "Aqua nostra est ignis," meaning, "our water is fire." It is the water of life which is at the same time fire. You remember certain pages in the Gospels that bear out what I say.

Now this fire looked at from a symbolical point of view is the outburst of passion; it is psychical intensity. Passion is intensity; it is of high value. Things are "hot" when they are urgent or impressive or difficult. Then you use such a term as *fire*. You see we are getting into a whole world of ideas and symbols which express the basic facts of life, namely, on the one side remoteness from the spring, remoteness from life, a low tension of life, little warmth; on the other side, an intensity of life, fire of life, flowing water of life, movement, vital energy, health, heightened feeling of existence. But a full life involves risk, danger; for whoever is near to the fire might get burnt; whoever is near to the water might get drowned. And now all of these ideas are most probably constellated in the unconscious mind of our dreamer.

In the next dream, the ninth, he is with his father again, meaning that he takes refuge with the father.[21] "I am a little child." You see we always become little children when things threaten to get hot. When we are in danger of getting into hot water, we prefer to be like children and act as if we were quite innocent, keeping on the safe side of things. Then one is not, of course, in possession of one's full responsibility; one has taken refuge with authority, with father, with the laws; and one is a perfectly good child. So here he is with the father, and the father is on a peculiar errand. He takes the son to an old-fashioned pharmacy, where very precious things, compounds, medicines, of course, healing stuff, can be bought at a very cheap price. Above all a particular water can be bought for almost nothing. They go there and buy some of that water, and his father tells him a long story of the country where the water originates. After having heard the story, the patient is in a train crossing the Rubicon.

Now the pharmacy in our days is the place where all the terminology of alchemy is encountered; in old-fashioned pharmacies you can still discover the divine stone, the *lapis divinus*. I don't know whether that is so in the English pharmacopeia, but in Switzerland we still have such terms. The old alchemists say you can buy that particular water at a very cheap price. The stone then is this *aqua permanens*, which so long as it is water is not yet stone and is sold publicly at a very cheap price. It is said that if it were generally known that this *aqua permanens* is that water out of which our most precious stone is made or is kindled or is generated, the merchants would not sell so much of it because they would realize what it was worth. This is the wonderful water, the miraculous water, that can be bought everywhere, found everywhere, and has no value. If one should know what it is worth, nobody would sell it because it is the most precious thing. It is also said, as I have already mentioned, that the precious prima materia is thrown out into the street, *lapis in via*, the stone is found on the road, *ejectus*, "thrown out." Prima materia is also very cheap in money value.

---

[21] Cf. "Dream Symbols," nr. 14, p. 142, and CW 12, nr. 14, par. 158. M 14 {0127}: "Visit to the pharmacy with the father; travel with train along the river Rubicon," April 29, 1932, CDM.

This is the kind of symbol that we find in the fifth chapter of my book on "types," where I speak of Spitteler's *Prometheus*.[22] In that story Pandora, daughter of the gods, realizes the misery and suffering of mankind and makes up her mind to create a wonderful, healing, miraculous jewel, a medicine to bring to earth to heal suffering mankind. So she brings down this jewel, more precious than any, and hides it under a tree. As Buddha is born under a tree, and the world is filled with the miraculous light of his birth, so the world is filled with the miraculous light of the jewel. A boy finds it and thinks it is beautiful. People advise him to take it to the high priest. The high priest thinks it is very pagan, probably immoral, and rejects it. Then the boy goes to the president of the Academy of Fine Arts, who says it is in bad taste. He goes next to the goldsmith, who says, "No, no, the metal is not even good." And the peasants who accompanied him and thought he ought to get a good price for it beat him up because they got nothing, and they finally throw Pandora's jewel out into the road. After they have gone, the wandering Jew comes along. He thinks it may have value and puts it in his pocket, where it stays for five hundred years longer. Nobody has really known its worth. That is the story of the stone cheap and valueless to those who do not know what it is.

You can see how the majesty of our conscious has risen out of the modest background of the unconscious, for the prima materia is everywhere; it is the cheapest thing in the world, on the earth, and nobody thinks of it. Yet it contains nothing less than the source of life. So you see his father, as the traditional mind, contains really the whole story, beginning I do not know when, in that century, before our era. And through this traditional mind, the story has been handed down throughout the ages. In many countries it is the story of the precious jewel. It is in their legends, in their hymns, in their sacred teachings, always the same old story. It is never understood, therefore it must be eternally told again. It is the story of the origin of the water, the story of that land in which the water originates. When the patient realizes the extraordinary importance of this story, the real meaning of it, he crosses the Rubicon. That was what Caesar did when he made up his mind to take the final step of his career; he had to decide to cross the Rubicon. So we use that metaphor when we make a fateful decision, make up our minds to go across, saying, "I will risk it." He actually dives when he makes up his mind, saying, "I will go for it. I will risk the adventure. I am now for it." This is indubitably

---

[22] Jung discusses the story of Pandora in the chapter "A Comparison of Spitteler's with Goethe's Prometheus," CW 6, par. 295.

the first moment in his analysis when he almost consciously makes up his mind to continue, to stick to it.

In the next dream, the tenth, there are four people in a boat traveling down the river.[23] They are floating down the river, following its course, that is, they are following the river of life, the protection of the water, following the fire, whatever the risk may be. And those four people are his ego, who is himself, the father, a certain friend, a man he knows very well, and the anima, the unknown woman.

Now in this instance, what is the proportion, the chance of the unconscious? What do you say? The unconscious has the chance of one to three. Three are on his side, and where did they come from? What do you think? It is very important. Three are on his side, and they have come because they took the chance. He made up his mind to cross the Rubicon, to risk it for better or for worse. Instantly the unconscious is on his side. "Well chosen! We are for you, except for that unknown woman." One does not know what she is going to do; however, the unconscious is reduced to one. He is three. He is now in possession of an important part of the unconscious. If he keeps on like that, he has power; he lives. But it might be that should he grow uncertain, get afraid, he could lose two souls right away; then it would again be one against three, and the unconscious could play a trick upon him and take him up into the air. He can be pulled down again, but to put his head under water, that is, not to keep conscious of the situation, only makes him do something terribly foolish. He is a victim if he does not choose to live, but now he is a living man, a Caesar who makes up his mind for better or worse with the uncertainty, the risk represented by that treacherous or doubtful anima. Well, one cannot say too much about her. She does not talk and is not talked to; in other words, he has no connection with her, that particular element of the unconscious. We wind up today with a very positive situation, and we will look then tomorrow to see what is going to happen to this achievement.

---

[23] Cf. "Dream Symbols," nr. 15, p. 142, and CW 12, nr. 15, par. 162. M 15 {0142}: "Elderly man travelling on a river with a young woman," May 10, 1932, CDM.

Lecture 6

Ladies and gentlemen: Yesterday I told you the dream, the tenth, of the four people traveling down a river in a boat.[1] This dream shows us that for the time being the dreamer is three to one, which means that on his side are three figures of the conscious, with only one figure representing the unconscious. His conscious personality moves along with or agrees with the unconscious. But one-fourth of his conscious personality is still left out of consideration. This does not mean that it is necessarily against him; it could be with him, because the majority is on his side; but it is possible that this one-fourth is against him. We cannot tell, but the outcome will show. One part of the consciousness, and only the part with which the dreamer has no contact, is personified by an individual who is more or less strange to him. It is the unknown woman whose relation to the others is always uncertain. This marks her as the personification of the collective unconscious.

Now in the next dream, the eleventh, there are many people walking around the edge of a square, anticlockwise.[2] The dreamer himself, to his amazement, is not in the center but somewhere on the side, and he is naturally interested in that center which is apparently empty. But a peculiar idea dawns upon him concerning this whole circumambulation, namely, that the gibbon is going to be reconstructed. The gibbon, you know, is an ape, a so-called anthropoid. Here the dream comes to an end.

Traveling down a river, as the previous dream said, means following the natural course of things, the Tao, as one would say in Chinese philosophy, following the line of potential energy, the path of least resistance. There is no particular effort about it; the boat is carried along by the movement of the water. This corresponds to a psychological condition in which there is no resistance to the normal development of things. The

---

[1] This lecture was held on September 25, 1936.
[2] Cf. "Dream Symbols," nr. 16, p. 143, and CW 12, nr. 16, par. 164. M 16 {0143}: "Walking the square. The Gibbon will be reconstructed," May 11, 1932, CDM. In *PsA* Jung has added a long passage on the squaring of the circle as an alchemical motif. CW 12, par. 165.

dreamer is just giving way and trusting that this natural flow will carry him to the right place. It is like the advice that Christ gives to his disciples in the saying which I quoted from the Oxyrhynchus Papyrus.[3] There He says that the animals and the fowls of the air, the fishes of the sea, are those who will show the way to the Kingdom. Or it is like the parable of the lilies in the field; they take no care, yet God provides for them.

So here it is the natural course of the water that is carrying him along. It is curious that a man who has a Christian education, a thoroughly Western white man, should use a simile which is absolutely Eastern, Chinese, in nature. The unconscious frequently uses language or similes that really belong to the East, not that there need be any kind of direct connection, but it is an illustration of the compensatory character of the unconscious. The Chinese mind in many ways represents the unconscious of the West. I often wonder whether many Western traits might not be discovered in the composition of the Chinese unconscious. I am not sure about it, but it is quite certain that our unconscious contains a lot of Chinese ways, manners, and similes, and so forth. This does not mean that these things are really Chinese, but simply that China has developed those principles which we call principles of the unconscious mind.

Now this movement leads him to a particular situation, namely, to the square. The square is again the temenos, that sacred or delimited space, in which rituals are carried out, a mysterious place. Usually in the temenos is the temple or the place of initiation or the fountain of the piscina,[4] the place of spiritual transformation, of magic rebirth or renewal. So you see the river leads him to this place, and this place corresponds to the idea of the Kingdom, or of the City. As the Oxyrhynchus Papyrus says, "Know thyself," learn to know, or try to know, thyself, make the effort to know thyself, because you are the city, which means yourself, the Self in you. The Self to which you belong, in which you belong, is the city, the square city. This peculiar square, this mandala, is also very often represented as a city, for example, the city of Brahma Meru, and the heavenly Jerusalem.[5] Also I have told you that the Monogenes in the Coptic treatise is called the city, the city with four gates. The four gates of that city symbolize the four

---

[3] See above.

[4] Piscina: in this case Jung must mean the stone vessel having a drain that leads directly to the ground, located near an altar of a church, and used for disposing of water from ablutions.

[5] This description of a city resembles Jung's mandala painting of a golden castle that he made in 1928. See *RB*, 163. It is also reproduces in his commentary on the Secret of the Golden Flower, where he presents it as a European mandala. Wilhelm and Jung, 1962 [1931], 137. Cf. *CW* 13, p. 56/A10.

limbs of the Monogenes, who is really a sphairos, an all-round, a fourfold being, with four limbs or four members. He could therefore be described in this form.

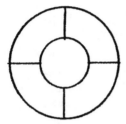

This is the form in which medieval alchemistic philosophy also represents what they call the *pelicanus noster*. Now the *pelicanus* is an alchemistic vessel used for certain kinds of distillation. It is a vessel of about this form.

The vapors which are developed become concentrated here (a), and flow back into the liquid. This is an opus circulatorium, that is, the process repeats itself continuously. It is called *pelicanus* because the pelican is said to rip open its own breast with its beak in order to draw blood to feed its young; therefore it is also one of the early symbols for Christ. Christ is often represented as a pelican in its nest, feeding the young with its blood. The central place (b) which is the miraculous place of rebirth is called the Mediator, that is, of course, the Redeemer, the mediator between God and man.

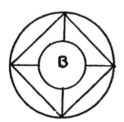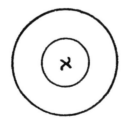

And it is said that four rivers flow out from the inner ocean, or the inner vessel into the ocean of the world, and return from the ocean into the center again. These are the emanating forces of the Chinese mandala I showed you yesterday; and the place at which the coming back, the return from the world, is initiated, is the dwelling place of the deity. This is the dweller, and this is the house of the dweller. "He is the house and the dweller in the house," as the Gnostics say. These ideas are well known practically as far back as the seventeenth century. You still find them in certain Latin tracts.

This is the kingdom to which the animals lead or to which the river flows. When you follow the river you might think that you would get nowhere, that you would be in a state of confusion; but that is only the case if you get into a panic. If you can hold to yourself you will land at that place where everything comes to rest. You will reach that center which is you or in which you are contained. This does not mean that it will be a particularly agreeable place; it can be a very hot place, as the pelicanus shows, for the pelicanus was heated, and it had sometimes hot water inside.

The idea of the square space starts, as you see in these dreams, from the fact that there are four people. You would place them like this and they would naturally form a square which you would surround with a circle.

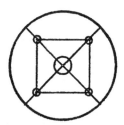

There you have the *quadratus circuli* mandala with the container or vessel, the pelicanus, in the center. This is the most simple form of the mandala. If you connect these four points, then you have the cross, so the basis of the mandala is the cross. There are, of course, irregular mandalas also, but they are very rare. In Mahayana Buddhism, examples showing three or five partitions are known; also you occasionally find three or five partitions in individual cases, sometimes even quite irregular mandalas, which however always denote gravely disturbed conditions. The three-partitioned mandala usually symbolizes a transitory or preparatory state. It is chiefly a development of consciousness, and is usually accompanied by certain disturbances because the fourth is excluded. You find this kind of situation illustrated in the Tantric Yoga, also in the second part of *Faust*. The question of three to one arises also in alchemy. There is always trouble in getting the three and the one together, as you can readily understand. That is just the trouble, to get the fourth into the gathering. The three go together, but the number four is difficult.[6]

The people in the dream are circumambulating the square. They are walking around the edge of the city, and they are walking anticlockwise. This circumambulation is a magic rite which has the purpose of making the center strong. To make something strong is primitive language, meaning to make it healthy, to give it medicine power, fertility, efficiency, prestige. So you make a circle around things. You move in a circle around the center, or around a person, which means concentration of attention upon the center and the heaping up of *mana*, or medicine power, in it.[7] You know that this is also an ordinary means used in religious rituals, a sort of concentrated effort to increase the power of the center. For example, circumambulation is one of the magic rituals used by peasants. There are still such rites in existence in Europe. In a certain part of Switzerland a procession rides around the whole estate of the community. All those taking part are on horseback. The priest leads the cortège. This is done in the spring in order to maintain and increase the fertility of the soil. By circumambulation, the people heap upon it, as it were, the grace of heaven, or in primitive language mana.

So you see when these people circumambulate the square then something must occur inside; something must happen. They are doing it for a certain purpose, and something must arise not from the conscious but from the unconscious, because the movement is going to the left, anticlockwise, and this movement to the left is *a parte sinistra*, to the "sinister side." The left also means unfavorable, uncanny, because the left side is the dark side, the unconscious side, the heart side, the emotional side, while the right side is really the right hand, the conscious. The right hand executes the conscious will, the left, the contrary. The left side is dark, as a

---

[6] Pauli later expressed that he was struggling with this problem of the three and the four when working on his exclusion principle in the early 1920s, for which he was awarded the Nobel Prize in 1945. "My way to the exclusion principle had to do with the difficult transition from three to four, namely with the necessity to ascribe to the electron a fourth degree of freedom (soon explained as 'spin') beyond the three translational ones." Pauli to Fierz, October 3, 1951 (1286), PLC IV/1.

[7] Mana: among Melanesian and Polynesian peoples, a supernatural force or power that may be ascribed to persons, spirits, or inanimate objects. Mana may be either good or evil, beneficial or dangerous. See in particular: CW 7, pars. 374–406.

rule, of dark omen. It is as if by an anticlockwise movement, toward the unconscious, something is produced in the conscious. Therefore this antique anticlockwise movement was used in black magic.

This circumambulation is a concentration visibly carried out. The circular movement always looks to the center, so it is an act of intense concentration upon that center, and whenever you give your exclusive attention to something, that something, whatever it is, develops a tendency to change, to transform, to move. For instance if you have a certain image in your mind and you concentrate your attention upon it for a while then it begins to move, something happens, you will do something with it, and it will do something, out of which you will develop a whole series of images. This is a sort of Yoga practice which we also use as a technique in analysis.[8] I think many of you know about it.

The ordinary Yoga also has such a concentrating purpose. The Mandala pictures in Buddhism are used in this way.

There are very exact descriptions as to how to make these drawings, which must have the right kind of color, form, design, and the like. There

---

[8] Jung developed the method of active imagination in the winter of 1913 as he "deliberately gave free rein to his fantasy thinking and carefully noted what ensued." It was not until much later that he gave it the name "active imagination." In the seminar of 1925 he uses the term in talking to a selected audience (see Jung, McGuire, Shamdasani, 2011, xii). In his published works before 1936 the method is often described without using the term explicitly (see, for instance, "The Relation between the Ego and the Unconscious," from 1928 [CW 7, par. 366, "fantasy of intensely visual character ... a vision perceived by intense concentration"] or in "The Aims of Psychotherapy" [1931, CW 16, pars. 98–108]). In his lecture "Yoga and the West," published in February 1936, he defines active imagination as "a special training for switching off consciousness, at least to a relative extent, thus giving the unconscious contents a chance to develop." This might be the first time he defines the concept publicly in print (CW 11, par. 875). The same year he gives the lecture "The Concept of the Collective Unconscious" to the Abernethian Society at Saint Bartholomew's Hospital in London, which is published in October in the hospital's *Journal* 44. There he describes it as "a sequence of fantasies produced by deliberate concentration." CW 9/I, par. 101. Jung acknowledges that he waited a long time before he decided to write about active imagination "to assure myself that these things ... really are produced spontaneously and were not suggested to the patient by my own fantasy." CW 9/I, par. 623 (1950).

are, of course, different mandalas, but they always have the same pattern. There are also different colors, changing in accordance with the meaning of the ritual. For example, the usual mandala in Mahayana Buddhism has a circle of fire beyond which an outermost circle represents all the horrors of the burial ground, where corpses are burned by devils or demons in the form of animals. This means that if you step out of that temenos you get into a state of dismemberment, into a state of disintegration. Whenever you get out of yourself, get out of your circle, then you are beside yourself, dismembered. When, for example, one side becomes identical with an emotion, that is, with the fire of emotion, you are simply disintegrated. In Buddhism the mandala is used as a means of reaching the center in order to become identified with the deity, as I have already explained. The important thing is that this ritual is always carried out in exactly the same way.

In the East you are taught how to make a mandala which has its traditional forms, its dogma, et cetera. You are not allowed to let your mind wander and invent anything different. The same thing is true of our Western Yoga. In the Catholic Church we have the Yoga in the Exercitia of Ignatius Loyola,[9] in the Jesuit Order. There you are taught to meditate, to contemplate traditional images or forms, such as the suffering of Christ and such things, and you are not allowed to let your mind wander from it. You have to concentrate your mind upon this particular form which is traditional and inevitable in a way; you really have to press your mind into that form. That is done all over the East; for all Yoga forms must follow a particular kind of pattern. In India usually the guru tells the pupil how to meditate, and also gives the pattern on which to meditate. You know in our deplorable imitation of these Eastern things, in theosophy,[10] we do the same thing. Even in the Rama Krishna[11] movement, the most

---

[9] Saint Ignatius of Loyola (1491–1622), Spanish theologian and one of the most influential figures in the Catholic Reformation of the sixteenth century, founder of the Society of Jesus (Jesuits) in Paris in 1534. In 1939–40 Jung dedicated his seminars at the ETH (Swiss Federal Institute of Technology) to a commentary on the spiritual exercises of Ignatius of Loyola, which followed from his commentary on Eastern texts. These are in preparation for publication by the Philemon Foundation. On this, see also Jung, 1996.

[10] Theosophy, from Greek *theos* ("god") and *sophia* ("wisdom"), occult movement originating in the nineteenth century with roots that can be traced to ancient Gnosticism and Neoplatonism. One of the founders of the Theosophical Society in London was Helena Blavatsky (1831–91). The international New Age movement of the 1970s and 1980s originated among independent theosophical groups in the United Kingdom.

[11] The Ramakrishna movement or mission was founded in Calcutta by Swami Vivekânanda (1863–1902) in 1897 with the purpose to spread the teachings of Vedanta as embodied in the life of the Hindu saint Ramakrishna (1836–86) and to improve the social conditions of the Indian people. Ramakrishna encompassed the Hindu tenet that all religions are paths to

modern form of Yoga practice, the same form used ten thousand years ago is still followed exactly. With us in analysis it is quite different. When you step beyond the universal Christian Church into the psychological movement, naturally you have no traditional forms and have to make the primordial experience; you have to take what the unconscious produces.

In this case I could not bring the patient back into the Catholic Church, for he was already beyond it and no longer had access to it. So his unconscious moved on and produced those things that have always been produced everywhere in the world, this peculiar pattern in which the animal instincts are trapped. We shall talk of that still further today.

The idea in the dream of our patient is that the gibbon, the ape-man, has to be reconstructed. Usually, or in nearly all cases of such ethnological mandalas, that which is in the center is not to be reconstructed; for it is already there and is a symbol of the deity. There is Shiva, or Buddha, or any kind of a great teacher in the center, and man becomes more or less spiritualized in growing into or identifying with that deity. Thus the idea of the gibbon in the center is rather paradoxical, even grotesque. The gibbon that is not there yet has to be reconstructed first. What does that mean? It can only mean that the archaic man, the ape-man, is going to be reconstructed, as if that being had to be called back into existence. This is a development which is quite against our expectation, and against our ideals. We don't like the idea that a gibbon or any kind of gorilla should be reconstructed.[12]

So you see something happens which I alluded to yesterday when I told you how old Moses who traveled to find the source of life and met with that Green God who said to him, "You are not able to follow me." But when Moses insisted on following him, he experienced marvelous things. He walked with Chidher, and after a while a nice young man came toward them, and Chidher went to that young man and killed him on the spot by strangling him. Moses got into a state naturally and said, "What are you doing? Here is a perfectly nice young man, and you have killed him." Chidher said, "Naturally you cannot understand." And they went on. After a while they came to the sea beside which was a village. In the harbor were two fishermen with their little fleet. Chidher glanced over these boats, then went down to the shore and bored a hole in every vessel

---

the same goal. Ramakrishna Mission. Jung had copies of several of Vivekânanda's works in his library. Jung, 1996.

   [12] Jung has expanded the text surrounding this dream extensively, compared to Eranos version (CW 12, pars. 172–73, 175).

so that they all sank. At this, Moses flew into a rage and said, "How can you do that? That is their only means of livelihood!" Chidher replied: "I told you, you could not follow me." Moses said, "Yes, of course—sorry—I will go with you." They walk on. Evening comes. They come into a noisy town and there seek shelter for the night. The people, however, are quite inhospitable infidels and chase them away from their doors so that they are forced, weary wanderers that they are, to leave the town at the other end. When they leave the gate of the city and go out into the desert again, Chidher looks up at the wall and says, "This wall needs repair," and goes to it and rebuilds the wall of the city of the infidels. Then Moses is through with him. "Now you have killed that young man, sunk the ships, built the wall of the city of the infidels; how can you explain that?" he asks. Chidher replies, "I told you you could not follow me; but now by the grace of the All Merciful I will explain to you. That young man was the son of believers in Allah, very righteous people, and he was on his way to commit a crime that would have brought great shame on his family, so I killed him first. That fleet of the fishermen was threatened by pirates. Pirates had put into the harbor on the same day seeking the fleet. In the evening the fishermen simply pulled up the boats I had sunk and saved them all. And didn't you notice that at the foot of the town of the infidels there was a little hut where two brothers lived, true servants of Allah, the only ones in town? The wall was crumbling. That night it would have fallen down and killed those two, so that I saved their lives."

There are many tales in religious literature. This way of the Green One, you can say the green river, or the way that plants grow or animals move, is by no means something chaotic or rebellious or wrong. It leads you to the right place. If you are shocked by the idea that the gibbon is to be reconstructed, you simply don't understand what it means. You know that center has a peculiar name in the Taostic or Syncretistic philosophy that began in China somewhere between AD 800 and 900. The center around which one circles or around which the light of consciousness circulates is called the land of the ancestors. This corresponds in the West to the place which is thought of as a vessel or bladder or womb where life is generated. This is the place in which the ancestral souls are collected. What are ancestral souls psychologically? The souls of which we consist. We have certain traits from the mother, others from the father. You have a nose perhaps from the grandmother, eyes from the grandfather, certain traits of character from a great-grandfather or uncle. Somewhere out of your ancestral tree, often reaching back for many centuries, certain elements may remain. Take for instance, the peculiar lower lip of the Spanish Hapsburg line, or the peculiar insanity in that line. There are many such cases known where certain peculiarities are transmitted from age to age. There is, for example, an English family by the name of Whitelock. Their peculiarity is that they all develop a streak of white hair in the middle of the head, from which the name Whitelock is derived. I have already told you that in certain cases there are such ancestral inclusions. If you had a unique ancestor, you might inherit that peculiarity, which you could not assimilate. It would then form a lump in your psychology and would cause you all sorts of trouble.

There are examples of how the psyche is made up. It is like a sack of grain or a handful of coins, a collection of inherited units, which primitives call ancestral souls. You are not conscious of that collection of units, but your unconscious projects it out into space, and then you behold the ghosts of your ancestors in the circle around you. The ancestors form, of course, a multitude, and as long as you are the victim of such a multitude, as long as you are such a multitude, you don't know who you are; no one knows. You are not a personality, because you are unconscious of a definite ego. Therefore primitives felt it to be an absolute necessity to compel everyone to pass through a kind of initiation in which they were given a particular personality. In this way they were redeemed from a state of disintegration, of unconsciousness, into a state of definite spiritual existence in which they were given new, different names, secret names. In Christianity, through baptism you are understood to receive the faculty of the vision of God, eternal life, et cetera. You receive certain qualities which those people who don't experience initiation don't possess. The missionaries in the Rondo country of eastern Africa, by telling the natives that the initiation ceremonies were all wrong, have simply helped the cowardly among the boys and girls to avoid passing through the rather painful initiation. Then the other Negroes of the tribe called these cowards "animals," because they believe that only that person who has passed through an initiation where he has experienced a kind of metaphoric death and rebirth is a *man* or is human.

These initiations are, of course, exceedingly drastic, but for primitive man something drastic is necessary, otherwise no impression at all is made. It can't be done with hymns and organs. Therefore, the British government very wisely tries not to interfere with such things. But the influence of the missionaries in that respect is not very favorable, I'm afraid. It undermines the morale of the primitive. By far the best kind of government for him is a military government. That is what the primitive understands thoroughly—when man meets man squarely. Some of the British officers in charge of lonely posts are really very fine people. I know a case in southern Sudan. A British officer in charge of a vast country of absolutely wild Dinka tribes had to make an expedition against them. He went there with a military escort. Then the chief of that hostile tribe came to him and said, "It is unfair of you; you have machine guns and rifles; we have only spears to fight with. Fight us with spears. Fight with me." So the European took a spear and fought a duel with the Negro. The natives had pledged their word that if the white man should win the duel then they would burn up their villages and leave the country.[13] And they did so. That is education. But the sweet stuff these mission stations produce is no good. Religion must belong to a certain blood and soil; the primitives can't obey something which is not even fully understood by the white man. How can we do missionary work? It is terribly ridiculous. It is more than ridiculous; it is a shame, because we are not Christians at all. Look at Europe that calls itself Christian!

In the dream before us, the meaning of the reconstruction of that archaic man remains completely dark. We must therefore go to the next dream, the twelfth.[14] Here he is now definitely in theatrical surroundings. There is again the delimited space which is like a stage, and there is stage scenery representing a house. The whole scene, whatever he sees around him, has a theatrical character. And there are also people about. Somebody mentions the name of Bernard Shaw. The play going on is very interesting and is enacting something in the future; it is a sort of anticipation of the far future. When he looks around he sees an inscription over the door of the house written in both English and German: "This is the universal Catholic Church, the Church of the Lord, and all those who feel that they are tools in the hands of the Lord may enter," and then in smaller print, "The Church is founded by Jesus and Paul." And he has a feeling as though that were a sort of firm, "Jesus and Paul," and as if by mentioning those names, one meant, "This is a very old firm, founded in the year zero." Now I will read a passage directly expressing a conversation that takes place in the dream:

> I said to my friend who accompanied me, "Now come, we must see that." And he replied, "I don't understand why so many people must be together in order to have a religious experience." And I said,

---

[13] The author Blake Burleson suggests that Jung became familiar with this story while traveling down the Nile in February 1926, passing by the village of the Dinkas. Burleson, 2005, 219n2.

[14] Cf. "Dream Symbols," nr. 17, p. 148, and CW 12, nr. 17, par. 176. M 17 {0151}: "The church dream": a church on a stage. In the end popular music, May 15, 1932, CDM. In *PsA* Jung has added a passage on the lack of the Dionysian element in Christianity. Cf. CW 12, par. 182.

"Well, being a Protestant you never will understand it."[15] And there is an unknown woman and she says, "Right you are," or "You are right." And then he becomes aware that there is again some advertising or an announcement printed on the wall which says: "Soldiers, when you feel that you are standing in the power of the Lord, avoid talking to Him directly. The Lord is not accessible through words. We advise you urgently not to arrange any discussion whatever about the attributes of the Lord. It is futile because the valuable and important is ineffable. Signed: Pope...." (Name illegible)

Then we enter. The interior is similar to a mosque, particularly to the Hagia Sophia, the great Byzantine mosque in Constantinople. There are no chairs or benches. It is a beautiful space, most impressive, with no images decorating the walls, but only framed sayings from the Koran [That is in reality so.] One of those sayings reads: "Don't flatter your benefactor." The woman that has accompanied me suddenly begins to weep and says, "Then nothing remains." I said, "I think this is all perfectly in order." Then she disappears. First I am in a somewhat unfavourable position; I cannot see anything of the ceremony going on because there is a pillar right in front of my eyes. Then I change my position and see a whole crowd of people. I don't belong to them and I am standing aside. But I see them very clearly and see their faces individually. All say *uni sono*: "We confess that we stand in the power of the Lord, the Kingdom of Heaven is within us." This is spoken very solemnly three times, then the organ plays a sort of Bach fugue with choir singing. The original text is omitted. I only hear repeatedly the words, "Everything else is just paper." It means "has no vital influence or importance." After this music is over a second part of the meeting begins in the way students hold their meetings. First there is the business part, when speeches and official transactions take place; then comes the second part and that is described by a word that cannot be translated—*Gemütlichkeit*—where all present drink and smoke and just have fun. Those people who were formerly there in the religious performance, although they are still in the Sofia, are very nice and joyful, quite human and well balanced. They walk and talk together,

---

[15] In 1951 Pauli returns to this dream and the motif of the Protestant friend and links this to the missing relationship to the feminine principle in Protestantism as well as in Western science. The missing feminine principle in Western science is according to Pauli a failure to encompass a holistic view of the relationship of psyche and matter. Pauli to Jaffé, November 11, 1951 (1304), PLC IV/i, 422.

and greet each other, while wine and all sorts of refreshments are offered from the Episcopal College of Priests. One even drinks the health of the Church and wishes the Church a further good development, many happy returns, et cetera. There is great pleasure and satisfaction over the fact that new members have been received into the society. In celebration of this a megaphone or radio begins to play a certain chanson with the refrain: "*Karl ist jetzt auch dabei.*"[16] This refers really to something that is sung in music halls. The priest explains to me that these somewhat secular amusements are officially conceded and admitted, that we have to adapt somewhat to American methods. [Don't you remember our reception yesterday evening?] We have to deal with such masses of people that it becomes quite inevitable to adapt to circumstances, but we are different from the American church principally because we have a pronounced anti-ascetic leaning.

Then he wakes up and feels a tremendous relief. I'm sorry I can't enter into every detail of this very beautiful and most witty dream. I must leave much of it to your own imagination. I have to restrict my attention to the specific symbolism, namely, the symbol of the temenos, and what is going on there. We learn something important in this dream, namely, that the temenos is a very sacred space. Our assumption that it is a sacred place is verified because it is here explained to be the Hagia Sofia—Greek for Saint Sophia—which is wisdom.[17] Also according to a certain sect of the early Church, Sofia was the mother of Christ. Mary was Sofia. That means Mary was the mother of Jesus, and Sofia was the mother of Christ. And Sofia is wisdom. So the sacred wisdom, which is the center of the temenos, is like the *Rosarium Philosophorum* or rose garden of the philosophers.

Then we learn something else, namely, that there are two aspects of that experience, one perfectly solemn and quite serious, the other *gemütlich*, a sort of social evening. Yet the wine which is offered comes from the College of Priests of the Episcopal Church. It is highly official, ecclesiastical wine, presumably the wine of the Communion. Yet it is for thoroughly worldly amusement so that the priest has to explain that this—well, has

---

[16] German: Karl (anyone) has become one of the group—he is now "one of us."

[17] Cathedral built at Constantinople (now Istanbul, Turkey) in the sixth century under the direction of the Byzantine emperor Justinian I. The original church on the site of the Hagia Sophia is said to have been built by Constantine I in 325 on the foundations of a pagan temple. It was rebuilt after a fire in 404 and enlarged by the Roman emperor Constans I. The church was burned again in the Nika insurrection of January 532, a circumstance that gave Justinian I an opportunity to envision a splendid replacement.

to do with American methods, of organizing masses of people, great masses. Also Americans play a particular role in this man's mind. The dream occurred when America began to control currency, when the devaluation of the dollar, which made a tremendous impression on the world, took place.[18] It was just as if the president of the United States had declared that from now on he was going to control the weather all over the earth, or something equally near to God. It seemed to us an extraordinary hubris and exaggeration of the power of a human being that he should presume to control Deus Terrae, the earth god of the yellow metal. So the American mind or mentality has that aspect to my patient, namely, an assertion of man over against the blind or the foreseeing but incomprehensible mind of fate. It was to him as if the president of the United States was representing the brain trust of the whole of America and as if he and the peoples of the world were going to compete with the divine mind, or the dark fate. So you see when the priest says we have to adapt to American methods this means we have to take into account that man has a consciousness, a belief in his conscious method, and it is this that enables him almost to compete with God. Therefore we must give a lot of credit to so-called common sense and even to an exaggerated consciousness of power, because it is a fact that mind, its rationalism, its methods and purposes assumes such a large part of the management of our world that we cannot overlook it. We cannot put ourselves entirely under the

---

[18] It is not clear what this refers to. This dream is dated March 15, 1932. On April 5, 1933, President Roosevelt, acting under the sweeping authority passed to him by Congress on March 9, invoked his authority to make it unlawful to own or hold gold coins, gold bullion, or gold certificates (Executive Order 6102). The export of gold for purposes of payment was also outlawed, except under license from the Treasury. It required all persons to deliver on or before May 1, 1933, all but a small amount of gold coin, gold bullion, and gold certificates owned by them to the Federal Reserve, in exchange for $20.67 per troy ounce. Violation of the order was punishable by fine up to $10,000 or up to ten years in prison, or both. Most citizens who owned large amounts of gold had it transferred to countries such as Switzerland. The price of gold from the Treasury for international transactions was thereafter raised to $35 an ounce, resulting in an immediate loss for everyone who had been forced to surrender their gold. On January 30, 1934, Roosevelt then implemented the Gold Reserve Act. The day after the passage of the act, President Roosevelt fixed the weight of the dollar at 15.715 grains of gold "nine-tenths fine." The dollar was thereby devalued from $20.67 to one troy ounce of gold to $35.00 to one troy ounce of gold—or 40.94 percent. The Treasury, which had become the possessors of all the nation's gold on the previous day, saw the value of their gold holdings increase by $US2.81 billion. The Treasury now "owned" the gold, and no one else inside the United States was allowed to own any gold except by the express permission of the Treasury. In B. M. Anderson, ed. and trans. (1949), *Economics and the Public Welfare: Financial and Economic History of the United States, 1914–1946* (New York: Van Nostrand).

management of our unconscious, but also we have to believe in the effectiveness of the conscious; for then we can do something about the course of life although we may not be able to control it entirely.

The most serious problem is to be found in the mystery and incomprehensibility of the Divine Will. That is the meaning of the part of the dream where soldiers are admonished not to discuss God, not to know anything about the attributes of God. By these attributes is meant all the things you might possibly say about God, for instance, God is, and God is not; God can only be good; God is the entirely different One; or that God is accessible or inaccessible. It is said that all those things which might be said about God are human assumptions, impertinences, because we cannot say anything about that of which we know absolutely nothing. There is only the subjective experience, and nothing else can tell an individual that he has experienced God. To discuss these matters is not allowed by the dreamer's unconscious. It is futile to discuss these most valuable and most important things because they are ineffable and cannot be formulated. Furthermore, if they are formulated, it is man's work, and it is futile. See how the unconscious speaks to this man in his dream and then you will see the meaning of the confession of that assemblage of people in the church, when they say: "We confess that we are in the power of the Lord," which means that we are overcome by it, that we have no power against it. And then, "The Kingdom of Heaven is within us." This is the confession of one who acknowledges that at times and in certain respects three are against one, as in America one is against three. In other words, sometimes your conscious is on top and ought to be on top. In other moments your conscious is at the bottom and is overcome by the unconscious. Only with such a formulation is it possible to deal with the factors of the unconscious.

The dream we are discussing is very important, and there is quite a lot to be said about it. It is also a difficult dream, and I will try to make it as plain to you as possible. Of course I am not aware of your preparation and readiness to see all the manifold historical allusions in this dream. I shall speak primarily in any case about its more general aspects. In this dream a peculiar contrast appears which is in a way historical, namely, the contrast between the principles of the Dionysian and Christian cults. They were in opposition. The cult of Dionysus is about eight hundred years older than that of Christ and is an orgiastic cult which came from the East and swept over Asia Minor into Greece. A struggle between the principles of the Apollonian and Dionysian religions then took place, and after a pretty long struggle Dionysus became copatron of the oracle of Delphi, which was formerly exclusively the sanctuary of Apollo. Now the Apollonian religion was a highly cultured religion, with measured, definite proportions, and laws, while the Dionysian was a reidentification with the animal, something very wild. As I have already told you there were many women adherents to this latter religion who cultivated a certain ritualistic mania, which is a state of raging, of religious exaltation of a very wild nature. I told you that these women often tore living lambs or goats with their teeth. We learn from Euripides that the cult was in part characterized by the fact that its adherents ate raw meat.[19] A fragment of Euripides reads, "after I had finished the raw-meat-eating meals belonging to the initiations of the Bacchic cult."[20]

When Christianity began in the third century to spread through the Roman Empire under Constantine the Great, it really became the universal Roman Church. At that time it assimilated a great deal from other prevailing religions. It drew chiefly from the cults of Mithra and Attis, but also from the rather numerous Dionysian initiations or mystery cults.[21] We have evidence in Pompeii, for instance, of the existence of cults in which Dionysian initiations were celebrated. Christianity took over many

---

[19] Euripides (ca. 480–406 BC), Greek dramatist.

[20] The correct translation of the fragment that stems from the tragedy *Cretans*, reads:

> "My days have run, the servant I,
> Initiate, of Idaean Jove;
> Where midnight Zagreus roves, I rove;
> I have endured his thunder-cry:
> Fulfilled his red and bleeding feasts;
> Held the Great Mother's mountain flame;
> I am Set Free and named by name
> A Bacchos of the Mailed Priests.
> Robed in pure white I have borne me clean
> From man's vile birth and coffined clay,
> And exiled from my lips always (or away??)
> Touch of all meat where Life hath been."

Euripides and G. Murray, trans. (1991), *The Cretans*, frg. 475, *ap*. Porphyry, *De abstinentia*, IV. 19. See discussion of fragment in J. E. Harrison (1991), *Prolegomena to the Study of Greek Religion*, 3rd ed. (Princeton, NJ: Princeton University Press). See also J. Campbell (2004), *The Hero with a Thousand Faces*, commemorative ed. (Princeton, NJ: Princeton University Press).

[21] Attis (also Atys), a beautiful youth and mythical consort and son of the Great Mother of the Gods (classical Cybele, or Agdistis). Having become enamoured of Attis, Agdistis struck him with frenzy as he was about to be married, with the result that Attis castrated himself and died. He was worshipped in Phrygia, Asia Minor, and later throughout the Roman Empire, where he was made a solar deity in the second century AD. Jung provided an interpretation of the Attis myth in *Symbols of Transformation*, in CW 5, pars. 659–62.

things from the Dionysian cults, as, for instance, the role which wine plays. Here in America is the famous Chalice of Antioch, which was buried during the persecutions of the Christians by the heretic emperor, Julian the Apostate.[22] In the filigree work around the goblet or chalice Christ is seen seated or enthroned, almost suspended, in vines full of grapes, exactly as Saint Augustine was represented in a similar relief. The work is done in typical Dionysian style. Then there are other symbols used by the early Christians such as that of the fish, which also occur in the Dionysian cult. There is an excellent collection of the fish symbols and a discussion of the questions concerning this symbol in Eisler's *Orpheus the Fisher.*[23] Another very important document is the cylinder of Berlin, which is a stone engraved with a crucifix, on which a man is suspended on the cross exactly like Christ, bearing the inscription "Orpheus Bakkikos," the Bacchic Orpheus, a mystery god. Christ has been compared with him in drawings in the catacombs, where he is pictured as taming the wild animals, or the instincts, by his music. Now, Bacchus is the same as Dionysus. Here, in the Berlin cylinder, you have the crucifix and the inscription, Christ-Dionysus-Orpheus, all the same.

That was the age in which things were assimilated. For instance, the origin of the Mass points quite clearly to the cult of Mithra. Excavations have shown it indubitably. You know Masses were unknown to the evangelists. The heathen influences, the religious cloth, the robes, are all ornaments of the Roman pagan priesthood. So close was the similarity in the forms of worship that even educated people of those days regarded Christ as a certain variant of Dionysus. So the early fathers of the church had to

---

[22] Julian the Apostate (331/32–363), Roman emperor from 361 to 363 and a noted philosopher and Greek writer. The Chalice of Antioch is a silver-gilt early Christian chalice made in the early sixth century. It is in the collection of the Metropolitan Museum of Art in New York City.

[23] Robert Eisler (1882–1949), PhD, Austrian Jewish writer on comparative religion, was said to have been a follower of Jung. Eisler was born and educated in Vienna, receiving his doctorate from the University of Vienna in 1904. He subsequently had a successful academic career in Austria and Germany, including time spent as a visiting lecturer in France, Britain, and the United States, until the Anschluss in 1938 when he was interned in Dachau concentration camp. Released shortly before the outbreak of the Second World War, he went to England and continued his research at Oxford and later in London, though his time in Dachau left him in poor health for the rest of his life. His research interests included classical archaeology, art history, and philosophy, as well as various aspects of the history of religious belief and superstition. He advanced the controversial theses that Jesus was a Zealot, i.e., a rebellious political prophet with a penchant for eschatology. There is a collection of his papers at the Warburg Institute in London. See also Jung to Eisler, June 25, 1946, Jung, *Letters*, vol. 1, 427. R. Eisler (1921), *Orpheus—the Fisher: Comparative Studies in Orphic and Early Christian Cult Symbolism* (London: J. M. Watkins).

say something about it; and they denied it, defending the uniqueness of Christ. You see there already existed in antiquity a contrast similar to that in the dream. Christianity was a religion, or is a religion, that goes clockwise, that develops into consciousness. If prescriptions of conscious intents are laid down, the psyche can for a while find satisfaction in these conscious forms and so long as that is possible, it is all right. Then the symbol adequately expresses the unconscious. When we study the dramatic symbolism of the Catholic Church we can see that it expresses the main process of our unconscious. So long as we can press the psyche into a form which works, it is the truth. It is the truth because the dogma expresses the empirical truth about the unconscious. We can translate the whole Catholic dogma into psychological language, and it fits marvelously well.[24] That is why the old fathers were so tremendously busy building up that symbolism, because they felt its expressiveness greatly. It expresses the truth about the basic structures of our mind as other religions do too, and that is where the difficulty comes in. A German Jesuit, a famous man, was once asked whether he would like to meet me. He said, "No, never. I know exactly what he will say; he will say that we are quite right and that everything else is also true." Now you see that point of view was too much for him. The weakness of the Catholic standpoint is that it can never grant that anything else might also be true. Mind you, it is very true that Buddha was also true. Buddhism expresses a basic truth of the mind, otherwise it wouldn't work. It would be dead and dry, if it did not express the living substance of the unconscious.

Now, of course, if you are no more able to press your mind into that form which is quite ready to accept it and express it sufficiently well, then you must accept that other things are also true. Then something else is demanded of you, namely, this development into the unconscious that I have been describing as the anticlockwise movement. You cannot go on with the conscious because you have no forms in consciousness beyond the Christian form into which to press the whole of your soul in a more or less satisfactory way. You cannot put it into science, into art, into politics. These things will not express the kind of experience that comes from your unconscious. It is only the Christian symbolism that contains it. But unless you swallow the whole thing, the virgin birth, the Trinity, and everything else, it does not express your unconscious. If, however, you go beyond Christianity, well then you come into that sphere which was originally swallowed by it, namely, into Dionysian, Mithraic, and Attic symbolism.

---

[24] Jung did this in his essay "Transformation Symbolism in the Mass" (1942), CW 11.

Since the symbols used by these cults are very little understood, nobody can explain what is happening to you, when you touch upon them in dreams, not even the parson.

I know of a parson, though not personally, who had a dream which he gave to a friend and the friend gave it to me. It was a very interesting dream which the parson did not understand and so wanted my interpretation. I do not know how he reacted to my interpretation, but the dream is very good anyhow. This parson, who is in charge of a church, is a man with many interests who really thinks and unfortunately thinks beyond. As a consequence he had some doubts and became restless because he didn't know where to find peace for his mind. He can no more remain in the lap of the church, although he tries to. He is, however, really hanging out of the window. Naturally when you are in such an uncertain, restless, peaceless condition, then the unconscious will most likely say something. It did. He had the following dream: He came to his church not in the daytime, but in the night, which he never had occasion to do. But in the dream he goes there in the night. Now just try to look at his experience not from the conscious but from the instinctual point of view. He enters and suddenly discovers that the whole choir loft behind the altar has crumbled down and that the ruins are quite overgrown with vines, enormous vines full of grapes. The full moon is shining into the church. This was the most wonderful answer from the unconscious. I told him right away, "Well when you have stepped beyond your absolutely male Christianity where the deity is masculine in all its three parts you go back into the past. Here is Luna, the Queen of Night; here is the sign of Dionysus." These things are not terribly far away from the Christian mentality. I do not know whether the dreamer has ever been to Rome, to Saint Peter's, where there is that famous tomb of Saint Peter, with four columns covered with vines. This is really the typical altar of the temple of Dionysus taken over into the church. So you see Dionysus is hidden within. If you step beyond yourself you are in the pagan world; but only your unconscious tells you that you have gone into the Dionysian sphere, into the unconscious that contains the mysteries. It is as if when we go forward, become enlightened or scientific, we really go back into the past. When our conscious mind goes forward in the direction of more consciousness, more science, more rationalism, our unconsciousness goes back into former stages and reveals them. So that dream came to him in typically Dionysian symbolism.

These two religions form an enormous contrast. The Christian goes toward the conscious; the Dionysian goes toward the unconscious, anticlockwise, and leads its adherents to reidentify with the animal man or the half-animal man. The Corybantes of Cybele, the satyrs, the centaurs, panthers, and so forth, all these play a great role in the Dionysian religion.[25] The adherents of this belief transformed themselves into such half-animal beings.

So you see when two such opposites appear in a dream, an enormous conflict between two worlds is stirred. On the one side are men of culture with a world full of learning; on the other side is the world of nature, of the woods and of the animals, where man is still embedded in nature, in the maternal earth. It is the fight between the wind or the heavens, and the earth, between the masculine principle of the Spiritus and the feminine principle of the moon, Luna, and the earth. This conflict is also contained in the symbolism of the church with its unequal rites. You know that the Mother of God, Mary, is not of divine nature. She is the supreme saint but not even an archangel. She represents more or less the female principle. She is defined as the Earth. Saint Augustine says in speaking of Mary, *illa terra nova*, "that virgin earth, or that earth, the virgin, not yet wetted by the rains of spring," and Tertullius mentions that Christ is born of Mary, which means he is born of the earth, which means that the truth is born of the earth, because Mary was the earth. The earth, however, is not contained in deity. It is outside.

So you see when this conflict becomes conscious in such a dream as we have been discussing, or influences the conscious through the dream, it causes a great struggle of the opposites. The animal identification in the code of Dionysus is parallel to the reconstruction of the gibbon in the dream. The unconscious has a tendency to reconstruct the Dionysian cult, one might say. That is, of course, tremendously against our Christian consciousness. The impact of that conflict when it becomes constellated is tremendous as you can well understand. So the unconscious makes an attempt to pull the two opposites together, to reconcile them, and this is already expressed in the choice of the place, the temenos. The Hagia Sophia was originally a Christian church but more recently served as a mosque. At the present time it is used neither as church or mosque, but as a museum.[26] With this peculiar history, the place shows already the reconciliation

---

[25] Corybantes: sons of Apollo and the Muse Thalia, mythical attendants of the ancient Oriental and Greco-Roman deity the Great Mother of the Gods. Satyrs: in Greek mythology, creatures of the wild, part man and part beast, who in classical times were closely associated with the god Dionysus. Satyrs and sileni were at first represented as uncouth men, each with a horse's tail and ears and an erect phallus. The race of centaurs were part horse and part man, dwelling in the mountains of Thessaly and Arcadia.

[26] Hagia Sophia was converted into a museum in 1934.

of the opposites, the Christian and Dionysian religious ideas. It is a remarkable fact that the old mosaics in the Villa dei Misteri in Pompeii were simply painted over and covered with framed sentences from the Koran, and now they are restoring the original mosaics again; it is neither this nor that.[27] It is no longer a church, this place where the hostile religions come together.

In this dream also one can say the Dionysian element is recognized within Christianity, and the whole thing expressed in an extraordinary and paradoxical way. On the one side there is a most solemn reference to the essence of religion, and on the other side, a perfectly harmless social gathering with wine, cakes, and refreshment. There is also a peculiar element, even within the solemn part, of a certain grotesqueness. You know when you read this dream in German, it is terribly funny. I am afraid when translating it into English, I cannot give you the peculiar taste of the German text. It is most witty and funny in the very choice of words.

This means that the two elements, solemnity and grotesqueness, do not hurt each other. According to our text they might be expected to injure each other, but in the cult of Dionysus, for instance, they do not conflict. Grotesqueness as an essential element in nature belongs with solemnity. There are many beasts in nature that do not look solemn; an elephant does not look solemn, a whale, or a poisonous snake, and there are also millions of animals that just look funny. Look at human beings, and you see the whole grotesqueness of nature, and it does not hurt seriousness. We have an idea that what is serious is very serious, only serious. Not so Dionysus. In the Dionysian rituals you are not sure whether these things are to be treated seriously or not. Why, for instance, in one of the Greek islands they have dug up a sanctuary of Dionysus and found a floor of mosaics with the inscription "Only no water."[28] If you were to express in English all that is in the German phrase *nur kein Wasser!* you would say, "For heaven's sake, give me something substantial, some alcohol." It might have that meaning; it might just be a joke. It also might be a medical prescription because these places were healing places. In such a case it would mean, "Please do not drink water because you will get typhoid fever or colitis or something of the sort." In some countries water is a very critical proposition. Probably it has both meanings. That natural stand-

---

[27] Jung or the note takers must have made a mistake here. He must refer to Hagia Sophia, not to the Villa dei Misteri in Pompeii. There are no framed sentences from the Koran at the Villa dei Misteri.

[28] Jung found this information in Eisler, 1921, 272.

point, that natural paradox which you find in the cult of Dionysus, is also here in this solemn part of the dream. When you come to the second part where that funny tune is played with everybody joining in the refrain, then the meeting becomes just carnival. It is the carnival in the church which was the last remnant in the medieval church of ancient times, when they celebrated the Saturnalia, the spring mysteries in Athens, which were even quite obscene.[29]

This was one of the first dreams that seriously tried to bring together the almost irreconcilable pair of opposites and shows this clearly to be a religious problem and not at all a moral or cultural one. The whole act of reconciliation takes place in the temenos, and there only. It does not take place somewhere in the marketplace or in a worldly place; it takes place in the temenos, the sacred place, within the temple itself. This means that it is not a worldly thing; it has nothing to do with the surface of our life. The surface of daily life is outside, not in the temenos; but our religious life ought to be in the temenos, always in the temenos. There only the opposites can become reconciled, not in life. Life is a battle; life is full of opposites, full of conflicts. You cannot become a believer in Dionysus in your daily life; it is absolutely impossible; you can become that only within the temenos. Carnival is still celebrated to some extent in Europe. Everything that happens inside of the carnival is "carnival," and nothing is said about it. "Well, yes, it is carnival, and you don't judge it." If the same thing happened outside of carnival, you would say, "How terrible, how awful, quite immoral."

As long as you are a Catholic you can accept this inconsistency; you can confess, "in the carnival I have sinned so and so, and so and so," and you repent and you get absolution. And next year you do the same thing again. Not so with Protestants. We have no confession, no carnival, no absolution. We think we have gained a lot. Sure enough we have gained a lot; but something is lacking for we have lost touch with the unconscious. We grew into consciousness, into a world of laws and conventions, and we do not know these other things anymore; they are lost from sight. They are no more in existence apparently. We look back on what we have lost as if it were a matter of the past. You see, however, how these things come up again in dreams, and in such a case you can also see what the return of such thoughts means to human beings. This man, the dreamer, came back to life through them; he lived again; he again had the feeling

---

[29] Saturnalia: One of the best-known festivals of ancient Rome was a winter festival celebrated December 17–24.

that his life made sense. You get the feeling that your life makes sense the moment it touches nature again. Therefore whenever you have a chance to return to nature, you feel better; at least to a small extent you return to the "mother." Instinctively your life becomes corrected; it gets the right balance. This is the great consequence of such a union of opposites.

Well, I should also mention that this reconstruction of the ape-man, or the half-animal man in the form of a gibbon, which is just an ape, has a particular connotation in Christianity; for he would be the devil. The devil is called "God's Ape," the one who distorts and ridicules what God has done well and perfectly. It is always the devil's work that distorts God's intentions. And you know, the devil has been represented as a satyr with the legs and horns of a he-goat. He is just an old priest of Dionysus. A parallel to this dream is found in the life of Nietzsche. He became, as he himself said, a new believer in Dionysus. He had a most extraordinary mystical experience of Dionysus, and out of that experience he wrote his famous *Dithyrambs of Dionysus*, some of his most beautiful poems.[30] This is about all I shall have time to say about that dream.

I want to add now another dream, the thirteenth, which immediately follows and this will be the last one we can take up.[31] The scene is laid in a square room, in which complicated things take place, sort of ceremonies that apparently had the idea of transforming animals into men or into human beings. In the beginning of the ritual or ceremony there are two snakes which try to run away in opposite directions, and they must be removed as quickly as possible. It was apparently quite wrong that they should run in opposite directions. Then there are other animals like foxes and dogs, which are chiefly in the corners of the square, as if arranged in a certain order. There are also many people there who circumambulate the room anticlockwise. Each time they pass around the corner where the animals are, they must allow themselves to be bitten on the calves by these animals. They are not allowed to run away. If one should run away then everything would be lost; the whole meaning of the ceremony would be destroyed. During that circumambulation nobler animals come into existence, namely, bulls and goats. Four snakes now go into the four corners. Then the whole crowd leaves the room, and two priests come.

[30] F. W. Nietzsche and R. J. Hollingdale, trans. (2000), *Dithyrambs of Dionysus* (London: Anvil Press Poetry).

[31] Cf. "Dream Symbols," nr. 18, p. 151, and *CW* 12, nr. 18, par. 183. M 18 {0153}: "Square room; animals are being transformed into people," May 16, 1932, CDM.

They are carrying a gigantic reptile. There appears now an amorphous substance, an awful accumulation of vital matter—mass *vitalis*—but quite amorphous; yet there is some sort of head to it. The priest now touches this head with the reptile, and then a human head appears in transfigured form, and a voice says, "These are attempts at becoming."

This is a further explanation of things that happened in that peculiar temenos. There is some amorphous, but vital, matter in the dream, which symbolizes the amorphous condition of the Self, the unconscious. And the peculiar symbolical act performed by the priests is an old initiation into the mysteries of Sabazios.[32] In Egypt they initiated people in a similar way. A Latin text says that a golden serpent is let down into the bosom of those that are initiated and is taken out again down near the feet. Obviously it means that the golden serpent is passed under the clothes and out again; that the serpent has transversed the body. In this way the body becomes filled with the god, because the serpent represents the *agatho daimon*, namely, the "good demon" or the "redeemer."

There was an early Christian sect of a Gnostic nature, the Ophites, who worshipped Christ in the form of the redeeming serpent, as Moses exalted the serpent on a pole in the desert.[33] So Christ said, "I myself will be exalted on a pole," referring to His crucifixion. The Ophites celebrated communion with the snake in a basket on the table and shared

---

[32] Sabazios: an originally Phrygian god who lent some of his traits to Dionysus. He was venerated as the supreme god in the Thracian Hellespont, a solar divinity, who was sometimes considered as the son of Cronos, sometimes of Cybele, whose companion he became. His wife was either the moon goddess Bendis or Cotys, an earth goddess analogous to the Phrygian Cybele. Sabazios was represented with horns and his emblem was the serpent. He is his often depicted riding a horse. The Sabazia, nocturnal festivals of orgiastic character, were celebrated in his honour. R. Graves, ed. (1993), *New Larousse Encyclopedia of Mythology*, new ed., 3rd impr. (London: Prometheus Books), 160.

[33] The Ophites (from Greek *ophis*: "serpent") were members of Gnostic sects during the second century AD flourishing in the Roman Empire and for several centuries thereafter. The Naassenes and Cainites were two of the many Gnostic sects designated as Ophites. Although differing in their beliefs in many ways, they all encompassed a dualistic theology putting a Supreme Being and origin of the cosmos in opposition to a chaotic, dark material world. Man is a mixture of these conflicting spiritual and material forces and only by gnosis, the knowledge of how to become aware of the unknown or hidden god, can man redeem himself. They regarded Jehovah of the Old Testament as a demiurge, or a subordinate "fallen" deity who had created the material world. The serpent holds special importance to their belief, because it enabled the gift of the all-important knowledge of good and evil that the demiurge withheld from them. Hence the serpent is the true saviour that taught men to rebel against the demiurge and seek knowledge of the true God. The Ophites saw Christ as a purely spiritual being who, uniting with the man Jesus, taught men of the true gnosis.

the communion with the serpent, symbolic of Christ. The healing serpent of Aesculapius at Epidaurus[34] is another illustration of serpent worship. Once when there was a terrific pestilence at Athens, nothing helped until the sacred snake was fetched from Epidaurus, the main sanctuary of the Esculapians. It was the healing serpent that brought the life power, the mana, and that again is the same serpent as in Egypt.

In the so-called Kundalini Yoga,[35] the serpent is spoken of as "the serpent power," and the idea is that it is a sort of dormant energy lying deep down in the bottom of the "small basin" and if aroused will shoot up and bring to consciousness and experience everything that is above: all the lotuses or chakras, all higher states of consciousness, all religious experiences which have a healing effect. In the Kundalini Yoga, you concentrate on the serpent and arouse it; and after arousing the serpent, you will have the enlightenment which is connected with this central experience. There is an interesting version of the snake experience in *Zarathustra*. Here the shepherd who slept in the open woke up to find a serpent trying to creep into his mouth and causing him to choke. Zarathustra shouted, "Bite his head off." So the shepherd bit his head off and got rid of the serpent. Translated into religious language this would mean that the god tried to enter the shepherd's consciousness in his sleep. Of course, that shepherd in *Zarathustra* is Nietzsche himself. The archaic man knew that the Zarathustra experience was a religious experience and that the god really tried to enter him. But the exalted consciousness of Nietzsche, which was overwrought and identified with the figure of Zarathustra, advised him not to let the god in, but to bite his head off; but this was, of course, fatal. It was exactly the same fatality that made the hero in Meyrink's *Golem* reject the offered grain, or our dreamer reject the golden coins. He thought it wrong, a danger to take them, and that was human. If Nietzsche had accepted the snake, it would have been an illustration of that archaic form of initiation in which the god enters man, meaning that the man becomes filled with god, he has God within. It is the Kundalini experience.

---

[34] Aesculapius (Lat.) or Asklepios (Greek), was the Greco-Roman god of medicine, son of Apollo and the mortal princess Coronis. The centaur Chiron taught him the art of healing. Asclepius was frequently represented standing, dressed in a long cloak, with bare breast; his usual attribute was a staff with a serpent coiled around it. There is a famed fourth-century BC temple of Asclepius at Epidaurus. Excavations have revealed that it contained, in addition to temples to Asclepius and Artemis, a theater, a stadium, gymnasiums, baths, a hospital, and an abaton, an area where patients slept.

[35] In the autumn of 1932 Jung held a seminar (mostly in English) on Kundalini Yoga together with the German Indologist Jakob Wilhelm Hauer. See Jung, 1996.

The dream we were discussing shows very beautifully something that I spoke of earlier today as a trap for the animal instincts. You see the square here acts like a net in which animals are caught, the animal instincts that try to be chaotic. They are, as a matter of fact, always chaotic; but if you go deep enough there is that trap which is set for them, namely, the geometric form in which the irrational, the chaotic, is caught. The pair of opposites (the two snakes moving in opposite directions in the dream) try to flee from each other, because the conscious disturbs the unconscious and the unconscious, the conscious. The conscious is a sense organ in a way; it is an organ of orientation in outer space. The unconscious is something quite different; it is the life of the soul, yet, it is doing something very similar to that which the world does. For the unconscious also is a movement, due to the circumambulation of images, a constant change of images. It is as if someone were sitting in a revolving art gallery looking at the pictures, seeing the continuous change of eternal images.

But what is our universe? Millions and millions of revolving stars. What is the life of the earth? A series of millions and millions of forms ever renewed and ever decaying. And somebody is looking at this spectacle and asking what it is all about. It is the same with the unconscious. But the two words are singularly opposite and the only place where sense is made is where the two come together in the temenos, in the square of individuation, where one knows what one is and why one lives.

New York Seminar, 1937

Lecture 7

Ladies and gentlemen:

Those of you who were present at that more or less famous Bailey Island seminar may remember that we discussed there the case of a scientist.[1] I cannot give you the particulars in regard to his personal life because he is a famous man and his case might be recognized. I have already with his complete consent published some of the facts, for naturally, in treating of his dreams, I have had to give you certain details about his life. I always find it a little awkward to deal with individual medical cases as the material is for the most part confidential so that in my writing I have often felt these restrictions as a very difficult handicap. I have seen so many things in my career about which I could talk, but the material is too delicate. The people concerned are sometimes in high positions, in the limelight, and so I don't care to say too much.

Now this case is exceptional since the man himself is a scientist and has given me permission to use at least a part of his material. You remember he is about thirty-three or thirty-four years of age. His neurosis, at the time of which I am writing, had extended over two years. During this period he produced a series of about fifteen hundred dreams and made a record of them with very careful self-observation.[2] The unique fact is that he started his analysis all by himself; for when he came to consult me, I talked to him for only about twenty minutes, just long enough to tell him that I would not touch his case because at first he could just as satisfactorily observe himself, being a very intelligent man. I added that later, when he had observed enough, I would tell him something about his case.

So he collected about four hundred dreams, all carefully observed and recorded, some of which I am using in these talks. Out of those four hundred, I picked fifty-nine, all of which contain a certain motif which we call, as you know, the mandala motif. This is a particularly important and

---

[1] This lecture was held on October 16, 1937.
[2] See introduction n. 86.

central symbol in dreams. I talked to you a good deal about it last year, so I won't repeat what I said then. But our next dream, which we will presently take up, contains that same symbol. For this reason it is more or less unavoidable to say something further about the mandala. We shall be concerned with this motif throughout these talks.

I want to state at the beginning, however, that the underlying processes which are demonstrated in these dreams and visions are quite general. It is also not only my own patients who have manifested such phenomena. Colleagues of mine who had no idea that such things existed have had similar instances of the appearance of the mandala in the dreams of their patients. I have also found this symbol in literature, as well as in historical material. The fact is we meet it practically everywhere in the profane and sacred literature of the whole world. We have it, for instance, in certain Pueblo rites, as in the Mountain Chant of the Navajos. But also we have it in the mosaic plaque discovered under the altar of the old Temple of the Warriors at Chichen Itza, and in the Calendar Stone of Mexico City, and I do not doubt that if we were in the possession of the texts of the old Mayan civilization we would see the same ideas expressed, with the same significance, as in the writings and art of the East. This motif of the mandala is neither an invention nor a tradition, although in certain civilizations it has been handed down from generation to generation. In Tibet they have special prescriptions in the sacred texts that describe exactly how such a mandala must be formed. We find the same thing in other places. For example, in the alchemy of the Middle Ages there was a traditional form for mandalas, very beautiful examples of which you may have seen in the famous church window of Chartres Cathedral. Also in old illuminated texts you find beautiful representations of Christ and the symbols of the four Evangelists, often arranged in the four corners with the Rex Gloriae, the King of Glory, the Triumphant Christ, in the center. We find it also in ancient Egypt, and—well, everywhere.

Now of course in the old civilizations the mandala had a traditional form, but we cannot say that the same is true now. With us, as a rule people have never been taught of such motifs and have no idea that they exist. They have been forgotten long ago. Yet we find that they come up all by themselves, quite spontaneously, in dreams, in dreams of normal people and of morbid cases, even in psychoses, and when they appear, they always have the same meaning. For the symbol of the mandala is always an attempt at self-cure, exactly as with the Pueblo mandala which was used in the Mountain Chant ceremony for healing, the sick man being placed in the center of the mandala to be made over.

To return now to the last dream with which we were concerned in the Bailey Island seminar, it was the dream of the church—that rather amusing dream—where, after the solemn part, there came a sort of second act which was quite funny, where wine was served.[3] That dream was again, one might say, the result of a peculiar situation which had preceded it. In this earlier dream there had been a square room, and somebody had said that someone was going to reconstruct the gibbon in that place. Now the gibbon is a monkey, an ape, and that thought was very disagreeable to the patient because he instantly had the feeling, "This is morbid; it is something awful"; and he tried to get away from it.

To understand this dream you must put yourself into the frame of mind of such a man. He came to me in a more or less disintegrated state; he had lost his self-control, had taken to drink, was doing everything wrong under the sun. He had lost himself completely. Naturally he had the idea that there must be something fundamentally wrong with him. Not being familiar with the structure of the neuroses, he had a suspicion that perhaps he might be crazy. To him the square room was a sort of cell in a lunatic asylum in which he was made into a monkey—a sort of regression was to be produced in him so that he would be compelled to go back into the state of an anthropoid.

It was after this that he had the church dream, that crazy dream which clearly showed that his attempt to cover himself with a traditional religion was ineffective. The dream is so ambiguous and ridiculous that it is quite obvious that it would not give him any protection against the threat of the monkey that looked to him so morbid and dangerous.

The next dream after the one of the church dream, as one might expect, is a return to the motif of self-cure, of course, coupled with the same uncanny idea of the remaking of the monkey.[4] Remember I told you then that this reconstruction of the anthropoid is merely a reconstruction of the instinctual personality, which ought to be made over, because when a man loses himself as he had, he has lost his guidance, his concept of himself. He has no central idea anymore; he obeys every impulse. He is really already the monkey who simply reacts to stimuli in his surroundings.

After his futile attempt then to protect himself by a religion that simply did not work anymore in his case, he is put again into the same situation

---

[3] Cf. "Dream Symbols," nr. 17, p. 148 {M 17, 0151}, and CW 12, nr. 17, par. 176.

[4] Cf. "Dream Symbols," nr. 18, p. 151 {M 18, 0153}, and CW 12, nr. 18, par. 183. In *PsA* Jung has added a small passage on the concept of the massa confusa in alchemy (CW 12, par. 185) and also a passage on concentration in alchemy (CW 12, par. 187).

as before, namely, in that square room so the dream begins with the statement: "I am in the square room again." All sorts of complicated ceremonies are going on which have the purpose of transforming animals into human beings.

That is very much the same idea as in dream eleven only in reverse order. There the idea was that a monkey should be made; nothing was said about the transformation. Now in this case, in dream thirteen, the idea is that animals, presumably monkeys or any other sort of animals, should be transformed into human beings.

That is soothing; it is just as if the unconscious were trying to introduce the same idea that had been so upsetting in the former dream, in a different way, a less offensive way. Of course this is only an introduction. Whenever the unconscious tries to introduce a new theme in such a nice soothing way, we can be sure that soon afterwards the same unconscious will say something that is very disagreeable. It is a sort of *capitatic benevolentiae*, a capturing of your goodwill before saying something very disagreeable. It sounds quite all right, that animals should be transformed into human beings, which means that the animal reactions, the animal instincts, should be transformed into human reactions. That is what we all wish, and every well-meaning person would say that is just the thing we should work for.

Now two snakes suddenly appear and try to run away to opposite sides, and the dream says they must be removed at once. You see snakes are relatively low animals. They usually represent the lower part of our psychology, that part which presumably reaches down into the spinal cord. Snakes are chiefly spinal cord animals; their brains amount to very little. So whenever snakes appear it must refer to a very deep-rooted instinct. This is a statement you will just have to accept. To give any proof of it would lead us much too far afield.

These two snakes represent a split, a dissociation. There should be one snake, as there is one spinal cord. There should not be a split; there should be a unified something. But in the case of our dreamer there is a split, a disagreement shown by the movement to the opposite sides. Also these snakes are obviously trying to escape. The dreams say they should be at once removed, which means there must be no split, no dissociation about it; nothing must be allowed to run away. The dreamer has an instinctive impulse to run away, just as anyone, faced with a situation which he feels to be impossible, looks around and asks himself, "Where is a hole, through which I can slip out?" That is the meaning of the two snakes. Instinctively you look to the right and to the left to find out where you can escape. And, it is for this reason, as the dream says, that they must be removed.

Such an interpretation sounds as if it might be a mere invention, a wild idea, and I make it tentatively for the present. We are playing with the material; later we shall see if the hypothesis is applicable to all. We have more material in the dream and perhaps we shall find a justification.

The text continues: There are animals present, like foxes and dogs. That is a new form of animal. These are higher animals. When you speak of dogs you speak of creatures with a kind of domesticated instinct. Foxes of course are wild animals, not domesticated, difficult to tame, but when you dream of a dog it always means a form of instinctual psyche that goes with you, obeys you, is under your control, not against you. So also with horses. The horse has, however, a different meaning in that it is a working animal and so represents that instinctual psyche which produces work. It represents the energy you can apply to work. While the dog does not actually produce work, he is used for many other things, as, for example, for his particularly refined senses. He smells, he has a keen ear, he is watchful; and so dogs frequently stand for acute sensitivity in man, and often, in particular for intuition. A dog in a dream may represent the quality you refer to when you say, "You should follow your nose" or "Somebody has a good nose."

Now he simply notices the presence of such animals. Then something happens, namely, that many people who were there as in the former dream walk around the square anticlockwise. You remember perhaps that we spoke of this as the circumambulation motif. Circumambulation is not usually anticlockwise, a turning from right to left, which is of course different from the clockwise movement. These two movements are clearly differentiated both in Buddhism and Lamaism; one is the right kind, and the other is the wrong kind. For instance, the *stupa* (which is a sort of sacred building usually containing some relics or saints or of Buddha himself) must be circumambulated but always to the right, never to the left. This latter would be most unfortunate. The movement to the left means to the sinister side, to the unconscious, while the movement to the right would be towards consciousness, because movement to the right expresses consciousness. The right hand is the conscious hand, the left the unconscious—that is, if you are not left-handed.

As these people move around the square in anticlockwise way, the animals that are stationed at the four corners show a disagreeable tendency to bite their calves. It seems, indeed, to be necessary for the people to expose themselves to that injury because if they tried to run away then everything would be lost—that is what the text says. So it seems to be all important that the people circulating around the square should not run away. Now you see that is the answer to our question about the snakes. The snakes ran away; they tried to escape, and here it is stated that one should not run away in spite of the fact that one may be bitten; in spite of the pain. These animals get at you; they put their teeth into your flesh; and that is painful. So the dream suggested that one can't avoid a certain painful interval; it has to happen. These animals must get at you, and that is exactly what the dreamer tried to escape. He did not know that he was already completely swallowed by the animal, by an unconscious condition. He was afraid of becoming conscious of the fact that he had already been bitten, so he had to learn to expose himself consciously to the assault of the animal. The dreamer needs to learn to expose himself to the knowledge and to the understanding that he is emotional in a certain way; that he has certain instinctual impulses. He should confess that he is a victim of his own condition. He should see it consciously, and that is painful. If he could say, "I am just rotten; I am completely degenerate," he would have gained something. That is the great value of the confession of sin which the Catholic Church has known for a long time. You must be able to distinguish where you are wrong and to confess it, in order to maintain your human condition. If you cannot, you are identified with your sin which is an animal condition. You lose the human rapport.

You see, that is the great difficulty with this particular patient. He didn't try—he didn't dare—to expose himself to a complete understanding of his condition, and if he can't stand the pain of seeing himself, well, everything is lost. This means that whatever he tried to accomplish hitherto, whatever happened in his dreams, whatever he understood and learned will be lost if he can't overcome himself to this extent.

Now after this, nobler animals appear in the dream, namely, bulls and goats. Then four snakes, I should rather say serpents, arranged themselves in the four corners of the mandala. I cannot go into every detail of such a dream; it would need much closer research to take up all the nuances; but at least you get the general idea, that through his submission, he comes to understand or accept the fact that he should look at himself and that he should be conscious of his condition. This change of attitude has a differentiating effect upon him or his instincts. These animal instincts symbolized at first by snakes transform into a higher class of animals. Then suddenly four snakes appear as if *he* were going back to a former condition in which there were two snakes that had to be removed. Now, however, there are four.

This symbol of the snake has many surprising aspects. It is a very primitive, and at the same time a very complicated and highly sophisticated, symbol. As you know, the serpent may represent the devil himself, or the lowest form of sinfulness, and yet the serpent may also represent the Savior, so-called Agathodaemon, God or the Redeemer, and this is true not only of Gnosticism, but also of certain Christian sects, as, for example, the Ophites. The snake also, curiously enough, often represents a perfectly abstract idea; for example, the idea of the famous so-called ouroboros, that is, the tail-eater, the snake that bites its tail. That is really a philosophical idea. The same is true of these four snakes in the dream which symbolize four abstract notions. They are in the four corners of the square. This mandala is similar to the one which was discovered in the Temple of the Warriors by the American expedition to Chichen Itza. There you find the plumed serpent Quetzalcoatl also in the four corners. Now, as you may know, the plumed serpent is a symbol of the Redeemer. But in the dream the snakes merely designate the importance of the four points of that peculiar square room. They would convey the meaning of four different living entities which designate the four corners of a mandala.

These four different living entities, which we consider as being functions, are represented in the Lamaistic mandala as the four different ways to reach an orientation in psychological space. The square room with the four snakes is the primitive form, the scheme or diagram, one could say, of the psychological functions, which are not yet, however, differentiated from each other. They are only indicated as different psychological and living entities. That they are presented as living entities is because of the fact that the psychological functions have specific energy. This simply means that you cannot deplete a psychological function. For example, you cannot get along without thinking. Of course, it is quite possible that you live by feeling only, that you forget about thinking; but thinking nevertheless exists. It goes on without you because it has the specific energy which cannot be disposed of. An intellectual type can get detached in his thinking; he can handle his world by mere intellect, and he can suppress or repress or forget about feeling altogether, but nevertheless feeling is going on and manifests itself indirectly in certain attacks he suffers from, such as violent emotions and bad moods; or perhaps he falls in love with his housekeeper or such things. The same holds true with the other functions. But it may be truly said that the forgotten function is always just the one that plays the most disturbing role on account of the fact that it has energy which cannot be disposed of. It has its specific energy which always works. So you see, no matter whether you dismiss your thinking or your feelings or your intuition or your sensation, their specific energy is always there, and it works against you insofar as you don't consciously make use of it. So, if you see only one snake in one corner, well, that doesn't mean that the other corners are not occupied by other snakes; for they are.

After this the crowd of people that has made the circumambulation leaves the room, and two priests enter carrying an enormous reptile, presumably again, a serpent. And in the center of the room now is a sort of substance which the dreamer calls a living mass, a mass of living substance, whatever that may mean. The priests next touch the unformed mass with the snake, and it immediately begins to take on a definite shape. It becomes like a human head, but in a sort of exalted form. The dreamer uses the German term *verklärt*, which means enlightened, exalted, illuminated. At this same moment he hears a voice. You remember the phenomenon of the voice which always makes absolutely irrefutable statements has appeared in previous dreams. The voice now says: "Those are the attempts of the becoming," which if translated literally, would mean, those are attempts at the creation of something. That is the final statement. Then the dream comes to an end.

In this dream the priests are bringing in one snake which is no longer split, but is an integrated, instinctual being. This means, that by the proceeding ceremony, through the creation of a complete mandala, his instinct had been caught, concentrated, organized, synthesized, and is now a unified thing of magic importance. The magic character is indicated by the priests. The whole process is demonstrated as in a mystery play, which is of course very mysterious in this case, for he is a scientist and knows nothing of mystery plays or such things. However, he might easily have known that there were Gnostic cults, for example, that of Sabazious, in which a ritual of initiation was practiced for the creation of a divine condition, the making of the initiant into a being designated as *entheos*, that is, a being filled with the God, containing the God. This was done in a way similar to that in the dream. The priests brought in a golden snake and put it into the garment of the initiant under the upper part of the clothing. It was then pushed down and pulled out from below. This was also the act of adoption by the god, according to antique adoption rites. When a child was adopted by a woman, he was put under her garment and drawn out below. Then he was fed with milk, and the woman was obliged to give her breast to the child in order to complete the act. There is a famous picture by an Italian painter—it is somewhere in this country—which really represents "the Adoption of Heracles by Juno," or Hera.[5] It is mistakenly called a love scene between Mars and Venus, which comes from a lack of historical knowledge. In the picture, Ercole, Heracles, is lying on the floor in front of the queen or the deity, Hera. Because he looks like Mars, the picture was thought to represent a peculiar love play between Mars and Venus—people have such fantastic notions. But, it is the same adoption scene that is in the initiations of the Sabazios mysteries, in which the divine snake representing the healing God, the famous snake of the ouroboros, entered man and filled him with divine power, thus making him entheos. After this he is supposed to be cured, which means that he is lifted up in a different condition.

Now in this dream you have exactly the same idea, only it is not a human being that is to be transformed or exalted or filled; it is an unformed shapeless mass of living substance, which might easily represent the dreamer himself. At the time of the dream he was in a dissociated, disintegrated psychological condition which could be compared to a heap of living matter which ought to be given shape. He himself, of course, has shape. He is a man of remarkable mind, so that nobody would think that such a one could be symbolized by a shapeless heap; but when you look at him from another side, from the standpoint of feeling, you can easily see how completely disintegrated he was. He had a very powerful mind, but on the other side he was threatened with utter destruction. Now, inasmuch as he is only a heap of living matter, completely dissociated, having no human shape, he needs that contact with the unified instinct. That was originally the purpose of creating the ape, namely, creating the instinctive man, which is a unity. That would heal him because it would give him a backbone. He has no backbone any more. Therefore he needs more snake, to be more centered, and that is represented in the dream exactly in the same way as has always been done throughout all centuries and in very different civilizations. But this, of course, doesn't come from any tradition; this is a genuine re-creation of an archetypal image. That is why we speak of archetypes. They exist in the blood, that is, in the very structure of the brain, so that he produces the same ideas that were always made use of under such conditions.

The interesting thing is that this transformation is represented as a sort of sacred ceremonial. It is just as if the unconscious were trying to give it

---

[5] It is unclear which painting Jung is referring to.

a particular flavor or a sort of mystical character. The unconscious is, however, only presenting it in this way because it actually has such an aspect. This type of transformation has always been called a magical or mystical performance, which means an inexplicable, almost superhuman, process, because it is done beyond man. He doesn't do it; I don't do it; it happens; it is done as if by a superhuman agency or a superhuman consciousness. I say "as if"—it is just as if there were priests who knew about his psychological state and were doing the right thing to cure it. Now, this is surely a most upsetting idea, that, when I am seemingly in a bad neurotic condition, a magic performance or ceremony is performed somewhere in order to cure me against my will, against my understanding, and against, indeed, every bit of common sense.

But, you know, that is the thing that always has happened in history. Look at the primitives—how they cure their patients. The primitive medicine man performs his mysteries and his magical ceremonies, which appear to us as a mere play on ignorance. But they rise from a psychological activity which is very meaningful and beyond consciousness. It is this activity which is portrayed in the dream, and if you can see something positive in it, if you can say, "Well, I accept the fact that such a thing happens," then, it has a good effect upon you. You know man has really been cured through just such performances.

To show him that there is some intelligent agency at work, the voice explains to him, "And those are the attempts at becoming," which means, attempts at the re-creation of the individual. Remember that I haven't influenced him in the least. I simply helped him to understand the ceremonies that were carried out on him, in his dreams; and through this process he came together and became a perfectly normal being. For those among you who believe that no real solution to life is reached until one is happily married, I can tell you that he is happily married.[6] [*Laughter*]

The patient drew his own conclusions from the dreams without any analysis from me. He saw, for instance, that in this dream there were allusions which contained something terrifying to him. He saw that something strange which hadn't been in this world hitherto was approaching him.

You see, you must put yourself into his frame of mind. He was a hard-boiled scientist in whose world such things do not exist. When he came to me, we went through some very critical moments when such dreams as these brought this strange world to his consciousness. Again and again he tried to escape because he simply couldn't cope with it. He felt that

---

[6] Pauli married Franca Bertram April 4, 1934.

these things had some reality, but he didn't know where to locate them in his physical world. So whenever he had such a dream, he had a pretty bad reaction afterwards because he couldn't accept its peculiar content. I have to admit that the assimilation of such a dream really is a very difficult problem. How can we integrate it with our empirical world? We thought that we had overcome long ago that kind of thinking which we still call "superstition." But while we call it by fresh names we really cannot permit such things to exist. I wish I knew how to formulate them differently. I can only formulate them in the way in which I have tried to do it tonight. But the formulation of the meaning of such a dream has something offensive to our scientific mind. It sounds strange, and I shouldn't wonder if some of my audience would ask, "But do you really believe that there are agencies that apparently, all by themselves, try to improve such a man in an intelligent and purposive way? I can't believe it, and I don't believe it."

To these objections I would answer: "These happenings are facts. Facts don't need to be believed. One knows about them, or one doesn't. It is just a fact that things developed within the dreamer in such a way. We can only try to formulate these happenings, and if by chance they do not coincide with our philosophy, *tant pis pour elle*,[7] the fault is with our Weltanschauung.[8] We cannot explain those facts away."

This dreamer often asked me, "What do you think about it?"

I said, "What do *you* think about it?" I simply handed the question back to him: "I wonder how you are going to deal with it," and I also wonder how I am going to explain those facts.

Now, of course, he had more and more dreams of the same kind. He had already had, as you know, quite a series, and they always aroused a conflict in him.

The next dream pictured a wild battle between two primitive peoples—that was the entire content of the dream.[9]

This is again a conflict like the two snakes that parted from each other; it is again a dissociation. This time it is the people, who had appeared before in the dream of the crowd. When this particular motif arises, it refers to the collective man in us; we feel ourselves to be one of the crowd like everybody else. In this case it means also that he is a multiplicity. He is not one; he is many. He is to a certain extent disintegrated. The fact that

---

[7] French: too bad for her.

[8] Weltanschauung: worldview, world conception.

[9] "Dream Symbols," nr. 19, p. 157, and *CW* 12, nr. 19, par. 194. M 19 {0172}: "War between two parties, the dark and the light," May 27, 1932, CDM.

he had had a previous dream, in which he couldn't cope at all, produced this effect on him. The earlier dream had come to him as a shock, and this had led to the present dream of conflict: two peoples engaged in battle, a wild war.

Whenever there occurs in the dream a situation in which the active figure is represented by a crowd, it refers to a disintegrated condition; with a preponderance of the unconscious you see when the unconscious gets on top of you, and you lose your self-control; you become merely like the rest of humanity; you develop a morbid psychology. For you are like the many, and you consist also of many. The conscious has lost energy. It is what Janet called an *abaissement du niveau mental*.[10] The flight in the dream was on dual terms, which means that his conscious is no more on top of the unconscious or, in other words, that his unconscious instinctual personality is no more controlled by the conscious personality, for there are now two peoples fighting each other on equal terms. It is a dissociation between his conscious and his unconscious attitudes. Whatever the unconscious is after is clearly shown in the dream before, namely, a peculiar attempt at a self-cure.

In this case you could represent his personality by this diagram

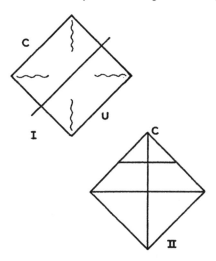

You remember, the square with the four snakes occurring in an earlier dream. That is now divided. There is a war between the two sides on equal terms. Let C represent the conscious side and U the unconscious, with a line making an equal division in between. In diagram II, it might

---

[10] See above.

be that consciousness is here (C) in just one function. When one function is conscious, three are unconscious. In this second case there would be an absolute preponderance of the unconscious, and the conscious would be overwhelmed. However, his actual condition is that there is a war on equal terms taking place, with a disintegration of consciousness, shown by the presence of the many. You will see how that develops in the next dream.

In the next dream he says, "There is a cave. In that cave there are two boys, and there is something like a tube in the ceiling of the cave. A third boy falls from above through the tube into the cave where there are already two."[11]

Now, we haven't heard of the boys before. Since the boys are little boys, he regards them as children. These little boys in the dream belong to the so-called dwarf motif or little men motif. The little men are, for instance, those mysterious forces in the house which do the housework for the housewife—the little dwarfs whose feet you shouldn't see. Or they appear in mines as the so-called *Heinzelmännchen*, or in Greek, the *homunculi anthroparia*. They appear also in alchemy as the personification of the vapors arising from the melted metal. The old texts contain drawings or pictures of these little men jumping out of the fire or out of the melting metal, personifying the spirit of the metal. They are also supposed to live in mines, where the miners often see them. In old tales and folklore, they appear on ships at sea, where they are of bad omen, indicating danger or disaster. They represent part of our psyche—split-off parts, autonomous elements. They always indicate a certain dissociation.

In this case of the patient they derive from the fact that the dream consciousness has become aware of this condition, and instead of seeing snakes, it seems it sees now little human beings, and as you may know, these anthroparion homunculi have always been understood to have no human souls. There is a very beautiful Danish story, which you may know, of a parson who, late in the night, was returning home from a visit to a sick man. He was very tired, and as he went over that is [*sic*], they suddenly heard faint music coming from the morass where it was humanly impossible for anybody to walk without getting drowned. Then he discerned in the distance, in the moonlight, two little figures coming across the moor, playing the fiddle. They came nearer to him until he saw they were elves. They asked, "Who are you?" He replied that he was the parson. They then asked him what a parson was, and when he told them they

---

[11] "Dream Symbols," nr. 20, p. 158, and CW 12, nr. 20, par. 196. M 20 {0177}: "Cave with two boys, with a third falling down through a tube," May 29, 1932, CDM.

began to complain that they didn't have any souls and asked him what to do about it. And the parson said, "Well, you should pray." And they asked him what they should pray. He replied: "Our Father who art in Heaven," and so forth. And they said: "Teach us." He tried then to teach it to them, saying: "Our Father who art in Heaven," but they always repeated after him: "who are *not* in Heaven." They couldn't say, "art in Heaven," only "not in Heaven." You see, they must deny that prayer by which he hoped to give them souls, because they are partial souls only. You see, folklore knows.[12]

Now, these partial or fragmentary souls, these fragments of human personality are also functions. So anybody who identifies with only one function is necessarily a fragmentary personality, only a part of himself and all the other parts are missing. Naturally they are there, but they are unconscious; they function on account of their specific energy, but they are none the less unconscious.

To return to the dream: the two boys in the cave are the two functions in the darkness, in the unconscious, and he sees how a third one falls into

---

[12] There is a story very similar to this called "The Fairy's Enquiry," listed as a story from the Scottish Highlands in T. Keightley (1975 [1870]), *The Fairy Mythology: Illustrative of the Romance and Superstition of Various Countries* (Detroit: Gale). A clergyman was returning home one night after visiting a sick member of his congregation. His way led by a lake, and as he proceeded he was surprised to hear most melodious strains of music. He sat down to listen. The music seemed to approach coming over the lake accompanied by a light. At length he discerned a man walking on the water, attended by a number of little beings, some bearing lights, others musical instruments. At the beach the man dismissed his attendants, and then walking up to the minister saluted him courteously. He was a little gray-headed old man, dressed in rather an unusual garb. The minister having returned his salute begged of him to come and sit beside him. He complied with the request, and on being asked who he was, replied that he was one of the Daoine Shi. He added that he and they had originally been angels, but having been seduced into revolt by Satan, they had been cast down to earth where they were to dwell till the day of doom. His object now was, to ascertain from the minister what would be their condition after that awful day. The minister then questioned him on the articles of faith; but as his answers did not prove satisfactory, and as in repeating the Lord's Prayer, he persisted in saying *wed* instead of *art* in heaven, he did not feel himself justified in holding out any hopes to him. The fairy then gave a cry of despair and flung himself into the loch, and the minister resumed his journey.

Just before coming to New York Jung had attended the Ninth International Medical Congress for Psychotherapy in Copenhagen, arranged by the ÜAÄGP (Überstaatliche Allgemeinen Ärztlichen Gesellschaft für Psychotherapie), of which Jung was the president. This was a conference arranged by the Scandinavian groups of the ÜAÄGP, Sweden and Denmark. Could he have heard a version of this story at the conference in Denmark? There were thirteen nationalities represented at the conference. See also Jung, "Presidential Address to the Ninth International Medical Congress for Psychotherapy, Copenhagen, 1937," *CW* 10. Herbert Read, Michael Fordham, Gerhard Adler, and William McGuire, eds. (1970), *Civilization in Transition* (London: Routledge), 561.

the darkness, too. That means that the unconscious increases: two functions were already there, and now a third one is dropping into it. The threshold of consciousness (in diagram II) rises up to (X), and consciousness then consists of one function only. In other words, he has withdrawn into that function which is most differentiated, into his intellect. He tries to shield himself by his intellect and to keep out all that threatens the rational. Before that he had tried to rescue himself by adopting the traditional religion, but that didn't work. This time he tries to rescue himself by means of his intellect. If he could talk in his dream he would say, "What is this all about? It is all nonsense. The world is thus and so, you see." He would use our magic, scientific language, in order to explain it away.

Well, after such a dream, which shows him that he consists of one-fourth of himself, only one quarter, giving a preponderance to the unconscious, which amounts to a sort of disintegration, we should expect a new attempt at a wholeness, an integration, a synthesis.

The next dream is he sees a great globe, containing many small globes.[13]

You see, here is the idea; there should be a wholeness. The globe is a perfect form; it is the perfect form of the soul. Therefore the entire philosophical world has always assumed that the anima mundi, the soul of the world, is the human soul and has the perfect form, that is, is perfectly round. Certain heretics in early Christianity assumed that at the day of resurrection the soul with its glorified body would be spherical. According to the Symposium of Plato, the original man was round, *spherogenous*, meaning perfect.

And then the dream continues: From the top of the globe that contains many small globes, a green leaf appears.

This means that if that wholeness which contains the parts is reached then life, one could say, begins to sprout again. This idea of the globe comes after the dissociation, to compensate it, and to overcome that very one-sided condition where he is only one function, where he has lost three-quarters of himself. The dream presents the idea that you ought to be, or the ideal thing is to be, like a globe that contains many units. These units shouldn't split off by themselves; they should all be contained in one wholeness. That would be a new spring, a new life, symbolized by the green shoot.

---

[13] "Dream Symbols," nr. 21, p. 158, and CW 12, nr. 21, par. 198. M 21 {0189}: "Transparent globe with many small globes; a plant," June 5, 1932, CDM. In *PsA* Jung has added an illustration of the Indian Trimurti. Cf. CW 12, par. 199.

This dream is, of course, a bit abstract. It probably didn't touch him profoundly. It was a vague general idea which possibly left him in a dissatisfied condition. I know nothing about that, whether it was so or not, but I should assume that it was, because the next dream, which is pretty long and complicated, is again occupied with functions.

The place or the country in which this next dream takes place is America. He is in an American hotel, and there he goes up in the lift to the third or the fourth story.[14] There the lift comes to a stop, and he finds himself waiting with many other people. A friend, a man whom he knows very well, appears and says that the dreamer has left a dark and unknown woman on the ground floor and that he should not have made her wait so long. He should have taken care of her. The friend had given the woman into the dreamer's care. There was a sort of reproach, an offensive reproach in his remark: "You should have taken care of her. You left her alone too long, and you made her wait." He now gives him a letter, which probably, as he says, is meant for that dark and unknown woman. He reads the letter, which says, "Redemption does not come from not going with it." (That means, from not accompanying, or from running away.) "Redemption also does not come from a state in which one allows oneself to be merely driven. Redemption comes from a complete devotion, during which, or connected with which, the eye should always be concentrated upon the middle, upon the center." And as if that idea should be made clearer there was a diagram on the edge of the letter, consisting of a sort of wheel or a wreath, which looked about like this—a wheel with eight spokes (diagram III).

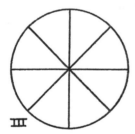

A little boy appears and says that the dreamer's room is on the eighth story. So he goes up in the lift again to about the seventh or the eighth story, with the same uncertainty as before when he did not know whether it was the third or the fourth floor. Now there is some doubt as to whether

---

[14] "Dream Symbols," nr. 22, p. 158, and CW 12, nr. 22, par. 200. M 22 {0192}: "A lift in an American hotel. Note with message to the dark one," June 7, 1932, CDM.

it is the seventh or the eighth, but his room was definitely on the eighth floor. Arriving there, though still not sure whether he has reached the seventh or the eight story, he meets an unknown man, a red-haired man, who greets him in a very friendly way. Suddenly the whole scene changes. We shall take up the first part now and deal with the second part later.

The situation is an American hotel. It is always important in dreams to pay attention to locality. Very often, or indeed, usually, in the beginning of a dream, you have a suggestion of the locality as in a drama. America means something definite to the dreamer, as I had already learned from him. To him it is a sort of exalted commonsense country which consists chiefly of straight lines and quick movement, a place where only reasonable things happen—nothing else. As you see, he has a very perfunctory knowledge of America, but that is his impression—a place where everything is organized and working smoothly. Nothing happens that is untoward; everything is explicable and reasonable. You see, that is also a sort of description of his own world which, curiously enough, is projected by the dreamer into America. If the scene were laid in Europe, then he would have to be concerned with his situation, with his reaction as a European, and then, you see, he would find himself in that mixed-up situation where he would be unable to deny the existence of the unconscious. In Europe you can't say, "There is no unconscious." But in America you might be able to say it, because here the head is cut off from the body so that most people are entirely unaware of the deeper layers of the irrational and the instinctive. You can't go up beyond a certain point in Europe; but here you can go up indefinitely, leaving something below yourself. That was his idea of America. Of course, it isn't so in reality.

In this dream then he is going up, which means that he is trying to pull himself out of the European situation, where he cannot deny the presence of these awful things. His idea was that if he were in America, he could go up and leave all that below. So it comes about that he goes up; but he gets stuck. He doesn't reach the fourth floor, or at least one doesn't know whether he has reached it or not. Perhaps he stopped at the third. Here again are the ominous numbers four and three suggesting the question, Is it three or is it four? In the diagram the question would be: have we all the four together, or is one missing? He would be sure to have his differentiated function. He might know that he had his two auxiliary functions, but the question is: Has he got his fourth function, too? For his problem is the very anxious question of whether or not the totality has been established. Does the globe contain all the other units? He might have left out something, and that omission would be symbolized in this dream by his doubt as to whether he had reached the third or the fourth floor. He was stopped for an unknown reason and then comes the explanation, brought him by his friend.

This man is a very positive figure. He is a learned and very nice man, who is older than the dreamer and has often in reality played a sort of paternal role so that the dreamer used to talk to him when he was in difficulties. When that friend appears in the dream it means that his advice will presumably be good and sound advice. He explains, "Well, naturally you got stuck because you have left that dark and unknown woman down below."

Now, who is that dark and unknown woman? Well, we have encountered her several times before. It is the female side of the man. This is perhaps a peculiar notion for many people, but if you were in the Middle Ages, you would understand what I am talking about because people then knew that man carries his female part in himself. It is the feminine minority that every man has within him (as women have a masculine minority and sometimes it isn't even in the minority; at least it doesn't look like that when it gets on top of a woman).

So you see, a man's feminine side can be a very obnoxious thing. If it gets on top of him it makes him moody. We call that state "animosity." We aren't 100 percent masculine. If we are men, we have so much in common with women that during a certain period in our embryonic life as far as any outward evidence would show, we might have turned into females. Everybody contains much of the other sex, both in his body and in his mental makeup. This minority of the other sex present in each one of us is always a typical personification of the unconscious. This is most clearly demonstrable in literature, as in Benoit's *L'Atlantide*,[15] and Rider Haggard's *She*.[16] I could give plenty of other illustrations. A wonderful anima story is to be found in a recent novel by William Sloane, *To Walk the Night*.[17] The anima of a man is characterized in a very typical way, and most men, when they have once grasped what is meant by the term *anima*, can recognize that figure in themselves right away. It is just as if every man had a definite idea of the woman that is in himself. That woman

---

[15] Pierre Benoit (1886–1962), French novelist and member of the Académie Française. Jung often referred to his novel *L'Atlantide* (1919) to illustrate the anima concept.

[16] Sir Henry Rider Haggard (1856–1925), English writer of adventure novels set in exotic locations, predominantly Africa. Jung often referred to his novel *She* (1887) to illustrate the anima concept.

[17] William Milligan Sloane III (1906–74) was an American author of fantasy and science fiction literature, and a publisher. *To Walk The Night* (1937) has been described as a science fiction novel with horror elements.

personifies the unconscious, and the friend who gives the good advice simply tells the dreamer, "Well, you have again left your unconscious behind you, below you. You went to America, and you tried to jump into the air in order to escape that other side of yourself."

It was simply too difficult for the dreamer to recognize or accept it, or to digest it, and therefore he tried to jump into the air in order to escape. I remember the case of a compulsion neurosis which began at the age of about sixteen or seventeen. I saw the patient only when he was forty-five; obviously he was absolutely incurable. His mental disturbance began with the following dream, which occurred twice:

He dreamt that he was going home pretty late at night when the streets were deserted. Suddenly he heard steps coming up behind him. It seemed somehow uncanny to him, and he walked faster; but then the steps also went faster. Then he began to run, and he heard somebody running after him. Suddenly he turned around to see who it was; and when he saw he was overcome with terror; for it was the devil. He jumped right into the air, and there he remained suspended while the devil stood underneath waiting for him to come down. He said, "I can't come down. I can't afford to be cured. For if I should be cured, I should have to admit the fact that I have lost twenty-five of the most precious years of my life. I can't admit that. Therefore I prefer 'Happy Neurosis Island.'" Those were his words, "Happy Neurosis Island"—his happy condition. His main symptom was that he always felt himself to be in a state of suspension. He called that state, "the state number one of decontamination." In that state he always had to wear an absolutely white suit and to sit on a chair with his arms held out, so that he didn't touch anything. He had no clock in his room; that was absolutely taboo. He wouldn't shake hands with me because I was a doctor and a doctor has to do with death and with sick people. He couldn't bear to see anybody dressed in black because that meant death, which suggested "time." This state of mind was what he meant by "condition number one." He spent all his time trying to "decontaminate." Yet, on the other hand, he felt compelled to keep touching something that reminded him of time and decay, thus torn in his mind he was held in a state of complete suspension. That was his life, a very unusual condition indeed.

Our dreamer in a similar suspended condition gets a suggestion of the way out from his friend who symbolizes an intelligent agency in his own unconscious. This says to him: "Well, what are you doing? You are simply leaving behind your female side," which is, of course, the inferior function. As he is an intellectual type the opposite function would be, of course, feeling. He has left his feeling side below, downstairs on the ground floor. His friend had trusted him with her, and he should have taken care of her, of the feeling point of view. It would be by means of this function that he could understand his dreams. The intellect doesn't help him to understand such dreams. Only his feeling can tell him, "Well, but after all, I am influenced by these subjective states, the psychological facts. I think this dream is perfectly marvelous." That is feeling. He can't cope with this side of himself intellectually, but he could from a feeling point of view. But, since he is very intellectual, he has naturally to apologize for his feeling because it might hurt his intellect. That is the reason why you have to exclude thinking, when you are a feeling type, because you mustn't think too much about things that you believe to be beautiful or dear. You might discover a flaw in the crystal or a hair in the soup or something like that.

The advice this intelligent agency is giving to him is expressed in the dream through a very remarkable observation, namely, that "redemption does not come from not going with it." The German word used for "redemption" is *Erlösung*, which isn't exactly "redemption." It means rather a "liberation," also a "liberation from." This doesn't mean refusing to share an experience or keeping away from it, or running away even. Neither does it mean that one should surrender completely to one's impulses without self-control and without reason, which would be the other side. Rather does "redemption," in the sense of *Erlösung*, consist in a complete devotion, in a conscious submission to the facts as they are, to that which you are. If you can do this, if you can submit in this way, then it would surely not be mere blind acceptance.

You also should keep your eye directed upon the center. Now, here you have the very idea of the mandala. The mandala is a circle with a center, and the center is usually characterized by the highest values, usually by divine attributes. As a rule the mandala is used as a so-called *yantra* for contemplation. You see, the circle and the center should catch your attention. It both expresses and produces a state of concentration. If you have that concentration, then you can fuse everything together into that one act of devotion, and this is the thing that transforms. Then it is just as if you were contained in the center, or in the circle, and as if you had been made over in the act of devotion, which the old East Indians called *tapas*, meaning "brooding" or "hatching." It is what the hen does with the egg. It is a term taken from Yoga, where it means a concentration within oneself which causes such a warmth that you become hatched, that the Self develops in you. And that is what his friend means in the dream.

Lecture 8

Ladies and gentlemen:

There seems to be some misunderstanding concerning the personal material in the case about which I am speaking.[1] As I have already told you, these dreams are selected from a series of four hundred, out of which I picked those which contain the so-called mandala motif. You already have a certain idea of what we understand by it; it is the circle, the rotation, the circulation, the circumambulation, the center, the middle; also the square and the four, because the square and the circle always belong together. It is the famous problem of the *quadratura circuli*, the squaring of the circle of medieval times, a terrible abstruse problem over which we naturally smile in a very superior way, because we don't understand it. You see we always turn up our noses at things we do not understand and think they are very stupid, projecting our own idiocy, which is of course easier than to grapple with such a problem.

Many people have dealt with problems like the *quadratura circuli* or the *perpetuum mobile*, which are of course very abstruse problems. We think them only matters for madmen or for those dark, troubled minds of the Middle Ages, when people were all asses. For us there are no such problems, which means that we simply haven't understood them as men did once. We prefer to forget about them, because it is of course much easier not to know about such things. But unfortunately I dig up all these problems from our dreams, and people have to get busy over them again. It is really too bad that such things exist; it would be so much easier if there were some simple scheme so that we could tell people exactly what these dream contents are about. But nature isn't simple. Nature has always been the greatest problem to man, and we never shall arrive at the complete truth about it; still we have to cope with it.

These dreams I have chosen, which contain this particular motif, are, of course, sandwiched in between dreams of a very personal nature, but

---

[1] This lecture was held on October 17, 1937.

as I have already told you I am not allowed to talk about the personal psychology of the dreamer. You know in his own mind he had nothing but personal psychology, and that is just what he suffered from. You see a personalistic psychology is an unconscious psychology, approaching the animal kingdom. As long as you have such a psychology you deserve to be neurotic; for the more personalistic your psychology is the more you approach the morbid level until, when you get entirely personal, you are simply a victim of your own emotions, and of your own animal impulses. For instance, one says to people who get emotional, "Now don't get personal," which simply means, "don't behave like an animal, be reasonable," because one is not reasonable when one is personal.

So you see the kind of psychology which causes one to suffer moves exclusively in the field of the personal emotions, and so the great psychotherapeutic systems of the past, namely, the religions, always tried to heal man through depersonalizing his psychology. For instance, take Christianity. What would Christianity say to the suffering man? It would say, "Sure you suffer, you are sick; but look at the wounds of Christ, how he suffered, and how He was healed and how He heals you. You are not the only one who suffers; many people suffer; look at them; and they are all healed by Christ." That is depersonalization of personal suffering. You do it also quite instinctively when you talk to people who complain about personal and subjective ailments. You say, "Yes, of course, it is difficult, or painful, but look at Mr. and Mrs. So and So; they also have a bad time; they also suffer. Don't make such a fuss about it; you are not the only one." That is only an attempt to depersonalize that particular psychological fact, to get the individual out of a too personal psychology.

Here I am attempting to show you those dreams that definitely contain attempts at self-cure. I want to show you how nature, or the unconscious agencies, try to depersonalize the dreamer's psychology, and release him from the web or confusion or *enchevêtrement*[2] with personal relations. Of course, he is full of relations of a personal or morbid nature. He has a family, as everybody has. He naturally had a pathological dependence of fixation on his parents, and there was an infantile fixation to his sister. All these situations made his life miserable.

Now, you never will cure that man by turning round and round in those things; and as I told you, I did not even touch him; I had not even seen him. I only took his dreams, so that I might see what nature herself

---

[2] French: entanglement.

had tried to do to that man. In that respect the case is unique for it has not been touched or handled at all; this man was absolutely uninfluenced. So there was a really unique chance to observe what nature does when a man is set upon the right track. The first time I saw him I said to him, "You are a man of a certain intelligence, so you will know how to deal with your own material after a relatively short time. Therefore I don't want to interfere. I will tell you only this much. You are, as you yourself know, completely disintegrated and are on your way to hell right away, and you are in despair. Whenever a man is in such a predicament then helpful powers arise from the unconscious. You don't need to believe in the unconscious, or to think anything about it, only to observe your dreams, because your dreams express your unconscious condition. Then after a while when you feel that you have gained a certain insight, when you feel that the unconscious really has done something for you, then you can come to me and show me your dreams; and we will talk about them." That was the instruction.

Being an intelligent fellow he has quite understood that when a man is in trouble, and his conscious mind is upset or deranged, the unconscious, being the more instinctual part of the psyche, or whatever you want to call it, could perhaps produce certain compensations. The body does the same; it works in a compensatory way because the organic system of the body is a self-regulating one. For example, if you have kidney trouble the heart compensates it. There is no reason to believe that the mind is entirely different. The mind is so bound up with the body that we must assume that it is also a self-regulating system which will presumably follow exactly the same laws as the body.

So the hypothesis that both body and mind have compensatory functions was not strange to the dreamer as he is a scientist, without prejudices, and could accept that possibility. Indeed, this hypothesis is as good as any other. It is not nonsense, so you too can accept and follow it. Observe your dreams and see what happens.

Now you see I had to separate the material I could speak about from his personal dreams and his personal material. We do not need to talk of what his relation was to his aunts, his sister, and his grandfather; of how he was thwarted in this way and that or of what he was not allowed to do when he was a child. We leave all that behind, as the dreams had already tried to do. From time to time he had a big dream. I make exactly the same classification as the primitives make with their dreams. They say there are small dreams and big dreams, and only big dreams count; small dreams count for nothing. Small people have small dreams; but this fellow is a big man, so he had more big dreams than usual. The primitives say that their big man is the chief and he has big dreams.

Big dreams have usually a peculiar character, namely, a lot of mythological material peeps through the veil of the dream, often in the form of allusions. Of course it is necessary to know such material; the dream does not say what it means; it does not give you the references, any more than a fish will tell you to what species it belongs. No flower ever told a scientist what its name is. There is a story, I have often quoted, of a man, a great admirer of astronomy, who used to say: "Astronomy is really the greatest science; they have found out how far the stars are from the earth, which is marvelous; and it is still more wonderful how they found out what the weight of the stars is; but the greatest discovery, which I myself cannot even understand, is how they found out what the stars are called, what their names are."

So the analyst who deals with dreams must needs have a certain education; he must possess a solid knowledge of historical symbology, otherwise he does not know what big dreams are nor where archetypal material shines forth. He simply overlooks it all because of his complete and profound ignorance. I must say I could not have dealt with the dreamer if I had not had a certain idea of his material. If I had left him to his own ideas he would have got stuck, because his knowledge was too little. He could not understand the big dreams, despite the fact that many things are of astonishing clearness. There were certain symbols where he simply said, "Well, I must give up; I don't understand it." This happened in one of the greatest visions he had, which made an enormous impression on him; it was really the turning point in his whole development, but he could not understand it at all. Therefore, every big dream he had produced an evil impression on him because he could not understand it. He said: "It is impossible that I contain things I don't understand. Only a mad man has such experience. A reasonable person understands his whole psychology." It is just as if you should say that every reasonable person knows all about his body and its functions. Plenty of people live in a body and don't know how it functions, nevertheless it functions. But they always forget to apply that very banal truth to their own psychology. Psychology can function without the individual knowing how. Psychology is not what a man knows of his own psychology. That is only his conscious point of view. Yet his conscious is a little speck of light on this or that point, a little lighted up area; that is all, and the rest is complete darkness.

You see our conscious is like an island in a vast ocean, whose extent we don't know because it is unconscious. The very word unconscious means we don't know it; it is profound, abysmal; we can't say it comes to an end anywhere, because we don't know the end. When we say the unconscious, we think we have said something. We have said nothing, except that we don't know. We know nothing about the unconscious. But that is where our real psychology is. Objective psychology is not what people know in the conscious mind about themselves. You would not assume that when a man says, "I know my heart is here," that he has any knowledge of anatomy. If anatomy consisted of what people know of their own anatomy, where would we be in medicine? This is why we have science, and make researches, and establish definite facts. That is exactly what I am trying to do, namely, to acquire knowledge of the objective mind or the objective psychology of the human mind, which is not what people think of themselves. That would be a psychology of human illusions and childishness, and this is exactly what everybody suffers from. If you want to have a sane mind you must get away from these very incomplete things; you must not turn round and round in them. Now I hope I made that point clear.

Well, I think we are now ready to continue with our dream. I have already told you that it is as if there were an intelligent agency at work in our unconscious mind which produces the healing effect. This is a careful formulation of observable facts; it is not a theory by which we assume that there are or must be or ought to be such agencies; it is simply a formulation of actual experience. There is evidence of this in the dream we have begun to deal with: the letter the dreamer receives from his friend, in which there were remarks or observations about redemption. In this letter it is said that redemption is not due to a sort of running away from difficulties or disagreeable things; redemption cannot take place when you avoid disagreeable difficulties; also that redemption cannot come about when you surrender blindly without self-control to unconscious impulses, which is the other extreme. Either you go with the unconscious without self-control, you surrender completely to its intimations; and you behave like an animal, driven by instincts; or you keep away from all that. Those are the two extremes, and redemption has nothing to do with either of them. You can let yourself go in emotion. That is wrong. Or avoid emotion. That is wrong, too. The right thing would be something else. The letter tries to illustrate this point, therefore it says redemption can only take place when it is a matter of complete devotion, namely, a complete concentration of your willpower upon a certain goal, and that goal is characterized or explained as the middle.

If you realize what such a message means, you will come to the conclusion that it is something like a bit of Eastern philosophy. You see that *middle* sounds peculiarly Chinese. This man has never been busy with Eastern philosophy. The Tao to him is an unknown quantity. But if I should tell this to an educated Chinaman he would say, "Here we are right in the midst of it; this is the Taoist philosophy; this is Laotze; this is Eastern wisdom."

Now where does it come from? He has not thought it, yet this letter sounds as if somebody had thought it, as if he himself had consciously thought these sentences. But actually he dreamed them and was himself baffled by them and could not understand how he got such ideas; yet there they were. If you got a letter with such contents you would naturally conclude that somebody with a certain amount of intelligence and consciousness had written it. Now why shouldn't we draw such a conclusion here, too? We are forced to do so, because if we say this was due only to organic cerebration, and these things coagulated accidentally—well, I should reply that if they coagulate in such a way that an intelligent message comes through, it is a pretty intelligent coagulation! So don't play with words; we don't need Greek or Latin words to designate the process; we simply say this is very intelligent, and that is all there is to it. It is intelligent, and it is mighty good advice.

If you translate the message into ordinary language it would amount to something like this: you find a man in a disintegrated condition, and you say, "Come on, old fellow, pull yourself together; let's be interested in something. Concentrate your mind upon a goal. Pull all your powers, your whole personality, together, and get ready to do something." That would be about the same. Yet curiously enough it isn't expressed in the dream in the form of such a commonsense admonition but is stated in almost hieratic[3] language, familiar to anybody who knows anything about Oriental texts. Perhaps you already feel a certain likeness to biblical language or something of the sort, but if you have a certain knowledge of Eastern texts then you see the exact similarity. This is a product of the unconscious mind; a perfectly reasonable and very wise exhortation.

So we are forced to the assumption that there must be a pretty intelligent agency at work in his unconscious to help this man, to pull him to-

---

[3] Spoken in a language associated with sacred persons or offices; sacerdotal. From Greek *hiertikos*, see also *hieros*: holy.

gether, to make him concentrate upon the middle. Now I want to remain with that word "middle" for a while. It is important because it refers to the mandala, to the center of the circle. The center of the circle is the middle ground between pairs of opposites; it is the reconciling symbol, which reconciles dissociations, controls contradictions and conflicts. It is the black and white stream coming together; in Chinese language it is the Tao. The Tao is the middle, the middle way. Now this is a concept we don't possess in our Weltanschauung; in medieval philosophy, born about 1100, it was still going strong, but we have no such concept because we went off on an intellectual tangent; we began to speculate with our intellect rising up to the seventh or eighth floor, high above odious realities, as the dreamer tried to do in the American skyscraper hotel.

So that problem of the pairs of opposites practically escaped our Western philosophy. Any European philosopher of our day would be gravely offended if one talked to him of pairs of opposites, because he doesn't understand that; it doesn't exist in his world because his philosophy got away from it long ago. Of course that is due to a peculiar development of our Western mind which began with Scholasticism. I don't want to go into that, but we should understand such historical origins in order to know where we are now, for without understanding this we shall never understand what the origin and conditions of our neuroses and mental disturbances are. For instance, I had to go out of Europe, out of the civilized world in order to get a glimpse of the real European. You can only get that when you go to primitive countries where you can look at the white man through other eyes; then you get an idea of what he is. But if you are in the white crowd, you are just one of those specimens, and you share the psychology of the crowd by *participation mystique*;[4] and you are submerged by all the prejudices of the white man, and you cannot see him from the outside.

In the same way we have to go into other mental circles, into other philosophies, other creeds, other religions, in order to see what our trouble

---

[4] Concept coined by Lucien Lévy-Bruhl, mystical participation, denotes a peculiar kind of psychological connection with objects and consists in the fact that the subject cannot clearly distinguish himself from the object but is bound to it by a direct relationship which amounts to partial identity. Lévy-Bruhl, 1985, 345. Jung read this work around 1910, but he only later started to use the concept in his own works. He adopted it to describe the unconscious identity between a person and an object, which is a natural state for infancy, but with increasing age this becomes a problem, and one needs to realize that this experience of identity rests on projection of psychic content on outer objects. See Shamdasani, 2012, 55, and "Concerning the Archetypes with Special Reference to the Anima Concept"(1954), CW 9/I, par. 121.

is, and then we behold that the white man has climbed way up in his intellect and left his other side to complete darkness. This is a fact; and it is
also the case with the dreamer. He has a powerful intellect, and he mas-
tered his world with his intellect exclusively, and then more and more it
dawned upon him that he was not master of himself. He wasn't master
of his destiny. He could do what he wanted to do in his intellect, but that
could not help him in the least when it came to the living of his human
life. There he got into no end of trouble because one side of him was absolutely undifferentiated. His feeling was just as far down as his intellect
was up, and that, of course, caused a tremendous conflict. Now this man
was a bachelor, and life pushed him into a situation where he should have
been able to use his feeling function, but the inferior function usually
shows itself first in a very disagreeable way.[5]

To such a man the feeling function would naturally be represented by
a woman. So his feeling, being completely in the unconscious, would be
projected upon a woman, and then when one turned up and got near him,
he would get the full impact of his unconscious. Then he would either fall
for her quite blindly, although she might be worth nothing, or less than
nothing, or he would run away from her, being afraid because she represented the unconscious with ten thousand horns, an elephant or a monster. But, of course, the woman would not understand why that fellow
should run away, and he could not understand it either because he did
not see it. That is the usual story of how an intellectual gets into trouble.
When his feeling comes up it carries the whole power of the unconscious,
and his feet become entangled in a web he doesn't understand. Then he
gets dreams of this kind, and if he doesn't understand them, he cannot
disentangle his feeling from the unconscious. It doesn't help at all to say,
"This is all nonsense, or it is infantile, or something like that." He himself
feels that the material contains gold no matter how ugly it looks. He was
clever enough to see that, and not for one single second would I have tried
to convince him that it was all bunk, or childish fantasy stuff. Of course
his consciousness would have rejoiced at such an idea, but the next night
he would have had a dream that would have blasted him to pieces.

Well now, you see, in this dream the message, that very wise, helpful
message, was beyond him somehow. He couldn't grasp it apparently. I
must call your attention to the fact that in order to make it clear what the
"middle" meant, there was a drawing of a wheel with eight spokes added

---

[5] For Jung's definition of the feeling function, see CW 6, par. 723.

to the letter. You see, it is just as if that unconscious agency would point out, "Now, look here, what I understand by the middle is the mandala." The mandala has eight spokes, just as you go up to the eighth floor, but the eight, or the four, if things are normal, are always arranged symmetrically in a squared circle, the quadratura circuli. But in this case the whole was represented symbolically by his trip up in the elevator, so that instead of circumambulating the mandala, making a circle with four or eight partitions, as it ought to be, this man goes straight up in a vertical line, for this is the prejudice of our intellect, that we can lift ourselves out of humanity, out of the slime in which we are, and can soar somewhere above.

So, he follows the invitation of the lift boy who had told him that his room was on the eighth floor. But to him the lift boy is, of course, a miserable little quantity, a *quantité negligeable*. Yet the lift boy is part of his personality, that part which is absolutely incapable of dealing with these problems and which naturally thinks of nothing but lifts. So he steps in and goes up and expects to arrive on the eighth story, where his room is, but the same difficulty occurs again: he doesn't know whether he has landed at the seventh or the eighth floor. But when he steps out of the lift, a man with a pointed red beard is there, who greets him with a friendly smile. Now we have encountered that fellow before; he appeared in the earlier dreams as the devil. The dreamer had recognized him right from the beginning as Mephisto, the typical Mephisto from *Faust*, and had himself thought, "This must have to do with my intellect. This is the intellectual fellow." And mind you, if you study the story of Mephisto in *Faust*, he is the intellect, a sort of Luciferean intellect, that depreciates everything, reducing it to a "nothing but." So you see, when he rises to a height where he thinks, "now we are safe," up comes the devil and says, "Here we are, my dear fellow," and takes him into custody.

But, why that peculiar idea, that there should be trouble between three and four or seven and eight? Well, anybody who knows German literature can't help remembering that same difficulty arose in the second part of *Faust*. There in the so-called classical Walpurgis Night, a parallel to the German *Walpurgisnacht* where the witches ride to the *Blocksberg*,[6] but in the witches' Sabbath of classical antiquity, instead of witches, there

---

[6] Walpurgis Night, usually celebrated on April 30 or May 1, is a pre-Christian traditional spring festival celebrated with bonfires, music, and dance. During the Middle Ages it became associated with the witches' Sabbath. Blocksberg or Brocken is the highest of the Harz Mountains of north central Germany.

appear all the figures of Greek folklore: Sirens and Nereids and Tritons and gods, and so on.

The Sirens above in the rocks sing:

What do we see in the far distance, lifted high above the surface of the water, as when by the purpose of the wind the snowy sails are billowing forward; such is the brightness of the transfigured sea-nymphs! Let us hurry and climb swiftly downward, for listen! They are singing!

The Nereids and the Tritons:

That which we are carrying upon our hands shall be to each and every one a source of pleasure; reflected from the immensity of the tortoise-shell are definite images, symbols of the gods whom we are bringing. Chant to them your lofty songs of praise!

I quote from a translation in prose which I owe to the kindness of Mrs. Eckstein, translator of the first part of *Faust*, an excellent translation by the way.[7] Now though English is, of course, a very perfect language, it doesn't exactly render the peculiar magic of Goethe's verses, so I must read you this particular passage from the German text.

Sirenen:
 Klein von Gestalt,
 Gross von Gewalt,
 Der Scheiternden Retter,
 Uralt verehrte Götter.
The Sirens: These tiny deities, powerful in strength, are the gods,
 primitively revered as saviours of the shipwrecked.
Nereids und Tritons:
 Wir bringen die Kabiren,
 Ein friedlich Fest zu führen;
 Denn wo sie heilig walten,
 Neptun wird freundlich schalten.
The Nereids and the Tritons: We bring you the Cabiri, to initiate this
 festival in peace; for wherever they hold sacred sway, there
 Neptune will be propitious.

This is a very dark passage. The idea is that the sea gods or demons bring a peculiar symbol in a tortoise shell. The second part of *Faust* is an alchemistic drama, and the old alchemists had an apparatus called the *testudo*, or tortoise shell; it looked like a sort of spoon.

---

[7] See the introduction to this volume concerning Alice Raphael (married Eckstein). She was also convinced that the second part of *Faust* dealt with an alchemical problem.

The bowl would be the shell of the tortoise and the handle the tail. It was used for melting metal over the fire. Now when the alchemists melted metal over the fire, peculiar vapors arose, and the colors of the rainbow appeared on the surface of the metal, which they called the *cauda pavonis*, or peacock's tail. As they were so deeply concentrated on their world, expecting the great miracle to happen, they began to see visions in the vapors that arose, and there they saw, not the miracle that was in matter, but the miracle that was inside themselves, just as when you look intently enough into the unknown, you discover the unknown in yourself and see the bottom of your own soul, not the bottom of matter; and so they projected the secret proceedings of their own unconscious into those vapors. Now that is the vision to which *Faust* alludes, namely, a peculiar symbol appears out of the alchemical vessel. But we don't know what that peculiar symbol was, perhaps a particular demon or fate.

There is a passage in a Zosimos[8] text which Goethe could not have known because it was not printed then. There the *periekonismenon* is spoken of. This term comes from the word *eikon* meaning image; *peri* means round, and the periekonismenon is the thing that is built round. In the famous visions of Zosimos the periekonismenon is brought in during the alchemical procedure by an angel or demon. And that word *periekonismenon*, the round object, recalls the German word *Gebilde*, which is in the testudo in our passage from *Faust*.

So you see, we have ample evidence (I could add any amount of documentary evidence) that this is the so-called round of elements which plays a very great role in alchemy. It is the alchemistic mandala. So we are quite safe in assuming that the peculiar symbol that appears here was a mandala.

Now in the verses the mandala is explained as being "little gods," and you will see how Goethe defines these gods. He says, "These tiny deities, powerful in strength, are the gods revealed from primitive times as saviors of the shipwrecked. To initiate this festival in peace, we bring you the Cabiri." This peculiar word in Latin is the *Cabiri*; in Arabic it is the *el*

---

[8] Zosimos, a Greek alchemist, lived in AD 300. Jung had just given a lecture on the Visions of Zosimos at the Eranos conference in August 1937. Cf. Jung (1938), also in CW 13, "The Visions of Zosimos."

kabir, the great one, the powerful one, or the mighty one.[9] It is a relative of Akbar-Kabira. These are then the great ones, yet they are tiny deities. Now these are the homunculi; the little dwarfs that belong to the alchemistic miracles.

Do you remember he had before this a dream of the dwarfs, or little boys who fell into the cave? There were two already in the cave, and one fell into it. They correspond to the parts of the mandala, the four corners; also to the four snakes. Now these Cabiri are unconscious, fragmentary souls, fragments of personality, personifying helpful, intelligent agencies. Therefore, in Greek folklore, the Cabiri were those who brought wisdom to men, who taught them how to dig up metals, and to produce metal out of the rough ore. They also taught them all kinds of crafts; they were sort of thumblings and so are relatives, near cousins, of the so-called Daktyls; meaning thumblings, or fingers, and in particular the Idaean Daktyls[10] were famous. Heracles was a Daktyl as a child. Faust says: "as to size, small, but as to power, big."[11] They are the dwarfs in fairy tales, too, the Heinzelmännchen, the brownies. You find them everywhere. These helpful powers are the agencies that are parts, the four or the eight parts of the mandala. Now you will presently hear something about exactly that.

The Sirens sing: "We readily admit your greater powers; whenever a ship has foundered, irresistible in power, you protect the crew."[12]

This is the great helpful power.

Then they sing: "But three have we brought with us, the fourth refused to come; he claims to be the genuine god, who for all of them does the thinking."[13]

---

[9] The Cabiri were the deities celebrated at the mysteries of Samothrace. They were held to be promoters of fertility and protectors of sailors. Jung already discussed the Cabiri in *Transformations and Symbols of the Libido* (1912), CW B, pars. 209–11. The motif of the kabir had accompanied Jung from his earliest childhood, and he describes how he as child manufactured a little manikin from his wooden ruler that represented a hidden and secret part of himself. *MDR*, 5–38. Later the Cabiri confronted him in his imaginatory material rendered in *The Red Book*, where they present themselves as "We are the juices that rise secretly, not by force, but sucked out of inertia and affixed to what is growing. We know the unknown ways and the inexplicable laws of living matter." Cf. *RB*, 320; see also n. 310; see also the Cabiri in Goethe's *Faust*, part 2, 308 (par. 8180). J. W. V. Goethe and S. Atkins, trans. (1984), *Faust I and II* (Cambridge, MA: Suhrkamp).

[10] A member of the group of mysterious beings who dwelt on Mount Ida on the island of Crete; as a group they are referred to as the Idaean (Idaian) Daktyls. Apollonios Rhodios and P. Green, trans. (1997), *The Argonautika* (Berkeley: University of California Press), book 1, line 1129.

[11] Goethe and Atkins, 1984, 308 (par. 8175).

[12] Goethe and Atkins, 1984, 308 (par. 8185).

[13] Goethe and Atkins, 1984, 308 (par. 8180).

You see, here you have three. Where is the fourth? This is the beginning of the temenos, you know. There are, however, only three; where is
the fourth?[14]

Now, what does that mean? You see, these little dwarfs, whose power
is so great, being the unconscious functions, the real foundations of the
structure of our conscious personality, these Cabiri are four or perhaps
eight. Now one always seems to be lacking, therefore, the question, "There
are three; where is the fourth?" And there is something particular in the
case of the fourth. That fourth one won't come. He refuses to join in somehow. Now which function would refuse to appear? Well, the one that isn't
welcome. Now, you see, when Goethe, in the first part of *Faust*, says,
"Feeling is everything," "Gefühl ist alles," he is declaring that feeling is
the highest value, the best, the most important function, that which expresses the whole world.[15] Now this is the confession of the feeling type;
no thinking type would ever say such a thing. He would say, "Feeling!
That is my housekeeper, or that is my wife, or my mother. That has nothing to do with the Weltanschauung. Feeling for New Year's Day or a birthday or perhaps occasionally in a concert, but not otherwise." Feeling is
nothing, you see. He would never say, "Feeling is everything." But when
somebody says, "Feeling is everything," instantly number four goes to hell,
for then thinking is nothing, because these two functions oppose each
other, and when you feel exclusively then you have to check your thinking. It is not healthy to think when you want to feel exclusively. That is
the reason why the fellow who thinks will exclude feeling as much as
possible. Of course, he believes that he has a lot of feeling. Naturally! But
when you ask him what feelings consist of, you will hear of emotions,
and mind you, emotions are not feelings. It is a great mistake to think
that feeling consists of emotions. Emotions are states that have you, but
if you have feeling, *you* have the feeling; the feeling does not have you. If
it has you, it is an emotion. Mark that difference.[16]

Now when Goethe declares, "Feeling is everything," then you can be
sure that his thinking has gone deep down, that when he needs it, it won't
be there. Three have come; where is the fourth? The fourth refuses to
come, and yet he says that he is the one who claims to be the genuine God

---

[14] Compared to the EYB 1935 Jung has added two paragraphs in *PsA* on the problem
of getting from the three to the four, and on the axiom of Maria Prophetissa from alchemy.
CW 12, pars. 209–10.

[15] Goethe and Atkins, 1984, 140 (par. 3455).

[16] For Jung's distinction between emotion/affect and feeling, see "Psychological Types,"
CW 6, par. 681.

who is doing the thinking for everybody, who would think for all of them. This means that the fourth function in Goethe's case is thinking.

Now, of course, if you take a thinking type, then number four who refuses to appear will be feeling. That will be the case with our patient. You see he has been maneuvered by his life into some funny relations to women, where he needed his feeling judgment. Feeling is a function of values, and his feelings would have told him, "Now, look here, this girl is just wrong you see; that won't work at all." But there he got his feet in the wrong place, and, of course, it upset his apple cart completely because he couldn't understand it by means of his wonderful intellect. You never can make out a woman by intellect. That is the mistake that so many men make. They think that the way to see through women or to do anything with them is by thinking, but that isn't the way. The only function that can help is feeling.

Well, when he was challenged in his feeling function; there was nothing doing. Feeling, number four, would not come, which explains why he had so much difficulty when he arrived at the third or the fourth floor. He gets into an unconscious condition so that he doesn't know whether this is three or four, and it always seems as if four hadn't come; and when he went higher up there was the same confusion about the seventh or the eighth story. Now, let us listen to Goethe again:

The Sirens sing: "So it may happen that one god holds the other god up to scorn; do honor to their beneficence, but beware their powers of evil."

The Nereids and Tritons: "In truth they number seven."

The Sirens: "Where stay the other three?"

The Nereids and Tritons: "That we cannot answer; on Olympus they may be questioned; there perhaps is the eighth god, of whom no one has thought until now. They are disposed to do us favors though not yet consummated; these incomparable beings, always striving further, are consumed by a yearning hunger for the unattainable."[17]

Now, you see, we hear that it is not four; we hear it is seven, exactly as in the dream of our patient, only with him it wasn't a matter of Cabiri, but a matter of stories. And here we are told that the three or four other Cabiri are way up on Olympus. Is the story seven or eight, and, of course, is it three or four? Again the same uncertainty, and the question in *Faust* is, "Where is the eighth?" exactly like "Where is the fourth?" The question simply is repeated. It remains the same problem; there is always that uncertainty. He could go up to the sixteenth, and the question would still

---

[17] *Faust I and II*, 309 (par. 8200).

be is it the fifteenth or the sixteenth, where is the sixteenth, and so on? Where is the thirty-second? We shall see later on that he has the thirty-second, but in a different arrangement.

I hope I have succeeded in making clear what is meant by this peculiar first part of the dream. It concerns the question of how to deal with the four functions, or with the totality of the functions, which means the totality of the personality, for he would only be a whole if he were able to assemble the four, but there is always the difficulty that number four refuses to come, that is, the fourth part of himself, the inferior function, is hesitant about appearing, and this reluctance brings with it a sort of unconsciousness, so that he doesn't know whether he is on the third or the fourth story, or the seventh or the eighth. Now this simply comes from the fact that the fourth function, being the inferior function, has descended into the unconscious because it wasn't tolerated in the conscious. In the conscious there was a prejudice in favor of the differentiated function, in his case thinking, and thinking doesn't tolerate equally important feeling, for if feeling were to persist in consciousness, it could only be or live in the same right, and with that same competence and authority, as thinking, but thinking will only tolerate as much feeling or feeling of a kind, which coincides with or obeys and adapts to thinking. That means that thinking will allow a certain amount of feeling with pleasure, but it must be feeling that fits in with the thinking. Now practically that means that only those values are allowed to exist that fit in with preconceived intellectual statements. Anything beyond, anything independent, anything autonomous, will not be tolerated but will be wiped out; which means that feeling of a kind or value which would not contradict an intellectual statement would simply not be valid. It would have to disappear, because the differentiated function always has to be absolutely valid, absolutely right.

There was once a philosopher, with whom I discussed the problem of functional types, who said, "Well, of course, any other mental function is relative, but thinking can never be wrong." Now what can you do against that? Of course, I could do nothing. I said, "Well, we will just wait and see, my dear man." But he got my goat. [Laughter] For when a fellow makes such a statement, I find myself thinking, "Well, perhaps he is right," and I feel very small. And then I get spiteful because I cannot go below my own size, and when somebody makes me feel like nothing, then he gets it in the neck somehow. So, I will tell you what I did. Of course, it was terribly mean, but it was psychological. [Laughter] Well, I knew he had a wife. I said (you see my reckoning was simple), "Thinking cannot be wrong; therefore, way on top. Feeling is quite inferior, quite low, quite archaic, savage, somewhere in the cellar, in the slime, and his wife has to represent it because he has projected it into his wife." I didn't know her at all. I thought I must find out something about his wife. Now I happened to know where that man lived, and not very far from that man lived a patient of mine, and that patient was well acquainted with another patient (also a lady) who happened to be a friend, and per chance the intimate friend of Mrs. So-and-So. So I asked that lady to do me a favor and to inquire about Mrs. So-and-So.

Now, the story we heard was very interesting. His wife is a very nice and intelligent person, and she was a bit annoyed with that "thinking that is never wrong" [*laughter*], and she entered into enterprises on her own account and disappeared occasionally for four or five weeks, and she confessed to her intimate friend, who, of course, hastened to betray that little secret wherever she could, that she had an affair with a student whom she visited during the four of five weeks when she disappeared from home.

I said, "Now, that is the thinking that never can go wrong." He didn't think that about his wife, and there he was wrong. [*Laughter*] Then, in the meantime (I hadn't seen him for a long time) it came to his notice, and the whole thing blew up, and when I met him again he didn't repeat that statement. He had a hole, and he didn't know how to stuff it up. He was disorientated in this world. You see, that is what the inferior function can do; it can work extraordinary things to a Weltanschauung.

In the case of my patient, his feeling was below in a primitive condition. Whatever is in the unconscious is contaminated with everything that is in the unconscious, and that is, of course, a tremendous mix-up. All the unconscious contents, the archaic, historical things are interwoven with the feeling, and when you try to pull up feeling for use, why you pull up a whole world; the whole world shakes when you try to pull it up, and that is why the fourth won't come up. He doesn't refuse to come; he can't come. You can't pull him up, and therefore, you have to bow down to him.

You see, it is that story of Heracles, who went down into Hades, and there he found Theseus and Pirithous, the two friends held fast to the rock.[18] They had gone down originally on a peculiar errand, to bring

---

[18] Heracles (Greek Herakles, Roman Hercules), one of the most legendary Greco-Roman heroes. Heracles was traditionally seen as the son of Zeus and Alcmene, granddaughter of Perseus. Zeus swore that the next son born of the Perseid house should become ruler of Greece, but by a trick of Zeus's jealous wife, Hera, another child, the sickly Eurystheus, was born first and became king. When growing up Heracles had to serve him and also suffer the vengeful persecution of Hera. His first exploit, in fact, was the strangling of two serpents that she had sent to kill him in his cradle. It was Eurystheus who imposed on Heracles the

Persephone up from Hades. They descended for a long time, and then they got tired and sat down on a rock, and when they tried to get up again, they couldn't; they were held fast to the rock, and there they were. Then Heracles came down to liberate them, and he took hold of Pirithous first, who was the lesser hero but couldn't tear himself loose from the rock. Theseus, being a big man, a big hero, a first-class man, was, of course, held much faster to the rock so that when Heracles shook him to tear him loose, the earth shook to such an extent that even the gods got frightened, and he had to leave him below and himself go up again. Since then, Theseus is down there tied to the rock. This is a psychological story which means that the same thing can happen when you go down in order to get the inferior function. You see, the dreamer was forced, more or less, to go down in order to bring up his feeling, and then when he saw what the condition was down there he got frightened out of his wits, because he saw the whole underworld slowly opening up. And that contact which he had established was sufficient to bring up the contents of the unconscious, and so he got the big dreams. Now, if you do not understand what such dreams mean, you only can drop them, and then the only thing that might help, the inferior function, drops down again into the unconscious, and there it remains like old Theseus, and you are deprived of number four.

Now in order to heal him, the unconscious had to make the proposal to bring up number four, or to do something about it, and this is an attempt in a way, yet it is an attempt in the wrong direction. You see he tried to get away from the problem, yet the problem followed him up but in a distorted form, so that instead of making the squareness of the circle, that is, assembling the four around himself, he put them up like a sort of ladder into Heaven, and at the end of his going up—well, there is Hera, who catches hold of him. Now, the scene changes in the dream; this is the end of the first part.

---

famous labors, later arranged in a cycle of twelve, usually as follows: (1) the slaying of the Nemean lion, whose skin he thereafter wore; (2) the slaying of the nine-headed Hydra of Lerna; (3) the capture of the elusive hind (or stag) of Arcadia; (4) the capture of the wild boar of Mount Erymanthus; (5) the cleansing, in a single day, of the cattle stables of King Augeas of Elis; (6) the shooting of the monstrous man-eating birds of the Stymphalian marshes; (7) the capture of the mad bull that terrorized the island of Crete; (8) the capture of the man-eating mares of King Diomedes of the Bistones; (9) the taking of the girdle of Hippolyte, queen of the Amazons; (10) the seizing of the cattle of the three-bodied giant Geryon, who ruled the island Erytheia (meaning Red) in the far west; (11) the bringing back of the golden apples kept at the world's end by the Hesperides; and (12) the fetching up from the lower world of the triple-headed dog Cerberus, guardian of its gates.

Then comes another part; there is no interruption; the scene simply shifts in the dream. It is no longer America; it is now Switzerland, and he hears that a revolution has started. There is a military party which makes a terrific propaganda, whose tendency is, as he hears, to strangle the Left entirely (that means the political Left). Somebody says, "But the Left side is already quite weak." But others reply, "For that very reason, the Left side ought to be strangled entirely."

Now, without further explanation, you see that the Left side is the unconscious side for that is the sinister side, and the dream says, that his unconscious should be strangled, suffocated. Mind you, he is here to answer the devil, and it is, of course, the tendency of the superior function to deny the unconscious entirely and so to suffocate it, suppress it, annihilate it. And now soldiers appear in old-fashioned uniforms, and they all look a bit like the man with the pointed red beard, all devils, but in old-fashioned uniforms. Now uniforms always mean *uniformitus*, uniformity; that is, of the same opinion, the same way, the same style. It is collective opinion, old-fashioned and traditional. These soldiers are the representatives of old-fashioned traditional tendencies to strangle the unconscious completely, denying even its existence. That is, of course, a most radical measure. It frees the individual right away from discussing with the unconscious the series of negatives or of taking them into account at all. Now, these soldiers who have old-fashioned rifles prepare to fire. They form a ring, and all make ready to shoot into a center. But the shooting doesn't begin, and it seems to the dreamer as if the soldiers were finally walking away, but nevertheless he wakes up in a state of fear. And that is the end.

Now you see, what the last part of the dream says is merely the conclusion. It is a picture which shows in a vivid way what is going on in him, the acceptance of a traditional collective opinion, that the unconscious has no right to exist; that there is no such thing as an inferior function; that feeling, the dark woman, who is so awkward that she has been left below on the ground floor or in the cellar, does not exist; and that the idea of a center upon which one should concentrate is to be executed, to be shot to pieces by these collective tendencies. You know, as soon as he gets into the hands of the devil, then, of course, he is disintegrated. The devil is the disintegrator par excellence, the destroyer. Then he becomes one of the many who have only a personal psychology and no center at all. He has only those views that move the masses, which everybody has. He is a particle of a newspaper perhaps, but nothing else, and that condition is represented by these uniformed soldiers who extinguish the idea of a center, in other words, of a reconciling symbol which would bring together the parts. They simply deny the existence of something which could compensate. To them there is only one thing, and that is intellectual truth, and outside of that intellectual truth, well, there is the end of the world. There is nothing. Thinking cannot be wrong, therefore, everything else is wrong, and it must be wiped out.

This is a dream that is morally negative in spite of the fact that it contains again hints at the real problem, namely, how to arrive at the place where the four would be together, where the four would be accomplished or put together.

Now, we will see what this dream produced in him. The end of the dream is slightly less unfavorable, inasmuch as the soldiers do not actually shoot and seem to walk away. So we can assume that the attempts at the collection of the four will be continued or renewed.

The next dream begins with the statement that he is again in the square room, which means that he is again in the mandala, in the place where the four ought to be or can be put together, where the synthesis can take place.[19] And here, he finds himself sitting opposite the unknown woman, the one who had been left downstairs in the dreams before. This means, that his opposite, his female counterpart, representing the inferior function is now on the same level with him. Now that is, of course, an important step forward. He is confronted with his inferior function. Presumably the preceding dream has left a definite impression; things cannot go on like this. The letter with the important advice still has a certain effect. At first, it was apparently denied because refused, but it seems as if that letter had some influence because this dream now begins in a most positive way. He is confronted with his inferior feminine side, with his anima, representing the feeling function, and this is exactly the situation which he has always tried to avoid. He is afraid of such a confrontation on an equal level, and in the dream he has the task of making a portrait or drawing of that lady.

Now, he is not an artist, and it seemed a very strange thing to him that he should be called upon in a dream to make a portrait, and as a matter of fact, what he was actually drawing in the dream (he then had pencil and paper) was not a portrait or a face; it was a design of clover leaves, always in three parts, like distorted crosses, but in four different colors, namely, blue, green, yellow, and red.

---

[19] "Dream Symbols," nr. 23, p. 164, and CW 12, nr. 23, par. 212. M 23 {0194}: (figs. 14, 15, 16) "In the square room again. Has to draw," June 8, 1932, CDM.

Now, if you pay attention to the text of the dream, you see again the problem of the three and the four. This shows a peculiar parallel to certain statements of medieval alchemistic philosophy, for the philosopher's stone has three qualities and four natures, or, it has three colors and four elements, elementary qualities, warm, cold, dry, and humid; or four colors, red, yellow, green, and blue, or according to the original and ancient formulation black, white, red, and yellow. But often the texts say, "the prima materia," the primal matter, which is a sort of mystical idea, or the philosopher's stone, has three colors and four natures, namely, the nature of fire, of earth, of water, and of air. You know the statements of alchemy shift a great deal, but the thing which is invariably there is the same peculiar contradiction between the three and the four; that never varies.

So you see, the plant, the clover leaf with three leaflets, represents a Trinity, as do the crosses, because the crosses and the leaves he drew were like this.

Now that, of course, emphasizes the Trinity. You see, our cross has this form on account of the Trinity, while the earlier cross, the primitive pre-Christian cross, is a cross of equal branches surrounded by a circle, which has, of course, an entirely different meaning. It is the cross of space; it is east, south, west and north, or it is the triumphant Christ in the center and the four Evangelist symbols in the corners.

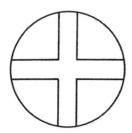

Now you see, the Trinity again means the three functions together, and the fourth is represented by the four different colors. That is not a union; it is not a synthesis. The things haven't come together. But the Trinity symbols are given four different colors, in what is at least an honest attempt to bring the two apparently absolutely contradictory statements together. The fact that the four is not represented by a four-leaf clover or by a cross of equal branches, but by four colors, so that the four is represented by something totally different from the Trinity, refers to an incommensurable factor. This points, as Goethe has already indicated, to the fact that the fourth or the eighth is represented as in some way very peculiar, and we can infer that it is the genuine or the most important function; the fourth is something totally different from the third. It is just as if that substance or function which was rejected is more important and is different in principle from the three already existing. Now that can only be explained by the fact that the fourth function, being contained in the unconscious, has become contaminated with the collective unconscious and has therefore taken on an entirely different quality from the three functions which were capable of being conscious.

In our dreamer's case, the fourth function, his feeling, if it could come up into consciousness, would be entirely different in character from the three functions of which he is conscious. His thinking, his sensation, his intuition, would be psychological functions, as we know them, but his feeling would be something quite different, something important and, presumably, unrecognizable. He would not recognize it as a psychological function. When we speak of the fourth function as being the feeling, we assume that it is a psychological function just as thinking or any other function is and that all we have to do is to detach it from the unconscious, to tear it loose and bring it up into the conscious, and then it would be the usual feeling; but that is not true. This is an important point: for people always suffer from the prejudice that the fourth function can be simply detached from the unconscious and that then this would have the characteristics of usual feeling or thinking, as the case may be, because this holds true of every other function that is not contaminated with the unconscious. But when a function once has been contaminated with the unconscious, it is quite different from one of the conscious functions and is psychologically something very dangerous even. Therefore, people are absolutely afraid to touch it. When they think they have liberated the inferior function from the unconscious, and haven't yet gone through God knows what, you can be sure it has been a hoax, just an illusion, because to bring up the fourth function means to bring up the whole of the unconscious, and that is no small matter.

Therefore, Goethe rightly says, "The fourth, that is the real thing! That is the God! That is the one who functions for all!" This means that it is really the superior thing. Well, it is the stone that the builders rejected; it becomes the head stone of the corner. This is also the philosopher's stone of the old alchemists, which is the *lapis angularis*, the cornerstone, and it is also called the light that is greater than all lights; they even call it *lux moderna*, the modern light. The light greater than all light means a new manifestation of the deity almost. Therefore, the philosopher's stone is identified with Christ, because Christ was always "the light that lighteth every man that comes into the world."[20] The fourth function is the Redeemer because if you succeed in getting up the fourth function and you can stand it, then you are cured, because the fourth function brings up everything of which you are afraid. If you want to find the fourth function, go where you are the most afraid. Follow your fear to find your destiny, and there you will find your fourth function. It is destiny; it is fate; and it is real life. It is a reality, an attractive reality, and so, quite often, it is most advisable *not* to seek it.

We assume, of course, that carrying on their laboratory experiments with melting ores, and so on, was a peaceful occupation, but nevertheless the old alchemists said, "There are some who went under in our work." And this is true of the problem of the fourth function. It is the whole adventure; it is the whole risk of life, because if you bring it up, then the whole earth shakes up to the heights of Olympus, which means that the whole system shakes. You remember that cool man who thought that thinking could not be wrong. He was completely shaken when he encountered the feeling reality because he hadn't thought that such a thing could be in the world, but there it was right under his nose, and that is, of course, our dreamer's case too. He had a vague idea that there was something very dangerous which one had better not touch, but he felt it was absolutely necessary for his life to touch it and to bring it up. He felt it came up to him, and he had to face it no matter what the risk was.

This dream is then an attempt to characterize the fourth as something by itself, entirely different from the ordinary functions, because that function is now a factor which is no more in my possession. I can say, "I want to think! I do think! I will think!" I can also dispose perhaps of my other functions. I can say "I want to observe." I can actually see reality and adapt to it. I can take it into account. I also can take into account my intuitions. But I cannot take into account the feeling, inasmuch as it is the inferior function. One can't say, "I can face it," because one can't.

---

[20] John 1:9, King James Bible.

You see, this opens up an abyss of problems which chiefly comes from the fact that we have a medieval education. We were shielded by a church from the immediate experience of real human nature. Of course, real human nature was everywhere, but we believed that something was always kept at bay. The worst things were projected into the heavens, or they happened somewhere else, and not in us. We are all convinced that we are frightfully decent people, and if the world only consisted of people like ourselves, there would be no war and no terrible things could happen. We wouldn't go out and slaughter innocent children. We are human beings and wouldn't throw dangerous bombs or fill the streets with poisonous gases; for we are perfectly nice people. But we are just those people who would do it, and that is what escapes us, and what we can't face. We can't face ourselves as such beings. We only can say in general, "Yes, of course, we admit that people who throw bombs have our anatomy. They are all called *Homo sapiens*, but they live somewhere else. They aren't here; here, there is nothing bad. It happens in newspapers, or God knows where, but not here, not with me, not with my family, not with my dear friends." But we are exactly those who do it. We are in no way different from them, and that is what we have to face, and nobody can do it if he's honest. It's too much; it's murder.

So man has always had religion to shield him from such insights, and these religions had helpful inventions, such as the devil, who is the evil principle, so that a lot of evil could be shifted over into the devil, or into demons, and thus we learned to build up a quiet and peaceful world in which we are the masters of fate, where nothing could happen which wasn't reasonable, until somehow we were badly shaken up by more recent events. We understand that nobody really wanted the Great War, but yet everybody helped the war to be, for the war was a being in itself that went on, and everybody served it while nobody wanted it. Who then did make the war? Human beings made the war, and so you see, any horrible destruction can come, any horrible epidemic. Nobody wants it, and everybody is doing it. But this situation is only possible when our psychology is such that we control only a certain part of it, while another very important part, which we can't face, escapes us. And it is this very part that we have no control over. This is an insight that slowly begins to dawn upon humanity, but it will take a long time before it is completely realized.

Lecture 9

Ladies and gentlemen:

I am unable to answer all the questions I have received, particularly since some of them are beside the mark.[1] I have chosen therefore those that really have to do with what we are dealing with now.

QUESTION: If the individuation process sets in as a corrective to over specialization of one function, what causes it to happen in the primitive, whose functions are equally conscious and unconscious?

DR. JUNG: Well, you see the individuation process is simply unconscious, as it is in nature. That is just the difference.

QUESTION: How is it that some men seem to persist all through life in a one-sided attitude, without becoming neurotic?

DR. JUNG: Some can stand it, and some can't. There is such a thing as a disposition to a neurosis. There is a little political implication following this question, but I don't want to speak about political personalities, otherwise I should get into the papers.[2]

QUESTION: Does the individuation process in exceptional cases take place in the first half of life, even in early youth, as in certain young saints and mystics?

DR. JUNG: Now don't make the mistake of thinking that the individuation process has anything to do with saintliness or with mysticism. Nothing of that kind takes place in the individuation process, for it is a

---

[1] This lecture was held on October 28, 1937.

[2] Jung is probably referring to the interview he gave in 1936 when coming to the United States, where he was cited to have made statements about Roosevelt and world politics, such as " 'Before I came here,' he said, 'I had the impression that one might get from Europe, that he was an opportunist, perhaps even an erratic mind. Now that I have seen him and heard him when he talked at Harvard, however, I am convinced that here is a strong man, a man who is really great.' [A]nd 'Dr. Jung paid his respects to dictators, explaining their rise as due to the effort of peoples to delegate to others the complicated task of managing their collective existence so that individuals might be free to engage 'individuation' (sic)." "Roosevelt 'Great' Is Jung's Analysis," *New York Times*, October 4, 1936, 4.

natural event or course of events, while mysticism or saintliness is something absolutely different which is incommensurable with the problem.

The individuation process, the normal process, naturally begins with the second part of life, because there consciousness begins to detach itself slightly, and then only are you able to understand. As long as your consciousness is absolutely bound up in your personalistic psychology, you cannot understand; you cannot see clearly; you cannot objectify. So usually this change begins at about thirty-five or thirty-six or thirty-seven, sometimes even later. There are exceptions, of course, but as far as I have seen, these have to do with young people who have a very short life, who will die in a relatively short time. I have seen a few cases where the difficult individuation process began in the twenties, and these people died shortly after. Ordinarily, in normal cases, no signs of any individuation process are visible before the middle of life.

Young saints and mystics make no exception. They also belong to humanity and follow the general rules, for saintliness, like any other gift of nature, has nothing to do with the problem of individuation; you could just as well speak of young artists, young doctors, young craftsmen, young seamen, or any other kind of occupation or talent, because saintliness is a certain gift, just as high morality, for instance, is a sort of art. It isn't general; if it were a general quality of mankind then we should all be ashamed that we are not saints.

QUESTION: Would you be good enough to tell us how intuition of that which is not conscious manifests itself?

DR. JUNG: In the form of dreams like these I am dealing with. That is unconscious intuition.

* * * * *

Well, you remember yesterday we remained with that dream of the square room, in which the dreamer is concerned with the unknown woman, with the anima. He ought to draw her portrait, but instead of drawing her portrait he produces a number of crosses. I have already told you several things about it, but, of course, that is not sufficient to elucidate the dream. We have to explain why he doesn't draw, or at least make an attempt to draw a portrait, and why instead he makes that almost foolish attempt to draw such crosses.

Well, when people make the sign of the cross, then you already know something. When do you make the sign of the cross? Well, when you suppose that the devil is somewhere about, and of course that unknown woman is just the thing he fears most. She is the representative of the dark side; she is the personification of the unconscious of which he is as afraid of as the devil; and he makes the sign of the cross against it. It is a so-called apotropaic sign by which one conquers the evil influence arising from it.

Now I can say this much of his personal psychology: the unknown woman here is a sort of abstract of many women who really confronted him in his personal life, and always, after a while, he made the sign of the cross and ran away. So you see the dream takes them all in a bunch and simply marks them with an abstraction, the unknown woman, because to him they are all the same, they are just "the woman," not women or Miss So-and-So. It is always one and the same woman, the unknown woman, the uncanny woman, the dark woman, the animal figure, the projection of an archetypal image he had of the woman, as it was born with him. He projected that image into the mother, so the mother became the all power-ful one; this is the reason why mothers, who are, as a rule, perfectly harm-less beings, attain such enormous power over their boys, because boys have an archetypal figure of the woman. It is the same, of course, with the father; the father is, as a rule, a relatively unimportant being, but a daugh-ter can make a god of him. But she can only do it by way of the projection of that powerful image which is formed by her and with her. It is a struc-tural element of her mind, and later on when that image becomes de-tached or autonomous, there is a chance of realizing it as it is in itself, but so long as it is projected into other human beings she is not aware of its existence; she is only aware of the person who carried the image.[3]

And so you see the first figure, that female figure, which carries the image for the son, is the mother, and that gives the mother a sort of divine or demoniacal aspect, an overpowering aspect, so that each time she re-curs he is hit below the belt and collapses. This is the usual influence which causes the normal fixation to the mother. And then children who are par-ticularly under the influence of the mother and of this archetypal figure develop a precocious sexuality in order to free themselves from the image of the mother, because if they proceed to attach sex fantasies to the mother that depreciates the mother; it brings her down to the level of nature; she is only woman.

I have seen pictures, for instance, in which people, all by themselves be-fore I ever touched them, had represented this depreciation of the mother

---

[3] All this personal information on Pauli is not included in other works where Jung dis-cusses Pauli.

by mutilating the mother's image, cutting off her fingers or hands or feet, or ripping her open, or beheading her, which were all attempts to depreciate the powerful mother in order to make her human. If they succeed in depotentiating the mother either by sex fantasies or by magic means, such as making a wax figure of the mother and destroying it, then the anima is detached from the mother and can go on and project itself into other female figures, perhaps the sister or aunt or any other woman, until the projection reaches a fairly feasible possibility. And then they may even marry the projection. Of course it is the same thing with a woman.

Now in the dreamer's case it became obvious in the course of these earlier dreams that the image of the anima had detached itself from his sister. The first inklings of an anima had appeared in dreams in connection with the sister. The mother had already been largely depotentiated, although from time to time she appeared in his personal dreams with still a good deal of power, but the main figure was decidedly the sister. And then in the later dreams even the sister lost the fascination; she was no more a magic figure; she had lost her power, and the anima appeared as the unknown woman causing quite a number of pretty misshapen love affairs in his personal life which all had a bad end.

So when in his dream reports he writes "the unknown woman," he always means this figure whom he knew quite well. It was a definite figure with very definite characteristics, like the character in Rider Haggard's *She*, and in other books which I have quoted previously. It is a literary figure, which, however, has a grand power in our psychology; and this figure in the dreams has the quality of an uncanny demoniacal being of whom he is deadly afraid.

Now, that the unconscious puts this woman in the same square with him, of course, has the meaning of an attempt to reconcile him to the fact that there is another side of himself with which he ought to be able to cope. Making the portrait of her would mean assimilating her, making a picture of that other side. This would be something like realization; we say, for instance, "You have to face it." That is making a portrait; you have got to make for yourself a picture of the situation. You must look it squarely in the eyes so that you may know how it looks. You must have a certain idea of the thing, and the idea is, of course, an *ideos*, an image.

So you see to draw the portrait is a sort of metaphor which means, "Realize that figure; have an idea of that figure." But instead of realizing her he makes apotropaic signs of the cross to ward off that terrible thing, to hold her away. Of course, this means that he regresses to his former tendency to revivify his Catholic education. But his Catholicism never meant much to him; he never went to church although he had been baptized according to the Roman Catholic rite, but it meant nothing; he had never practiced it and did not think on it, but when things became critical, then even the Catholic Church might do.

Now, as I told you, he used different colors to make the crosses. And here another element comes in. The crosses are characterized by the Trinity, while the colors are four, so you see the idea of the four over against the three insinuates itself. It is just as if while he was making the crosses in an attempt to draw apotropaic pictures, the unconscious flowed in, suggesting, "Why not the four, take four colors." One would think he would take three colors, but no, it is four, and here you have again that peculiar transition from the three to the four; the four against the three.

In that little bit of symbolism you see a very important development of modern times. Of course it is not merely modern; it is age old, that four; but the three has had great preponderance as a symbol through the idea that God, the *Summum Bonum*, the Highest Good, the most important figure and center of the world, was characterized by a Trinity.[4]

So you see there is a sort of inborn imprint in us, not only through the Christian era, but also through immeasurably old antiquity, that the gods, or certain gods, usually the highest gods, appear as three. That is not only so in our ancestry; it is the same in Egypt, and with the primitives, while in the East you have the Trimurti. But, the four is not only a modern invention, it is a very important item in medieval symbology. It insinuated itself into the Christian cult very early. There are representations of the *Rex Gloriae*, the Triumphant Christ, with the four symbols of the Evangelists. You find the same four already in the Egyptian cult, namely, Horus and his four sons. Not infrequently these four sons appear in a funny way, quite analogous to the Christian way of depicting the Evangelists, namely, three have animal heads and one has a human head. Now you remember that these four animals, or four symbols of the Evangelists, are the eagle, the ox, the angel, and the lion. In medieval manuscripts, usually of an early time, the seventh or eighth century—well, I know one that is even twelfth century—the Evangelists appear as human figures with animal heads, exactly like the four sons of Horus. So you see that is also an archetypal idea which assumed a new form and a new interpretation in the Christian era. In modern times the four naturally assumes a new form,

---

[4] Jung published his ideas on the Trinity in 1940, "Attempts at a Psychological Interpretation of the Trinity," *CW* 11.

and inasmuch as the four seems to be asserting itself in our unconscious products, in dreams, and in fantasies, and particularly in all these mandala motifs, it will produce a new interpretation. Of course, we do not represent the four any more in the form of four animals. You have seen one dream where they appeared as four snakes, or four animals, or occasionally, demons, but these animal symbolizations get stripped off pretty soon, and people usually develop a tendency to give definite interpretations to the four sides of the character or four functions. We find exactly the same development in Lamaism, where the four are no more the four directions of space, the cardinal points of the horizon, which presumably they were originally, but have also developed into the idea of psychological functions. Since the time of the Pythagorians the four has been a symbol for the human soul. The Pythagorians attributed to their master, Pythagoras, the statement that the soul is square. Others say the soul is a circle or a globe. They had the idea of the quadratura circuli as a characteristic symbol of the soul.[5]

Now the unconscious produces the idea of the four spontaneously, as you can see in these dreams, as a sort of abstract fact which is here suggested, at least, by the four colors that slip in. It is just as if the unconscious were trying to say, "Yes, you can make your sign of the cross, you can use that apotropaic gesture, but do it please in a fourfold way," as if that were better or more efficient. At all events, the unconscious succeeds in slipping in the idea of the four over against the three.

After this dream something curious happened. You know when one has a series of such dreams as these one begins to sit up and ask oneself the question, "Why should I dream like that, why these numbers, why these peculiar abstract symbols, the four, the three, et cetera, the crosses and circles and all that?" And one naturally gets accustomed to such thoughts and begins to speculate about them. This is exactly what happened to the dreamer. Immediately after this dream he began to make drawings. First he made a circle and divided the circle into four parts, then he took colored pencils and gave the four parts of that circle the four colors of which he had dreamed. Then he made another variant of the same idea, a wheel with eight spokes, and even put something into the center of the well, namely, a blue flower with four petals.[6]

---

[5] Compared with EYB 1935 Jung has in *PsA* added passages concerning the symbolism of the wheel in alchemy and in Jakob Böhme. *CW* 12, pars. 214–16.

[6] As a matter of fact Pauli started to illustrate his dreams already in connection to his sixth dream {0006} of the veiled figure on the stairs. But after this dream {0194} he drew several figures one after the other, figs. 14–22. These were (in order) a colorless torus, a torus

Now you see here comes in quite naturally the idea of the lotus, which the East calls the *Padma*.[7] And as if these picture had not been satisfactory, or if he had gone on with his speculations about these flowers, he now made quite a number of other similar drawings which were all concerned with the structure of the center which he had characterized as the flower with the four petals. He made a larger flower, for instance, with eight petals. Then he made the picture of a lake in a crater surrounded by four mountains. Then he drew a red ring lying on the earth, and in the center of the ring stood a dead tree. And a green snake was coiled around the tree in an anticlockwise direction. The green snake symbolizes the greenness which is life and the snake is alive. He is not a dead snake, which means that the principle of life begins to creep up around the dead tree.

All these speculations show an interesting development: First, he realizes the fact that the four can be expressed in many different forms and that these four have a peculiar center or they designate a center; they are not without a center. But he also realizes that the center is dead. There should be really a green tree, a living tree, which would mean growth or development. But there is no such thing. The tree is dead, it doesn't live anymore; but now a new life is coming into it.

Now you see, the tree is an archaic symbol which always designates a process of inner growth.[8] Therefore the tree is used as a symbol in Yoga, the Yoga Tree. Also it was used in Paradise, to lay a trap for the first parents, while the *Arbor Philosophica*, the philosophical tree, is a well-known symbol in the medieval Hermetic philosophy. The tree is dead, which means the spiritual or inner development is dead. The snake always symbolizes life which comes from below; it is a chthonic symbol, an earthy symbol. Therefore in alchemy it represents Mercurius, that very peculiar being which lives, as they say, in the caves of the earth, or in the center of the earth, and represents the split-off part of the anima mundi which originally created the earth and the universe. It is really a god and is therefore symbolized by a Greek god. Mercurius or Hermes, the leader of souls and initiator or revealer of secret wisdom. For this reason the final authority for that whole philosophy is Hermes the Thrice Greatest, Hermes Tris-

---

with a blue flower, a blue flower divided in eight sections and a mountain lake, an erupting volcano, a snake coiled around a tree. Information from forthcoming publication of complete dream material, CDM.

[7] Padma: the sacred lotus in Hinduism, Buddhism, and Jainism.

[8] Jung published an essay on the Philosophical Tree in 1945 and published a greatly revised version in 1954. See *CW* 13. The motif is already present in the *RB*, 273, 351.

megistos.[9] This Hermes is the same as the medieval Mercurius, the life giver; this is the healing serpent which comes up from the depths, from below our feet, which is, of course, a projection of the fact that our head has grown far above the unconscious, so that it appears as if the unconscious were right under our feet. And so the serpent, as the representative of the spinal cord, is an apt symbol to express the fact that our head, our brain, or our consciousness had detached itself pretty thoroughly from its instinctual basis.

I could give you a number of alchemistic parallels to this peculiar series of symbols, but that would lead us a bit far away. I might perhaps call your attention to one interesting item. You remember I told you yesterday about the three and the four, and the seven and the eight Cabiri. That scene in *Faust* is followed by a little intermezzo with the old sage, Thales,[10] who appears in the classical Walpurgis Night, and at the end after the arrival of the Cabiri, the Sirens sing of the Golden Fleece.[11]

Note that the Golden Fleece is mentioned in connection with the Cabiri. But the Golden Fleece is a symbol of the precious thing difficult to attain, which is always the goal of the quest. So the goal of the alchemical quest is the philosophical gold, that which they call gold. All the world thought that they really meant gold, but they say, "Our gold is, of course, not the gold of the vulgar people. Our gold is a philosophical gold. It is a metaphorical gold." It means simply the precious substance or the precious thing, the jewel, that is difficult to attain. This is not just my own impression. I can give you plenty of documentary evidence for this fact. It is only our ignorance that makes us believe that alchemy was merely

---

[9] The figure of Hermes Trismegistus was formed through the amalgamation of Hermes with the Egyptian god Thoth. The *Corpus Hermeticum*, a collection of largely alchemical and magical texts dating from the early Christian era but initially thought to have been much older, was ascribed to him. Cf. *RB*, n. 267.

[10] Thales of Miletus (ca. 624–546 BC) was a pre-Socratic Greek philosopher from Miletus in Asia Minor, and one of the Seven Sages of Greece. Many, most notably Aristotle, regard him as the first philosopher in the Greek tradition. Thales attempted to explain natural phenomena without reference to mythology and was tremendously influential in this respect. He was also the first to define general principles and set forth hypotheses, and as a result has been dubbed the "Father of Science."

[11] In Greek mythology, the Golden Fleece is the fleece of the gold-haired winged ram, which can be procured in Colchis. It figures in the tale of Jason and his band of Argonauts, who set out on a quest by order of King Pelias for the fleece in order to place Jason rightfully on the throne of Iolcus in Thessaly. The story is of great antiquity, it was current in the time of Homer (eighth century BC), and, consequently, it survives in various forms, among which details vary.

a fraudulent attempt to produce gold. So, you see, these Cabiri, being the fragmentary personifications of the unconscious, are really the ones who bring up the precious symbol called the "round thing" or the "gold" or the "Golden Fleece."

Thereupon, the old sage, Thales, makes a remark. He says, "Der Rost macht erst die Münze wert," which means, "The rust or the oxide gives the real value to the coin." You see, the coin is supposed to consist of precious metals, silver or gold, and there is a certain patina on it, a certain oxide, which one would think was just a bit of dirt that one could clean off, but Thales says, "That is the real value. That, alone, gives the real value to the coin."

Goethe was deeply interested in alchemy and had read a good deal and had very probably learned that the precious substance was also called *nummus* by the Latin alchemists.[12] *Nummus* means a coin and was one of the metaphors for the precious substance. There is a Latin tract which says that the oxide, and not the metal, is the precious substance, bearing out what Thales said. I will quote the original; it is quite interesting. The text says, "Our gold is not the gold of the vulgar people. Thou hast asked about the greenness, viriditas, meaning the green oxide of the copper, assuming that the ore or the copper is a leprous body having a skin disease on account of that greenness, but I will tell you that there is nothing more perfect in the copper than that greenness, for the greenness is the thing that will be transformed into our gold through our *Magisterium* (which means, through the secret of our art)."

Here we have the absolute evidence that in alchemistic thought the greenness is the leprosity, the skin disease of the metal, and the oxide is the substance from which the philosophical gold is derived. In the dreams of the patient we are, however, concerned with the green serpent which suddenly appears and brings in the motif of the greenness, and this is a sign of vegetation. It is the green of the chlorophyll, again an alchemistic thought (I haven't invented it). In their books the alchemists make a great story of that *benedicta viriditas*, the blessed greenness of spring and vegetation, which is an analogy for their procedure. It seems as if the dreamer were following old paths of associations, as if he were really thinking like one of the old alchemists, and we have to be mighty careful not to miss that particular suspect because it explains so much of the secret tissue in

---

[12] See Jung's "Faust and Alchemy" (1949) in *CW* 18, par. 1692. Apparently, Goethe was also an ardent collector of antique coins.

which our dreamer's thinking is caught. I will briefly give you, then, some other examples where you can see the same fact.

The dreamer is obviously trying to produce that precious substance, the center of the ring or of his mandala, which in one case was a lake in a crater. The word "crater" is a Greek word, *krater*, meaning a vessel; it was the jar in which the wine was mixed with water. This word is used by one of the old Greek alchemists, Zosimos, to designate the marvelous vessel in which the process of transformation takes place. He used it in a way which can be understood as an alchemical procedure, but he also used it in another way, namely, as a mystical term. Many of those old philosophers had found out that there is no real philosophy if you don't face the anima, so many of them had a so-called soror mystica,[13] a friend in God, a woman friend. Women played a very great role in the early alchemist tracts. There were quite a number of them: for instance, one of the oldest is Maria the Jewess, or Maria the Egyptian; then Paphnutia; then Zosimos dedicated his works, or addressed his works, as if they were written to this woman friend, his soror mystica, Theosebeia. The name means, "the one that worships God." And he gave her good advice in the form of alchemistic prescriptions, how to produce changes in metals, how to melt the ores, and suddenly, in between, he tells her also that he should advise her to go right away down to the krater, to dip herself or to get baptized. To be dipped in the krater means to transform into a new kind of human being, a pneumatic being.

We know something about this krater from another source too, namely, from the *Corpus Hermeticum*, a collection of about seventeen Greek tracts, ascribed to the legendary Hermes, Hermes Trismegistos, in which is a tract where the krater is mentioned. The tract is even called *The Krater*, and in it there is the legend that in the beginning, when the Demiurgos[14] made the world, he also created human beings, but he didn't create them perfectly. He created them in a state of *anoia*,[15] of not knowing,

---

[13] Latin: mystical sister.

[14] Demiurgos: Greek, literally "public worker," originally a common noun meaning "craftsman" or "artisan," but gradually it came to mean "producer" and eventually "creator." The philosophical usage and the proper noun derives from Plato's Timaeus, written ca. 360 BC. In the Apocryphon of John ca. AD 120–80, the Demiurge arrogantly declares that he has made the world by himself: For he said, "I am God and there is no other God beside me." J. M. Robinson and Coptic Gnostic Library Project (1988), *The Nag Hammadi Library in English* (San Francisco: Harper and Row), 111.

[15] *Ánoia* (from privative meaning "no" and "*noús*," "mind")—properly, "no-mind" referring to *irrational* behavior (*mindless* actions).

of mindlessness, unconsciousness, we should say they had no nous, no mind, but there were some among them who were not quite satisfied with their condition. They were miserable in the state of anoia, of not knowing or of being unconscious, and so he invented something for them. After the world had been created and the human beings therein, he created a wonderful vessel, a krater, and filled it with nous, with mind. The word *nous* is the equivalent of *pneuma*, which is the word for spirit; he filled it with spirit. It is nothing unheard of that you can fill a jar with spirit; we still do it. For instance, bottles are filled with spirits. We still use that word. You see, the original mind could not conceive of an abstract spirit, as we speak of it. The spirit originally was a sort of liquid, a more or less ethereal liquid, which could, however, be poured into bottles. So God filled the vessel with nous and sent it to earth for those who were not satisfied with their state of anoia, and they could then dip themselves in the krater in order to be transformed and to attain a new state of *ennoia*, that is, as state of consciousness, of being conscious or away of, which would mean mindful of, or, filled with mind, by means of which they really became spiritual beings.

From this text we can understand why Zosimos should advise Theosebeia to seek the aid of the krater. For it is in the alchemical vessel, in which the philosophical gold is found or in which the transubstantiation takes place, where physical beings are transformed into *volatilia*, which means, into a volatile substance called *spiritus*, spirits or ghosts. The alchemists depicted such spirits personified as homunculi, meaning little men, who jumped out of the alchemical vessel. This is like the early Christians who went down into the piscina, into the baptismal water, and came out reborn, being now *pneumatikoi*, spiritual beings, new, changed, immortal beings. This mean substance had been transformed into a noble substance.

If we remember such historical facts as these, and keep in mind that the unconscious is perhaps still capable of thinking in these old ways, we can understand the choice of peculiar symbols, such as the lake in the crater. Now one of the most famous ideas of the alchemists was that in this vessel the philosopher's stone could be made. This stone is said to be as clear and translucent as a diamond and has therefore often been called a diamond or crystal, a marvelous crystal, so clear that it was even invisible, and was, therefore, called *lapis invisibilitatis*. So you see, the idea of the wonderful vessel, the circle, the krater, in which a transformation takes place, is closely linked up with the idea of a precious stone, as for instance, a diamond.

The next dream says, "There were two people, unknown people, talking together. It was as if he were overhearing a conversation. They talked about crystals, and quite particularly about a diamond."[16]

If we don't know of these age-old connections, we shall be at a complete loss to understand how he now suddenly comes to such a dream. But, you know, it is exactly as if he had been listening in to the proceedings of the unconscious, where the people down there, the agents, were discussing, "Now what could we say next? What would be suitable? Let us see; we've got something in our records." And then they look at the rows of old books and say, "Oh well, there—there is the idea of the diamond. Let us talk of that. Now what about it?" He listens in and hears them talking about another symbol, which is absolutely along the lines of an ancient type of thinking.

So you see, this bears out what I say, that the old kind of thinking and the old symbolical connections are still living entities in his subconscious mind, and he just listens in to a continuous process of deliberation about what could be done in order to give him the suitable idea in consciousness. "That idiot up there, who doesn't understand, to whom one has to talk in a lot of practical symbols saying, 'Now, look here, it is, for instance, so-and-so or so-and-so.'" It is the same predicament that Christ was in, when he had to talk to his disciples who were a pretty poor lot intellectually. When he wanted to talk of a very different idea, namely, His idea of the Kingdom of Heaven, it was too much for them, and so, He had to use a number of similes, saying that the Kingdom of Heaven is like this, or like that; it is like the pearl or the treasure in the field or the mustard seed, the grain of mustard, and so on, in order to make it plain to them what he meant. And that is how the unconscious proceeds, just trying to teach that tough mind up here what there is meant.

The next dream is again a continuation of the same theme.[17] In the dream he found himself strenuously occupied with a mathematical or geometrical task; he could only make out that it was a question of the

[16] "Dream Symbols," nr. 24, p. 167, and CW 12, nr. 24, par. 221. M 24 {0207}: "Conversation between two Jews about crystals and especially diamonds," June 14, 1932, CDM. This dream was preceded (in the same night) by a dream about Hitler winning the election with a small majority over Hindenburg. In reality Paul von Hindenburg (1847–1934, president of Germany at the time) won with a small majority over Hitler in April 1932, appointing the latter to chancellor of Germany in January 1933. Jung erased all links to politics and Pauli's Jewish descent from the dream material, presumably to protect his identity, but Jung might also have had other reasons to erase all links to Judaism during this time. See Cocks, 1985.

[17] "Dream Symbols," nr. 25, p. 168, and CW 12, nr. 25, par. 223. M 25 {0212}: "Construction of a middle point. Mirroring a shape," June 18, 1932, CDM.

construction of a central point with a complicated something around it, which had to be symmetrized, to be made symmetrical through mirroring in that one point. The idea is, there is something around a center. Perhaps it is chaotic. It should be made symmetrical.

Now remember, he has two sides; he has a conflict, the left and the right, which in his case are asymmetrical. The one is all in the foreground, and the other is apparently nonexistent, and it is even a question whether he shouldn't strangle the left side altogether. Now the task is to make the thing as symmetrical as a mirror would do, namely, an exact replica, a mirror image, and he tries to accomplish that task through a sort of geometrical design in the dream. Of course, he couldn't carry it out in reality. The interesting point is that if the indistinct, complicated something can be mirrored in the center, then the center must be a mirror. It must be a sort of glass. Now if you remember, the dream before said, "diamond." Now there you have the thing that is mirroring, that is a glass. Moreover, the alchemists say that the lapis is a *vitrum*, namely, a glass, or the process that brought about the philosopher's stone was called the *vitrificatio*, the making of the glass.

There is at the same time another idea in this dream, namely that the right condition would be that this center would produce a new Weltanschauung. For he has on the one side, the right side, this world, the world of a scientist, and on the other side, only despised objects or nothing. And now this peculiar ensemble has to be made absolutely symmetrical, so that the left side shall be a mirror image of the right, or the right side the mirror image of the left. If you imagine a new Weltanschauung to result from this basic idea, then you would reach the conclusion that the correct image of the world would be a double image: on the one side, this world; on the other side, an absolute replica. But you know, this replica is, of course, reversed. Whatever is right here is left there; and whatever is left there is right here. So everything is in the reverse order. This is an extraordinarily peculiar idea, but surely an idea which tries to establish a complete symmetry and a complete balance between the two worlds, the world of the conscious and the world of the unconscious. Now this man has the Weltanschauung of the scientist, which naturally envisages the whole cosmos, the whole physical world. This symmetrical standpoint must include a vision, which would also embrace even the galactic systems.

The next dream continues the argument.[18] It begins: it is night. The sky is full of stars. And the voice says, "Now it will begin." And the dreamer

---

[18] "Dream Symbols," nr. 26, p. 169, and *CW* 12, nr. 26, par. 227. M 26 {0213}; fig. 23, "Starry night. Fight about left and right," June 18, 1932, CDM.

asks, "What will begin?" And the voice says, "The circulation can begin." In this moment a meteor falls in a very peculiar curve, about like this.

In the dream the patient didn't realize what that curve was. He was only struck by something peculiar about it, but afterwards, when he was writing down the dream, it suddenly came to him that this curve was exactly the one he had made several days before when he drew the petal of the blue flower. You see, the meteor was falling like this, and then he understood what that circulation was, for the meteor is an apparition of life, and the life begins to circulate around the flower of the four petals, which shows that this flower is extended all over the firmament.

Now this is the same as the vision in Dante's *Paradiso* where the Rose is formed in Heaven by all the saints with the Deity in the center.[19] It is a cosmic mandala. From this he realizes that the mandala is a cosmic thing; an idea of complete symmetry between the physical and the psychological realms, that is, between the conscious and the unconscious cosmos.

This dream is again one of those I have designated as "big" dreams. It made also a big impression upon the dreamer. He couldn't help realizing that this idea was widening out beyond the ordinary limits. Whenever that was the case things became uncomfortable to him, and it was as if he recoiled. Then he usually made a regression into something that was just the opposite, just the contrary of what he had experienced. Naturally, such a countermovement, such a regression or reaction, can take place in the dream. So, without waking up in the dream, suddenly the situation changes, and instead of being under a starry firmament, he finds himself

---

[19] Canto 30, lines 110–15, in Dante's *The Divine Comedy*: "Of verdure and of flowers; so, round about, Eying the light, on more than million thrones, Stood, eminent, whatever from our earth Has to the skies return'd. How wide the leaves, Extended to their utmost, of this rose, Whose lowest step embosoms such a space Of ample radiance! Yet, nor amplitude Nor height impeded, but my view with ease Took in the full dimensions of that joy."

in a luxurious nightclub. It is to just such places that his neurosis always pushed him, and that was where he got into trouble. So he makes a sort of neurotic regression.

He finds himself suddenly in this curious place, and there is a sort of manager there, and a dubious-looking, unscrupulous fellow, apparently a tough kind of personality, and there are also girls of the same character and in a pretty dejected condition. In that place there is a row going on between two parties; the one part is apparently the right wing, and the other, the left wing. The dreamer doesn't like it and leaves the place and finds himself again in a different situation. He is in a taxi which drives with him around the square, anticlockwise. He makes what is called a circumambulation of the square; this means that he repeats the movement of the meteor which described the curve around the mandala, which is, of course, also the square; this means that he repeats the movement of the meteor which described the curve around the mandala, which is, of course, also the square; but, you see with him the square is usually a square in a town, or a square room or something like that. Here it is a town square, and he is driving around it. And suddenly, he is again in the bar of the nightclub.

Now you see, he tried to escape from that evil-looking place; it was a bit too strong for him. And then he had to circumambulate the square. This is the square, you remember, where there are the dogs and foxes that bite, and he has to expose himself to all the disagreeable happenings in the square. This means that this is the place where he belongs, from which he should not get away, because the square is the alchemical vessel of transformation out of which the one who is inside should not escape. Therefore, the eternal prescription of the old alchemist, "Keep your vessel well shut, so that the one who is inside can't fly away," although what goes on inside is torture.

Having circumambulated that place in an anticlockwise sense which means going towards the unconscious, he approaches the unconscious again and necessarily must find himself again in the bar. For this is also a part of the unconscious, the contrast to the things above; the old alchemistic truth, you know, says, "As above, so below." First he ascends, and then he descends, and that is also one of the alchemical rules.

And now the manager, talking to him, says, "What these people here have said about the right and the left hasn't touched my feeling. Is there really a right and a left wing to human society?"

And the dreamer replies, "The existence of left doesn't contradict the existence of right. Both are in each man. Left is the mirror reflection or the mirror image of right, and always when I feel it as a mirror image (or a mirrored image) then I am at one with myself. There is no right and no left wing to human society, but there are symmetrical and oblique human beings. The oblique ones are those who only possess one side, either the right or the left. They are still in an infantile condition."

Then the manager, thinking for a while, says, "Now that is already much better," and goes away to look after other things. And the dreamer wakes up.

This story again contains important realizations, as you have probably seen already. The contention is between the right and the left wings. The idea is, of course, to create a symmetrical universe where right is the mirror image of left, and left, the mirror image of right, but that can't be because he is in the universe. He is part of it, and he cannot be his own negation. He cannot deny his position, or be positive and negative at the same time. He cannot be this visible man with such-and-such a name, and so on, and over there be that unknown thing. These two things are not compatible. The one exists, and the other is not allowed to exist. That is his standpoint, but the unconscious urges that he is at the same time both the one and also the other.

This is the great difficulty: the ordinary mind can only think one thing and cannot at the same time think the other thing. He cannot think of a thing that is and is not, for that is impossible; but the man of superior mind is superior only because he can think in paradoxes. This is one of the highest achievements of the Eastern mind. In the West, one cannot think, "I am good; I am bad"; to think those things could be together would be dangerous. Such a thing can't be. Therefore, you see, we are forced to be oblique, as he says. But there are those who can think paradoxically. They are symmetrical beings; they think in terms of paradoxes, while all the others are oblique, which means that they are lopsided. They are either right or left, and because they hold that their particular point of view is *the* point of view, they always quarrel with each other. In his dream he realizes all that. It sounds as if it were an absolutely conscious thought, but all these conscious thoughts are only those which he gathers in consciousness. The dream speaks of just the thing he doesn't want to be; there he thinks according to the intimations of the unconscious. You see, the unconscious idea of the symmetrical universe has caught hold of him and made him think as it wanted. Now that is the situation in the dream. Soon this idea will come to the surface, and then, even on the surface, namely, in consciousness, he will begin to think paradoxically, and that is, as the manager says, "already much better."

In this dream again he tried to escape from a big world where one might have feelings. It suggests that there are certain people who have feelings, and a heaven full of stars, where one might realize a sort of poetical thought, but he thought he would be safe in a nightclub where, of course, such feelings don't count. Yet even there, it gets at him; even there, people are divided. There is a discussion between the right and the left wing, and the manager, a most despicable person, begins to philosophize and put awkward questions to him about a right and a left wing of human society and forces him to realize that he himself thinks that those people who have only the one point of view are oblique, and others, who can think paradoxically, are symmetrical; in other words, he is forced to believe in a symmetrical universe, whatever that means.

This dream made a certain dent, so that the unconscious could go on and try again, and this time it shows something pretty positive, for the next dream is almost like a vision.[20] There is a circle. In the center, there is a tree, and the tree is now green and full of leaves. Within the circle, around the tree, are many primitive savages who are fighting each other murderously. They don't see the tree. He looks at it and knows that they don't see it, assuming that if they were to see the tree, or if they could see the tree, they wouldn't fight like that. But they fight because they are all weak and can't see the center. They can't see that the tree, which is now green, is the center. The greenness means that there is now life in the tree. The tree has been made alive by the green serpent; the life got into the tree. The inner, or mental, development, or whatever you like to call it, seems to be again working, and he realizes now that those people who fight the opposite point of view are really savages; that it is barbarous to think on the right side only or on the left side only, and that such an attitude inevitably leads them to quarrel; but if these people—which means if he, as a savage, as an oblique one—could only see, they would realize that the real life process is not in the quarrelling, but is in the center. It is in a growing tree, a growing understanding, a growth of philosophy.

This is, of course, a different concept of philosophy from the usual one. You see, philosophy in the West usually means talking about words. But philosophy originally meant a truth that is lived and is still understood in that way in the East. Not very long ago, an Eastern guru, an old man of seventy years, paid a call on me. He had just come from Paris, from the

---

[20] "Dream Symbols," nr. 27, p. 171, and CW 12, nr. 27, par. 232. M 27 {0214}: "Vision: Circle with a green Tree in the middle. A fight amongst wild people," June 18, 1932, CDM.

International Congress of Philosophy.[21] There he had read a paper about the concept of truth from the standpoint of a philosophy that is lived. He was completely crestfallen because all these intelligent philosophers hadn't understood a word of what he said. That unfortunate man, of course, didn't know that, with us, truth is a concept, a logical idea. To us it is only an intellectual concept, and he, in his infinite naïveté, spoke of truth as of a life lived. Naturally, none of the Western philosophers could understand such a thing. They have made a new world consisting of printed paper, a world of two dimensions, consisting of pages of books! Words, nothing but words. But for Heaven's sake, not a life lived! A famous scientist, who inquired about certain of my ideas, once said to me when I had explained a little of them to him: "That is very interesting, what you say. Indeed, most interesting, but dangerous." [*Laughter*] "You had better leave these things and keep away from reality. So keep away from the world of feeling, from the world of values, or if you talk of values, talk of words, but don't apply to life. Don't get into any contact with realities, for that is dangerous."

Then after this dream comes another.[22] There again is a circle, and within the circle there are steps leading up concentrically to a basin, in which a fountain wells up. Here we have an attempt of the unconscious to make clear what it means. We can safely conclude that he hasn't understood what the dream meant by the tree; he has not realized the feeling quality. The tree is the thing that draws vital forces together from the depths, from the roots, and brings the life up in one shaft, and it even unfolds like this [*making the movement of opening out*]. You see, when you make this movement, then you know what the tree symbolizes. It is an unfolding, and that is also the fountain, the water comes together below and rises up in a shaft and falls down like this.

---

[21] The conference in question must have been the Ninth International Congress of Philosophy, called the Descartes conference, held in Paris, August 1937. *Philosophical Review* 47 (1) (January 1938). The guru in question is in all probability V. Subrahmanya Iyer from Mysore. He contributed with a paper called "Pure Philosophy in India." Travaux du IX congrès international de Philosophie no IX, Analyse réflexive et Transcendance, IIme Partie, XXIII, p. 162. There he says: "truth is what makes for life perfect. What is perfection? It is the life in which none feels any pain ... the 'totality' of data alone can give truth.... They think that the experience of the waking stage is all that is of value, and ignore that of the dream and the deep sleep states."

[22] "Dream Symbols," nr. 28, p. 171, and CW 12, nr. 28, par. 234, is called a visual impression, not a dream. M 28 {0218}: "Vision: circle with inner steps leading up to a basin, with a fountain," June 20, 1932, CDM.

In alchemy, for instance, they speak of a tree that sheds its leaves on either side. They fall down into a fire and are burned, and the fire goes into the roots of the tree, and the tree sucks it up and blossoms again, and the leaves fall down and nourish the fire. You see, that is the circulation. That is the so-called *opus circulatorum* or *rotundum* or *rotatorum* of alchemy. They did it like this: they constructed a very complicated *alembic*, in which the sublimate or the condensed product always flowed back into the receptacle. For instance, this is the pelicanus.

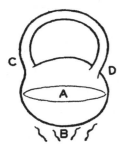

You see, (a) is the liquid, (b) is the fire, and the vapor rises up here (c), condenses here (d), and falls back to (a). That is an apparatus for rotation or for the opus circulatorum.

They made all sorts of variations in these apparatuses because they believed that when you have accomplished the distillation a thousand times, you will have brought out a quintessence, which is so fine and so refined that it is spirit-like. With that spirit-like substance, which is equivalent to the anima mundi, the world soul, you can transform matter.

So the idea of the water rising up is also an alchemical idea. The chief substance with which they operated was the so-called *hydrotheion*, the divine water. This is the Greek name. Later on, it was called in Latin the *aqua permanens*, which means the everlasting or the eternal water. This was the humid anima mundi prepared or sublimated out of matter, forming a sort of liquid, by which one could bring about these transubstantiations. And so they often used the symbol of the fountain, for there the invisible liquid gathers itself together out of the elements down in the earth and rises up and appears on the surface, producing fertility, the wonderful greenness of a new spring in which the metals began to transform.

The dreamer had already had a dream in which he discovered a square garden.[23] In the middle of that garden was such a fountain. He had also had the symbol of the *aqua permanens* in a former dream, where his father went with him to a drugstore where one could buy a water that was particularly cheap. This is almost a literal quotation from one of the texts, because that precious substance, they say, is the cheapest thing you can imagine. You find it everywhere. It is thrown out into the road. If the merchants in the market knew what it was worth, they would never sell it at such a low price. The alchemists even spoke of, *lapis vilissima res*, the stone, as the cheapest thing, or the most unassuming thing. They called it the *lapis exilis*, a thing with no appearance, no show at all, a vile thing. And, curiously enough, this word, *lapis exilis*, is the peculiar name which Wolfram von Eschenbach, a man who couldn't even write and who didn't understand Latin, gave to the Holy Grail, and he probably made a mistake.[24] He said, "lapsit exillis," which means nothing in classical Latin. It is probably the "lapis exilis" of the old alchemy. We have documentary evidence for the existence of this term as early as the beginning of the thirteenth century, about 1220.

So the philosopher's water is a very cheap thing, and it can be had everywhere, and this is the motif that occurs in his dream. Usually the garden, in which is this fountain, is a rose garden. That is the typical expression which occurs in Latin alchemistic literature, the *Rosarium Philosophorum*," the rose garden of the philosophers. It occurs in numberless pictures. There is a famous tract which was first printed in 1550, though

---

[23] Cf. "Dream Symbols," nr. 13, p. 139, and *CW* 12, nr. 13, par. 154; see above.

[24] Wolfram von Eschenbach (ca. 1170–ca. 1220), German poet whose epic *Parzival*, distinguished by its moral elevation and its imaginative power, is considered one of the most profound literary works of the Middle Ages. Likely based on an unfinished romance of Chrétien de Troyes, *Perceval; ou, le conte du Graal*, it introduced the theme of the Holy Grail into German literature. Its beginning and end are new material, probably of Wolfram's own invention, although he attributes it to an unidentified and probably fictitious Provençal poet, Guiot. The story of the ignorant and naive Parzival, who sets out on his adventures without even knowing his own name, employs the classic fairy-tale motif of "the guileless fool" who, through innocence and artlessness, reaches a goal denied to wiser men. W. von Eschenbach, and C. Edwards, trans. (2004), *Parzival, with Titurel and the Love-Lyrics* (Cambridge, UK: D. S. Brewer). Jung's wife, Emma Jung, worked on the Grail legend for many years; the work was finished after her death by Jung's coworker Marie-Louise von Franz. E. Jung (1986), *The Grail Legend*, 2nd ed. (Boston: Sigo).

the tract itself belongs to about the middle of the fifteenth century, and parts of it are much older, called the *Rosarium Philosophorum*.[25]

The next dream of our patient is: He sees a beautiful bouquet of roses, and then a peculiar symbol appears which looks like this.[26]

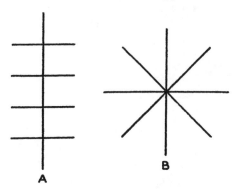

There is a vertical board with four partitions (a), and it shouldn't be like that. In the dream he finds it should be like this (b). Now remember what I told you yesterday about the three, and the four, and the seven and the eight all stretched up in a vertical line. They shouldn't be like that. I told you it should be round, or with four corners, and here in his dream he makes that correction himself. It goes with that bouquet of roses. The bouquet of roses is a collection of roses, of flowers, which are of ancient tradition, the famous roses, the white and the red, are symbols of the aqua, the water by which the transformation is produced.

Now, these dreams are really manifestations of a tissue of thinking that was on the surface about four or five hundred years ago. It is just as if these old fellows were still discussing the red and the white rose, the rose garden, the fountain, the *aqua permanens*, and he listens to them, going back in time, by a sort of time machine, such as H. G. Wells described; in other words, these discussions of the Middle Ages seem to be still going on.[27] Can one really go back in time, or is it perhaps that he really has

---

[25] Cf. *Psychology of the Transference* (1946) in CW 16, pars. 402–539.

[26] Cf. "Dream Symbols," nr. 29, p. 171, and CW 12, nr. 29, par. 236. M 29 {0226}: fig. 27, "Vision: a bouquet of roses, symbol of a flower in eight partitions," June 25, 1932, CDM.

[27] H. G. Wells (1866–1946), English novelist, journalist, sociologist, and historian best known for such science fiction novels as *The Time Machine* and *The War of the Worlds*. His first novel, *The Time Machine* (1895) was an immediate success. H. G. Wells (1946 [1897]), *The Time Machine: An Invention and Other Stories* (Harmondsworth: Penguin Books). Jung met Wells in 1924. Michael Sherborne (2012), *H. G. Wells: Another Kind of Life* (London:

archetypal contents in his unconscious that always, since eternity, talked and are still talking like that, and he just catches the nearest, the historically nearest, forms? For this series of dreams is just one continuous alchemistic argument, and I could read you alchemistic texts where there is that same connection, only in the Latin, and of the year 1450 or 1350 or 1250, and, of course, by entirely different people of whom we think, when we meet them historically, that they were old fools; but, apparently, they are immortals, whose discussion is still quite as alive as it always was.

Well now, after these performances and discoveries, he finds himself back again at a round table, and opposite to him sits the unknown dark woman.[28] Now it almost seems as if he has made his peace with her. After the careful preparation of those very intelligent unconscious agencies and after all the *synonima* brought up by the unconscious, he is now able to face that woman. It is just as if these unconscious agencies had said, "Now, look here, it is like a rose, or like a bouquet of roses, like a rose garden, like a fountain, like a tree." And by that they insinuated more and more the idea of the squareness, the roundness, the spacing, the reconciliation of pairs of opposites. And so he is brought again into relation with the dark woman.

Peter Owen), 273. In his novel *The World of William Clissold* Wells describes a conversation with Jung at a party in a London flat, allegedly after one of Jung's lectures at the Queen's Hall in London. (Jung was in the UK during the summer of 1925 giving lectures on "Dream Psychology" at Swanage, Dorset. See Burleson, 2005, 21). Jung also describes his meeting with Wells in the Jaffé protocols, where he does give a rather negative description of Wells's personality, comparing him to Thomas Mann, as a person of so much differentiated culture, intellect, and feeling, who can see everything with accuracy, but without being gripped by it in his personal life. He compares them both to vampires that sucked every word he said out of him, a feeling that made him avoid their company. Maybe this is what Wells himself means when he says, "I buttonholed the great man because I wanted to know how he regarded this conception of a sort of supermind of the species, and he said that it was entirely sympathetic with his views." H. G. Wells (1926), *The World of William Clissold* (London: E. Benn), 1:92. Jung recounts that he told Wells what happens in the mind of a paranoic, a description that inspired Wells's story *Christina Alberta's Father*. See AJ Protocols; H. C. Wells (1925), *Christina Alberta's Father* (London: Cape). See also Jung, McGuire, and Hull, 1978, 58, where Jung in an interview mentions the example of *Christina Alberta's Father* by his "friend, the great English writer."

[28] Cf. "Dream Symbols," nr. 30, p. 171, and CW 12, nr. 30, par. 238. M 30 {0228}: "Sitting with the dark woman at the round table," June 27, 1932, CDM.

Lecture 10

Ladies and gentlemen:

QUESTION: You have given us a good deal of historical evidence for the fact that the mandala is an ancient symbol of integration, but in the last two sessions you have made a very specific interpretation of this old symbol as referring to integration through the reconciliation of the four psychological functions.[1] This is puzzling, because so far as I know the systematic representation of the personality in terms of thinking, feeling, intuition, and sensation is your own work. Is this just a case of new wine in old bottles [*Dr. Jung: "That is sometimes quite advisable!"*], or is there historical evidence for the identification of the four points of the mandala with a fourfold classification of human functions?

DR. JUNG: This question is quite interesting. You know integration or individuation or concentration of human personality does not happen in a schematic way, but in a rather complicated and individual way, so individual as a matter of fact, that it is exceedingly difficult to find a rule or a regular course for it. The process can begin at any angle with any kind of problem, so naturally the process itself falls along very atypical lines. However, there are certain stages which we can designate definitely. Medieval philosophers worked for a very long time to establish an orderly sequence of events in that process, but even they did not arrive at any unanimity, and the writings are full of the most varied kinds of attempts to find a suitable formula.

Older attempts in antiquity are to be seen in the sequences of mystery pictures. I don't know whether you know these mystery images. Let us assume that you don't. They are a somewhat unknown matter anyhow. Of course, it would take the whole hour to describe them or their sequences, but I can give you a hint. Perhaps you know the Tarot cards, by which the gypsies prophesy.[2] They are descendants of the mystery pic-

---

[1] This lecture was held on October 25, 1937.

[2] Tarot, first known as trionfi and later as tarocchi, tarock cards, today mostly used for divination, is a deck of cards containing seventy-eight cards. Fifty-six cards consist of four

tures, and the twenty-one picture cards of the Tarot will give you an idea of such a sequence of images. There are other sequences of that kind, as, for instance, the sixty-four hexagrams of the *Yi King*, but of course that is more difficult.

True enough the process follows through all the functions. I could give you a scheme, a diagram, for the typical way in which the integration process usually takes place. We have here our cross of the functions. Let us assume that we are dealing with an intuitive type.

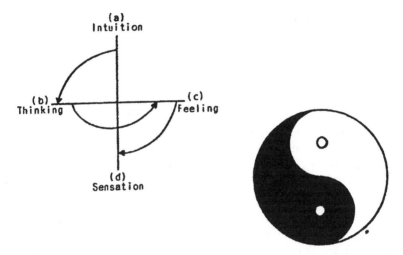

I shall put intuition up here at (a) to designate it as the superior or the most differentiated function. Then we usually have one or two auxiliary functions. In this case it would be one of the rational functions, and so here is thinking at (b), and feeling at (c), and then naturally down here at (d), we would have sensation.

Now usually the process of individuation begins with a very decisive experience, namely, you fall down through your most differentiated function; you meet with a situation you can't handle. An intuitive will discover

---

suits (usually coins, cups, wands, and swords) from ace to ten and four face cards, king, queen, page, and knight. Additionally there are twenty-two trumps with motifs illustrating among virtues like justice, strength, and temperance, other well-known principles like fortune, death, love, and judgement, as well as cosmology (world, moon, sun, and star) and powerful personages (magician, high priest and priestess, emperor and empress). These cards were from the beginning probably used for playing card games, a custom that we have references to from the fourteenth century. The oldest preserved tarot deck is the Visconti-Sforza deck from fifteenth century. There is no documented evidence that the deck was used for divination before the eighteenth century and the hermetic/spiritist revival with movements such as the theosophists and the Golden Dawn movement. S. R. Kaplan (1979), *The Encyclopedia of Tarot* (New York: US Games Systems; distributed by Aquarian).

that he always overlooks reality; he walks over it or stumbles upon it. And then he breaks his shin bone or gets ulcer of the stomach, and then most certainly if his next auxiliary function is thinking, he will begin to think and ask himself, "How is it? Why?" So he makes the movement from intuition (a) to thinking (b). Then a split, similar to the one we had before between intuition and sensation, occurs between thinking and feeling. He will find that his thinking comes to a standstill when he meets a feeling situation. He will most surely meet the feeling situation because he is now thinking. Instantaneously the feeling will be constellated, as the somewhat inferior function over against thinking; for he is an intuitive-thinking type, with thinking, the first auxiliary function, not as differentiated as intuition. So when it comes down to (c), because he has run into a feeling situation where his thinking is inadequate he will be in contradiction to thinking. Naturally this attempt will be followed by instant regression to intuition. He is once more back at the beginning and goes on again to thinking and then inevitable gets into contradiction with his feeling. Thinking is not in contradiction to his intuition and, since feeling is more or less contaminated with sensation, because it is a slightly unconscious function, so they go together. Then, if he discovers the possibility of dealing with a situation through feeling, there is a chance to get across from ab to cd. Inasmuch as thinking and feeling are auxiliary functions, the conflict between them is not so marked as between intuition and sensation, so he can get across here from (b) to (c) and understand feeling, which is, however, slightly in the unconscious and out of his control. Now sensation is contaminated by feeling and is quite in the shadow, so the movement will be (a) to (b) to (c) to (d). Thus he arrives at the inferior function.

If you draw this graphically it forms the sign of Tao. (See diagram.) It really goes that way, showing that this must be a sort of archetypal movement. It is the way of the serpent, and the serpent is always a symbol for the way through the mysteries, through the transformation. Even the hero who anticipates you and goes ahead of you as the *Psychopompos*, the leader of souls, is the guiding serpent. Therefore Christ was also identified with the serpent, and he was also supposed to be the guiding hero who goes through the transformation of the zodiac, taking the serpentine way through the whole zodiac. The Gnostics, the Christian Ophites, took Christ to be the serpent in Paradise, the One who was sent by the Father of the spiritual world to teach consciousness to the first unconscious human pair in Paradise. Their teaching is that the creator of the visible physical world, the Demiurgos, Jehovah, was an inferior daemon who had created an incomplete and very imperfect world. On the seventh day he took his seat in a high place and complacently looked down at the creation and found it very well done. But it was not very well done, because human beings could not stand erect and were creeping like worms and were unconscious. That is the teaching of the Gnostics, particularly the Christian Ophites. Their Christ was an apparition in the form of the serpent, and they had communion with the serpent on the table. They had a special gospel, the so-called Gospel of the Egyptians, in which there is the famous dialogue between Christ and Salome.[3]

Now you see this diagram is a reconciliation of pairs of opposites. It is an archetypal pattern of the whole, namely, the original four back of the four functions in consciousness. I have often been asked and have more often asked myself, why four, why not five, three, or seven? It can be any number, but we have here to do with four qualities of existence, and I don't know of any other quality. Sensation, when you put it quite simply, is that function which tells you that there is something. Thinking tells you what it is. Feeling tells you what that thing is worth for you, whether you like it or dislike it, whether you accept it or reject it. And intuition gives you a hunch about where that thing comes from and where it goes to, which is not given by sensation or by thinking. Occasionally you can think it, if you already know it, but sometimes you can't. So we get four qualities of any kind of conscious experience.

Now I told you that the idea of four functions is based, as it were, upon a subterranean archetypal pattern. I am willing to admit that I have been influenced by that archetypal pattern, though when I discovered the four functions, I didn't know it was an archetypal pattern. I only found out later on. To my great astonishment I found very similar diagrams in old texts and naturally asked myself, "Now what about that? Presumably I have been the victim of the operation of an old archetype." Then I found out that formerly they spoke of the four elements, or the four points of the compass. I began to seek in the literature to find out whether these four were understood to be psychological functions, and I found such a text, the *Bardo Thodol*, the so-called *Tibetan Book of the Dead*.[4] There

---

[3] In this very short gospel Salome asks when the things concerning which she asked should be known, and the Lord said: "When ye have trampled on the garment of shame, and when the two become one and the male with the female *is* neither male nor female." See Montague Rhode James (1924), in *The Apocryphal New Testament* (Oxford: Clarendon), 10–12. The figure of Salome was of special interest to Jung as he had encountered her in his fantasy material written down in the *RB*, 245.

[4] In 1935 Jung wrote a commentary to the *Tibetan Book of the Dead*. In the revised version of 1953 he lists these four aspects of wisdom as (1) White = the light-path of the mirror-like wisdom, (2) Yellow = the light-path of the wisdom of equality, (3) Red = the

you find the explanation that these four points or four functions or four colors are the four Light Paths of the Four Wisdoms. That has to do with the initiation ritual in which you follow the four paths. This text has not been subject to the slightest European influence; it is a very old Tibetan or Buddhist text that already gives the explanation that the four are really psychological functions. Of course they don't use that word, because they have no psychology such as we have. There, in the East, is the metaphysical philosophy, and that is what we call psychology. It is exactly the equivalent, only with the difference that they always hypostasize, namely, they act or think on the assumption that these four are not merely a figure of our thinking to explain psychological facts, but that they are cosmological, that they have a metaphysical existence.

In Europe during the Middle Ages, the mystery process had to go through the four elements. The philosopher's stone, or whatever the goal was, had to be composed of the four elements, and the four elements had four qualities, and these qualities were, of course, couched in physical terms; the hot, the cold, the humid, and the dry; or the four points of the horizon. It was put in such terms, but when someone said that the process had to start in spring and would ripen in summer and be mature in the fall and finished in the winter, did he refer literally to the seasons? Rather, he would have said, "Well, you know that is just a symbol or an allegory." You could express it just as well by the peculiar transformation of the four elements or of the four qualities. All those were synonyms. The medieval philosophers had no other language, so they used the terms taken from their knowledge of nature, as the East used the terms taken from their knowledge of nature, as the East used the terms they found in their metaphysical philosophy. But, as a matter of fact, they were always expressing the same underlying archetypal pattern.

So you see when I explain an antique mystery, or the use of mandalas in other civilizations or in other times, I would not say that those people thought that they referred to psychological functions. They couldn't think as we do; they thought differently, and so I am forced to explain in their language. But you see that is not a real explanation; I am speaking merely

---

light-path of the discriminative wisdom, (4) Green = the light-path of the all-performing wisdom. "Psychological Commentary to the 'Tibetan Book of the Dead,' CW 11, par. 850. Recently Donald Lopez has shown that the *Tibetan Book of the Dead* is a Western construction. He also emphasizes that Jung (and many others) have read the text in the light of their own theories (in Jung's case the theory of the collective unconscious) and thus grossly misinterpret the text. D. S. Lopez (2011), *The Tibetan Book of the Dead: A Biography* (Princeton, NJ: Woodstock/Princeton University Press).

in symbolical terms. But to us it seems that it is an explanation when we say that what those people meant by the four waters, the four winds, et cetera, was really the psychological functions.

Now I admit that this may be a new kind of symbolical language, by means of which we are continuing the process of human thought, that is, the transformation of human consciousness. Perhaps in one or two thousand years or perhaps less, people will again express these things in a very different way. It will always be the same pattern, however, and every new race or new civilization will invent a new terminology, will give a new name to an old thing. In this sense we can say it is putting new wine in old bottles; but I would rather say, giving a new name to an old thing. We never get away from archetypal patterns; they are simply structural elements of our mind, and if we try to explain psychology in terms that do not fit the mental structure, we have not explained the human mind. We must find a terminology, a way of envisaging things, that really expresses the structure of the human mind, so we are forced to use these archetypal terms. If we were to invent an entirely new theory of the mind, it would perhaps only explain the most recent and superficial psychological layer. There are such theories, and they only explain the uppermost layer of up-to-date consciousness, but nothing about these structural elements, so these theories have no appeal. The unconscious does not follow them unless they contain an archetypal pattern. Insofar as they do, they influence the unconscious. You only feel that something has gone home, has hit the nail on the head, when the archetype is sufficiently expressed. Otherwise it has no appeal at all.

QUESTION: Does the progressive mandala dream indicate that it is necessary to go after the fourth function?

DR. JUNG: It doesn't indicate anything of the sort. When you have a dream containing a mandala, as this dreamer had, then it simply means that the process of integration or individuation is about. It may be that you ought to, or that you can, or that it is perhaps advisable to do something, but the dream doesn't say so.

You see, nature doesn't suddenly shout into your ear: "I am gold or I am a diamond." If you find it, well, all right, but it may be there for a hundred thousand years, and nobody ever looks at it, because it doesn't say so. Dreams don't tell you what you should do with them, and they don't give you advice. The dream is not a sort of well-meaning teacher, a father, or something like that, who tells you what you ought to do. The dream is a symptom, a manifestation, a natural event. It is like, as a matter of fact very much like, the compass. The compass doesn't tell you to which goal you have to sail. It doesn't even tell you where north is. It simply moves, and it doesn't even point to the north pole. You must be very careful if you go by compass. You must know, for instance, the degrees of declination of the compass, and all that. It is just a natural phenomenon, and if you learn to make the right use of it, it is useful. But there is no "ought to."

I am really impressed by this demand for an "ought," this is a side remark, but in these days I have had ample opportunity to become a little acquainted with the peculiar mentality of America. I have been asked time and time again in relation to my lectures at New Haven whether I meant that one ought to be Catholic or ought to be Protestant. I don't know what one ought to be. So I came to the conclusion that one can hardly say anything without having people in the audience think that "one ought to."

I say nothing of the sort. I say it is so, and not that it means one ought to. It is always as if the great majority of people were under the eternal impression that they are in school or in Sunday school, where somebody says, "Now, you ought to or you must." Nothing of the kind! I wish you would learn to look at a thing in a dispassionate way and see how it moves and what it does. It is nature. Psychology is not something that a teacher once invented and tried to put over. Psychology, the psychological process, is a piece of nature. It is like a plant, like a tree or an animal; and you have to study its nature if you want to know anything about it, and draw your conclusions. There is no "ought to."

And so, you see, dreams can be very progressive, but that doesn't mean that they have an intention to tell you what you ought to do. So when you dream of a mandala, it can mean something to you or it can mean nothing to you. You find a diamond. You can say, "It means something to me," or you let it go. If you realize what it is worth and you want to make some money, you had better take it with you. If you don't want it, well, throw it away. The process goes on without you, if necessary. You see there are plenty of people in whom the individuation process, with mandala dreams and all the most beautiful stuff, just goes on without consciousness even. There are plenty of lunatics with the most wonderful individuation dreams, and nothing comes of it because there is nobody home.

So when you have such a dream, well, admire the grace of God that has given you such a thing, and marvel at it. Think what it could mean. Allow yourself to be impressed by it.

What could I say to my dreamer? What ought he to do now? Nothing can be said. I can say, "Don't you see what is happening? Now, cock your ears and try to understand what is going on. Meditate on your mandala, give interest to it. Ask yourself what that thing might be, or, if it is not clear to you, hope and wish for more enlightenment about it. But let it grow."

You would not dream of a mandala if the fourth function were not already there. If you dream of a more or less complete mandala, it means that the unconscious is preparing the stage in which the four functions really can come together, but it would help you not at all to seek for the fourth function. Moreover, I told you, you can't seek for it. You can't make for it. It already has you by the neck. It is just as if a lion in Africa should jump on you, and you were looking to see where the lion might be. The lion has eaten you long ago. You don't go lion hunting anymore!

I don't want to enter into the question of a person who has no sensation. To be blind, deaf, and dumb is not to be idiotic at all. Sensation has nothing to do with intellect. Sensation is just sensation. So when you have no eyes, you can nevertheless hear, or you can think. These functions are absolutely independent of each other. They are definitely organized psychological systems with even a specific energy, which means that if anyone prefers not to be conscious of a function in reality, then that function goes on nevertheless; it is unconscious but produces results. You can even be guided by such a function, by unconscious thinking, for instance it influences you, only in an archaic way, and then you might find suddenly that you disagree with it or that it disagrees with you, and you are in trouble, because everything will then lead to the unconscious. It is always functioning, but in an archaic manner and in such a way that it can hurt you as soon as you begin to deviate from it.

* * * * *

Well, we will now go on with our dreamer. You remember, we left off with the dream of the unknown dark woman with whom he finds himself at the round table. As I told you, he is now again confronted with the dark personification of the unconscious. He designates this figure as dark, and that is meaningful, because it is a specific form of anima. There are two forms of anima, a white one and a dark one. This is the archetype behind those famous words "Gentlemen prefer blondes but marry brunettes." You see, the blondes are the white, and the brunettes, the dark women. Now the darkness designates a peculiar kind of anima in the sense that this anima chiefly symbolizes the so-called chthonic side of the unconscious, namely, that side of the unconscious which has to do with the body and with the earth, with tangible realities, while the fair anima is a sort of celestial being and prefers to live on glaciers or on clouds and is something short of an angel.

These two figures are found, for instance, in a book, otherwise not particularly interesting, but intensely read by theosophists, by Schüre, *La Prêtresse d'Isis*.[5] I guess there is an English translation—I shouldn't wonder. She is the white anima, and then there is another one just the opposite, the black anima.

Surely you know, also, the story of *Hypatia*, don't you, an English classic?[6] She is counterbalanced by another one? Hypatia is the good, the spiritual, the white woman, and the other is the black woman. That is a clear anima story. It is projection. Often the two are together as in Rider Haggard's *She*. "She" is a twofold figure. She has both sides; but in one person. It is not so clear in Benoit's *L'Atlantide*. She has a bit too much the French style, a bit too much of the boudoir. There are plenty of others, for instance, the most modern edition, *To Walk The Night* by William Sloane, a young American writer, is a most commendable story, quite fascinating. That anima is a sort of derivative from *She*, of course, not consciously, but the author had read *She*. I myself asked to make sure. The heroine is also a figure containing both sides.

In my dreamer's case the dark anima is the critical one. If there were a fair one, that wouldn't be so bad. He had the fair one in other dreams, and there she always played the role of a guide, even of a mountain guide, a mountaineer, but in female form, she was guiding him through high or dangerous places. She gave him very valuable advice. She was a sort of revealing goddess to him, you know "une femme inspiratrice" of the best sort. But the dark one appeared often in the form of a colored woman or a primitive, or a dangerous woman, associated with gangsters, with bad tricks and all sorts of things, and he always got a shock when he discovered such a figure in his dream.

This darkness of the anima, particularly when it has a moral undertone, comes from the fact that the dreamer has left his own darkness to the unconscious and then the morally indifferent unconscious becomes suddenly colored by the admixture of his own dark substance, which we call the "shadow," his own shadow. He is not conscious enough of his own

---

[5] Eduard (Édouard) Schuré (1841–1929), French philosopher, poet, playwright, novelist, music critic, and publicist of esoteric literature. He published *La Prêtresse d'Isis: Légende de Pompeii* in 1907. See É. Schuré (1913), *La prêtresse d'Isis: Légende de Pompéi* (Paris: Librairie Academique Perrin et Cie).

[6] Charles Kingsley's novel from 1853. See C. Kingsley (1913 [1853]), *Hypatia—or New Foes with an Old Face* (London: J. M. Dent). Hypatia (ca. AD 350–70 to March 415) was a Greek Neoplatonist philosopher in Roman Egypt who was the first notable woman in mathematics.

dark side, of his own inferiorities, but likes to have a decent idea of himself. Therefore, he insists very much upon his achievements, and his position, because that gives him a pretty good persona,[7] and whenever you are the fortunate proprietor of a respectable persona, you dwell upon it. You always take shelter in it and not only point to it over against public opinion, but also against your own criticism. You pat yourself on the back and say, "But after all, I am so and so. I can do such-and-such things, and I have a wonderful voice. I am a singer, or a good actor, or a good doctor. It is self-evident; I have, at least, my diploma in my pocket." You see, it is always a temptation to have an undeniably splendid persona. You can take shelter, or refuge, in it over against your shadow. You can defend yourself. You have perhaps sufficient arguments against the possibility of having your attention called to the shadow side.

So you see, anybody who has good luck in the world, who is successful, is always in the greatest danger of becoming a two-dimensional personality, namely, one who has lost his shadow. Then you are made of paper, which means that you consist of what people say or print of you, and you are not a three-dimensional human being because you cast no shadow anymore. Many people are always busy rubbing out their shadow, so that they are only a façade with nothing behind it. Of course the shadow can never disappear to such an extent that nobody can see it. Perhaps the whole world will believe of such a fellow that he is a wonderful man throughout, 100 percent splendid, but, at least his wife will not be convinced. Therefore, there is a saying that no wife has ever been convinced that her husband was the superman. Somewhere the shadow will come through, no matter how you try to make it invisible.

The fact that my dreamer is now confronted with that black anima and that he can stand it, and can remain there, and doesn't run away from that side, is a great step forward, because it will help him to understand something more about himself, namely, he will now learn of what that dark anima really consists. Of course, he won't learn it from that dream. When he meditates on that dream, he will say, "Oh, what is that? Why is my unconscious so black? Why is it so uncanny?" And he probably wouldn't get any further. But, you see, the unconscious is going further. When his conscious process is getting too thin, he has an unconscious process of deliberation going on, and his unconscious is drawing exactly the same conclusions as I have just drawn from this dream.

---

[7] For Jung's definition of persona, see *CW* 6, par. 800.

The next dream says that he is sitting again at a round table opposite a certain man whom he knows, but who is an entirely negative figure to him.[8] That is the same dream situation practically as the last, but instead of the dark woman, there is now the man with negative qualities. Now, that man is a fellow who has all those qualities which the dreamer has but which he denies, which he would not have; he wouldn't acknowledge them. But, of course, he would point them out in everybody else and would be perhaps very critical of such qualities, not seeing that they are really his own that he has projected into other people. You know, we always criticize other people in the most severe way when they have the nerve to impersonate ourselves because they always impersonate the backyard of our consciousness, and that always gets our goat quite particularly.

So this is an important step forward. He is now confronted with himself, and he sees for the first time his own negative aspect. That fellow is his "bête noire" as the French say, his black counterpart which has all those qualities, obviously, which he denies in himself. Now, this is a situation which is promising; anybody who can face himself in his own negative aspect has overcome himself to a great extent. He is willing to accept the fact that he is not a wholly positive figure, but that he has a very negative side, and that that makes him, of course, a different man. Then people know that he knows and that he is a gentleman, because when anything happens, he won't insist upon being right absolutely and unconditionally. He will be able to admit that he might be wrong because he always thinks of the picture he once had of himself, where he cut a pretty deplorable figure, and when anybody has something to say about him, then he says, "Well, I remember, perhaps you are right. I don't know, but let us admit it; I will see."

At least he is accessible to a critique. And often, other people don't demand more of you than to have an opportunity to say something disagreeable to you. And when you accept it, then they have lost the motive; it makes no fun. They only get their real object when you are hit. You see, there are many people who are just born for that kind of business. They are sort of social wasps who must sting other people. As Socrates himself once said, "I am put upon the Athenians as a wasp or as a horsefly,"[9] to make them nervous and restless by his more or less pointed remarks.

---

[8] Cf. "Dream Symbols," nr. 31, p. 172, and CW 12, nr. 31, par. 241. M 31 {0229}: "Sitting with a questionable man at the round table. A glass with a gelatinous mass," June 27, 1932, CDM.

[9] From Socrates, *Apology*, line 30: "For if you kill me you will not easily find a successor to me, who, if I may use such a ludicrous figure of speech, am a sort of gadfly, given to the

Now this situation in a dream is positive, inasmuch as it gives him the chance of seeing his other side, of agreeing with it perhaps, because it makes no sense when you say, "I have rejected it; this is just the fellow I reject." You must sit together with him at the table, which is simply a symbol of communion or relationship. When you eat with somebody, or invite them to dinner, or luncheon, then you mean to express relationship. He is related to his shadow. Such a man is all round; he is approaching completeness, and that is about all we can wish for, to be at least complete. He agrees with himself; he agrees with his enemy.

And so, the situation in the dream is a positive and promising one and is now characterized by a further detail, namely, that in the center of the table there is a glass filled with a gelatinous mass. This points right back to a dream which I dealt with in a former seminar (I also mentioned it in this seminar), concerning the heap of gelatinous living matter. That albuminous stuff is like a matrix for hatching germs, and it surely refers to the experiment alluded to in former dreams, namely, the organization of the chaotic matter.

Now I think I should say something about this idea of the living chaotic matter, if I haven't already done so. I have said so many things these days that I don't know what I have said. I told you about the medieval idea of the earth as chaos?

Well then, you see, that is again an archetypal idea. We can follow it up as far as about the first centuries of the Christian era. It is the idea that there is somewhere, hidden in matter, a certain substance that is called "Earth of Paradise" or "Red Earth." This the alchemists were always seeking. You see, it was their quest to seek this matter, this Earth of Paradise, which was also called *massa confusa*, which means confused matter ("mass," matter; "confusa," confused).[10] Also, it was called the "chaos" or the "primordial chaos," and it was understood to be a remnant of the original matter which existed, when, in the beginning, the spirit of God incubated the waters of the world. You see, before the solid had been separated from the liquid, there were the celestial waters of the beginning,

---

state by God; and the state is a great and noble steed who is tardy in his motions owing to his very size, and requires to be stirred into life. I am that gadfly which God has attached to the state, and all day long and in all places am always fastening upon you, arousing and persuading and reproaching you. You will not easily find another like me, and therefore I would advise you to spare me." From Plato, author, and B. Jowett, trans. (1892), *The Dialogues of Plato*, vol. 2. (Oxford: Oxford University Press).

[10] In *PsA* Jung has added a paragraph concerning the prima materia as unformed matter in alchemy. Cf. *CW* 12, par. 244.

incubated by the spirit, the breath of God, and the idea was that when matter, earth, and the universe were created, then this original matter that contained the living breath of God did not disappear but was the constant originator of new life. These people thoroughly believed in a sort of *generatic aequivoca*, a spontaneous generation of life. They had no idea, as we have now, that all life comes from the egg, which means that all life comes from life. They assumed that life comes from dead matter. For instance, if some corruptible matter is left about, after a while, all sorts of things will grow out of it. A piece of meat rots there, and there are worms in it; they assumed the worms came out of the transformation of the meat. You see, that was an old observation of nature. So they assumed that there is such a generating matter, and it was the long-sought-for prima materia, the primal matter of the alchemists. It was, of course, a sort of psychological projection; therefore, it was always semimaterial and at the same time semimystical. That is the particular secret of alchemy, and the fact which we don't understand anymore, unless we are psychologists, and therefore it has caused no end of trouble in the comprehension of these old writings.

Now this living matter, this primordial matter, ought to be vivified, ought to be transformed from a sort of dormant condition into an active, flourishing, or developing condition, and therefore, it ought to be impregnated by the anima mundi. That is alchemistic thinking but was actually presented in the dream, where the heap of living matter was touched by the serpent. The alchemists say that Mercurius, which they called quicksilver, which was also nous, mind, *pneuma*, a diving breath, that Mercurius in the form of a serpent had to touch the Earth of Paradise, to penetrate it in order to make it into the substance by which the transformation of ordinary metal into precious metal, or ordinary stones into precious stones, or the ordinary medicine into the panacea, the elixir vitae, the elixir of life could be brought about. So that first formulation in the previous dream, that heap of living matter touched by the serpent, is an alchemical symbol. It is an archetypal image, and here again, we have the same. This time the archetypal matter is no more a mere heap, which it was before. It is not contained in the alchemical vessel. Of course he says "a glass," but in former centuries, this was the marvelous vessel of Hermes. We could say, doing no violence to the text, that Hermes was the nous, the Mind in the vessel of the mind. We find in this dream the original Earth of Paradise, the original chaotic massa confusa. In the former dream, the problem was still quite unconscious and, therefore, in a chaotic condition;

it could disappear again; it was not caught. But here, where the dreamer could stand the confrontation with his shadow, he has attained such an inner connection, such an inner continuity, such a wholeness and roundness, that his mind becomes the vessel, the miraculous vessel, the so-called *Vas Hermetis*, in which he can conceive the matter, and then the matter can transform. As soon as the alchemist gets the primordial matter into the miraculous vase, then the process of transformation begins.

Here is another question which I would like to answer right away.

QUESTION: The trinity, fire, air and water, exclude earth, the feminine, according to the alchemistic law that there are three that exclude the fourth. This is a demonstration of the exclusion of the fourth, the inferior function, and in alchemy, the fourth is always the earth or the feminine. Does not the psychological quaternity, as over against the trinity, include the feminine side or anima?

DR. JUNG: The three that excludes the fourth is, of course, clearly the formulation of a masculine mind. All these things have been formulated by men's minds, though there were quite a number of women active in alchemy, but because the whole problem was then projected into matter, it was immaterial what the formulations were because no person was implicated. So you see, the psychological structure simply didn't matter, and those ladies who were busy with alchemy, alchemical philosophy, simply took up the terminology of the men as is often the case, as you know, even in this country.

Now, how would this be expressed for the woman? Would the fourth function be spirit or animus? Would not this also make her trinity different from the man's? You see, as soon as you ask such a question, then, naturally, the tables are turned. Then it is not the earth that is excluded. Then, most probably, the air is excluded, because, you see, a woman, by her natural constitution and her whole creative faculty, her ability to create and build up bodies, belongs more to the earth, and her trouble is the air, and the animus, being the wind, the air, the *pneuma*, would be the inferior function, which, as a rule, is projected into the father. So her problem is not an anima problem, but an animus problem, and her fourth function would presumably be the air, if you express it alchemically. That, of course, gives a very different aspect to her problem. It also casts an interesting light upon the human relation between man and woman. Very often, man and woman are ships that pass each other in the night, and they don't even wink at each other. They are going in opposite directions, as a man transforms into his feminine character, so the woman transforms into her masculine character. That is, of course, a very interesting problem which I had better skip, also one of those problems one can hardly discuss dispassionately.

Now, you remember I told you that the dream just dealt with contains something very important, namely, that the Earth of Paradise is now caught in the vessel of the mind, and when it is in the vessel, according to the rule of alchemists, it will develop. Something is going to happen; a transformation is taking place which ultimately leads, according to the alchemistic law, to the birth or creation of a being, consisting of body, soul, and mind or spirit, as they said. That means a living being, to which they gave a very peculiar name and which they characterized in hundreds of ways. Usually it was called *rebis*: *re, res*, a thing; and *bis*, twice. A thing made of two things refers to the opposite being made one, for instance, man and his shadow or the male and the female, or the black and the white, or whatever you like to call the pairs of opposite. It is a bringing together of pairs of opposites into one. It is, in other words, a reconciling symbol, as I have described it in my book about psychological types.

The next dream reads: He receives a letter from an unknown woman (you can safely say from *the* unknown woman).[11] She writes that she has a pain in her womb. Enclosed in the letter is a design, a drawing.

Now this is the drawing that is included in the latter. It is mentioned that this point (a) is the womb, and this line leads towards it in a sort of serpentine way with the suggestion of a snake, but it also can be a road that goes in a serpentine way. And here at (b) is a primeval jungle, and in the jungle are many monkeys. And somewhere in the background is a beautiful view of glaciers. That is the whole dream.

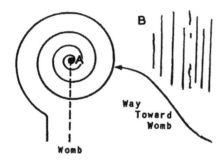

---

[11] Cf. "Dream Symbols," nr. 32, p. 174, and *CW* 12, nr. 32, par. 245. M 32 {0230}: fig. 28, "A letter from a woman, who has pain in her uterus. A map," June 27, 1932, CDM.

In that last dream we had the wonderful vessel. That vessel, the Vas Hermetis, was always compared to the womb by the old alchemists. This is again such a continuous thought, an alchemistic thought, going on in the unconscious. The thought passes from the vessel, the Vas Hermetis, to the uterus or matrix, and here it is called the "uterus."

Also, the unknown woman complains about pains, presumably labor pains, in her womb. This must refer to a possible pregnancy, a possible birth. At the same time, this place here (a), the uterus, the vessel, is encoiled by a line. We don't know what it is. The dreamer has no idea about it,

Now, this is an Eastern symbol. In India, it is like this. (See diagram)

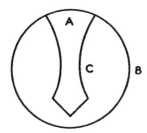

There is a snake's head (a) on top of an egg, or a globe (b). The center (c) is the Bindu, the symbol of Shiva, the creative god in the state of becoming; which is really the state of the unextended, the state of nonbeing, about to transform into the state of being, thus appearing as Hiranyagarbha. Hiranya is the golden germ or also the golden child, because it is the God *in statu nascenti*, in the state of becoming, hatched by Kundalini, the goddess who is coiling around the god.[12] She encircles him three and a half times. That is his story.

Now, mind you, the dreamer had never conceived of such a thing. He had no idea of anything like that, yet he produced the symbol of the becoming, of the beginning of all worlds, the eternal beginning of all existence, like the Orphic egg that was encoiled by the serpent, hatched by the serpent; and the serpent puts its head on top of the egg, exactly as the

---

[12] In *The Red Book* Jung painted an Image on page 59 around January 1917 with the title "hiranyagarbha." Jung owned copies of *Sacred Books of the East*, and the only section that is cut of vol. 32 is the opening hymn, "To the Unknown God," which begins, "In the beginning there arose the Golden Child (Hiranyagarbha); as soon as born, he alone was the lord of all that is" (1). In the *Rig Veda*, hiranyagarbha was the primal seed from which Brahma was born. In his copy of the *Upanishads* in the *Sacred Books of the East*, there is a piece of paper inserted near page 311 of the *Maitdiyana-Bdhmana-Upanishad*, a passage describing the Self that begins, "And the same Self is also called ... Hiranyagarbha" (vol. 15, pt. 2). *RB*, 59 and 285, also n. 130. On hiranyagarbha, see also Jung, 1996, appendix 1, p. 78.

Kundalini in India puts her head either on top of the creative organ or on the Shiva Bindu.

This serpentine way would mean going through the mystery, in the way of the serpent, to the place of becoming, to the place of birth, through the wood that is full of monkeys. That points back to the dream where he got the shock, namely, the dream in which the ceremony was being performed to reconstruct the gibbon; that means to reconstruct the anthropoid, the subman, the subhuman self, which is the animal or instinctual man. And this dream repeats it again, and says, "Your way is going the snake's way, the serpent's way, the way that isn't straight, that goes through this primeval jungle, where you are among ape-like beings, and in this way you come to the place of transformation."

The Hermetic vessel is the egg—was actually called the "egg"—in which the world or the wonderful substance or the gold is made. There is a Greek tract that has directly the title *Oochrysopoiia*,[13] which means, the making of the gold in the egg or through the egg. You see, this womb, this marvelous vase, is the vase in which the perfect being, the mysterious, complete being is made. You know, perhaps, that in the Lauretanian Litany, dating from the fourteenth century, Mary is three times called, "the vase."[14] I should assume, not without a certain hint from the kind of philosophy that was then current, she was in the *vas in signe devotionis*, the excellent vase of devotion, and so on. She was the vase or the womb in which the Deity was conceived, into which the Deity descended. She was the Earth of Paradise, and was called *terra virgo*, the virgin earth, by the fathers, Saints Augustine[15] and Tertullian.[16] She was that massa, that chaos or earth, in which the divine seed was planted.

And so we have here plenty of analogies that are, of course, exceedingly meaningful. Since it is the dark and unknown woman who writes

---

[13] The Chrysopoeia refer to two alchemical manuscripts; the first consists only of a page of symbols, containing the famous ouroboros snake with the inscription "εν το παν" = "one the all" (Cf. CW 12, par. 404, fig. 147, inscription removed) attributed to Cleopatra; the second is a lecture on the same subject attributed to Stephanus of Alexandria (seventh century Byzantine philosopher). They are to be found in the Codex Marcianus 299, which is said to be from the tenth or eleventh century. F. Sherwood Taylor (1930), "A Survey of Greek Alchemy," *Journal of Hellenic Studies* 50 (1): 109–39.

[14] The Lauretanian Litany is a litany (general prayer) of the Blessed Virgin Mary, the only approved Marian litany in the Western church.

[15] Saint Augustine (354–430) is one of the Latin Fathers of the Church and perhaps the most significant Christian thinker after Saint Paul. He adapted classical thought to Christian teaching and created a theological system of great power and lasting influence.

[16] Quintus Septimus Florens Tertullianus (born ca. 155, died after 220) was an important early Christian theologian, polemicist, and moralist.

the letter, it means that his anima is pregnant and that she is presently to bring forth. She is the marvelous vessel that contains the miraculous substance. She plays the role of the so-called Shakti, the female consort of Shiva, the Shakti Kundalini, the serpent; and the anima is also Mary. She stands in the place of Mary.

When you look back in history, you can understand the Christian mystery, the virgin birth, and all that, as a psychological mystery, for we don't know how the anima has conceived. The father is unknown. She simply seems to be pregnant and ready to give birth. We don't know to what.

Remember that the above dream follows the dream of the bringing together of the dreamer and his shadow. Making a composition or compound of man and his shadow is a particularly important act, as if it were the decisive thing, and we can really understand it because when a man can see his dark side, he then becomes complete. And, moreover, if he accepts his own dark side, and agrees that there is such a side to himself, and draws conclusions from it, if he takes over responsibility for this fact, then he instantly takes away that burden of darkness, that heaviness of the flesh, and of that dark matter, from his anima; and then something further can happen to her, for she has no longer that bondage to the earth. She is only the dark woman when she is not detached from earthly matters, or from this physical world. Now the dreamer has no longer an attached anima, at least theoretically. Let us be hopeful and optimistic and believe that such a thing is possible. The man who is ready to accept the fact that he has a shadow cannot get excited if somebody makes a remark about him. He will say, "Why, yes, of course, I most probably am this or that." He is quite ready not to flare up anymore, not to insist upon his point of view. He has no animosity, and so the anima has no place, because animosity is the real abode of the anima and the great temptation for her to jump into visibility. As soon as a man can accept his shadow, he can dismiss his anima; similarly a woman, when she accepts her other side, doesn't need to have any animus. She does not need animosity any more, and then her animus is also alleviated, is liberated from the shadow. The shadow had weighed down the personification of the unconscious, but now the personal face of the unconscious, or the anima, can turn away from the reality towards the unconscious, and then something new happens. So then according to this dream, and according to many, many dreams I have seen, the pregnancy begins, or then the birth begins, and the anima can function in a creative way. But as long as you have the shadow in the unconscious, nothing can happen because it is a blight; it destroys; nothing can grow. As soon as the unconscious is released from something which really belongs to yourself and which you can take care of, the unconscious can function in a proper way and then it is creative. Then a birth can take place.

Of course, we all are, I assume, curious to know what the unconscious is going to bring forth, what is to be born out of the woman, the Virgin Mary, the anima. According to the Christian legend, it is the Redeemer, the incarnation of the Deity. According to the alchemistic tradition, it is the marvelous substance, the panacea, the elixir of life; it is the red stone; it is the thing that makes the gold; it is the philosophical gold; it is, the "lapis invisibilitatis," the stone of invisibility, or the "lapis etherius," the stone that is ether-like, of heavenly substance, or as the French alchemists called in, *Notre Ciel*, Our Heaven, the quintessence that was as blue as the blue of Heaven. Those are synonyms, designating that wonderful thing which is to be born.

We have a certain hint in this dream as to the nature of the thing that is to come. Often we use a sort of speech figure. We say, "And here a new view opens up, a new vista appears." And so, at the end of the dream, it is said that then, somewhere in the background, a view upon the glacier opens up. We suddenly see the glaciers appear. Now, the glacier is an old archetypal image in itself. We naturally must refer to the individual associations of the patient, and he has the same association that he had to a former dream which is on record, namely, he instantly thinks, even in the dream, of the Milky Way in the sky. He had had the vision of the Milky Way during a conversation with another man, about the problem of immortality, that took place in a previous dream.

By that detour, the conversation about immortality, and the association of the Milky Way with glaciers, we know that the glaciers indicate immortality, the problem of immortality. Now that problem is indeed absolutely linked up with the problem of the precious substance in alchemistic thinking. It was always sad that the great art, or the royal art or the Magisterium, is the bringing forth of the panacea or the elixir vitae, the incorruptible body, namely, the body that will be glorified on the Day of Judgment. In Chinese alchemy, we have exactly the same idea of the formation of the so-called diamond body. The diamond body is a precious stone, and absolutely transparent like water; it is the crystallized divine water, and it is incorruptible. It is the hardest substance one knows of. It is a symbol for the incorruptible body, and so the medieval alchemists in the West also called the wonderful substance "the diamond," meaning the incorruptible body that should be produced by the *Opus Magnum*, the Great Work.

So you see, we also get indirectly in this dream a hint of the very nature of that peculiar thing which is to be born. We are quite safe in assuming that the dream wants to convey the idea that the product will have to do with the problem of immortality. This is not very astonishing. It is only in our conscious mind that we assume that the problem of immortality is an utterly unscientific one, that it is absolutely excluded, and that there is certainly no such thing as immortality, but our psyche has nothing to do with science. Our psyche produces such ideas, whether we have such a science or not. Science is a transitory phenomenon, while the idea of immortality or something equivalent to it is an age-old problem of man that surely won't die out, because it is an archetypal idea.

The dreamer already had a peculiar allusion to this problem in the series of dreams, almost in the beginning, when he had a dream of a clock that was a *perpetuum mobile*, a clock that worked without friction. Now, to any scientist, such an idea is most obscene; it is a terribly shocking idea that a reasonable individual should think about the possibility of a *perpetuum mobile* at all. But his unconscious is quite shameless in that respect, and it produces such a shocking idea because the unconscious wants to bring the problem of immortality nearer to him. We should be badly mistaken if we excluded such an idea, because it is a generally human one which we can never ignore. It would be just unscientific to refuse to consider such ideas. They belong to the human race from time immemorial, and, sure enough, they must have their place somewhere. You see, this does not prove the existence of immortality; it proves the existence of the idea of immorality, which, of course, is a very important face. If you have this idea, it is doing something to you, because if you have it really, then, you have feeling of it, you are in that state, you are in the state of immortality; and if you don't have such an idea, then you are not in the state of immortality.

Now, you can choose whatever you like, but it may be that it chooses you! Perhaps you might prefer the idea of mortality, but the opposite idea chooses you, and tomorrow you will be in a state of immortality, and there is nothing to be done against it. It may be stronger than you are. And, you see, whether we are really immortal or not doesn't matter at all. It is, at all events, not left to our decision; we have nothing to say about it. The only important thing is whether we are gripped by the idea, overcome by it, or not. Now usually, when people are overcome by the idea of immortality, they feel that they have received a particular grace, or they feel ever so much better. It is a very wonderful experience, and so there were millions of people (and are still millions of people) who seek that experience, who are only too eager to get that certainty. Our means to get there are, of course, very unreliable, despite the fact that the church provides many rites to this end, but they don't always work. But, nevertheless, the desire is there, and the fact that it happens to many people, relatively many, is also there, but we don't know exactly what we can do about it.

Well, this idea of immortality and the peculiar impression that something should be born, these exceedingly archetypal, exceedingly universal symbols, were very uncanny to my patient. He grew quite excited over them. They got him into a state of panic, as, naturally, a reasonable mind would be awfully impressed if he should find himself confronted with such ideas. Of course, it all sounds quite harmless. You can swallow that stuff easily, perhaps. But, you know, if it really happens to you, when you are all alone with yourself in a reasonable world, and suddenly you have the most unreasonable, the most irrational ideas, which you laugh at, and they come to you with all the paraphernalia of something serious, well, that just almost explodes you. And so, naturally, our patient ran away from it, and now see what happened.

For always when he had such ideas, he got frightened like anything and tried to escape. Then, the next dream would be a fight among savages, in which they committed the most beastly cruelties, or something of that sort, and he would wake up from such a dream completely shattered, because he was right in the midst of that slaughter, or whatever it was.[17]

Here then comes a clear regression to the dream or type of dream we have already seen a number of times. He always comes into conflict, after a particularly interesting or important dream. He gets into violent conflict between the yea and the nay. You see, he says, "Oh yes, very well, I will agree with that other side." Then it comes up and brings a basketful of the most amazing things, and then he gets the creeps and tries to get out, and so he naturally gets into a conflict between the right and the left side. It is the eternal problem.

Now, he couldn't remain forever in that condition of conflict, and so the next dream begins with the statement that he is talking to a friend, whom he knows very well in reality.[18] He is about ten years older than the

---

[17] Cf. "Dream Symbols," nr. 33, p. 178, and CW 12, nr. 33, par. 250. M 33 {0231}: "A polar expedition. People cut off from the source of life," June 28, 1932, CDM.

[18] Cf. "Dream Symbols," nr. 34, p. 179, and CW 12, nr. 34, par. 252. M 34 {0242}: "Conversation with a friend on the bleeding Christ," July 3, 1932. The friend in question was his paternal friend, the pianist Artur Schnabel (1882–1951), the renowned Austrian classical pianist. It is interesting to note, especially as the conversation in the dream is about the bleeding Christ, that Schnabel was of Jewish descent. He had to flee Berlin in 1933. There

dreamer and a very friendly man, who occasionally played the role of older brother or father figure to whom the dreamer often turned when he was in a difficult situation, to ask advice. This man had proven himself to be helpful in many ways, and he is the one who now appears in the dream. Remember that the dreamer is in a frightful conflict. He doesn't know what to do. He is torn to pieces over these peculiar ideas. And then the dream says, "Now, look here, talk to your friend. He is sensible; he is reasonable, and he will perhaps give you good advice."

And now, as often happens, it is not the friend who gives the advice, but the dreamer himself confesses something which is the helpful attitude by which he can surrender to that other side. Hear what he says to his friend in the dream, "I must endure in this situation, in front of the bleeding Christ, and I must work at it (namely, at my redemption)."

Now, you see, that scientist talks such a style! It is almost a hieratical, or a biblical style. He is forced to go back to such language in order to formulate the attitude which is really needed, and from that you can see how serious his conflict is and how terrible it is to him to submit to the other side. Of course, when you know all about that other side, you say, "How interesting, how nice, how beautiful!" But when it comes to you in such a nakedness, just so and nothing else, and with all the weight of a most important experience, well then, naturally, you doubt your sanity, and then you are forced to an extraordinary attitude, namely, an attitude of complete submission, identification with Christ, who simply surrenders to his suffering. The dreamer understands that he has to surrender to the extraordinary mental torture of undergoing thoughts that tear his intellect to shreds, and it is a mental torture. That is the *sacrificium intellectus*.[19] He must give up his idea that his intellect is valid. We shall see such things; he must be able to overcome his most cherished function. When anyone has to give up his differentiated function, then he has to go through all the torture of crucifixion, because he has to go the way of the Cross.

So, this dream is no exaggeration at all; you never get anywhere near to individuation if you can't go through that intense mental suffering of the way of the Cross. That is another insight into the Christian mystery. And what happens when you don't confess an external Christ and an external crucifixion, it is a crucifixion that happens to you in that place where you are the most sensitive, where you believe the most in yourself.

---

are many allusions to the political situation in Austria and Nazi Germany, and to Pauli's Jewish roots in his early dreams, on which Jung chooses not to comment. CDM.

[19] Latin: Sacrifice of the intellect. Jung discusses this in *CW* 6, pars. 19–20.

There you will be crucified, and there you will undergo the worst torture. In the mind or in the intuition, or in the feeling of a feeling person, it is just as if the best fruit of all your attempts had to undergo the crucial pain, and that is again a repetition of the Christian mystery, but in your own psychology.

Lecture 11

Ladies and gentlemen:

Here is a question about the functions: You remember I said that the inferior function can be thinking or feeling or any function at all, and the question is whether sensation and intuition can also occasionally be inferior functions.[1]

I can almost leave that question to you. Sure enough, any of the four functions can get into your unconscious. There are plenty of people right here whose inferior function is sensation, and they stumble over those awful realities like cooks and clothing and household and I don't know—perhaps husbands!

Then there is another question: Can the individuated person or the person who struggles or works towards individuation ever allow himself to relax into the unconscious, or is a relaxation into the unconscious always a regression? In other words, should a person who achieves individuation attempt to be conscious during all his waking time? If not, on what occasion besides sleep may he relax into the unconscious? [*Laughter*]

You see this unmitigated mirth released by that question shows that there must be something in it. This is a precious example of how things are taken in this country. You hear a statement, and then it becomes an "ought." You "ought to." In this kind of process, the analytical process, you struggle or make an effort to become more conscious, but you can't be in a state of continuous tension for fear you may lose yourself in a state of unconsciousness. Nature takes care of this. Every evening you lapse into a state of unconsciousness (at least I hope you do—otherwise you must take a sleeping draught), and in the day there are intervals when you sink down into a more or less unconscious condition. That is self-evident. If you observe carefully what happens within, you will see that you cannot do more than your ability permits you to do.

---

[1] This lecture was held on October 26, 1937.

QUESTION (CONTINUED): Is the burden of consciousness the cross that is meant in the phrase, "Take up thy cross and follow me?"

DR. JUNG: That phrase never meant "the cross of consciousness," because it is a quotation from the Bible. You know that the New Testament was written about two thousand years ago, and it referred to the suffering of Christ and not to consciousness at all. But if we interpret that myth in light of our present consciousness, then we can fairly say, "Yes, it is consciousness with its fourfold aspect, because we now have developed so far that we know these problems which were formerly projected into metaphysical entities, into a Son of God who appeared in the flesh—all these metaphysical ideas have been psychological in our day. We can't assume any more that the Son of God appeared in the flesh. Millions of people believe this as a fact, and we must not disturb them in such a belief. That belief is perfectly all right as long as people belong, say two thousand years ago, but we have layers of population that belong not only two thousand years back, but perhaps five thousand, six thousand, or eight thousand years ago. They still walk about among us: we still have cavemen. Right here in New York you do not have to go very far to meet cavemen. The population not only extends backward into the lap of time, into the ages, but also extends forward. People are living at the present day who don't belong in our age but who belong one hundred or five hundred or a thousand years hence. Such people are not easily understood. Advanced minds don't exactly belong in our time. When you look back there were fairly modern people in the past who did not belong in their age. So you see humanity is a very complicated thing, that is, with individuals living at levels corresponding to periods distributed over perhaps twenty thousand years. Of course here we are in a democratic country and can speak quite freely. I come from a democratic country too. That democracy is quite good for social purposes, but nature is not like that. Nature is thoroughly aristocratic, and she distributes people in different ages and different layers of intelligence, of modernity, so that the real structure of society looks quite different if viewed from a psychological angle.

You remember we read that dream yesterday in which the dreamer confesses himself in a very peculiar and striking way. It is quite unusual with him to come out with such a very important and outspoken confession. Usually it is a voice that makes such a remark, or it is the unknown woman or the old woman who says such things; but here he is almost forced to say those words himself. Now that is quite a step forward for him. By making such a confession he puts himself in the place where he really belongs; he tells the truth; he tells the truth about himself, which he never would have done in this way in his waking state. It was a dream in which he could talk as he really felt, although to say the same in the conscious state would have been too much for him, because he could not imagine himself speaking such words. He would have denied that he ever thought such a thing. It was necessary for him to have a dream in order to say such a thing.

When he tells the truth, he can't help saying how he feels, then he is in opposition or contradiction to his conscious state of mind. And so the next dream derives from this peculiar kind of conflict.

The next dream says an actor throws his hat violently against the wall, and the hat looks very peculiar there, in that it is absolutely round and has a dark center, in the place where the head goes, and there is an eight-fold division there.[2] You can easily see that this represents a mandala. This the dreamer himself perceives with surprise.

Now what does this dream mean? The hat that this man has worn before was a mandala, but he was not aware of the fact. It only became obvious when he threw it against the wall. You know the motif of throwing something against the wall from fairy tales, for instance, the prince who was an ugly frog or toad, and who wanted to eat with the princess. She got angry at his presumption and threw him against the wall, when he suddenly transformed into the Prince Charming. That is such a beautiful gesture!

The man who throws the hat is called an actor. The actor impersonates something, he creates the persona. The Latin word means *mask*. The actor of antiquity wore a mask, and because the antique actors playing in open theater had to fill an enormous space with their voices, they had a sort of megaphone inside the mouth of the mask to make the voice more resonant. *Personare* means to "sound through." The sound of his words is carried by this trumpet-like megaphone in the mask. Our word *persona*, personality, comes from that antique concept of the mask. Now we use that word persona in order to designate the adaption system everyone carries with him. It is sometimes such a clear system that you can see people put on the mask when they are called upon suddenly, particularly people who have to show themselves in public frequently. For instance, you know a very famous person in this country who has a very famous smile which can be put on instantly; then you can see the mask everywhere

---

[2] Cf. "Dream Symbols," nr. 35, p. 179, and *CW* 12, nr. 35, par. 254. M 35 {0243}: fig. 31, "An actor throws his hat at the wall," July 4, 1932, CDM.

in all the newspapers.[3] Other famous statesmen in Europe have the same. Also there are any number of professional masks, as that of the person who preaches, in contrast to the parson at home; the doctor with his patients— the bedside manner and all that. This is persona, which is the product of the man himself and of the public that expects a certain type of mannerism from him. The public has a typical expectation of how one must behave when one represents a certain office; the man who is called upon to personify (there is no verb "to person") that office must wear suitable robes. One wears those robes to denote the particular kind of personality one expresses. Clothing is a sort of mask one puts on—a costume, and the face must correspond to the dignity of what one wears; the actor is capable of impersonating many characters; he is typically the man who can put on a mask, can produce different personalities; and you would call a man an actor when he can put on such a persona.

Now when our dreamer dreams of an actor then surely it refers to a certain side of himself, that is, to the personality, or even individuation of a sort, the person he wants to be or the person who he wants to produce before the public. And this man, like all others, naturally has such a conception of himself, and of what he is and how he wants to be taken; and he is identified with that persona.

There are many people who perform a certain office and then get stuck in it, and they can't get out of it; they always act as if performing. We say of such people that they already live in their biographies, which is a rather expansive condition and somewhat awkward. You can't talk properly to these people for they always talk to you as if you were an audience; they take you as representative of a crowd, and so they show this typical behavior.

Here he suddenly becomes aware of the fact that he has played a role, that he has been identical with the character which he wanted people to see in him, and that he was not really himself. In the dream before when he made that confession, he had really been himself, and this reality naturally comes into a sort of contradiction with that which he performed or impersonated; this latter person of course would not like the self, the real

---

[3] This probably refers to President Theodore Roosevelt: "TR was known as 'the first president that smiled,' and he was typically photographed and illustrated grinning from ear to ear. His flashing white teeth, wide smile, and engaging openness became welcome symbols of national and international acceptance." A. G. Christen and J. A. Christen (2007), "Theodore Roosevelt's 'Presidential Smile' and Questionable Dental Health," *Journal of the History Of Dentistry* 55 (2): 85–90.

personality, for the total personality is anything but the personal, so the person in the mask throws away the hat because the hat symbolizes the self, the total man, namely, the totality of the conscious and unconscious personality.

Right in the beginning of this dream series, the very first dream in which the roundness or so-called mandala motive appears, was a hat. The dream was that he was at a social gathering, and when he left he put on the wrong hat. Then he woke up. Now this is a motive which was unconsciously drawn from, or at least parallel to, one contained in a pretty well-known novel by the Austrian author Meyrink, who wrote *The Golem*. There the hero of the story by chance puts on the wrong hat, the hat of a stranger. Later he finds the name inside, Athanasius Pernat. That name *Pernat* means nothing; at least I was unable to find out anything about it.[4] But *Athanasius* means *the Immortal One*. The hero of that story, under the strange hat, undergoes the most fantastic adventures. The most extraordinary things happen to him; in other words, he gets into the collective unconscious, and the story consists of a narration of the peculiar adventure he goes through—all adventures of the collective unconscious. In other words, when he put on that hat he got under the influence of a strange mind, the mind of an immortal one.

We are perhaps allowed to draw a parallel here and to assume that when the patient had that dream right at the beginning, the unconscious tried to convey to him, "Now peculiar things are going to happen to you. You will have the experiences of an immortal one, namely, the experiences of the collective unconscious," because the collective unconscious is the immortal substance in man. Conscious is mortal; we shall discover that there will remain nothing of that which our consciousness has acquired. But our mind is based upon a layer of the psyche that is everywhere and always there. So long as there are living beings, human beings, there will be the collective unconscious; and so we might call it the immortal part of man.

---

[4] Pernat seems to have been an ordinary family name of Dutch origin. Pauli had positive associations to Holland; he liked most of his Dutch colleagues. He visited the country for the first time in 1939. Later in life Pauli developed a countries mandala, where different countries symbolized different attitude types in Jung's typology. Germany symbolized thinking, England intuition, France feeling, and Italy sensation. He considered Holland to represent a "redemptive symbol" unifying feeling and intuition into intuitive feeling (unpublished letter to C. A. Meier from February 25, 1942, to be published in a forthcoming supplementary volume in the PLC series; see also Pauli to Jung [October 23, 1956, 69P], *PJL*).

If the dreamer puts on the hat of a stranger whose name is Athanasius, then he is quite likely to experience the contents of that immortal personality. At the same time he will realize something of the immortality of that being. We have seen in one of the subsequent dreams that he really experiences something of immortality, in the vision of the glaciers. Also, there is a hint of immortality, of something that never comes to a standstill, in the peculiar kind of simile used in a former dream where the unconscious was compared to or expressed by the clock that never ceases, really the *perpetuum mobile.*

You see in the present dream he is the actor, he is the persona, an utterly transitory figure, because whatever is performed in this world through consciousness is transitory and opposed to the everlasting unconscious. There is a deep gap between the two. Therefore if you speak to the collective unconscious, it takes about twenty years for people to become more or less acquainted with the term, and then they resist it because it seems to them something mystical, something unheard of. They don't resist the fact that our anatomy is somewhat the same all over the world, but they resist the fact that our unconscious is the same. There must be some reason why people want the conscious to be the only thing in man. Arrogant people with traces of megalomania usually have a deep-rooted inferiority complex, and therefore they always try to convince themselves and everybody around them that they are really big personas. So they make themselves noticeable; they are noisy; they insist upon their importance; they are touchy because they are all the time afraid someone might step on their toes, and they desire to anticipate that by playing an apparently very important role. The same is true of our consciousness, which is a relatively late acquisition in our evolutionary tree. If you go a little further back, to the primitive man, take the Bushman, the Aruntas[5] of central Australian origin, there you find very little consciousness. If they are conscious for half an hour they sink back into nonexistence. They do not even dream but are just unconscious, and when they are called upon to be attentive, they become terribly tired after a very short time.

This was also my own experience with African primitives. After I had the easiest kind of a talk with them for about an hour, they would say, "Oh, we are so tired. We can't stand it any longer. Why do you ask so

---

[5] Arunta, also spelled Aranda, Aboriginal tribe that originally occupied a region of twenty-five thousand square miles (sixty-five thousand square kilometers) in central Australia, along the upper Finke River and its tributaries. On Jung's sources of information about the Aruntas/Arandas, see above.

many things? We want to sleep. We want to go home." At first I thought they just had resistance, that they didn't want to be investigated or something of the sort. But I soon found out that they liked it. When they heard "There is a palaver today," they flocked to it. I always had a large audience. (Well, not so many as this!) They liked the performance because it was a solemn thing and satisfied their curiosity as to what the white man was going to do next, for to the primitive, he is a sort of miracle, and they liked to talk; but to be attentive or to listen to something or give precise answers, that is most fatiguing to them, because consciousness means to them a definite effort. It means the same to us, only we have better training. Our brain is capable of more awareness than that of the Negroes. If you go back to the Negroes, you are soon quite close to the gorillas where even the language seems to be pretty poor. Such tribes are like the lower animals which we assume have no consciousness, or at least no noticeable conscious whatever.[6]

So you see, consciousness is a late acquisition; it is pretty weak. We can only be continuously conscious for a few hours every day, and we soon relapse into a state of seeming or complete unconsciousness, in order to restore ourselves after the extraordinary exertion of having been conscious for a couple of hours perhaps. This means that consciousness is still threatened by extinction, by being overcome by the collective unconscious, that is, by a state of nonthinking in which people lose themselves.

We can say that to be unconscious is a pretty blissful condition. It would be quite nice if the unconscious were something which didn't move, which produced nothing; but when all our conscious functions drop into

---

[6] Jung's view of black and so-called primitive people (premodern, indigenous people) and so-called primitive psychology is linked to his views on the development of consciousness through evolution, where man, according to Jung, moves from a collective, nonreflective way of life toward increasing individualization and intellectualization of consciousness as seen in modern man. Although consciousness is a valuable but also quite new acquirement of man, Jung does not regard this development as solely positive. Modernity cuts man of from the intensity of life, from a living relationship to the unconscious and to the self, whereby something very valuable is lost. On the other hand, Jung criticizes "affect driven" crowd psychology, i.e., an "acting out" of this unreflected unconscious layer that exists in all men. In the above statement Jung uses the word "Negro" as synonymous to "primitive" psychology. As a comparison, a citation concerning the "mob" from a lecture held at the Zarathustra seminars on June 17, 1936, is illustrative: "Anyone in his sound senses must know that the mob is just a mob. It is inferior, consisting of inferior types of human species. If they have immortal souls at all ... [they are] presumably far away, as far away as they are in animals. I am quite inclined to attribute immortal souls to animals; they are just as dignified as the inferior man." Jung, 1988, 2:1003. For a thorough analysis of Jung's intellectual position on these issues, see Sherry, 2010. See also Shamdasani, 2004, 311–14.

the unconscious, a condition results which Janet called an "abaissement du niveau mental." When the functions are in the unconscious they nevertheless produce effects so that instead of thinking something consciously you think it unconsciously, and instead of having willpower or energy or impulse in a conscious way so that you do what you want to do, you do something of which you are unaware. This is what happens when people come under the domination of the unconscious. It is for this reason that primitives, much as they like to be unconscious, are at the same time afraid of it. For whenever they sink into the unconscious, it can make them do something which they never intended. Therefore they try very hard to keep awake. This is also one of the most important motives for the invention of taboos; for instance, you cannot speak a certain vowel or consonant; or if you belong to the water totem, you cannot drink water unless a man from another tribe hands it to you; you cannot drink water by yourself.

These exceedingly complicated taboos are attempts at consciousness. You must be conscious if you are not to produce certain vowels or certain words, or cannot instinctively take water, but must wait until a man of another tribe comes to give it to you. The life of primitives is just full of such things, of which, of course, we would not think, yet we have the same. In crossing the street, for example, we observe a certain ritual. Our taboos are represented by the police, by laws, by notices, in which it is forbidden to do this or that. Certain areas are not open to the public; and we know that we must not transgress. That seems to us to require no particular effort of consciousness. But the primitive has to keep all that in mind so that his life is pretty complicated, yet that is just what keeps him going; he has absolutely no other means of keeping himself properly awake.

So I hold that when the missionaries convert such people to Christianity and tell them that it is sufficient if they go to church on Sunday and sing hymns, they have deprived them of the only means of becoming conscious, and what they substitute is not sufficient. The primitives then disregard their taboos; they disregard dangerous areas; there are no ghosts or witches anymore. Happily enough these things are more deeply rooted than missionary teaching. Witchcraft is one of the most potent powers in Africa; you must be careful not to say this or that, because you fear a sorcerer. Missionaries are doing everything under the sun to remove their fears from the poor primitives, as if you could relieve humanity from fear. You would do humanity a poor service if you could, for that is the only thing that keeps people in reasonable form. There must be fear. Unfortunately man will only develop if he is in a state of dire need, otherwise he does nothing at all. So you see God has given us a lot of fear and worry.

You might suppose that the primitives would not need such stimuli; yet you find that they are just the ones who are the most *gêné*,[7] embarrassed and hindered by what seem to us utterly absurd taboos. But you see we are ignorant, and we do not realize why these taboos exist.

So, when primitives undergo the influence of Christian education, they degenerate. If you employ a boy in Africa, you are advised never to take a mission boy. They will all steal and lie and be fresh; for they have lost their taboos. When I was interviewing such a boy in Nairobi the boy said, "I am good; I know those fellows Johnny, Marky, Lukey—the Evangelists." I said, "You go to hell," and I thought a good deal about the effect of missionary training. The other boys are decent; they are afraid; but these mission boys are afraid of nothing. They are dirty and unreliable. Why? Because they have lost their taboos.

To return to our dream: The hat in this case is the mandala. This is a characteristic symbol for that strange second personality which is coming into the life of the patient. When that second personality appears there will be a conflict in the dream! Shall I be my second personality and go that way or remain in my persona? In the dream before he took a step forward and identified with his second personality, that personality which told the truth, how he really felt. But then, of course, the actor who represents himself shows that he dislikes the idea of the mandala and throws it away.

This would mean that if the patient is identified with the actor (we are not sure of that) he shows by his gesture resistance against the mandala, against the self. Then another rite will be needed, namely, a sort of circumambulation, in order to form a new mandala. I think that this really describes the case; he had identified with the actor; and this becomes clear in the next dream.

The next dream shows him driving in a taxi to the town square near the city hall, which means about the center of the town.[8] In reality it is called the Square of the City Hall; but in the dream it has the name "The Yard of Mary."

Now Mary refers to the Mother of God. You remember that in illustrating the former dream where we had the womb and the spiral around it, I told you that this was also like the Christian myth of Mary who is the Mother of God. She is called the vase, the vessel, the alchemical vessel;

---

[7] French: embarrassed.

[8] Cf. "Dream Symbols," nr. 36, p. 179, and *CW* 12 nr. 36, par. 256. M 36 {0244}: fig. 32, "Cab drive to the Courtyard, called the 'Court of Mary' (Marienhof)," July 7, 1932, CDM.

she is the creative womb in which God created the shape of man. It was just as if I had known what the dreamer was going to dream afterwards. Of course, I really did know it, but that was not the reason why I explained that former dream in the way I did. I simply gave you the natural materials, the alchemical materials, which were at the basis of his dream. And, you see, he himself comes to the square, which always means the temenos, the sacred tabooed area in which the transformation is going to take place, and he himself in the dream calls it the "Yard" or the "Court of Mary," as if he had been aware of the whole underlying symbolism. Of course, he was not; he had no idea of it. His unconscious itself interprets the temenos in the way in which I have explained it to you, and in the way in which it was always explained by the medieval philosophers, for which I am surely not responsible.

So this dream would mean that he has to go again to the place where the transformation is supposed to take place, where there is a possibility of a transformation. This obviously implies that he had left the place; that he had escaped again, probably because he identifies with the actor and showed his resistance against this accursed thing, which he simply won't have. His conscious mind rejects it because he can't understand the symbolism.

So the next dream again takes up a new variation of the same theme. There is a dark center, obviously referring to the dark center of the temenos, and there are curves around it (that reminds us right away of the symbol we had before, that of the womb or the vessel encoiled by the spiral).[9] Upon the curves light is circulating. It is as if light were a sort of liquid running along these curves.

Light always points to the consciousness, as if conscious energy were circulating on these spirals round the dark center, obviously in order to bring light, to bring energy, into the empty center, naturally for the purpose of a creation in the center. You could say straight away, his libido is circumambulating or coiling around that center in order to fill it. Then he finds himself wandering through dark caves, which means that he is now in the place of transformation. He is now in the womb, in the darkness of the unconscious, represented in the form of caves, and there he notices a wild battle between the good and the evil people. Again such a conflict as we have seen before. But there in that darkness is also a prince, a powerful prince, who knows everything, and this prince gives him a ring with a

---

[9] Cf. "Dream Symbols," nr. 37, p. 180, and CW 12, nr. 37, par. 258. M 37 {0245}: fig. 33, "Good and evil in a dark cave fighting. A diamond ring," July 5, 1932, CDM.

diamond and puts the ring upon the fourth finger of his left hand, and then the dream ends.

Here we have something new, namely, in the darkness which is filled with the din of a battle is also a prince who is superior to the battle, detached, like the tree under which the savages were fighting each other without even seeing the tree. So here the fight between good and evil takes place under the eyes of the prince who knows everything. He is a sort of reconciling symbol, a reconciling personality, far superior to those people who fight each other. He is beyond the conflict, *au-dessus de la mêlée*,[10] and he would represent a superior being in the dreamer himself, namely, that superior or true personality which is different from the persona, with which he had been identical hitherto. The prince gives him now a ring.

The ring refers again to the mandala, to the totality. The ring, furthermore, is decorated with a diamond. That diamond is the stone of the philosophers. It is the precious substance. It expresses the fact that the ring is the precious thing. To give someone a ring means to join him in something or to unite him with somebody or something. As you know, the fourth finger of the left hand is usually the place where an engagement ring is worn. In receiving this ring he becomes engaged; which means that he is now wedded to the diamond or to the prince, perhaps wedded to the secondary, and superior, personality. It is placed upon the fourth finger; it actually is in a sense the fourth finger. We might leave it at that, or we might say, "Well that is rather typical. It is just the fourth, because that means the fourth function. That is the inferior function in the scheme and he is wedded or connected or chained by it."

And this is really the case. We like to think that our human relations are chiefly based upon our achievements; for instance, upon our differentiated functions. That is what we wish to believe; but as a matter of fact, real human relations are based upon our inferior function. Where we are really related is where we are really dependent; but we hate to acknowledge it. It is very disagreeable to admit that we are dependent somewhere; yet our dependence, not our strength, forms the real source of a relationship. In our strength we can stand alone. We don't need other people. If a man has a good thinking function, he doesn't need the thinking of other people to help him when he thinks. On the contrary, he much prefers to think all by himself. If a man's feeling is strong, he doesn't need other people to make him feel. He has his own feeling. He can make others feel,

---

[10] French: above the fight.

if he likes, but he doesn't need other people to make him feel, and so on. So you see, through our strength we are, as a rule, rather separated from other people, because we prefer to act by ourselves and we are capable of so doing, but where we are weak, where we are dependent, where we are uncertain, there we need other people. There we even have a vital need of other people, and there we are related.

Everybody, then, has these two different sets of relations, on the one side, those which he likes to dwell upon, namely, those where he doesn't feel dependent, where he is his own free agent, and walks through the world without the help of others. That is why we insist that, "One shouldn't be dependent upon one's friends," and all that. But the other set of relations are the real relations, where we are dependent, where we are not free agents. This is exactly what we hate to confess, although in some cases perhaps we make a virtue of it, which is worse.

We learn from this dream that in a dark cave a prince was in possession of a precious stone and that the dreamer becomes wedded to that figure. This is again a medieval thought which in the form of a story goes back many hundreds of years, perhaps to the time of ancient Alexandria. We don't know exactly. The tale concerned a hidden king, who was at the bottom of the sea, and was called the "Rex Marinus," meaning the "king of the sea."[11] He is often described as in a state where he needs help. The philosophers should go down to the king; they should hear his lamentation coming up from the depth of the sea and should help him to reach the surface. This expresses a part of the philosophic mystery of the Middle Ages, namely, the attempt to rescue that spark of the deity which had fallen into matter and which cried out for help that it might be liberated, and be restored again to the light from whence it came.

After this dream another one follows, just a bit of a dream. In it, the dreamer sees a table, a round table like the one we have encountered several times previously. Four chairs are around the table, but they are empty.[12] Nobody is there, and there is nothing on the table.

---

[11] The *Rex Marinus*, "King of the sea," in alchemy is a metaphor for the process of dissoluting the raw matter or the gold that is to become the philosopher's stone, depicted in emblem 31 in Michael Maier's *Atalanta fugiens* from 1617. Emblem 31 of Jung's copy of *Atalanta Fugiens* from the digitized rare book collection of C. G. Jung (http://www.e-rara .ch/cgj/content/pageview/1906112). Jung mentions him in *CW* 12, pars. 435, 449, and *CW* 14, pars. 104–9 and 465. See also M. Maier (1989), *Atalanta Fugiens: An Edition of the Fugues, Emblems, and Epigrams* (Grand Rapids, MI: Phanes).

[12] Cf. "Dream Symbols," nr. 38, p. 180, and *CW* 12, nr. 38, par. 260, M 38 {0246}: "Round table and four empty chairs in a cave," July 5, 1932, CDM.

In an earlier dream, you remember, these chairs were occupied. There was even a glass with the matter of life in it. That isn't present any more. For this fact, we can conclude that his former confession, where he spoke the truth for the first time, has cost him dearly. He instantly made a bad regression, and the whole achievement or progress that was accomplished then has disappeared, and he has practically to begin again. But, at all events, there are the table and the four chairs ready to sometime occupy. Of course, the four chairs refer again to the four—the roundness and the four, the circle and the square, the totality and the function.

It is quite obvious that something ought to be done about this situation. At least that is what *we* would say. The dreamer, however, doesn't say that anything should be done about the empty table. As far as he is concerned, it might remain to all eternity. But if we think that this dreamer should get somewhere, then we would say to him, "No, look here, your table is empty. Those chairs are unoccupied. Is that right? Do you like it?" He might reply, "Yes, I like it." We should then have to say, "Well, all right, let it go." He can let it go, but we feel he ought to do something about it.

You know, at other times, under other circumstances with other people, the idea might legitimately be: "Let it go. It's nonsense anyhow, and you can manage things in this way, too." That is what people have always thought in the past. But I made another hypothesis, namely, that something might be done about it. Acting on this assumption, I might have said to my patient, if he had asked me (he was having no analysis at all when he had this dream), "Well, I think that these dream pictures should be used." Quite naturally! We shall see in the next dream what his unconscious is doing about it, and then we shall see why I say that something should be done about such unconscious situations, for his unconscious itself does not let the matter rest.

He is again in the dark place, and he falls to a great depth.[13] Obviously he is falling again into the role which he has always tried to avoid. When he arrives at the bottom, he sees a huge bear; which has four eyes; and these eyes are alternately emitting red, yellow, green, and blue lights. Then the bear disappears. The dreamer next goes through a long, dark cave or corridor at the end of which he sees a faint light, and there, he knows, a treasure is hidden. First he sees a sort of heap of something, and

---

[13] Cf. "Dream Symbols," nr. 39, p. 180, and CW 12, nr. 39, par. 262. M 39 {0253}: "Falling into the depth; a bear with coloured eyes. Guided by diamond ring," July 10, 1932, CDM.

concealed within it he finds his ring with the diamond. He is then informed, as you are informed in dreams where something seems to be just known, that this ring would lead him or guide him to the East, which means here to the Far East.

You see, he can't avoid that circle. Something must be done about it. The emptiness at the center is attractive. It draws him; he must fill it. All nature has this fear of empty space. Whenever there is an empty space in nature, something fills it or tries to fill it. It has been said, "natura abhorret a vacuo."[14] And so he falls into his own hole, namely, into that emptiness which is inside him, and there he discovers the bear. The bear is a symbol which plays a very great role in mythology, as you know. It is a sort of elemental man which is understood by primitives to be really akin to a human being. Therefore man, under certain conditions, might easily transform, or retransform, into a bear. You know the old legend that there were men who could transform into wolves in the night, that they were really wolves but they had the fur turned inwards. In the Germanic mythology, you have the so-called *Berserkers*, which means "bear skinners," not those who skin bears but those who wear the skins of bears.[15] They were a sort of bodyguard to Wotan, the Nordic king.[16] The Nordic kings wore bear skins because they could retransform, on certain occasions, into bears. They really belonged to a bear totem. They were bears with the fur grown inward, and at the times they could turn it out. There is plenty of evidence in the Germanic sagas of warriors who, in the heat of battle, suddenly turned into bears, which means they lost consciousness and became animal-like and behaved as if they were bears, developing supernatural animal powers. This is really a primitive phenomenon. It is exactly like running amok in the East, where a primitive man becomes the equivalent of a gorilla or some other anthropoid. This was his animal pre-stage, and when we realize his closeness to it we understand his fear.

When man "falls down" he falls into the past where he was still an animal; but this animal has four eyes. We have already met these four colors; they are the colors of the four functions. The animal, the personification

---

[14] Latin: Nature abhors (shrinks back from) a vacuum (emptiness).

[15] A fairy tale by the brothers Grimm, the title of Richard Wagner's first opera, and also the literal translation of "Berserker." Cf. Jung, 2008, 106.

[16] Wotan/Odin is one of the major father gods of Norse mythology associated with wind, storm, war, hunt, victory, and death, but also wisdom, prophecy, magic, and poetry. Jung later associated the rise of national socialism and World War II with the return of Wotan. Cf. "Wotan" (1936), and "After the Catastrophe" (1946), CW 10, pars. 371–99.

of the deeper layers of the unconscious, contains already the germs of the four functions, and that is the treasure. Then, in that underworld, behind the animal, much deeper than the animal, going back, one could say, down the long corridor of the history of animals until he arrives as it were at the mineral kingdom, he discovers the stone. In other words, that precious thing which has been there from eternity, from the time when there were no human beings, no animal beings, no plants even in the world, but only minerals. That is the idea of that long, dark corridor. And when he goes back like that into the depths of history, he goes back into his body until he reaches a place where there is no psyche anymore, where there is nothing but body, mineral organic body, and there he discovers the treasure, namely, that thing which is made of matter. He discovers a material body (whatever that means) and the ring that attaches him to his mystery. This ring will lead him to another country, namely, to the East. Now the Far East is the symbol of the *antipos*,[17] and the *antipodic* psychology is, of course, a psychology of the unconscious, that is, the other side. That stone will lead him to the other side, to the understanding of his unconscious side. Here, of course, comes the idea of a long voyage that isn't without risk, and, you know, he is afraid of that other side, that other world, and he might hesitate.

The following dream says: There is an idea of a great expedition under the guidance or leadership of a woman—that is the unknown woman, the anima—who is going to guide him to the North Pole, and he must try to reach the North Pole though it will involve grave risks, even of life. It will be a very dangerous enterprise.[18]

This is again a message from the unconscious, which says, "Now, you must get to that center, because the pole is the point around which everything turns." But here, the so-called cosmic aspect is added—it is no more just man's innermost center. There is at the same time something cosmic suggested, as we saw before when he had the dream of the stars. It is not only the microcosm, which is the innermost center of man, but it is also the macrocosm, namely, the greatest things in the universe outside. This is a somewhat new idea. Also, it suggests the idea of *perpetuum mobile*, the eternal rotation of the earth around the sun, the clock of the previous

---

[17] Greek: from *anti-* "opposed" and *pous* "foot," *antipod*: on the opposite side.

[18] Cf. "Dream Symbols," nr. 40, p. 181, and CW 12, nr. 40, par. 264. M 40 {0259}: "Being guided by the strange woman; going to great danger to discover the North Pole," July 14, 1932, CDM.

dream. This idea of rotation seems to be sticking in his mind, because the next dream speaks of yellow globes or balls that rotate in a circle, in an anticlockwise movement.[19]

Whenever the anticlockwise movement turns up, it means the movement towards the unconscious. In other words, he isn't sufficiently in the center or in the depth, and therefore, he must rotate to the left side in order to screw himself into the depth, to get right into the center.

The center is further emphasized in the next dream, where "an old master" is introduced.[20] The dream says that the word means an "old master" mind, a great sage, or philosopher, who shows or points out to him a particular spot that is shining red. That spot is on the soil or on the floor. He uses a term which leaves it open as to which it is.

This means that the old man, who is a representative of superior wisdom, is pointing out to him a definite place upon the earth, which is obviously important. Perhaps the dreamer belongs there, or something ought to happen there. It is a special place that appears in a red color. We don't know exactly what that means. We know that colors are of great importance, as the old alchemists realized when they spoke of a sequence of colors. The first was black; that is the darkness. Then comes the dim light, as if we glimpsed it in a dark cave which would be the first stage. The second stage is that a light appears, a white light, perhaps the diamond represented as a white light, and then comes a redness, the so-called *rubefacio*, the making of the red. The clear red color finally appears, and after it comes yellow. That is the ordinary sequence which most of the old philosophers believed in. And now, listen to the next dream.

He finds himself in a thick fog.[21] Then a light appears as if it were the sun shining through the mist. It is a yellow light. So you have the old sequence of the colors—black, white, red, yellow. But that light isn't clear; it is troubled. It is a sort of mist, and from the center of that light or the yellow disk, eight rays emanate, and the dreamer knows that this is the spot, where something ought to pierce or push through. The light should push through that place. You see, the light that was circulating before should reach this center and should push through there, in other words, should be born. But it hasn't happened yet, as he says.

---

[19] Cf. "Dream Symbols," nr. 41, p. 181, and *CW* 12, nr. 41, par. 266. M 41 {0260}: "Vision of the yellow globes circulating to the left," July 16, 1932, CDM.

[20] Cf. "Dream Symbols," nr. 42, p. 181, and *CW* 12, nr. 42, par. 268. M 42 {0261}: "Old Master shows a red spot on the ground," July 16, 1932, CDM.

[21] Cf. "Dream Symbols," nr. 43, p. 181, and *CW* 12, nr. 43, par. 270. M 43 {0263}: fig. 35, "In the fog. A yellow light with eight rays," August 17, 1932, CDM.

When the statement that it hasn't happened yet is made in a dream, we must assume that soon we shall have a dream where the attempt is made to bring it to pass, namely, to bring about the birth or the creation, or the piercing, the pushing through—whatever ought to happen in that center.

In the next dream, he is again in the square room.[22] This time it is not an open square. It is a room, in which he must now keep still; in other words he can't evade; he is caught. It is a prison for Lilliputians or children, or dwarfs, and there is a very bad woman, or a sort of witch, who watches them, gazes at them. Suddenly the children, dwarfs, or whatever they are, begin to move, to circulate upon the periphery of the square room in an anticlockwise way. There is a terrific tension in the place, and he wants to escape, to run away; but he knows he is not allowed to run away, even though things get worse. One of those dwarfs or children suddenly transforms into an animal which bites his calf. You remember that is the motif we already encountered before, where there were bad animals, dogs and foxes, in the corners of the square, and whenever he or the other people walked past those corners, their calves were bitten. This meant, as I pointed out, that they were compelled to expose themselves to the onslaught of those powers, those animals. We learn in this later dream that these dwarfs were also animals—like werewolves. They are the equivalent of the bears or the dogs and foxes. They can at any time retransform into their animal pre-stage, representing deep-rooted instincts which bite if you are not careful, if you try to run away, or to escape at the corners. Then they catch you. There the dream comes to an end.

There is still that tendency in him to escape the center. It must be very difficult for him to remain there because of his fear, his aversion, and mental inability to understand what is going on, so that he tries to avoid it, to run away and to have nothing to do with it, but he is caught in that peculiar underworld where there are these little things, these Lilliputians or whatever you call them. They are the Cabiri, whom we have already encountered in a former dream. These Cabiri are unconscious, creative powers, the dwarfs who produce the gold and the precious substance in the interior of the earth, or of the mountains. They are personifications of integrated creative tendencies, and by their circulation, they form the curve or the encoiling serpent. They are brought together into one movement, presumably in order to produce something in the center, because that circumambulation means a concentration of energy, a devotion to

---

[22] Cf. "Dream Symbols," nr. 44, p. 182, and CW 12, nr. 44, par. 272. M 44 {0304}: "Square room; jail with Lilliputians running in a circle," August 22, 1932, CDM.

the center that is circumambulated. You see, such circumambulations are carried out, for instance, around sacred places, around stupas,[23] and, you know, when the Jews couldn't climb or destroy the walls of Jericho until the walls came tumbling down. So they produced something in the center.

The bad woman, or witch that is there, is again the unknown woman. It is the anima that supervises this whole procedure, and this is so because he himself, his conscious side, wouldn't be in the game. He tried to get away and so left the whole attempt to produce the center to the unconscious, which takes care of it. So, you can say that when a man avoids doing something of importance, it falls into the hands of his anima, and then the anima takes care of it. The same thing holds true for a woman. When she fails to do something which she is aware that she should do, then the animus takes over the reins, and she will have an animus attack. In other words, when you fail to do something, fail to fulfill a duty, then you get into a state of animosity which amounts to an anima possession, and in the symbolism of the average dream this state is expressed by a woman in the case of a man, and in the case of a woman by a man, an animus. If, for instance, our patient could have made up his mind to accept this kind of symbolic thought, to say, "Yes, that is very meaningful. I must accompany it. I've got to go with it," then there would have been no anima to supervise the "circulation." He would have done it by himself. His devotion, his contemplation, his concentrated energy would have circumambulated the center, and the circumambulation would have amounted to a sort of meditation about the center, and this would be a normal mode of Eastern thought. That is why the former dream says that the ring will lead him to the Far East where they know about these things, where for thousands of years, these concentrations have been effectively used. In the Occident, we have forgotten about them. Yet we had pretty much the same thing in the West, too, although not exactly in the same form, but we had the mandalas, in front of the altar, and in the beautiful rose windows of the Gothic cathedrals. These were objects of contemplation, of concentration, and for this purpose they were painted upon the walls or were expressed in mosaics on the floor. Concentric buildings even were built as, for example, the famous *baptisteria*, the baptismal buildings which you still find in Italy, and which were usually separate from the churches, because they were places of mystery. You know, the Sacramenta

---

[23] Stupa is a Buddhist commemorative monument usually housing sacred relics associated with the Buddha or other saintly persons. The hemispherical form of the stupa appears to have derived from pre-Buddhist burial mounds in India.

were formerly, in the early church, called "mysteria." Later on these places were also built into the churches in the crypts below the choir, and in the Val d'Aosta in Italy, they are still called "mystae," a term presumably coming from the word "myster"—"mysterium."

The sacred mystery was something of which the early Christians did not speak in ordinary terms, but only allegorically. There was a time when Christ was not called Christ, but whenever His name was mentioned in the manuscripts, the papyrus fragments, it was simply written "X.R." This means Chi Rho in Greek. We still have a Greek inscription in which Christ was not called Christ, but Ichthys, meaning fish. Because he was a mysterious figure he belongs to the mysterious, therefore his name should not be mentioned. That only lasted a relatively short time, but it actually happened.

Now you see the *baptisteria* is just such a place. Perhaps some of you know the famous Baptisteria of Ravenna. Although these buildings are octagonal we can assume that they carry the same meaning as if they were circular. In the center was the piscina, the fish pond where the Christians, or those that were to be initiated, were submerged like little fishes in the water. Then, as in the miraculous draft of fishes, they were pulled out again, reborn, and became the little fishes of Christ. The pope's ring, that famous ring with the cut gem, the so-called fisher ring, shows the same symbolism. The *baptisteria* is the place where the center is, where is to be found the miraculous vessel containing the *aqua permanens*, that divine water with the procreative faculty. With that the water man is given a new spiritual nature; he is reborn *in novum infantilum*, born into a new childhood, as the text says in the *Missale Romanum*.[24] Also I don't know whether you are aware of the ritual of the *benedictio fontis*. This is still a special rite in the Catholic Church, though it isn't always celebrated. It is the mysterious rite of the *Sabbatum Sanctum*,[25] the Sabbath before Easter. In this ritual the priest causes the descent of the Holy Ghost into the water by invocation. He takes ordinary water which is first exorcised; then he adds salt to make seawater, salty water. This is carried out in the baptismal font. Formerly it took place in a large tank with space enough for quite a crowd of people. At present just the baptismal font is used. This is a round vessel which contains only salty water. The priest now divides the font into four parts. You see, he makes a mandala, after which he

---

[24] The liturgical book that contains the texts and rubrics for the celebration of the Mass in the Roman Rite of the Catholic Church.

[25] Holy Saturday.

breathes three times into the water. By this act he introduces the *pneuma*, the divine spirit, to descend into the water. This rite is still further developed when the priest takes a candle, symbolizing the light of illumination, and submerges it three times in the water until the light is extinguished. That is the moment when the fire of the Holy Ghost descends into the water, like the tongues of fire in the Pentecostal Visitation. Through this the water has obtained the procreative quality, namely the mystical power of giving birth to man, of transforming the ordinary, imperfect, sinful man into a new spiritual being.

This is exactly the idea of the alchemistic transformation. The interesting fact is that the alchemistic rite is much older than that of the church. This *benedictio fontis* dates from about the eighth century and is presumably of Gallic, that is, of Celtic origin, though we have traces of it earlier, for parts of the text were already known in the fifth century in practically the first *sacramentarium*, or collection of sacramental rites. The idea is undoubtedly very old, but the historical texts we possess of the early Greek alchemists are considerably older. They are, presumably, of pre-Christian origin. As you know, the baptismal rite is also pre-Christian, according to the evangelical record, for John the Baptist used it before Christ. Where did he get it? Well, you see, it is a pagan rite, a pagan idea of the wonderful water, the miraculous liquid that has the quality of giving rebirth, of transforming. This is another application of the mandala symbolism in the church.

To return to the dreamer. Here he is caught and put right into the center, into the room from which there is no escape. He is now caught in the unconscious, and there he has to stay until something happens.

The next dream is of an entirely different nature: There are barracks and a wide open field, in which are soldiers.[26] They are not preparing for war but are arranging themselves in the form of an eight-rayed star which is slowly rotating. They march in an anticlockwise direction as if they were a wheel. The process isn't finished yet. He must still go down into the unconscious, and his elements, his units, which were symbolized before by the children, the unconscious constituents, are now soldiers in formation. All his unconscious creative powers are now arranged in the form of a mandala. That is happening in his unconscious. And so he gets that structure of the mandala, as it were, within himself, below the threshold of consciousness, and against his will. He himself in his innermost sub-

---

[26] Cf. "Dream Symbols," nr. 45, p. 182, and *CW* 12, nr. 45, par. 274. M 45 {0305}: fig. 38, "Troups on parade ground, rotating in star formation," August 22, 1932, CDM.

stance becomes transformed into the eight-rayed star, and that is now rotating horizontally upon the Earth. That spot on the Earth was indicated
by the old wise man who conveyed the idea that he isn't in the heavens,
but right upon the Earth.

In the next dream, he is again or still a prisoner, caught in the square
room, but instead of children, there appear lions.[27] Far more dangerous
creatures are introduced just because of his tendency to run away. These
children are now lions in order to prevent him from escaping.

In the dream immediately following, "the old wise man" appears and
shows him a particular spot on the earth which he designates quite specially, a very particular, definite place on the earth, which, of course,
means: Here is the place where you presumably belong.[28]

The next dream says: The dreamer is informed that a friend of his has
received a prize for having dug up a potter's disc, a very old relic, a potter's wheel, that has been found in the earth.[29]

The potter's wheel is a rotating mandala. You make pots upon it. It is
a particular spot, we might say, that spot indicated by the old wise man.
Probably that was the spot where the wheel was buried or where it was
lost. It is a relict of former times, which has been evacuated, and the man
who has done this even receives a prize, because it is an important discovery. This means that the mandala is a very important archaeological
find, and it is also the instrument upon which potters' vessels are made.
It is mythologically the place or the instrument upon which, or through
which, human beings are formed. Therefore we speak of God as the great
Potter who has made the earthly vessels of our body to contain an immortal spirit.

The dream which follows is about a star, but it is not a star in the sky.[30]
It is a figure, like a drawing, and that figure is rotating, and in the cardinal

---

[27] Cf. "Dream Symbols," nr. 46, p. 183, and CW 12, nr. 46, par. 276. M 46 {0313}: "Prisoner in the square room with the evil sorceress and the lion," August 31, 1932, CDM. Jung
has added a sentence on the symbolism of the lion in PsA, CW 12, par. 277.

[28] Cf. "Dream Symbols," nr. 47, p. 183, and CW 12, nr. 47, par. 278. M 47 {0316}: "The
old wise man shows a particularly marked spot on the ground," September 2, 1932, CDM.

[29] Cf. "Dream Symbols," nr. 48, p. 183, and CW 12, nr. 48, par. 280. M 48 {0317}: "An
acquaintance receives a price for an excavated potter's disk," September 2, 1932, CDM.

[30] Cf. "Dream Symbols," nr. 49, p. 183, and CW 12, nr. 49, par. 282. M 49 {0320}: fig.
39, "Rotating star figure with depiction of the seasons," September 5, 1932, CDM. Jung has
added a few sentences on the symbolism of the year and the seasons, PsA, CW 12, par. 283.
Apparently this dream made a deep impression on Pauli: "Besonders auffallend und ein-
drucksvoll war mir das Bild mit den vier Jahreszeiten," Pauli to Erna Rosenbaum, September 11, 1932, JA.

points of the periphery are pictures illustrating the four seasons. So we have here a picture of spring, summer, autumn, and winter.

This is a kind of representation of the circle of the seasons which you often find in historical mandalas, for instance, in medieval mandalas, little medallions containing symbols or pictures representing the four seasons and coupled with the idea of north, east, south, west, and so forth.

The spot upon the earth, the place where the potter's wheel has been dug up, designates a definite place in space, while the star, the rotation sphere consisting of the four seasons, hints at time. We know that a definite existence has always two determinants, space and time. That was alluded to in a former dream where he was making astronomical observations in order to find out where he was both as to the time moment and the actual place he was occupying in space. This means definite existence, not just anywhere, not floating up in the air, but here on earth. This is in opposition to his consciousness, which liked to be unattached, under no obligation, without any inferior function which could catch him somewhere. He likes to think of himself as still young; so that anything can happen; nothing has come off yet because he is nowhere fastened down; he is in no definite place; and so everything is still possible.

This is a very typical mental condition, which I call a state of suspension. Many intuitive people, and others as well, are in such a predicament clinging to the illusion that anything is still possible. And so, they hover above fate. They are hanging in the air always promising themselves that anything may happen. Suddenly one says that they discover that they are just going to celebrate their fortieth birthday, or something of the sort, and then they come down with a bang. Up to then, no realization had taken place because they always lived in a state of suspension. This is the so-called provisional life, to which a man whose father is still alive and who is a bit *fils à papa*[31] is particularly prone, or a person whose mother is still alive and perhaps also the father. For such a person can leave things in suspension because the older generation is still going strong, and he is still a child and quite young, you know, and all that. Then suddenly the father

[31] French: father's boy. H. G. Baynes had written an essay called "The Provisional Life" where he describes this attitude as "it denotes an attitude that is innocent of responsibility towards the circumstantial facts of reality as though these facts were being provided for either by the parents or the State, or at least, by Providence." H. G. Baynes (1936), "The Provisional Life," *Zentralblatt für Psychotherapie und ihre Grenzgebiete* 8:83–85. See also H. G. Baynes (1950), *Analytical Psychology and the English Mind, and Other Papers* (London: Methuen).

dies or the mother dies. I have seen quite a few men completely collapse the moment that the father died. Of course, well-meaning people said, "Oh how he loved his father." He didn't really love him particularly, but he collapsed because he had lived a provisional life, and suddenly it came home to him with a crash that he had maneuvered himself into a condition which he never would have chosen, but had drifted into because he thought, "Well, father is still the backbone of the family. He pays; he will take care of it." These people often live in the most astounding way. They undertake things they never would undertake if they had to do so on their own account, on their own responsibility. But inasmuch as the father is still alive, well, they undertake it, always with that wonderful feeling, "We are supported, you see." They always have something very solid behind them. When the father dies, they suddenly become aware that there is nothing to hold them up and that they are in a situation they never would have dreamt of choosing.

Well now, that definiteness of time and space means, "Come down. Come into this reality. Don't assume that you can be almost anywhere. Now things are going to happen. You are going to come down to earth where you are going to take root." In the case of this man, he had never, for instance, felt under any obligation to a definite woman. Up to then, his women were ghosts, shadows, sort of wraiths. They were not quite real. He drifted into a woman and drifted away, and he never thought that this amounted to anything, and so he didn't become, he wasn't born. He didn't live in reality. He wasn't fastened down; and to be tied in any way was, of course, what he hated most. So you see, during all the time that he was having these individuation dreams that other problem came in, because you can never individuate if the process doesn't happen in reality. If you think, for example, that you can individuate in a suspended condition, living perhaps a provisional life, you are quite wrong. The individuation process cannot get into the right spot, the here and now. There is no escape from this fact. You cannot drift about and imagine you can individuate. Otherwise you might just as well sit on top of Mount Everest and think you have a beautiful personal relationship to humanity.

The next dream says: There is an unknown man, who gives him a precious stone, the beautiful jewel. But the dreamer runs away with terrific fear and is thus able to save himself.[32] The unknown woman then comes

---

[32] Cf. "Dream Symbols," nr. 50, p. 183, and CW 12, nr. 50, par. 284. M 50 {0326}: fig. 39a "A stranger gives him a gem, he is attacked by Apaches, September 9, 1932, CDM.

to him and says: "Well, don't think that you can always escape. When once the moment comes when you cannot escape any more, you must stand still."

The last dream, which I shall take up directly, is of a square which isn't really a square, but a rectangle. In each of the four corners, there is some kind of a cup.[33] One is filled with green, one with yellow, and one with red water. The fourth is filled with a colorless liquid. Blue is lacking.

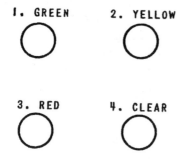

1. GREEN   2. YELLOW

3. RED   4. CLEAR

We arrive now just where I began my lectures at Yale. There I mentioned this dream. If you want to know more about the continuation and the ultimate outcome (I do not mean, of course, the absolutely ultimate outcome but the attainment of a fairly definite state) then please read my Yale lectures.[34]

---

[33] Cf. "Dream Symbols," nr. 51, p. 184, and CW 12, nr. 51, par. 286. M 51 {0338}: fig. 40, "A large rectangular place, in which people circulate," September 20, 1932, CDM.

[34] The Terry Lectures, "Psychology and Religion" 1937, CW 11. In the Terry Lectures Jung chooses to presents Pauli's dreams to illustrate how dreams reveal the unknown inner facts of the psyche, and especially demonstrate how a modern, scientifically minded intellectual, not at all interested in religious problems, in his dreams reveals an independent unconscious "point of view" containing religious tendencies. Jung chooses to present dream nr. 17 (M 17 {0151}) of the Catholic Church (he also mentions the dream preceding and following this dream) and dream nr. 54 of the Solemn House (M 54 {0382}: fig. 53, "In the House of the gathering (Haus der Sammlung), Wagner's fire music," October 16, 1932), and the vision of the world clock, nr. 59 (M 59 {0410}: fig. 61, "Great Vision of the World Clock," November 4, 1932), CW 11, pars. 38–55. Cf. "Dream Symbols," nr. 17, p. 148, nr. 54, p. 186, nr. 59, p. 189, and CW 12, nr. 17, par. 176, nr. 54, par. 293, nr. 59, par. 307.

Index

The Collected Works of C. G. Jung

Editors: Sir Herbert Read, Michael Fordham, and Gerhard Adler; executive editor, William McGuire. Translated by R.F.C. Hull, except where noted.

PSYCHOPHYSICAL RESEARCHES (1907–8)

On the Psychophysical Relations of the Association Experiment
Psychophysical Investigations with the Galvanometer and Pneumograph
    in Normal and Insane Individuals (by F. Peterson and Jung)
Further Investigations on the Galvanic Phenomenon and Respiration
    in Normal and Insane Individuals (by C. Ricksher and Jung)
Appendix: Statistical Details of Enlistment (1906); New Aspects of
    Criminal Psychology (1908); The Psychological Methods of Inves-
    tigation Used in the Psychiatric Clinic of the University of Zurich
    (1910); On the Doctrine Complexes ([1911] 1913); On the Psycho-
    logical Diagnosis of Evidence (1937)

3. THE PSYCHOGENESIS OF MENTAL DISEASE (1960)

The Psychology of Dementia Praecox (1907)
The Content of the Psychoses (1908/1914)
On Psychological Understanding (1914)
A Criticism of Bleuler's Theory of Schizophrenic Negativism (1911)
On the Importance of the Unconscious in Psychology (1914)
On the Problem of Psychogenesis in Mental Disease (1919)
Mental Disease and the Psyche (1928)
On the Psychogenesis of Schizophrenia (1939)
Recent Thoughts on Schizophrenia (1957)
Schizophrenia (1958)

4. FREUD AND PSYCHOANALYSIS (1967)

Freud's Theory of Hysteria: A Reply to Aschaffenburg (1906)
The Freudian Theory of Hysteria (1908)
The Analysis of Dreams (1909)
A Contribution to the Psychology of Rumour (1910–11)
On the Significance of Number Dreams (1910–11)
Morton Prince, "The Mechanism and Interpretation of Dreams":
    A Critical Review (1911)
On the Criticism of Psychoanalysis (1910)
Concerning Psychoanalysis (1912)
The Theory of Psychoanalysis (1913)
General Aspects of Psychoanalysis (1913)
Psychoanalysis and Neurosis (1916)
Some Crucial Points in Psychoanalysis: A Correspondence between
    Dr. Jung and Dr. Loÿ (1914)

Prefaces to "Collected Papers on Analytical Psychology" (1916, 1917)
The Significance of the Father in the Destiny of the Individual (1909/1949)
Introduction to Kranefeldt's "Secret Ways of the Mind" (1930)
Freud and Jung: Contrasts (1929)

5. SYMBOLS OF TRANSFORMATION
([1911–12/1952] 1956; 2d ed., 1967)

PART I

Introduction
Two Kinds of Thinking
The Miller Fantasies: Anamnesis
The Hymn of Creation
The Song of the Moth

PART II

Introduction
The Concept of Libido
The Transformation of Libido
The Origin of the Hero
Symbols of the Mother and Rebirth
The Battle for Deliverance from the Mother
The Dual Mother
The Sacrifice
Epilogue
Appendix: The Miller Fantasies

6. PSYCHOLOGICAL TYPES ([1921] 1971)
A revision by R.F.C. Hull of the translation by H. G. Baynes
Introduction
The Problem of Types in the History of Classical and Medieval Thought
Schiller's Idea on the Type Problem
The Apollonian and the Dionysian
The Type Problem in Human Character
The Type Problem in Poetry
The Type Problem in Psychopathology
The Type Problem in Aesthetics
The Type Problem in Modern Philosophy
The Type Problem in Biography
General Description of the Types

The Psychology of the Child Archetype (1940)
The Psychological Aspects of the Kore (1941)
The Phenomenology of the Spirit in Fairytales (1945/1948)
On the Psychology of the Trickster-Figure (1954)
Conscious, Unconscious, and Individuation (1939)
A Study in the Process of Individuation (1934/1950)
Concerning Mandala Symbolism (1950)
Appendix: Mandalas (1955)

9. PART II. AION ([1951] 1959; 2d ed., 1968)

RESEARCHES INTO THE PHENOMENOLOGY OF THE SELF

The Ego
The Shadow
The Syzygy: Anima and Animus
The Self
Christ, a Symbol of the Self
The Signs of the Fishes
The Prophecies of Nostradamus
The Historical Significance of the Fish
The Ambivalence of the Fish Symbol
The Fish in Alchemy
The Alchemical Interpretation of the Fish
Background to the Psychology of Christian Alchemical Symbolism
Gnostic Symbols of the Self
The Structure and Dynamics of the Self Conclusion

10. CIVILIZATION IN TRANSITION (1964; 2d ed., 1970)

The Role of the Unconscious (1918)
Mind and Earth (1927/1931) Archaic Man (1931)
The Spiritual Problem of Modern Man (1928/1931)
The Love Problem of a Student (1928)
Woman in Europe (1927)
The Meaning of Psychology for Modern Man (1933/1934)
The State of Psychotherapy Today (1934)
Preface and Epilogue to "Essays on Contemporary Events" (1946)
Wotan (1936)
After the Catastrophe (1945)
The Fight with the Shadow (1946)
The Undiscovered Self (Present and Future) (1957)

Psychotherapy and a Philosophy of Life (1943)
Medicine and Psychotherapy (1945)
Psychotherapy Today (1945)
Fundamental Questions of Psychotherapy (1951)

SPECIFIC PROBLEMS OF PSYCHOTHERAPY

The Therapeutic Value of Abreaction (1921/1928)
The Practical Use of Dream-Analysis (1934)
The Psychology of the Transference (1946)
Appendix: The Realities of Practical Psychotherapy ([1937] added 1966)

17. THE DEVELOPMENT OF PERSONALITY (1954)
Psychic Conflicts in a Child (1910/1946)
Introduction to Wickes's "Analyses der Kinderseele" (1927/1931)
Child Development and Education (1928)
Analytical Psychology and Education: Three Lectures (1926/1946)
The Gifted Child (1943)
The Significance of the Unconscious in Individual Education (1928)
The Development of Personality (1934)
Marriage as a Psychological Relationship (1925)

18. THE SYMBOLIC LIFE (1954)
Translated by R.F.C. Hull and others
Miscellaneous Writings

19. COMPLETE BIBLIOGRAPHY OF C. G. JUNG'S WRITINGS (1976; 2d ed., 1992)

20. GENERAL INDEX OF THE COLLECTED WORKS (1979)

THE ZOFINGIA LECTURES (1983)
Supplementary Volume A to the Collected Works.
Edited by William McGuire, translated by
Jan van Heurck, introduction by
Marie-Louise von Franz

PSYCHOLOGY OF THE UNCONSCIOUS ([1912] 1992)
A STUDY OF THE TRANSFORMATIONS AND SYMBOLISMS OF THE LIBIDO.
A CONTRIBUTION TO THE HISTORY OF THE EVOLUTION OF THOUGHT

Supplementary Volume B to the Collected Works.
Translated by Beatrice M. Hinkle,
introduction by William McGuire

Notes to C. G. Jung's Seminars

DREAM ANALYSIS ([1928–30] 1984)
Edited by William McGuire

NIETZSCHE'S *ZARATHUSTRA* ([1934–39] 1988)
Edited by James L. Jarrett (2 vols.)

ANALYTICAL PSYCHOLOGY ([1925] 1989)
Edited by William McGuire

THE PSYCHOLOGY OF KUNDALINI YOGA ([1932] 1996)
Edited by Sonu Shamdasani

INTERPRETATION OF VISIONS ([1930–34] 1997)
Edited by Claire Douglas

Philemon Series of the Philemon Foundation

GENERAL EDITOR, *Sonu Shamdasani*

Children's Dreams. Edited by Lorenz Jung and Maria Meyer-Grass. Translated by Ernst Falzeder with the collaboration of Tony Woolfson

Introduction to Jungian Psychology: Notes of the Seminar on Analytical Psychology Given in 1925. Edited by William McGuire. Translated by R.F.C. Hull. With a new introduction and updates by Sonu Shamdasani

Jung contra Freud: The 1912 New York Lectures on the Theory of Psychoanalysis. With a new introduction by Sonu Shamdasani. Translated by R.F.C. Hull

The Question of Psychological Types: The Correspondence of C. G. Jung and Hans Schmid-Guisan, 1915–1916. Edited by John Beebe and Ernst Falzeder. Translated by Ernst Falzeder with the collaboration of Tony Woolfson

Dream Interpretation Ancient and Modern: Notes from the Seminar Given in 1936–1941. C. G. Jung. Edited by John Peck, Lorenz Jung, and Maria Meyer-Grass. Translated by Ernst Falzeder with the collaboration of Tony Woolfson